TIDEWATER VIRGINIA FAMILIES:
Generations Beyond

TIDEWATER
VIRGINIA
FAMILIES:
Generations Beyond

Virginia Lee Hutcheson Davis

The Families of
*Bell, Binford, Bonner, Butler, Campbell, Cheadle, Chiles, Clements,
Cotton, Dejarnette, Dumas, Ellyson, Fishback, Fleming,
Hamlin, Hampton, Harnison, Harris, Haynie, Hurt,
Hutcheson, Lee, Mosby, Mundy, Nelson, Peatross,
Pettyjohn, Ruffin, Short, Spencer, Tarleton,
Tatum, Taylor, Terrell, Watkins,
Winston, Woodson*

Adding the Families of
*Alsobrook, Bibb, Edwards, Favor, Gray,
Hux, Ironmonger, Laker, Southern, Taylor and Woolfolk*

GENEALOGICAL PUBLISHING Co. Inc.

Published by Genealogical Publishing Company
3600 Clipper Mill Rd., Suite 260
Baltimore, Maryland 21211-1953
1998, 2004, 2009
Library of Congress Catalogue Card Number 98-72719
ISBN 978-0-8063-1578-2
Made in the United States of America

To
James Williams Davis, Senior
1906-1996
His quiet wisdom, his encouragement, and his enthusiasm
have made this possible

He has been the wind beneath my wings

*It is said that as a figure is sculpted by the hand
of the Artist, so is a man molded by those
who preceded him on Earth*

*We have a heritage of which to be proud
and much to learn
and impart to those who follow us*

TABLE OF CONTENTS

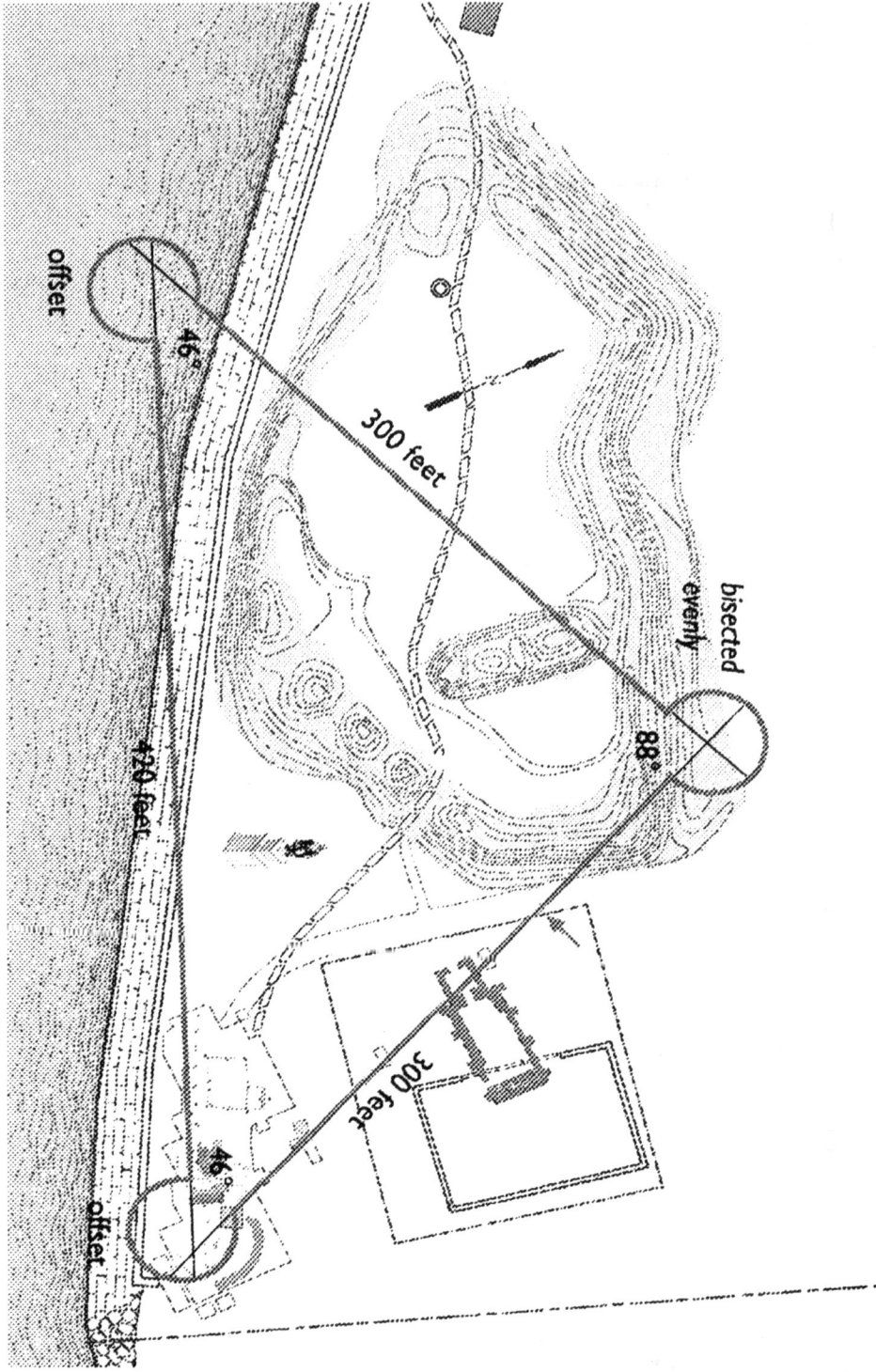

James Fort
As Plotted from Jamestown Rediscovery Archaeological Studies
(Used with permission)

READ THIS FIRST: HOW TO USE THIS BOOK

It is time for an update and revision of *Tidewater Virginia Families*, both as a social history and as a genealogy of more than forty Tidewater Virginia families. There have been a few corrections, based on records that have been found since the first book, *Tidewater Virginia Families: A Social History* was privately printed in 1989 and the second edition, *Tidewater Virginia Families* was published in 1990 by the Genealogical Publishing Company.

This book was begun as an addendum *Tidewater Virginia Families*, complementing the complete published book; however, it is also of value to others interested in tidewater Virginia settlers and history. The supplement is made up of additional information; both brief, vital record entries and more lengthy descriptions where new information has come to light. Some recently identified family connections are presented as family lines in the same format as those presented in the original publication. Some of these accounts include descriptions of research methods of general interest that are applicable to the analysis of data where primary source records have not survived. Homes and parish churches associated with these tidewater Virginia families, identified since the book was written are described. Some personal anecdotal notes have been included that provide insight of times past. There are also some corrections, which are presented in bold letters.

In each case the entries are keyed by page number to both the original, privately printed edition and the second edition published by the Genealogical Publishing Company. The page numbers are given in parentheses for the privately printed version first, followed by a semi-colon and then the page numbers for the published edition. If it is a correction, it is so noted. While the typographical errors in the first books are a matter of personal embarrassment; they are not dealt with, they will have to remain, much to this author's chagrin. Suffice it to say that your author has learned a great deal since writing and typesetting "the book"; still not as much as she would like, however. VLHD

Tidewater Virginia 1702

PREFACE

As an outgrowth of the book, *Tidewater Virginia Families*, your author has undertaken the publishing and editing of the magazine, *Tidewater Virginia Families: A Magazine of History and Genealogy*. This publication, begun in 1992, has elicited a number of contributions of additional information about descendants presented in the book with other lines also extended. Subscribers to the magazine have been generous in supplying their own family lines and where appropriate, will be included in this supplement. Some old record books have come to light, some loose papers have been found and connections have been made to family lines that were not known at the time of the first writing.

A significant aid to identifying family lines, and especially the elusive maiden names of wives, has come from the recent abstractions of early Tidewater records. Many volumes of very good county record abstracts have been published, as well as a number of very accurate transcriptions of records. These have also been thoroughly indexed, providing a cross-indexing that is not available when one searches the original records.

It has always been important to place these early settlers in their own environment, both geographically and culturally. A number of old homes and churches have been identified and visited and can now be described in greater detail than in the original account. As your author has become more knowledgeable through the publication of the magazine, so has an understanding of the history and ways of the people matured.

Documentation will be provided in the form of endnotes, following the format of the earlier publication. In some instances, where material has been contributed, the name of the person submitting the information will be noted, and whatever documentation that was given will also be noted. Further verification will not be sought in such cases. This will provide a direction for further research only. Where references are made to information in the first and second editions of the book, the references will not be repeated; however every effort has been made to accurately document new information presented.

ACKNOWLEDGEMENTS

Just as "the book" would never have come into being without the encouragement of my husband, Jim Davis, so would this supplement never have evolved. His confidence in my abilities, his insight regarding my research and his unflagging enthusiasm caused the book to take form. Whenever I lamented that I didn't know what to write he would always reply, "just sit down and start writing". His faith was unbounded as was his patience. These same qualities provided the inspiration for *Tidewater Virginia Families: A Magazine of History and Genealogy*. This was his contribution to the preservation of Tidewater Virginia's unpublished records and thus the heritage that belongs to all who have ancestors who first settled in Virginia.

James Williams Davis, Sr. was born in Laurens County, South Carolina on May 1, 1906. He died on November 20, 1996 in Williamsburg, Virginia. Not only did he spend sixty years of his life in Virginia, but he also had roots in Tidewater Virginia as well as in South Carolina. He was a southern gentleman of the highest order with a deep love for Virginia and an understanding of its rich heritage.

Through the magazine I have corresponded with and met personally many cousins and fellow researchers who share the desire to preserve the history and records of colonial Virginia. Their work has been both scholarly and dedicated. Throughout this work credit will be given to these generous people. Those persons acknowledged originally in the book have made many contributions.

The work of LtCol. James W. Doyle, Jr. is also greatly appreciated. With his knowledge of Virginia history and outstanding insight, "Pat" has spent many tireless hours researching the relationships of early Virginia settlers and sharing this information with readers. J. Thomas Wadkins, my son Tom, has again provided his expertise in formatting and has prepared this supplement for publication.

INTRODUCTION

As in the original book, the account of my life is followed by the lives of my parents, then grandparents. The organizational order is then reversed and each family is presented from the earliest date that family can be identified, to its entry into the appropriate family line. The generation numbers go in ascending order from my generation. This sequence was chosen because there are family lines shared by both of my parents, and they are not necessarily the same generation. Families are organized with the presentation of the paternal lines first, then followed by the maternal lines.

Family charts provide a guide for progression from one family and generation to the next. Roman numerals are used to designate more than one generation of the same name of the direct line. Such a designation was generally not in use during the lifetime of that person. Siblings with the same name are not designated with the use of the Roman numeral. The use of the "m" symbol to indicate marriage does follow some order: where it is known that they did not marry (sometimes for obvious reasons) the symbol has been omitted; where it is known that they married, but not to whom the designation is "unknown"; where it is assumed that they married but no information has been found the symbol is included and space for spouse is left blank.

It was not until I began to organize the book originally for the publisher that I realized that I had not followed the stated order of the families of the Lee ancestors. The closest relationships began with the family lines of Clements (Chapter 19), and were followed by the family lines of the Pettyjohn family (Chapter 20) and their antecedents. To follow the stated established order, the sequence of presentation was reversed in the published book, and this order will be followed in the supplement. The pagination will be presented to be correct for each book.

The same ground rules will be followed in presenting this material as were employed in the original book. A correction should be made concerning the custom of abbreviating the months of the year. (xiii;xiii) **correction: With the Julian calendar in use until 1752 the month of September would have been abbreviated to be 7ber (rather than 8ber as indicated in the first paragraph).**

One of the oversights in the publication of the original book was the failure to index the maiden name of a wife, where it was known, unless it appeared in the text. Because of the difficulty in working with such a large manuscript, it is not feasible to correct this. In this supplement, names will be indexed following the accepted format presently in use, with variations of names indexed. It was impossible to index place names because of the size of the book, and the length of the index of names. This has been a source of frustration to many of us. Perhaps the indexing of place names in this supplement will provide clues as to the location of a number of these in the original text.

Every attempt was made to document the information presented in the original publications accurately. In the instances where references contain typographical errors, they will be corrected. It must be understood that references listed ten years ago may have a different location at the present. In fact, references given in this publication may have different locations by the time this supplement reaches the publisher. The Library of Virginia holds many original documents that have not been catalogued and preserved. Some have been lost, others have had their location reassigned. Some of the records held by the Virginia State Library and Archives that were accessible to the public are no longer available for use by the public. My apologies, but this is the way it is in 1997 and 1998. The Library of Virginia does not make any projections regarding the preservation of records, nor of the time frame concerning their accessibility. Sources have been presented as they were identified at the time that the information was collected, *i.e.*, the name may have changed since that time.

While not claiming to possess a crystal ball or to have infinite wisdom, I feel that some greater latitude can be employed in the use of circumstantial evidence. Increased knowledge and understanding of the culture and history of the colonial times have provided a better ability to interpret information and taken together may provide insight concerning identities and relationships of these families. More liberties may be taken in drawing inferences from the existing records of Tidewater Virginia, simply because there are so few that have survived in a number of these counties.

Speaking of a crystal ball, one should keep in mind that it is extremely difficult to find the maiden name and parents of the wives of many of the early residents. When women's names appeared in court records it was the custom to refer to them by their given name, or even the diminutive of that name and if a second name or initial was used it was generally the middle name rather than the legal maiden name. Also very often only the names of sons appear in the records. Many times there were several more children than the number of children recorded in a will or estate settlement, as the mortality rate was high and children died young. The number of children found in the extant records may well not have been all of the children of a given family.

One must use the records at hand and the knowledge gained in a study of these records and people. This more liberal approach will be used, not to gather "people", but to offer a basis for further research that may provide primary proof and documentation at a later time. The more that is learned about the inter-relationships of these Tidewater Virginians, the more one realizes the extent to which their lives were inextricably linked by blood ties, marriage, business and politics. And the extent to which their lives were circumscribed by geographic limitations, and that when they moved, families moved together.

I am sure that readers have been disappointed with the few references made to Revolutionary War service of our ancestors. There are several reasons for this. Many of the ancestors living at that time were members of the Society of Friends who were pacifists, and did not serve in the War. A number of ancestors appear to have been too old or too young to have served. Some may be found among the public claims for service of goods and supplies. These have not been generally included in the biographical sketches. Which leads to the third reason that service in the Revolution has not been stressed, there simply were too many sons who had the same names to be sure I was giving credit to the right person, hence, rather than err, the information was not included.

It is unfortunate that the time and devotion to research could not be extended to this supplement that went into the original writing. It becomes increasingly difficult to extract information from the scant and scattered records and much time and energy has of necessity gone into the publication of the magazine. There are still many unanswered questions, some of which are just awaiting discovery. I commend this challenge to the descendants of these more than fifty families of early Virginia.

The accounts, as presented here, of my early ancestors and the siblings are uneven in detail and length. Some of the research has been pursued as I have had time. Many accounts have been contributed by descendants, and of course, all of the lines have not been identified or expanded. Perhaps this supplement will spur additional research and at some future time *Tidewater Virginia Families* can again be updated and enlarged. This continuation of *Tidewater Virginia Families* now includes the discovery of the relationship to Thomas Gray, *Ancient Planter*, who was in the colony of Virginia between 1607 and 1616. This extends this family history in the colony of Virginia to a span of almost 400 years.

SECTION I

THE PROGENY

VIRGINIA LEE HUTCHESON

Gen. 1

My first remembered experience occurred on a sandy road leading to Mobjack Bay, just off the York River, in Mathews County. Just as this memory opened my account of my life in the book, so did another experience along a river begin the genesis of the supplement to *Tidewater Virginia Families.* Having committed my memories and research to print did not quell the questions. They persisted in following me. Jim and I continued to search for answers. It was on the banks of the Pamunkey River in King William County that we decided we must share our later discoveries with readers.

We had packed a lunch and were contentedly finishing the last crumb as we watched the slow current of the muddy river carry a few leaves and sticks down stream. The fact that the Pamunkey was not a pretty river, and one that no self-respecting fly fisherman would drop a line in was well known to me. The Mattaponi, in contrast, was a beautiful river, as Jim had pointed out many times. These reflections did not diminish the satisfaction we experienced in having just discovered the homeplace (1794) of Thomas Butler of St. John's Parish, King William County. This exciting find led to our determination to share whatever records we found and the discoveries we made.

We felt that we should confine our efforts to the counties north of the James River, many of which had lost their early records to fire and the ravages of time, or to "the several enemy incursions", as has been euphemistically stated many times. We could enjoy "poking around" the Northern Neck and the Middle Peninsula countryside and perform a real service to researchers at the same time. Our plans were made with enthusiasm, and carried out with a great deal of planning and zeal.

We decided upon a quarterly publication with Tom Wadkins as our publishing consultant, who would format the magazine with each issue. We planned the marketing strategy together and made the leap of faith. It seems that we started something that grew beyond our expectations. *Tidewater Virginia Families* has filled a gap in the genealogical research community and has become recognized as an outstanding scholarly publication. It has provided us with a great deal of satisfaction. It has also meant that we have seen a lot of Tidewater Virginia and met a lot of interesting people from all over the country.

We gave up country living in Urbanna when services seemed to move farther away and when the yard grew larger each year. The early history, ambience and convenience of Williamsburg beckoned. *Kingsmill-on-the-James* in James City County beckoned more forcefully, and we found that *Littletown Quarter*, with all of the community services, was just what we sought. We moved in April of 1996, right into the middle of Tidewater Virginia's earliest history.

Soon after Jamestown was settled the colonists quickly staked their claims to the shore up and down river from Jamestown Island. They set about to make their fortune from the wilderness; the reason most of them came to Virginia. The Virginia Colony was above all, a business venture and land was a key to success.

From 1607 to 1624, it was governed by the Virginia Company of London, a joint stock company, and its Council in the colony. Investors or members of the company were granted fifty acres of land for each settler whose passage they paid to the colony. The settler was then obligated to work off the debt with seven years of service, at which time he could obtain land of his own.

In 1619 Richard Kingsmill, William Fairfax, William Claiborne, John Jefferson, William Spence, Richard Staples and Richard Brewster were the first company members to receive grants of land in what was later to become *Kingsmill.* From this series of speculative plots of land stretching along the James River in the 1620s, deeds were bought and sold, and inherited and consolidated by marriage, until a series of plantations emerged. Richard Kingsmill, a member of the General Assembly, expanded his holdings to 750 acres. He and his wife, Jane had one child, a daughter, Elizabeth (1634-1691) who married first William Tayloe and then

Colonel Nathaniel Bacon. The Kingsmill land was passed down through them to their niece, Abigail Smith and her husband, Lewis Burwell II.

In 1736 Lewis Burwell III chose a low hill along the James to build what was then one of the grandest of all James River plantations; named *Kingsmill*, it contained 1250 acres with its large brick manor house, dependencies, coach house and barns, fenced gardens, orchards, wells, warehouses, river landing and wharf. The two-story house, large for its time, contained eight rooms and 4800 square feet, with two large brick dependencies; a kitchen and office. The foundation of the house has been preserved and is outlined today, along with a storehouse and dairy, at the Kingsmill Plantation site. Both the kitchen and the office have survived and are restored on the site. Two well sites have been preserved also.

Kingsmill Plantation was the home of four generations of the Lewis Burwell family, from 1690 until 1781. The manor house burned in 1844 and after the Civil War, with the devastated economy and non-existent cash money, the other splendid buildings of *Kingsmill Plantation* deteriorated or were destroyed by fire. Only the office and kitchen remain to attest to the fine brickwork and architecture. It was purchased first by the Colonial Williamsburg Foundation, then later by Anheuser-Busch (1969). It was then that a series of archaeological excavations were initiated by the Virginia Center of Research Archaeology. Eight major digs from one old well shaft along the river bank, and from thirty-five minor sites were studied. Archaeologists have unearthed significant evidence of extensive seventeenth and eighteenth century occupation, including what was once the *Pettus Plantation* (Thomas) overlooking the James. Artifacts from these digs are on display today.

Kingsmill-on-the-James lies along almost three miles of the majestic James River, a residential and resort community. It is unique in its juxtaposition with the very earliest beginnings of Virginia and our country, and in the beauty with which this heritage is incorporated in its planning. It encompasses both a special, privileged history, spectacular natural beauty and a vibrant promise for the future. Richard Kingsmill could not have dreamed of the perpetuation of his plantation in such a manner. In many ways, it seems a revival of the impressions held by George Percy, fifth president of the Council of Virginia, and deputy governor of the Colony in 1611: *The twelfth day (of May, 1607) we discovered a point of land called Archer's Hope (Kingsmill), which was sufficient with a little labour to defend ourselves against any enemy. The soil was good and fruitful, with excellent good timber. There are also great stores of vines...in great abundance. We also did see many Squirrels, Rabbits, Black Birds with crimson wings and divers other Fowles and Birds of divers and sundrie collours...If it had not beene disliked because the ship could not ride neare the shoare, we had settled there to all the Collonies contentment....*

By 1648 the 350 acres of land originally owned by William Claiborne and John Commandres and variously called *Cosbie's, Mount's Bay* or *Quarterland* had been acquired by Richard Richards and renamed Littleton or *Littletown*. Around 1650 *Littletown* and John Wareham's *Hampton Key Plantation* (George Sandys' former *Utopia*) were acquired by Colonel Thomas Pettus. Pettus was from Norwich, England, and built his home on the bluffs overlooking the James River. Colonel Pettus was appointed by the crown to the Council of Colonial Virginia, where he served from 1641 to 1660, a Vestryman of Bruton Parish, and a colonel in the Militia. He died in 1669 and his property passed through his son's wife to her second husband, James Bray II in 1691.

James Bray built a new brick home and dependency complex in 1700, on a hill overlooking the James River. The home was substantial for its day, containing six rooms, several outbuildings and a well. The house was destroyed by fire in 1780, but the locations of the well and house have been identified and are outlined on the site, which is now a part of the Conference Center complex at *Kingsmill-on-the-James*. The Bray family retained ownership until *Littletown* was sold to Colonel William Allen and merged into his large *Kingsmill Plantation* in 1796.

Littletown had been a thriving plantation in its own right in colonial times, even before becoming a part of *Kingsmill Plantation*. Since a small settlement on a main property was called a "quarter", the name has been revived and given to the present community of cluster homes in *Kingsmill-on-the-James*, retaining the flavor of the homes of the colonial period.[1]

We arrived just in time to become a part of the Jamestown archaeological dig, sponsored by the *Association for the Preservation of Virginia Antiquities* (APVA). Over and over we were drawn to Jamestown Island, the site of the ongoing dig, just to stand and watch as artifacts were patiently uncovered and preserved. The APVA had embarked upon a major archaeological investigation, *Jamestown Rediscovery*. With the same determination and teamwork of the founders, the APVA has "pulled off" the major find in the archaeological history of our nation. Once again attention has been paid to Jamestown. This time the APVA had the distinct honor of announcing that the original 1607 fort had been found.[2]

The discovery dispelled the long held belief that James Fort, site of the first permanent English settlement in North America, was lost to the mighty James River.[3] On 12 September 1996, The Honorable George Allen, Governor of the Commonwealth of Virginia proclaimed before all of us and national network news coverage, the finding of the site of the original 1607 James Fort.

The Virginia Company, from which came the conception of Jamestown, was the first English commercial venture to survive in the New World. Thus, from the Jamestown Fort foundations we all are reminded that on this unequaled hallowed ground the foundation of free people and free enterprise was begun. From this birthplace rose the spirit that formed a great state — a great nation — and the ideals emulated by people all across the world. The ambitious, adventurous and enterprising spirit that gave rise to the original fort is the same spirit that has led us to its discovery today.

The original Jamestown Fort stands as an instructive reminder of America's humble, but courageous and noble beginnings. It is the symbolic "cornerstone of America": the foundation of our form of government, law and predominant language began in this place. It is a reminder of our unique and storied history. Jim and I felt privileged to experience the excitement of this revelation.

* * * * *

It is now three hundred ninety years since the first permanent settlers set foot on this soil. It may just be that somehow Jim and I felt drawn to this land. He enjoyed it well, but briefly. We had just "settled in" and noted the history and beauty of the area and the things we wanted to do. While death never comes at the right time; I wanted to scream, "wait, we have not done all that we wanted to do together". Jim died after a brief illness, on November 20, 1996, and was buried in Hollywood Cemetery in the Richmond to which he had contributed his talents and civic pride.

Jim Davis grew up in another era, in South Carolina. He was a gentleman in the truest sense of the word. He was a man of absolute integrity and honor. He lived with dignity and compassion and a great deal of humor. He not only looked for the best in people, he expected the best from them. He had a great love for his family and appreciation of his friends. He lived with faith and a quiet joy, and validated this in his love of the out-of-doors. His legacy lives on.

Because of him my contribution continues in *Tidewater Virginia Families,* and in serving as a volunteer at *Jamestown Rediscovery* and at *Colonial Williamsburg,* in acquainting visitors with their rich heritage in the history of Virginia.

Elizabeth Lee Wadkins Vliet M.D.

15-16;11-12) Lee continues to provide a caring and innovative approach to health and well being and is nationally recognized as Dr. Elizabeth Lee Vliet, an authority in the field of preventive and climacteric medicine. Her work with women's health issues has meant that she is sought by women with serious health issues from all over the United States. Her book *Screaming to Be Heard: Hormone Connections Women Suspect and Doctors Ignore* and her many national speaking engagements mean that women have been able to find answers to health questions that had gone too long unresolved. She is also well-known for her many professional medical articles, and is presently engaged in writing a second book, addressing and answering other pressing women's health issues.

Lee and Gordon are living in Tucson, Arizona, where they work together with Lee's medical practice, HER Place, Health Enhancement and Renewal for Women, Inc. HER Place also has a center in Dallas-Fort Worth, Texas and plans to establish similar programs in other cities. Lee's innovative model addresses overlooked hormonal connections in many illnesses, and brings together state-of-the-art Western medical approaches and the best of alternative medicine modalities.

James Thomas Wadkins III

(16;12) Tom is the J. Thomas Wadkins III, Publishing Consultant of *Tidewater Virginia Families: A Magazine of History and Genealogy*. Without his expertise the magazine would not be possible. Tom's primary employment is with the Richmond City Sheriff's Office as Thomas Wadkins, Major - Chief of Administration. Sheriff Michelle B. Mitchell, for whom he works, was elected to the position when she was only thirty years old. She is one of only seventeen female sheriffs in the United States and only two African-American females in that position in the United States, as well as, the first female elected to that position in the Commonwealth of Virginia.

Following Tom's divorce he met Anne Robin Perdue and they were married on September 27, 1997 at St. Michael's Episcopal Church in Chesterfield County. Their lives should have come together earlier, for she is the granddaughter of Mrs. Mildred Perdue (Mrs. Eddie Philip Perdue), the first grade teacher at Chester High School when I started school in the first grade in that school. Her father, Philip Sutherland Perdue grew up in Chesterfield County in the same community of the school I attended, and we know many of the same people. Philip Perdue married Pattie Burgess, a Virginian for most of her life. There have been so many family connections that it was destined that they meet and marry. Robin is a physical therapist at *Cedarfield*, a retirement community. They live in Richmond, in what was Chesterfield County close to where each of them had lived as children.

Richard Cleveland Wadkins

(16;12) Dick and Helen have moved to a beautiful part of Virginia, and are now living in Edinburg, in the Shenandoah Valley. They have a second daughter, Sarah Tyce Wadkins, born December 31, 1992 in Fredericksburg. Kyle Lee has been selected for the Gifted and Talented Education program in school. She has said that she really likes living near the mountains where they have snow, skiing and sledding nearby; Sarah is busy being a little girl. Helen is associated with the Shenandoah County School System in the field of Work and Family Studies. She has had the distinction of traveling nationally with her students who have been state officers in the Future Homemakers of America.

Dick is presently a staff manager with National Fruit Product Company in Winchester, a national corporation as the name implies, with Winchester being the corporate headquarters and one of their processing facilities for White House brand products. He is serving in the US Coast Guard Reserve as First Class Machinery Technician, currently assigned to the Coast Guard Station at Milford Haven, Mathews County, which is a Search and Rescue facility. He will have served thirty years in 1999, a record of dedication.

(19-30d;14-22)
Chapter 2

WALLER BERNARD HUTCHESON

Gen. 2

(22;16)   The society column of a Richmond newspaper provides a more complete description of the wedding of Nellie and Bernard:[4]   *Pretty Home Wedding*

>   *The home of Mr. and Mrs. Robert Emett [sic] Butler, at "Level Green", was a scene of a pretty marriage Wednesday morning, when their daughter, Nellie, became the bride of Waller Bernard Hutcheson, of Ashland. The Rev. D.M. Bishop, of the Methodist church, officiated, and goldenrod and ferns and candles were arranged in the parlor and dining-room, carrying out effectively the color scheme of yellow and green. The bride entered with her sister, Miss Grace Ruffin Butler, she was met at the altar by the groom and best man, Edward Hutcheson. The bride was attired in a going-away gown of midnight blue and wore a corsage bouquet of Sunburst roses. Miss Grace Ruffin Butler, the maid of honor and only attendant, was gowned in white net and carried Kilarney roses. Only the immediate families were present, and after the ceremony Mr. and Mrs. Hutcheson left for Asheville, N.C. and other Southern cities.*

The Waller Bernard Hutcheson Family

Gen. 1

1. Virginia Lee Hutcheson   m   (1) James Thomas Wadkins, Jr.
b 9 February 1925   b 30 April 1925
p Richmond, Virginia   p Atlanta, Georgia
m 7 August 1944, Chesterfield County, Virginia, divorced 1960
      Issue:
      Gen. 1A
      1. Elizabeth Lee Wadkins   m   Gordon Cheesman Vliet
      b 12 July 1946   b 4 August 1932
      p Richmond, Virginia   p Saginaw, Michigan
      m 13 July 1968, Wren Chapel, Williamsburg, Virginia

      2. James Thomas Wadkins, III   m   (1) Harriette Madelon Gray
      b 22 July 1948   b 4 January 1949
      p Richmond, Virginia   p Oak Hill, West Virginia
      m 29 June 1968, Oak Hill, West Virginia, divorced 1989
                                m   (2) Linda Martin Sowers
                                   b 29 November 1943
                                   p Richmond, Virginia
      m 23 December 1989, Richmond, Virginia, divorced 1991

                                   (3) Anne Robin Perdue
                                   b 18 January 1957
                                   p Richmond, Virginia
      m 27 September 1997, Chesterfield County, Virginia

      3. Richard Cleveland Wadkins   m   (1) Edith Allison Hall
      b 15 January 1951   b
      p Richmond, Virginia   p
      m 25 May 1975, Alexandria, Virginia, divorced 1977
                                m   (2) Helen Anne Struthers
                                   b 6 December 1957
                                   p Phillipsburg, New Jersey
      m 18 February 1984, Fredericksburg, Virginia
            Issue:
            Gen. 2A
            1. Kyle Lee Wadkins
            b 5 December 1987
            p Warren County, Virginia
            2. Sarah Tyce Wadkins
            b 31 December 1992
            p Fredericksburg, Virginia

Virginia Hutcheson Wadkins   m   (2) James Williams Davis, Sr
                                      b 1 May 1906
                                      p Laurens County, South Carolina
m 17 June 1972, Richmond County, Virginia

                                      d 20 November 1996
                                      p Williamsburg, Virginia[5]

Notes

1. William Brown, *Who's Who, Street and Subdivisions in Kingsmill-on-the-James*. Busch Properties, Inc. 1984. Markers at the sites of Kingsmill Plantation and Bray Plantation. See also Paul John, *Burwell Residents of King's Creek*. Privately Printed, 1982. 203 Live Oak, Baytown, TX 77520.
2. Governor George Allen, Press Conference, Jamestown. 12 Sept. 1996. Remarks announcing the discovery of the original 1607 James Fort to national and international media representatives and an assembled audience.
3. Samuel Yonge, *The Site of Old "James Towne"*. (Richmond: APVA, 1903).
4. *Richmond News Leader*. September 29, 1916.
5. Records of family of Virginia Lee Hutcheson can be verified from appropriate Bureau of Vital Records.

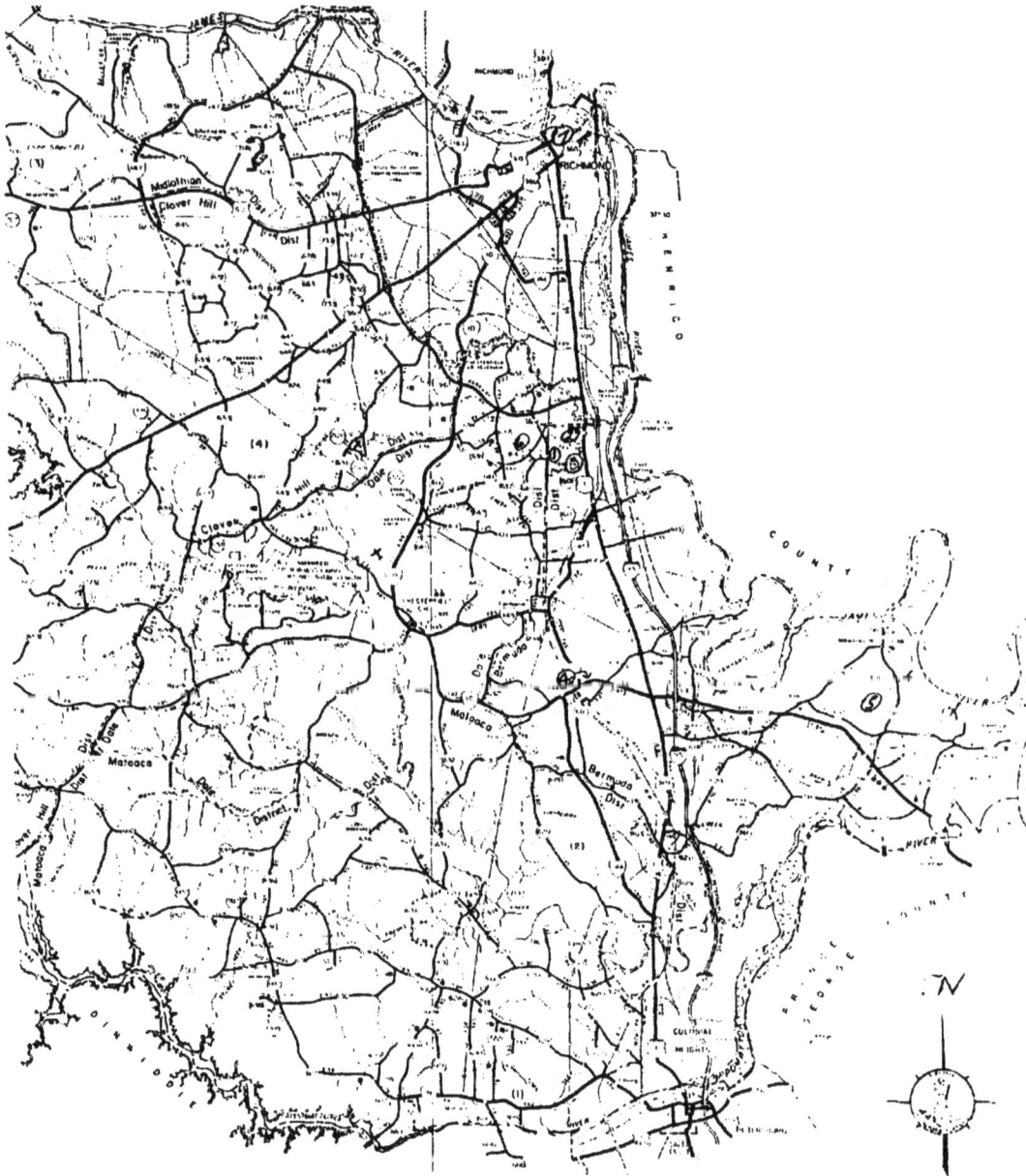

CHESTERFIELD COUNTY

RICHARD WALLER HUTCHESON III

Gen. 3

(32;23-24)   RICHARD WALLER and DORA PEATROSS HUTCHESON set up housekeeping at what was then known as The McLaughlin Place. It was originally a part of *Prospect Hill*, originally land that had belonged to James Harris and left to his daughter, Elizabeth who married Samuel Terrell. It became known as the Ricks home from 1779 (see biographical sketch of Elizabeth Harris Terrell).[1] The farm was owned by Richard A. Ricks during the Civil War.[2] A Legislative petition (1862) that stated: *We the undersigned do hereby certify that 'Ricks' Mill' is indispensable to the comfort of the neighborhood & we recommend that Richard A. Ricks (the miller) be exempted from military service.* It was signed by Dick's father, Richard W. Hutcheson and a number of his neighbors (namely, Henry Doggett, John G. Coleman, Richard H. Burruss, James C. Luck, Parthenia Hutcheson, Geo. M. McLaughlin, Matthew Peatross, Thos. C. Hackett, Joseph F. Robinson and Daniel Turner).[3] It was necessary that he be allowed to keep the mill in operation to supply both the residents of Caroline and the Confederate troops. The remnants of this mill can be seen today. It was later that the old home and a later mill assumed the name of "Shannon Mills".[4] Today the McLaughlin land and Ricks farm form a development called "Caroline Pines". Between the mill pond and the North Anna River is a campground, with the remnants of the two early mills still evident (1997).

Henry Edward Hutcheson
(38,28) Henry Edward Hutcheson and Susan Daniel Cross were married on October 21, 1919 at the home of her mother, Mrs. Nathaniel Benjamin Cross in Ashland. Nathaniel Cross had died the year before on January 26, 1918.[5]

(39;28) Susan Daniel Cross Hutcheson died May 13, 1991 and was buried in Woodland Cemetery with her husband and son, Edward, Jr.[6]

(41-42;28-29)   **Henry Edward Hutcheson Family**

Gen. 1
1. Henry Edward Hutcheson, Jr.
b 29 December 1924
p Ashland, Virginia
d 10 January 1931
p Ashland, Virginia

2. Susan Daniel Hutcheson   m   John Charles Jurgens
b 18 October 1932   b 19 February 1926
p Ashland, Virginia   p Brooklyn, New York
m 10 October 1953, Ashland, Virginia
    Issue:
    Gen. 1A
    1. Susan Carol Jurgens   m   Reza Esteki
    b 6 November 1955   b 30 August 1952
    p Fredericksburg, Virginia   p Isfahan, Iran
    m 9 July 1975, Chicago, Illinois
        Issue:
        GEN. 2A
        1. Jamil David Esteki

b 5 February 1982
p Fairfax County, Virginia

2. Danesh John Esteki
b 28 April 1987
p Leesburg, Virginia

2. Ellen Marie Jurgens	m	John Everett Ransone, Jr.
b 1 July 1959		b 22 January 1948
p Louisa, Virginia		p Richmond, Virginia
m 26 May 1978, Ashland, Virginia		

3. Benjamin Waller Hutcheson	m	Shirley Winston Mallory
b 4 December 1935		b 14 December 1934
p Ashland, Virginia		p Ashland, Virginia
m 15 October 1955, Hanover County, Virginia		d 31 October 1995
		p Richmond, Virginia

Issue:
Gen. 1A

1. Willard Edward Hutcheson	m	Trudy Lee Broyles
b 22 October 1957		b 25 March 1955
p Richmond, Virginia		p Richmond, Virginia
m 19 October 1985, Hanover County, Virginia		

Issue:
Gen. 2A
1. Benjamin Wilton Hutcheson
b 1 March 1987
p Richmond, Virginia
2. Rachel Lee Hutcheson
b 20 March 1989
p Richmond, Virginia
3. Trey Bennett Hutcheson
b 1 October 1990
p Richmond, Virginia

2. Phillip Maylon Hutcheson	m	Kimberly Ann Shaver
b 24 August 1960		b 20 September 1961
p Richmond, Virginia		p Richmond, Virginia
m 16 July 1983, Ashland, Virginia		

Issue:
Gen. 2A
1. Ashleigh Paige Hutcheson
b 3 April 1991
p Richmond, Virginia
2. Christopher Maylon Hutcheson[7]
b 20 May 1996
p Richmond, Virginia

Ilus Morton Hutcheson
(42;29-30)   **Ilus Morton Hutcheson Stebbins Family**

Gen. 1

1. Frances MacMurdo Stebbins	m	(1) John Barton Trevillian
b 24 June 1924		b 1922
p Richmond, Virginia		p
m marriage and divorce dates unknown		d 18 January 1998
		p Richmond, Virginia

10

Issue:
Gen. 1A
1. John Barton Trevillian, Jr. (adopted by Frank A. Shelton, 17 January 1955)

became John Stebbins Shelton	m	(1) Carolyn Lord Taylor Carneal
b 20 October 1947		b
p Richmond, Virginia		p Richmond, Virginia
m 1970, Richmond, Virginia		
John Stebbins Shelton	m	(2) Hilda Freeman
		b
		p
m marriage date and place unknown		
John Stebbins Shelton	m	(3) Deborah Kay Gross
		b 31 March 1961
		p

m 1 November 1985, Prince George, Virginia
    Issue:
    Gen. 2A
    1. Lorraine Frances Shelton
    b 21 January 1988
    p Richmond, Virginia

Frances Stebbins Trevillian	m	(2) Frank Aristidise Shelton, III
		b 31 July 1921
		p Louisa County, Va.

m 14 June 1952, Ashland, Virginia
    Issue:

2. Frances Ann Shelton	m	Gregory Ward Vaughan
b 28 November 1954		b 23 February 1958
p Richmond, Virginia		p Orange County, California
m 18 July 1987, Ashland, Virginia		

        Issue:
        Gen. 2A
        1. Anne Finley Vaughan
        b 22 February 1991
        p Richmond, Virginia

3. Richard Hutcheson Shelton	m	unmarried (1997)
b 15 June 1965		
p Richmond, Virginia[8]		

Richard Maylon Hutcheson

(42-43;31) Margaret Frances Edwards was the daughter of Walter Clayton Edwards and was born April 28, 1907. Margaret's second husband, Eugene Benjamin Crutchfield died May 10, 1991 in Richmond, Virginia.[9]

(41;30)   **Richard Maylon Hutcheson Family**

Gen. 1

Ann Livingston Hutcheson	m	(1) James Arthur, Jr.
b 5 February 1938		b
p Richmond, Virginia		p Richmond, Virginia
m 21 December 1959, Richmond, Virginia	divorced 1975	

    Issue:
    Gen. 1A

Margaret Elizabeth Arthur	m	George Alan Payne
b 28 January 1965		b 1960
p Richmond, Virginia		p Culpeper, Virginia
m 21 September 1996, Paradise Isle, Grand Bahamas		

Gen. 2A
Issue:
Tanner Andrew Payne
b 20 May 1997
p Richmond, Virginia

Ann Hutcheson Arthur   m   (2) William S. Field III
                                                    b 31 May 1935
                                                    p Hampton, Virginia

m 31 December 1986, Gloucester, Virginia[10]

Notes

1. "Prospect Hill" is a large three-story plantation home, the lower floor of brick and the other two of clapboard of English-type construction. It has been used as the club house for the Caroline Pines community but is now in need of repair. The community association is not willing to spend money on the necessary repairs and it is in danger of being used for training purposes by the local volunteer fire department (1997).

2. Herbert Ridgeway Collins, *Cemeteries of Caroline County, Virginia, vol 2* (Westminster, MD: Family Line Publications, 1995) 123.

3. Legislative Petition, Acc. No. 22656, Caroline County Court Papers. Archival and Information Services, Library of Virginia, Richmond, VA.

4. Papers of Arnold R. Ricks, Professor Emeritus, Bennington College, 370 Elm Street, Bennington, VT 05201. Sales brochure of *Shannon Mills Farm*, (Richmond: Whittet & Shepperson, 1926). Also deed, 1887 conveys mill to R.A. Ricks, Caroline County Deed Book 61, 412. See also account of James Harris' land in Caroline County.

5. Correction of date given in first edition. Reported by her daughter, Susan Hutcheson Jurgens.

6. Ibid.; Virginia Bureau of Vital Records (VBVR).

7. As reported by letters from family members of Henry Edward Hutcheson. Records can be verified through appropriate Bureau of Vital Records.

8. As reported by letters from family members of Ilus Morton Hutcheson. Records can be verified through appropriate Bureau of Vital Records.

9. VBVR.

10. As reported by letters from family members of Richard Maylon Hutcheson. Records can be verified through appropriate Bureau of Vital Records.

Gen. 4   **ROBERT EMMET BUTLER**

(45;32) ROBERT BUTLER felt his ties to his home state strongly, and his integrity and sense of duty demanded that he enlist in the "Cause" as soon as he was eligible. Otey Battery was a company in the 13th Battalion, Virginia Light Artillery, later becoming known as Walker's Battery, Virginia Artillery, organized March 14, 1862 and was enlisted in the Confederate States service March 22, 1862 for the war. The captains were listed as George Gaston Otey and David Norvell Walker. Light, or field artillery maneuvered with the troops in the field and employed light or mobile pieces drawn by horses. The most popular pieces used were twelve pounder napoleons, the three inch rifles and twelve pound howitzers.

The six pound smooth bore was used extensively in the early part of the war, but was replaced by rifled pieces; mounted, maneuvered with infantry with cannoneers riding on the ammunitions chest atop the limbers and caissons or the horse artillery, maneuvered with cavalry with cannoneers mounted on horseback. No account has survived as to which position Robert was assigned. The Thirteenth was one of the few recognized as a Virginia Regiment, most (those formed after 1862) were formed by the Confederate States Army.[1] Perhaps this was one of the reasons that Robert felt a continuing sense of loyalty to and pride in the Otey Battery. The men who fought together met often in comraderie to reminisce.

(46;33) In a letter from Robert's father to Dr. William Bates in Wheeling, West Virginia (the father of Marcia, the wife of William, Jr.) dated May 10th, 1865 he wrote: *I thank God I am able to report that my son Robert has been spared to us too. He was wounded thro the left arm (flesh) in a battle on the Saturday afternoon before Genl Lee capitulated Sunday, and taken to Lynchburg where he was kindly cared for be an old friend and brother Harris — and duly paroled as Lee's army. He is still there (and I suppose well by this time) enjoying himself visiting friends and relatives in and around the city; but he too cannot get home, nor indeed write to us — as the R. Road and Canal are for the present impassable — I get my information from members of his company who have been paroled & walked all the way from Lynchburg to this city....*[2] Perhaps ALICE LEE was still in Lynchburg and Robert lingered there instead of facing the long walk home; some 120 miles over devastated countryside.

Gertrude Lee Butler
(55;39)

John William Clay was of the Clay family descended from John Clay who arrived in the colony of Virginia on the *Treasurer* in February 1613, and was thus designated an *Ancient Planter*. He was listed in the muster as a resident on January 21, 1624/25 of Jordan's Journey, south of the James River in Charles City County. His wife, Ann arrived in the *Ann* in August 1623 and his servant William Nicholls, aged 26, arrived in the *Dutie* in May 1619. In 1635 he patented 1200 acres of land on Ward's Creek in what is now Prince George County, 100 acres being due him as an *Ancient Planter*, and 1100 due him for the transportation of twenty-two persons. He also had other lands south of the river and at least one tract near Westover on the north side of the James.[3]

John William Clay married second Gertrude Lee Butler. John Cole Clay was married to Lucy Elizabeth Winston on September 9, 1899 at Marysville Church. William Baldwin Clay died November 30, 1940.[4]

(39-42;54-55,62-64)   **The Gertrude Lee Butler Family**

Gen. 1

1. Alice Elizabeth Clay   m   Vernon Addison Hall
   b 25 December 1900   b 4 May 1900
   p Campbell County, Virginia   p Middlesex County, Virginia
   m 22 October 1924, Miami, Florida

d 26 January 1983   d 23 October 1983
p San Antonio, Texas   p San Antonio, Texas
    Issue:
    Gen. 1A
1. Cynthia Jane Hall   m   (1) Benjamin Leiby
b 16 September 1926   b 19 September 1919
p Miami, Florida   p Cuyahoga Falls, Ohio
m 23 November 1943, Miami Beach, Florida
        Issue:
        Gen. 2A
    1. Pamela Elaine Leiby   m   Douglas Bresler, Jr
    b 8 January 1945   b 3 June 1944
    p Akron, Ohio   p Omaha, Nebraska
    m 27 September 1963, San Antonio, Texas
        Issue:
        Gen. 3A
        1. Kimberly Anne Bresler   m   (1) James L Parkinson
        b 30 April 1964   b 25 Sept 1959
        p San Antonio, Texas   p
        m 26 May 1984, Lake Jackson, Texas, divorced
        Kimberly Bresler Parkinson   m   (2) Derek Alvin Wheeless Neve
                                                 b 9 July 1969
                                                 p
        m 3 May 1997, Texas
        2. Brian Douglas Bresler   m   Jacqueline Lee Raffensperger
        b 27 February 1969   b 23 November 1969
        p Lubbock, Texas   p
        m 14 August 1993, Lake Jackson, Texas
        3. Carey Elizabeth Bresler   unmarried (1997)
        b 14 June 1974
        p Lake Jackson, Texas
Cynthia Hall Leiby   m   (2) George Irving Urbach, Sr.
                                                 b 10 June 1925
                                                 p New York, New York

marriage date and place unknown
                                                 d December 1983
                                                 p San Antonio, Texas

    Issue:
    Gen. 2A
    1. George Irving Urbach, Jr   m   Marlene Rothman
    b 2 May 1954   b 16 December 1948
    p San Antonio, Texas   p Cleveland, Ohio
    m 11 May 1997, Las Vegas, Nevada
    2. Veronica Belle Urbach   m   (1) Jeffrey Brian Shadrock
    b 4 May 1955   b 14 Jan 1952
    p San Antonio, Texas   b San Antonio, Texas
    m 14 February 1971, divorced 1987, San Antonio, Texas
        Issue:
        Gen. 3A
        1. Sherri Louise Shadrock, LtUSA
        b 13 August 1971
        p San Antonio, Texas
        2. Jeffrey Brian Shadrock, Jr
        b 22 August 1977
        p San Antonio, Texas

Veronica Urbach Shadrock   m (2) Edwin Price Riley, Jr
                      b 18 June 1945
                      p San Antonio, Texas

  m 14 March 1992, San Antonio, Texas

2. Susan Irene Clay   m Leonard Allen Brand
 b 29 January 1903   b 25 July 1892
 p Campbell County, Virginia   p Nutley, New Jersey
 m 12 July 1923, Chesterfield County, Virginia

                 d 18 June 1934
                 p Miami, Florida

  Issue:
  Gen. 1A
  1. Leonard Allen Brand, Jr   m Marjorie Keil Hunt
  b 20 May 1924   b 26 November 1935
  p Miami, Florida   p Salem, Ohio
  m 9 April 1955, Miami Beach, Florida
    Issue:
    Gen. 2A
    1. Leonard Allen Brand III m Deborah Carol Smith
    b 18 March 1956   b 10 May 1956
    p Miami Beach, Florida   p Tampa, Florida
    m 14 September 1991, Lantana, Florida
    2. Clay Starling Brand   m Susan Reed Messner
    b 8 November 1957   b 27 January 1961
    p Miami Beach, Florida   p Miami, Florida
    m 27 July 1986, Rochester, New York
      Issue:
      Gen. 3A
      1. Clay Starling Brand, Jr
      b 29 October 1988
      p Palm Beach Gardens, Florida
      2. Reed Eldon Brand
      b 24 July 1993
      p Boynton Beach, Florida
    3. Hunt Keil Brand   m Rebecca Ann Burke
    b 1 January 1961   b 1 September 1964
    p Boynton Beach, Florida   p Sarasota, Florida
    m 14 July 1990, Palm Beach, Florida
      Issue:
      Gen. 3A
      1. Nathan Hunt Brand
      b 16 January 1997
      p Boynton Beach, Florida
    4. Keil Winston Brand m unmarried (1997)
    b 4 November 1969
    p North Miami, Florida
  2. Raymond Starling Brand m Mary Ann MacKenzie
  b 29 June 1926   b 27 March 1938
  p Miami, Florida   p Ann Arbor, Michigan
  m 8 April 1961, West Palm Beach, Florida
    Issue:
    Gen. 2A
    1. Raymond Starling Brand, Jr unmarried (1997)
    b 19 February 1962
    p Boynton Beach, Florida

2. John Robert Brand   unmarried (1997)
 b 31 January 1963
 p Boynton Beach, Florida
3. Robert Clay Brand   m Nancy Jean Hunt
b 29 June 1926 (twin)   b 15 November 1930
p Miami, Florida   p Salem, Ohio
m 5 May 1951, Miami Beach, Florida
   Issue:
   Gen. 2A
   1. Sandra Lee Brand m Reid Kurt Jacobsma
    (by adoption)
    b 3 June 1957   b 30 October 1952
    p Miami, Florida   p Sioux City, Iowa
    m 9 June 1979, Sioux City, Iowa
       Issue:
       Gen. 3A
       1. Paul Michael Jacobsma
       b 22 April 1980
       p Sioux City, Iowa
       2. Lee Soo Jacobsma
        (by adoption)
       b 9 September 1981
       p Pusan, Korea
   2. Nancy Jeanne Brand m Mark Stansberry
    (by adoption)
    b 18 September 1962   b 5 July 1956
    p Miami, Florida   p Iowa
    m 24 July 1982, Sioux City, Iowa
       Issue:
       Gen. 3A
       1. Conner Allan Stansberry
       b 12 August 1992
       p Sioux City, Iowa
       2. Bryce Allan Stansberry
       b 12 August, 1995
       p Sioux City, Iowa[5]

Alfred Lee Butler
(58-60,64-67;44-47)   The Alfred Lee Butler Family

Gen. 1
1. Alfred Lee Butler, Jr   m Norma Irene Gaspari
b 17 February 1919   b 26 December 1920
p Campbell County, Virginia   p San Francisco, Calif.
m 25 August 1948, San Juan, Puerto Rico
d 2 January, 1994
p Cocoa Beach, Florida
   Issue:
   Gen. 1A
   1. Alfred Lee Butler III m Molly Sue Risher
    b 4 September 1950   b 28 December 1950
    p Washington, D.C.   p Columbus, Ohio
    m 2 June 1978, Hubert, North Carolina
    d 8 February 1984, Beirut, Lebanon, Major USMC
       Issue:

Gen. 2A

    1. Alfred Lee Butler IV

    b 19 May 1979

    p Media, Pennslyvania

    2. Nicholas Xaviar Butler

    b 27 June 1981

    p Media, Pennslyvania

2. Melvin Gaspari Butler   m   Louise Francis

b 9 March 1952   b 19 November 1952

p Arlington, Virginia   p Cleveland, Ohio

m 1 January 1985, Cocoa Beach, Florida

    Issue:

    Gen. 2A

    1. Mark Melvin Butler

    b 16 April 1986

    p St. Petersburg, Florida

    2. Mary Louise Butler

    b 18 November 1987

    p New Port Richey, Florida

3. Carolyn Jane Butler   unmarried (1997)

b 23 August 1957

p Rockledge, Florida

4. Katherine Anne Butler   m   Charles McCabe Broughton

b 23 August 1957 (twin)   b 13 December 1958

p Rockledge, Florida   p Washington, D.C.

m 31 May 1986, Cocoa Beach, Florida

    Issue:

    Gen. 2A

    1. Charles McCabe Broughton, Jr.

    b 12 January 1988

    p Seattle, Washington

    2. Andrew Primo Broughton

    b 3 April 1989

    p Cocoa Beach, Florida

    3. Sarah Greene Broughton

    b 25 October 1991

    p Cocoa Beach, Florida

5. Virginia Grace Butler   m   Thomas Gibson Broughton III

b 17 October 1958   b 17 July 1957

p Rockledge, Florida   p Rockledge, Fla.

m 6 April 1985 Cocoa Beach, Florida

    Issue:

    Gen. 2A

    1. Amanda Leigh Broughton

    b 10 January 1986

    p Cocoa Beach, Florida

    2. Thomas Gibson Broughton IV

    b 1 May 1987

    p Cocoa Beach, Florida

    3. John Patrick Broughton

    b 1 August 1991

    p Cocoa Beach, Florida

2. Bess Jacquelin Butler   m   Robert Samuel Vandiver

b 22 August 1920   b 11 December 1917

p Chesterfield County, Virginia   p Florence, Alabama

m 22 April 1943, Sebring, Florida
d 29 August 1962
p Omaha, Nebraska

    Issue:

    Gen. 1A

    1. Carol Lee Vandiver   m   John Dale Lark
    b 9 September 1946   b 27 January 1947
    p Tampa, Florida   p St. Louis, Mo.
    m. 30 September 1966, Andrews Air Force Base, Maryland

        Issue:

        Gen. 2A

        1. Jenifer Elizabeth Lark m   Brian Baetz
        b 22 March 1968   b
        p St. Louis, Missouri   p

            Issue:

            Gen. 3A

            Zachary Baetz
            b July 1996
            p

        2. Jonathan Peter Lark   m   Annamarie Espares
        b 10 September 1969   b
        p St. Louis, Missouri   p
        m
        3. Scott Jeremy Lark   unmarried (1998)
        b 2 July 1974
        p St. Louis, Missouri

    2. June Elizabeth Vandiver   m   (1) William Bruce Burchard
    b 15 March 1948   b 27 July 1942
    p Monterey, California   p Springfield, Missouri
    m 27 July 1972, Knoxville, Tennessee, divorced, 1989

        Issue:

        Gen. 2A

        1. William Bruce Burchard III   unmarried (1997)
        b 17 May 1973
        p Lexington, Kentucky
        2. Walter Pinson Burchard   unmarried (1997)
        b 25 May 1975
        p Lexington, Kentucky

Gen. 1

(3) Robert Hardy Butler   m   Charleton June Galloway
b 20 October 1928   b 22 April 1928
p Sebring, Florida   p DeSoto City, Florida
m 24 November 1950, Sebring, Florida

    Issue:

    Gen. 1A

    1. Patricia Ann Butler   m   (1) William Vitter
    b 31 December 1951   b 7 September 1948
    p Gainesville, Florida   p Pennsylvania
    m 2 December 1978, Orlando, Florida divorced June 1988
    Patricia Butler Vitter   m   (2) James Thomas
                                     b 27 September 1947
                                   p Lake Butler, Florida

    m 29 February 1992, Florida

        Issue:

        Gen. 2A

1. Robert S Vitter
b 2 September 1980
p Inverness, Florida
2. Brittany C Vitter
b 23 November 1985
p Inverness, Florida
2. Deborah Sue Butler   unmarried (1997)
b 19 April 1954
p Orlando, Florida
3. Stefanie June Butler   unmarried (1997)
b 10 September 1958
p Tampa, Florida

Ann Crawley Butler

(61;47) While Ann Crawley Butler did not leave any descendants, it has always been of interest to the family as to the origin of her name. All of the Butler "children" were given family names, apparently of those relatives of whom they were fond. Aunt Crawley's name stood out as "different", and no one seemed to be able to identify its original owner, least of all Aunt Crawley. She was probably named for Ann Crawley Winston (probably born between 1810-1820), the daughter of Peter Winston, the son of Peter and Elizabeth Povall Winston. The first wife of Peter Winston was Susan Jones, the daughter of Elizabeth Crawley (the great granddaughter of William Claiborne). Ann Crawley married James B. Jones, the son of John Winston Jones.[6]

Notes

1. Lee A. Wallace, Jr., *A Guide to Virginia Military Organizations.* 1964. (Lynchburg, VA: H.E.Howard, rev. 1986) 1,6.
2. From the papers of Dr. Andrew Butler, Wheeling, West Virginia, a grandson of William Fleming Butler, Jr. and his wife, Marcia Ann Bates. See also William Fleming Butler, Sr for the rest of the letter.
3. Robert Young Clay, from a talk presented to the Jamestowne Society, May 1995.
4. Clay Family Bible Record, Acc. No. 22700, Virginia State Library and Archives, Richmond, VA.
5. As reported by letters from family members of Gertrude Lee Butler. Records can be verified through appropriate Bureau of Vital Records.
6. John Frederick Dorman and Claiborne T. Smith, Jr., MD, *Claiborne of Virginia Descendants of Colonel William Claiborne.* (Baltimore: Gateway Press, 1995). 234,237,242.

Women's Clothing 1900s

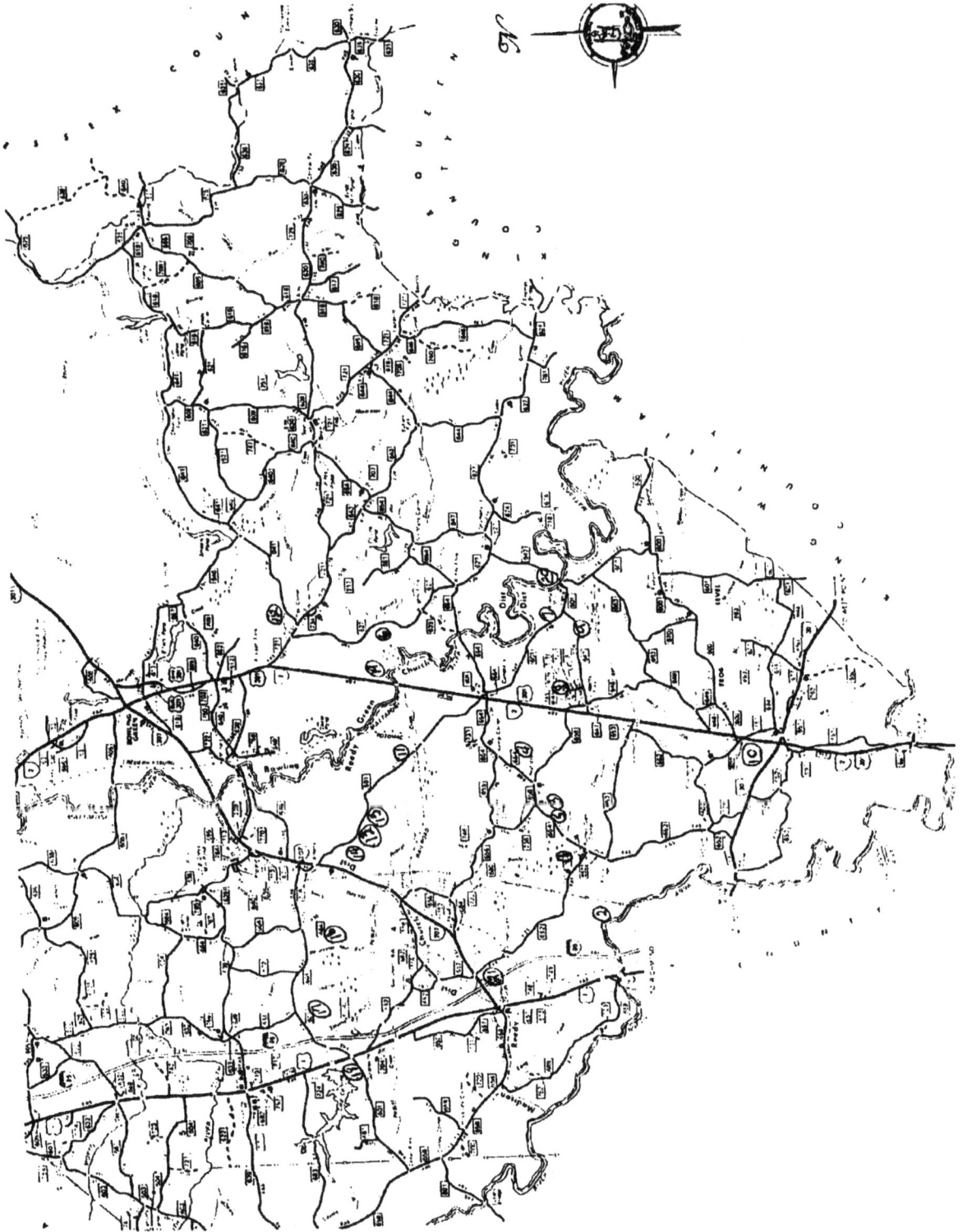

CAROLINE COUNTY

20

SECTION II

THE PROGENITORS

RICHARD HUTCHENS

Gen. 9

(72;53)   No record has been found of a Brock family in either Essex or Middlesex counties. It is known that William Broocke was one appointed to appraise the estate of RICHARD HUTCHENS.[1] Given the variant spellings entered in the court records, it is worthy of note that he and his wife, Ann Cardwell had a daughter, Ann born January 21, 1693/4 in Christ Church Parish in Middlesex County. Another entry in the parish register provides a further link between the families in the marriage of John Brookes and Mary Hutchings on January 23, 1680.[2] One or both of these may provide the link with Richard Hutchens' gift to his god daughter.

(71,75-76;53,56-57) No further information has come to light to identify the origins of Richard Hutchens. A Richard Hutchinson was listed in the Public Records Office of London[3], (among others) as *Shippers by the Concord, Mr. Thomas Grantham, bound from London for Virginia: [Thomas] Baker, Thomas Jaques, Richard Glover, Robert Johnson, George Baker, Richard Hutchinson.* 29 August-11 September 1676. (75;56) There are a number of entries of headrights with the name of John Hutchinson (varied spelling) from Bristol or other English ports. (90;70-71) If the progenitor of John Hutcheson of Caroline County entered the colony from an English port this does not in any way disprove the belief that the Hutcheson family was of Scottish origin. Whether it was a John, the father of Richard, or Richard himself who first came to Virginia, he may well have left the British Isles through an English port, as did many Scottish emigrants. No parish records for the time frame and area of Scotland in question appear to have survived to further this research.

(74,56) While it was not stated clearly in the original text, it is clear from the recordation of the deed of gift (1722) by Rebecca Hutchens of one-half of the 175 acres of land, that she was in possession of the full amount of land left by Richard Hutchens I to his two sons. It is further clear that the land deeded by Andrew Hardee and his wife, Jane to Thomas Smith constituted one half of the land that had been owned by Richard Hutchens II. Thomas Smith would have owned the other one-half by virtue of his marriage to the widow Rebecca Hutchens. That Jane Hardy was Jane Williams before her marriage, and very probably the step-sister of Richard Hutchens is revealing; however, a further search of the Essex County records has failed to produce evidence that Jane Hutchens married a second time a man named Williams.

(75;57) The William Hutchinson, who was a burgess in Isle of Wight County in 1632, left a son William. While no mention can be found of any male heirs, a record has been found for October 30, 1673, where William Hatcher appeared before the Governor and General Court on behalf of the orphans of William Hutchenson concerning Hutchenson's 300 acres of land on the north side of the Rappahannock River.[4] The orphans are not named, nor have their names been identified in later records.

(75,77;57,58) It is unfortunate that the two references that provide information about the Hutchings of Lancaster County that disprove the descent of Richard Hutchens from William Hutchings of that county were the victims of typographical errors. This has led researchers to question the validity of this information, and to perpetuate the inaccuracy of this line of descent. The correct references should have been: Will of John Hutchings, recorded 13 December 1727; **Endnote 34, Lancaster County Will Book 12, pages 41 and 42, also see page 46**. The will makes it quite clear that John Hutchings had a son, William who was living and a grandson, John Hutchings. **Endnote 35 should have read Lancaster County Will Book 18, page 21**. To this should be added Lancaster County Deed and Will Book 18, page 169. This last reference clearly shows that the estate of John Hutchings, deceased had gone to his son, John Hutchings. This entry was dated the 15th September 1768. If one follows the references in the Lancaster County records from 1727 until the probate of the will of John Hutchings of 1785,[5] one will confirm the fact that the John Hutchings of this family remained in Lancaster County.

(76;57) It has been suggested that the son of Joseph and Mary Needles Hutchinson married on January 2, 1705[6] was the John who was later found in Caroline County. Their first son John, was baptized November 17th, 1706 and apparently died since a second son, John was baptized on February 25th, 1710. From the later record of Joseph's death, this John must have also died, since he was not mentioned as an orphan of Joseph along with his other children.

(78-86;59-67)
Gen. 8

JOHN HUTCHESON I

(80;61)   The reference to log houses should be corrected to frame houses. Log houses as one envisions them from the mountains of Virginia were not built in colonial tidewater Virginia. Houses may have been originally post-in-the ground houses, with rough clapboard construction. As bricks or stone could be obtained the foundation would have become more durable with a solid foundation. In any case, many families began life on their new land with a simple lean-to, until tobacco could be planted and harvested.

The reference to Chesterfield Church states that the date of construction is not known. It is known that St. Margaret's Parish was created in 1720 and that the "new church" at that time was the Mangohick Church, built prior to 1732, and referred to as "the chapel" in Caroline County records. The second parish church in St. Margaret's Parish was a brick building, located east of South River, southwest of Bowling Green, and north of Chesterfield.[7] It became known first as Chesterfield Church, with the earliest reference found in a Caroline County court order of June 1738. Later the church became known locally as "Bull Church", a name that continued until a petition was filed (1821) to return the property to the county after the Disestablishment of the Church of England.[8] The petition stated that *Bull Church is unfit for religious purposes being so far in a state of decay that it will not afford a shelter from snow, rain or inclement weather.* Bull Church was located several miles west of what is now Penola, on the north side of the road leading from Ladysmith eastward. It is said to have acquired its name from the bulls that the workmen killed and ate while they were building the church.

Charles Hutcheson
(84;65) The children of Charles Hutcheson: John married Sarah, the daughter of James and Agnes Baugh. John moved to Montgomery County, Tennessee and died there before 1856. Collier married (1) Sarah, the daughter of John Collier of Charlotte County, and (2) on September 18, 1804, Sarah Williams, the daughter of Thomas and Frances Williams of Charlotte County. Collier settled in Charlotte County. Joseph married (1) Rebecca, the daughter of Sterling Neblet and Mary Chappell of Lunenburg County; he married (2) November 17, 1825, Mary Clifford Valentine of Richmond, in Mecklenburg County. Sarah, born March 13, 1771, died 1853, married her cousin John, the son of Peter and Elizabeth Brame Hutcheson. Lucy, as recorded. Susannah and Deveriux Hightower moved to Texas. Martha, born March 10, 1782 married Dabney Phillips, Jr, born August 9, 1780, son of Dabney Phillips. Hannah married John, the son of David and Ann Taylor Moore of Lunenburg County. Elizabeth married in Mecklenburg County.[9]

John Hutcheson
(84-85;65) The children of John Hutcheson: Jemima's husband, James, the son of James and Millicent Ferrell, Mecklenburg County, died before October 26, 1818 in Halifax County. Mary and her husband moved to Williamson County, Tennessee. Chiles married Frances Moss the daughter of Ray Moss. Chiles Hutcheson died in 1803, his widow, Frances married (2) July 16, 1804, Young Hudson. John married December 24, 1793 (1) Anne Stone, daughter of William Stone, died on January 16, 1801; John married (2) September 1, 1801, in Mecklenburg County, Mary Jones Suggett, the daughter of Stephen Jones, Brunswick County and widow of Edgecomb Suggett. John Hutcheson died in 1848. Samuel married Hannah Brame the daughter of Thomas and Elizabeth Rolfe Brame and the granddaughter of Richens and Susannah Chiles Brame. William

Hutcheson was born January 12, 1776. Susannah married William Stone, the son of William Stone. Elizabeth married John Stone the son of Thomas and Mary Nethery Stone. Richard married Wilmouth Malone Turner, born January 16, 1774, the daughter of George and Lucy Carter Malone, Mecklenburg County, and widow of Matthew Turner, Jr. Richard and Wilmouth moved to Franklin County, Georgia.[10]

Peter Hutcheson

(85;65) Peter Hutcheson, born December 30, 1743, died October 16, 1820, married Elizabeth Brame, born September 2, 1751 and died February 17, 1821, Mecklenburg County. She was the daughter of Richens and Susannah Chiles Brame. Peter established himself some three miles west of Boyton on the west side of what is now County Road (CR) 691. John Hutcheson, born June 26, 1768, Caroline County, died April 17, 1825, Mecklenburg County. He married on November 22, 1786, his first cousin, Sarah Hutcheson (daughter of Charles and Frances Collier Hutcheson); born March 13, 1771 and died 1853. Thirteen children died in infancy, their names unknown. Peter Wesley Hutcheson, born March 17, 1794 (died December 9, 1875) and married March 1818, Mecklenburg County, Eliza Fisher Carleton, who died October 6, 1875 in Oglethorpe County, Georgia. Elizabeth Whitfield Hutcheson was born November 6, 1795, married (1) December 20, 1819, Daniel Jones, and (2) Hiram Hayes, Clarke County, Georgia. She died July 9, 1870.[11]

Richard Hutcheson

(85;66) Richard married c.1766 Mary Chiles; he died January 1806. Their children: William married Amy, the daughter of Thomas and Mary Brown. Sally married William, the son of Thomas and Mary Brown. Richard, the son, married Sally, the widow of Charles Turner and he and Sally moved to Franklin County, Georgia. Peter married Lilly, probably the daughter of John and Rebecca Hudson Wagstaff. Anna married the son of John and Mary Norment Brame, a grandson of Richens and Susannah Chiles Brame. Ambrose was born June 12, 1782 in Mecklenburg County, married (1) Hannah Wilson of Lunenburg County. He married (2) Elizabeth Baldwin and (3) on March 30, 1815, Rachel Robins (born October 4, 1796 and died August 13, 1886) in Greene County, Georgia. He died November 18, 1861.[12]

It is interesting that the Brame and Hutcheson families both moved to Mecklenburg County and there were a number of marriages among the Brame, Chiles and Hutchesons, probably both before they left Caroline County and after they settled in Mecklenburg. The Brames, Chiles and Hutchesons all lived in the same area of Caroline. This can be seen from later court records and land plats, showing them all as neighbors. The plat of land at Reedy Mill of Samuel Norment of a later date gives a drawing of the Reedy Mill Meeting House, the land given by Melchezedick Brame, the brother of Richins Brame, for the Presbyterian Meeting shortly after it was established in Caroline County.[13] A court order book entry records the permission of the court for leave to erect a house on the lands of Melchezedick Brame for their public worship, that is a dissenting group, the Presbyterians.

(87-91;68-72)
Gen. 7   AMBROSE HUTCHESON

(88,332;67) A Petition was presented to the Virginia Legislature on December 17, 1821 requesting that the property of the disestablished Anglican Church, that is, Reedy Church in Caroline County be returned to people of St. Margaret's Parish, Caroline County.[14] It was stated that the church "had fallen". Permission to build Reedy Church had been secured in 1741.[15] Reedy Church has been conclusively identified as having been located at what is now the intersection of CR 656 and CR 654. The site is now known to adjoin the present day location of St. Paul's United Methodist Church. It would have been Reedy Church that Ambrose and his family attended. One can follow what must been the road to the church today.[16]

(88;69) It would appear from the ages of the known children of AMBROSE HUTCHESON and from the assumed age of his father that Ambrose was under the age of forty when he died.

(89;70) The final resting place of Ambrose and his wife was surely on his property, in the family burying ground that can be identified to this day. All of the research concerning burial customs of this time period would indicate that they would have established the graveyard for their family, at the edge of their garden.[17]

(94-95;75) correction: The paragraph concerning JOHN and SARAH HUTCHESON's attendance at church was unfinished, and the next three paragraphs were missing from the second edition. They should read as follows:

Church was important in the lives of John and Sarah, as with their neighbors. Not only had they initially defied the Church of England in their attendance, but they traveled great distances in many cases to attend. After the Disestablishment of the Church of England, John and Sarah could attend the church they chose in freedom, but they still traveled a long way. It was at least six miles from Signpost to Burruss Church (later, Carmel Baptist Church). Eventually John did have a gig, a two-seated, light-weight, two-wheeled vehicle, drawn by one horse. It would not have accommodated his whole family. Before that time there was only John's cart and oxen, and walking. Most people walked to church, even what seems today to be a very long distance. For Sarah, the church was likely the only opportunity that she had to be with other women and not be working.

John appeared in court on at least two occasions to collect debts owed him; one time in 1767, in a suit against Chapman, and again, in 1796, in a suit against Thomas Burk and John Gatewood. John recovered against the defendant in the second case, £32.7.8, along with interest and court costs. This was one-half of the amount owed him.[18]

In 1810 John reported that he and Sarah were over forty-five when the census taker came around.[19] This would be consistent with the birth dates already mentioned. Four children were living at home at that time, among them a boy and girl under the age of ten. Sally may have been the girl, and the boy may have been a grandchild. Nancy and John may have been the other children still at home.

John had prospered by this time; he now owned fourteen slaves and was the master of a well-managed plantation. Two of the daughters of John and Sarah were married. Polly married James Eubank, the son of a close neighbor, in December 1806. He was a Baptist minister and preaching at Bethel Baptist Church.[20] Jenny married Mr. Hodges, and must have died soon after her marriage, leaving a small son.[21]

Ambrose Hutcheson
(96;77) Mary Jane Hutcheson, daughter of Mr. Ambrose Hutcheson was married in Henrico County by the Rev. M.T. Sumner to Norborne E. Sutton, Esq. October 15, 1846.[22]

Nancy Hutcheson
(97-98;78) Nancy Hutcheson married Thompson Hodges October 24, 1812 with the consent of her father, John Hutcheson, who signed with his mark on October 25, 1812. Witnesses were Richard Hutcheson and Thomas Butler. Security was provided by Thomas Butler, who signed with his mark, witnessed by Pitchegrue (sic) Woolfolk.[23] One might conclude, in the absence of an extant marriage record, that Jenny may have been the first husband of Thompson Hodges, based on the information in the will of the father, John Hutcheson.

Sarah Hutcheson
(98-99;78-79) The complete transcription of the Legislative Petition requesting the legality of Sarah's marriage to James Luck has been secured by this researcher. It is quite interesting and revealing of the sentiment of the times. For anyone interested in social history and evolving customs, this makes for interesting reading. It should be pointed out that James Luck was a nephew **by marriage**, not a blood relative. In light of the number of marriages in Caroline County that were contrary to the Levitical Laws still in effect, the stand taken in this particular case is unusual.

RICHARD WALLER HUTCHESON I

(103;83) The Richmond, Fredericksburg and Potomac Railroad, affectionately called "the RF&P" was sold in 1995 to the CSX Corporation, ending an era. A passenger train still operates between Richmond and Washington, under the Amtrac regulations; CSX operates freight trains along the same tracks. The passenger train stops only at the towns along the way, the small communities are no longer served, having to depend upon highway and bus travel today. Many of the small communities evidence only remnants of their former activity, but much of the route is through countryside of Caroline County that is still rural (1997).

(104;83-84) Emmaus Church was located beyond the Samuel Chiles homeplace. Its exact location has been described by Herbert Collins as being one-tenth of a mile north of the old Penola Post Office on CR 601. Herbert places the date of establishment as 1837, a branch of Antioch Christian Church, which may account for the earlier date of 1826.[24] The school house in which they met in winter was across from *Palestine Farm*, on the south side of Polecat Creek. The arbor tree, an ancient white oak still stands at the gate to the farm on the opposite side of CR 601 (1997). The church burned during an ice storm on a Sunday in February 1943 and was never rebuilt. Evidence of the cemetery remain, with a few graves identified, and many unmarked graves.

(105;84) **A correction:** Slaves were considered to be personal property, and were so listed in the Personal Property Tax Records of each county, but deeds of ownership and the transfer of ownership were drawn up and recorded as deeds were also executed for real property. Also to clarify a wife's right to land, it should be understood, that while the husband held legal title to the land, he could not give clear title to that land if he were to sell it, without the voluntary relinquishment of the dower right of his wife.

(107;86) John Wilson Hutcheson's grave is marked with a Confederate marker with the inscription: *John W. Hutcheson, Co. E, 30 Va. Inf., C.S.A., (Died May 1902, age 84).*[25]

RICHARD WALLER HUTCHESON II

(111;89) The membership roll of Emmaus Church included this entry: RICHARD HUTCHESON, restored to membership, August 1872.

(111,89) It is interesting that a newspaper announcement has been found placing the marriage date of RICHARD W. HUTCHESON and Miss FRANCES ANN PEATROSS as February 4, 1844, at the home of William Mallory in Caroline County.[26] This seems to be more in keeping with the date on which the marriage bond was issued. The Mallory family lived in the Signpost (present-day Ruther Glen Corner) community with the Hutchesons and Lucks.[27]

(113;91) Richard enlisted in the 30th Regiment of Virginia Volunteers, the Caroline Grays, Bowling Green, organized December 12, 1859. It was accepted into the Confederate States on July 1, 1861 and reorganized April 16, 1862, under Captains Richard Olin Peatross and John W. Scott.[28] When Richard re-enlisted in the Cavalry it was under Captain Littleberry Wilson Allen. This cavalry regiment was formed by the consolidation of the 32nd and 40th Battalions, Virginia Cavalry forming the 42nd Battalion, two which two companies of the Eighth Regiment were later added.[29]

Edward Hebious Hutcheson
(115;93)
  Permission was granted for Edward to be buried in the Sweeny plot at Hollywood Cemetery, and he was buried beside Jennie, his wife.

Anna Morton Hutcheson
(116;93)

The listing for Anna Morton Hutcheson appeared in the Richmond City Directory for the year 1890; she would have married John Henry Rice after that date.

(118;93-94)   **HUTCHESON FAMILY**

Gen. 9 RICHARD HUTCHENS		m	JANE (—?—)
Issue:	JOHN	m	MARY (—?—)
	Richard	m	Rebecca (—?—)
	Catherine	m	
Gen. 8 JOHN HUTCHESON		m	MARY (—?—)
Issue:	AMBROSE	m	UNKNOWN
	John	m	Elizabeth Chiles
	Peter	m	Elizabeth Brame
	Charles	m	Frances Collier
	Richard	m	Mary Chiles (p)
	Mary	m	
Gen. 7 AMBROSE HUTCHESON		m	UNKNOWN
Issue:	JOHN AMBROSE	m	SARAH BUTLER
	Peter	m	
	Susanna	m	
Gen. 6 JOHN AMBROSE HUTCHESON		m	SARAH BUTLER
Issue:	Ambrose	m	Mildred Brown
	Polly	m	James Eubank
	Jenny	m	(—?—) Hodges
	RICHARD WALLER	m	MARY PERNALIA CHILES
	Nancy	m	Thompson Hodges
	John	m	Mary Dudley Brown
	Sarah	m	(1) Pleasant Chiles
		m	(2) James C. Luck
Gen. 5 RICHARD WALLER HUTCHESON I		m	MARY PERNALIA CHILES
Issue:	John Wilson	m	Parthenia Wright
	RICHARD WALLER	m	FRANCES ANN PEATROSS
	Ambrose Anderson	m	Sarah Ann Worshing
	Charles Elliott		unmarried
Gen. 4 RICHARD WALLER HUTCHESON II		m	FRANCES ANN PEATROSS
Issue:	Edward Hebious	m	Jennie Sweeney
	Henry Chiles		unmarried
	Mary Pamelia (Molly)		umarried
	Sarah Frances (Sally)		unmarried
	Anna Morton (Motie)	m	John Henry Rice
	RICHARD WALLER	m	DORA LIVINGTON PEATROSS
Gen. 3 RICHARD WALLER HUTCHESON III		m	DORA LIVINGSTON PEATROSS
Issue:	Frances Campbell		unmarried
	WALLER BERNARD	m	NELLIE BUTLER
	Henry Edward	m	Susan Daniel Cross
	Ilus Morton	m	Charles Stebbins
	Richard Maylon	m	Margaret Frances Edwards

Gen. 2 WALLER BERNARD HUTCHESON	m	NELLIE BUTLER
Issue: VIRGINIA LEE	m	(1) JAMES THOMAS WADKINS, JR
	m	(2) James Williams Davis, Sr.

Gen. 1 VIRGINIA LEE HUTCHESON	m	(1)JAMES THOMAS WADKINS, JR.
Issue: Elizabeth Lee	m	Gordon Cheesman Vliet
James Thomas Wadkins III	m	(1) Harriette Madelon Gray
	m	(2) Linda Martin Sowers
	m	(3) Anne Robin Perdue
Richard Cleveland	m	(1) Edith Allison Hall
	m	(2) Helen Ann Struthers
Virginia Hutcheson Wadkins	m	(2) James Williams Davis, Sr

Notes

1. *Essex County Will Book 14.* 84.

2. National Society of Colonial Dames of America in the State of Virginia, *The Parish Register of Christ Church, Middlesex County, Va. from 1653 to 1812.* 1897 (Baltimore: Clearfield, rep. 1990). 35, 52, 20.

3. Peter Wilson Coldham, *Complete Book of Emigrants, 1661-1699.* (Baltimore: Genealogical Publishing Co, 1990). 270.

4. H.R. McIlwaine, ed., *Minutes of the Council and General Court of Colonial Virginia.* 1924. (Richmond: Virginia State Library, rep. 1979). 357.

5. *Lancaster County Wills, Etc.* 22 29.

6. *Christ Church Register.* 80.

7. "The Colonial Churches of Spotsylvania and Caroline Counties, Virginia." *Virginia Magazine of History and Biography (VMHB).* 58(1950): 465.

8. Reedy Church and Bull Church, Legislative Petitions, Caroline County, 1821. Archival and Information Services, Library of Virginia, Richmond, VA.

9. Joseph L. Dean, Unpublished Mss., 1993. 2878 Avalon Meadows Ct, Lawrenceville, GA 30044. Mr. Dean has compiled the family lines of each of the four sons of John Hutcheson of Caroline County that moved to Mecklenburg County: Charles, John, Peter and Richard, to the present generations.

10. Dean.

11. Dean; Peter Hutcheson Family Bible, dated 1828. Copy in possession of Swepson O'Neil Hutcheson III, 1497 Mt. Vernon Road, Dunwood, GA 30338.

12. Dean.

13. *Caroline County Wills, 1742, 1762, 1830, Platts 1777-1840* 158. Dr. T. Marshall Smith, *Legends of the War of Independence and of the Early Settlements West* (Louisville: Brennam, 1855) 108-115; *Caroline County Court Order Book 1771* 300.

14. Reedy Church and Bull Church, Legislative Petitions, Caroline County, 1821. Archival and Information Services, Library of Virginia, Richmond, VA.

15. "The Colonial Churches of Spotsylvania and Caroline Counties, Virginia," *VMHB.* 58(1950): 466.

16. *Petition, Caroline County, 1821, Reedy Church and Bull Church, TVF.* 1(1992): 33-36.

17. Herbert Ridgeway Collins, *Cemeteries of Caroline County, Virginia, Private Cemeteries.* volume 2. (Westminster, MD: Family Line, 1995). 89.

18. *Caroline County Appeals and Land Causes, 1777-1807* 345.

19. US Census, Caroline County, 1810. The census information listed the number of people living in a household, in each age category, but did not identify relationships. Inferences may be drawn concerning these relationships, in light of other known information, but it must be kept in mind that no relationships are defined.

20. Marshall Wingfield, *History of Caroline County, Virginia.* 1924 (Baltimore: Clearfield, 1991). 318-319.

21. Hutcheson Family Papers. Accession Number 30739. Archival and Information Services, The Library of Virginia, Richmond, VA.

22. Virginia Genealogical Society, *Marriage Notices From Richmond, Virginia Newspapers, 1841-1853.* (Richmond: Virginia Genealogical Society (VGS), 1997). 122.

23. Robert Vietrozoski, *Magazine of Virginia Genealogy.* 31(1993): 102.

24. Herbert Ridgeway Collins, *Cemeteries of Caroline County, Virginia, Public Cemeteries.* vol 1. (Westminster, MD: Family Line, 1994) 42.

25. Collins, 2: 89.

26. Virginia Genealogical Society, *Marriage Notices from Richmond, Virginia Newspapers, 1841-1853.* (Richmond: VGS, 1997) 62.

27. Mark Anderson Sprouse, *Caroline County, Virginia Federal Census of 1850.* (Athens, GA: Iberian, 1997) 1.

28. Lee A. Wallace, *A Guide to Virginia Military Organizations.* 1964 (Lynchburg, VA: H.E.Howard, rev 1986) 63.

29. Wallace 114.

(119-124;96-100)
Chapter 6

MATTHEW PEATROSS I

Gen. 9

(119;96) It seems fairly conclusive that the entry concerning John Pedros of Lancaster County (1652) does in fact refer to a JOHN PEATROSS. While the transcriptions by Nugent gave the name as Pedros, an inspection of the original document of 1692 shows the name to be John Petro. The person with whom he was selling the land was named **Evan Davis** (not Dane, as originally transcribed by your author). The location of the land is described in detail in several land patents, of land belonging to land owners adjoining the land of John Pedro(s). The land is described as being on the south side of the river (Rappahannock River) beginning as the mouth of a little creek near Nimcock Creek (now Urbanna Creek) and in another patent the land is described as being on Sunderland Creek (now Lagrange Creek). From this it is known that John Pedros (Petros) was in Lancaster County prior to 1650, the date of the first patent describing an adjoining land owner (Bertram Obert).[1]

This is the same area in which Matthew Patre were living in 1679. Each time there is an entry for the name Peatross in the early records the name is spelled differently. When one considers the customary naming patterns, it would appear that John Petro was in all likelihood the father of Matthew. John and Elizabeth Patre, the son and daughter of Matthew and Elizabeth Patre were baptized **7th Xber (December) 1679.**[2]

(120;97) Middlesex County was cut off from Lancaster County about 1669; however, a church was ordered to be built on the south side of the river prior to that time. *On January 29, 1666, a General Vestry meeting was held at the house of Sir Henry Chichley (Rosegill). We doe accord and agree... Lancaster and Pianketank parishes unite and be called Christ Church, and that a Mother Church be built in ye small Indian field next ye head of Capt. Brocas his ground, and that ye Mother church be called by name of Christ Church.*[3] The Upper Church of the new Middlesex County, Christ Church Parish was apparently begun as the upper chapel of the original parish, and completed to serve the residents of the new county by 1667. It would have been this church that Matthew and Elizabeth attended as regularly as they could. It needed to be enlarged by 1687, as the settlement had grown.[4]

(125-127;101-103)
Gen. 8   **JOHN PEATROSS I**

(125;101) The date of baptism of John and Elizabeth Peatross, son and daughter of MATTHEW and ELIZABETH MAYO PEATROSS should read **7th December 1679.** It is sometimes confusing to translate the abbreviated Xber to the correct month, keeping in mind that the tenth month was actually December at that time.

(128-136b;104-111)
Gen. 7   **MATTHEW PEATROSS II**

(128;104) The site of the home of MATTHEW PEATROSS in Caroline County has been found in the woods on the east side of State Route(SR) 2 (US 301), just south of where CR 653 intersects SR 2 on the west side of the highway. There is evidence of the foundations of two house sites and two cemetery sites; the graveyards covered with periwinkle, but with no visible gravestones (1995). The wooded area is located off a dirt road behind the Thomas home (on the east side of SR 2), the home designated as #28179 for emergency identification.[5]

(128;104) Once again your author has erred with regard to the nature of early homes; Matthew and Amey did not live in a log house; they probably initially lived in a one-room post-in-the-ground house, with clapboard siding, and would have added on, room by room as the family grew. The log cabin as is visualized today was not the early homestead of colonial tidewater Virginia families.

(130;106) While it has been conjectured that John Hutcheson I and his family may have attended Mangohick Church, there is also the possibility that they attended Ivy Church which was built in 1727 near Sparta in Drysdale Parish. This may have been the church attended by Matthew and his family before Reedy Church was constructed. While the location of Ivy Church has survived, there is no remnant of the church today. It is believed that it stood on a hill overlooking a bridge crossing Marrocosick Creek.[6]

(131;107) Entries in the Caroline County court orders would indicate that the will of Matthew Peatross was recorded prior to the order to appraise his estate. Amey Peatross, William Peatross and Joseph Campbell, Executors of Matthew Peatross, deceased, were plaintiffs in a suit against Joseph DeJarnette in a debt of £18.6 (that had not been curtailed since August 1761), this entry was dated September 15, 1769.[7] The re-recordation of the will took place when Matthew's estate was finally settled.

Richard Peatross
(132;108) Richard Peatross and Agnes Hurt were married in Spotsylvania County on May 3, 1787.[8]

Mary Peatross
(135;110) Mary Peatross and Joseph Haden were married before April 30, 1774. Their children, as recorded in the *Douglas Register* indicated with (dr) and submitted by Mrs. Ethel Haden White were: Matthew Peatross, born c.1773, died after February 17, 1807; (John) Nelson, born April 30, 1774 (marriage date based on date of birth entry of first child), baptized December 17, 1775(dr), died October 5, 1822, married Susannah Payne July 24, 1793; Amy married Samuel Hopkins, March 15, 1798; Polly, born February 1781(dr), baptized October 22, 1781, married June 27, 1803, Reuben Martin; Joseph, born September 23, 1783, baptized July 8, 1787(dr), married before 1807 Nancy Ann Porter; Jeanie (Jane), born October 1785, baptized July 8, 1787(dr), married Mr. Stratton September 8, 1808; Rhode (sex not identified in entry), born September 1786, baptized July 8, 1787(dr) (Rebecca, married William Morton, December 2, 1805); Richard D, died before 1835; Joannah married (1) Turner Moon May 1798, (2) Matthew Rice, June 2, 1808.[9]

(137-141;112-115)
Gen. 6   **MATTHEW PEATROSS III**

(138;113)   The statement that the exact location of the house in which MATTHEW III and ANN HURT PEATROSS lived can be modified to read that it is known that the land Matthew's father left him was on the road from Reedy Mill. While the exact site of this Matthew's home has not been found, the general description of the location of the Peatross property can now be more definitively located. As well as a later entry concerning the land owned by Matthew's son, John. It was described as lying on the road from Reedy Mill to White Chimneys.

(140;114) The two cemetery sites already described on the homesite identified as that of Matthew Peatross I would very probably have been the final resting place of the Peatross descendants who lived in the area of Reedy Mill for several generations.

Note: There are many records of marriage bonds and marriage licenses that are extant. With the use of the same given names it is difficult to identify the individuals. Rather than assign the wrong bride or groom, only where those that could be verified have been given.

John Absolom Peatross
(144;118) Henry Peatross, Wren Saunders (Wren married Mary D. Peatross June 2, 1842, she was living 1853, but had died prior to September 9, 1866 when he married Sarah H. Peatross)[10] and others contributed $445 for the purchase of merchandise for the benefit and support of Suberta Peatross, wife of John and her children. John was to have control of the merchandise to use or sell, but could not use it to pay his debts.[11]

James Peatross
(146;119) Charles Asher Peatross married Annie Lee Carter on December 18, 1912; he was 21 and single and she was twenty and single. Her parents were R.W. and Mamie F. Carter.[12] Parthenia Virginia (born January 1, 1888, died September 23, 1967) married William Irving Covington in 1904. He was born April 1882, and died September 1, 1941. They are buried in Woodland Cemetery in Ashland. He was the son of William and Nanny Pavey Covington. Fannie Edna married, in 1884, Ernest Green Donahoe (born April 24, 1868 and died October 29, 1962). He was the son of James Donahoe.[13]

(148-156;121-128)

Gen. 4   **HENRY COOK PEATROSS**

(148;121)   The location of the land that HENRY and FRANCES CAMPBELL PEATROSS purchased from Elizabeth Dicken has been found to be on the road to Penola (CR 601) across from the James Collins place, *Hickory Grove.*[14]

          Further exploration of the area and of deeds of the time of Henry Peatross show that their home adjoined the Reedy Church site, which was just beyond the corner where St. Paul's Church now stands (CR 654 at the intersection of CR 656), and just across the road and north east of the home of Frances Peatross Lane, his granddaughter; now owned by her grandson, Stuart Lane). The deed of 1853 from Wren Saunders states that it is *the land on which Henry C. Peatross resides, the said land is contiguous to the Reedy Church and is bounded on the west by lands of the late Col. Booth Brown, on the north and east by the lands of Messers John A. Richardson and John W. Peatross and the south by the lands of the late Thomas Southworth...containing 183 acres.* Henry Peatross, the son had his store just across the road in front of the homeplace, on the same side as the home of Frances Lane. Evidence of a family cemetery has been found, but there are no gravestones. This Peatross cemetery is adjacent to the Lane home and what was the Peatross store site. According to Mrs. Lane, both Henry Cook Peatross and Frances Campbell Peatross are buried in this family plot. By tradition there are no stones; both Frances Lane and her husband, Frank Lane have been buried there in the twentieth century with unmarked graves.[15] The exact death date for Henry Peatross has not been determined because the death records for the years 1869, 1870 and 1871 are not extant.

(150;123) Henry Peatross enlisted in the 47th Regiment Virginia Volunteers under Captain William Timothy Chandler. This regiment was accepted into the service of the Confederate States on July 1, 1861. Company K began as the Tyranny Unmasked Artillery and served at Acquia Creek, but was reorganized April 30, 1862 as infantry.[16] No record has been found of how long Henry served with the Confederate States Army.

Katherine Marvin Peatross
(152;124) A correction: The statement that the first wife of Lewis Jacob was Mary Gregory came from *The Jacob Family* by Henry Aylwin Jacob and is not correct, so reported by his granddaughters, Elizabeth Jacob David and Virginia Jacob Chiles. Lewis and Kate lived in Caroline County for several years then moved to Richmond.[17]

(152;124-125) Information about the family of Lewis Jacob, the husband of Kate Peatross has come to light because of the effort to save the *Jacob House* in Richmond (610 West Cary Street, at Cherry Street) that was to be torn down by Virginia Commonwealth University (VCU) in its expansion plans for a new School of Engineering (1995). The father of Lewis Jacob was John Jacob, Sr. born May 7, 1790. He married first, Virginia Campbell Mitchell on November 26 1812, born February 15, 1796, died June 10, 1832. They had Benjamin, born September 22, 1814, died May 2, 1846, married December 13, 1838, Olivia Tinsley; John, born August 4, 1816, died December 17, 1898 and married October 31, 1839, Ann Adalaide O'Brien; a son born and died in 1818; Joanna Catherine, born January 17, 1820, died December 3, 1893, married 1839, George Willis; Caleb, born March 13, 1822, died September 16, 1904, married October 31, 1847, Lucy Colburn; Joseph, born January 24, 1824, died April 16, 1887, married 1842 (1) Mary Willis, (2) 1852 Samantha Wood; William Kerr, born May 16, 1826, died December 31, 1831; Lewis, born November 5, 1828; and twins who were born in 1832 died on the same day as their mother.

George Winston, a noted Quaker and a Richmond contractor built the Jacob house (as it came to be called) in 1817, in the "new west end of Richmond", in what was called the "Town of Sydney". This area was later to become "The Fan District" and "Oregon Hill". The preservation of this house provided an important window on the past and link to the early Quakers, apprenticed free-blacks, and innovative architectural features brought together in a simple small brick house. It is the only surviving house built or owned by two of the founders of the Town of Sydney.

John Jacob owned and occupied the house from 1832 until 1853. He was an early assistant superintendent of the state penitentiary, located on Oregon Hill a few blocks away. John Jacob worked closely with Samuel Parsons, also a Quaker, who built a contemporaneous home in Oregon Hill (601 Spring Street). The Quakers were active in the movement to build penitentiaries during this period in order to reform criminals. Both Parsons and Jacobs were ahead of their times in the humane treatment of prisoners and prison reform. Caleb Jacob, John's son who also lived in the Jacob house, owned a carriage manufacturing business later in the 1800s.[18]

Virginia Commonwealth University was unwilling to preserve the house on its original site, even though its history was especially related to their modern Engineering School. The house was moved across the street in September 1995.[19]

Seth Campbell Peatross

(152;125) Rozelle Burruss was born December 24, 1861. Their first child, Henry Lee ran a store at Peatross.[20] Edna Parrish Peatross, the wife of Erin Peatross was born October 12, 1896 in Fluvanna County, she died July 31, 1983 in Richmond.[21] Frances Peatross Lane reported the death dates of those family members buried in the family cemetery: Rozelle died September 1, 1918, Henry Atwell died November 6, 1953 and Frank Lane died January 17, 1963.[22]

William Henry Peatross

(152;125) William Henry Peatross was born March 18, 1863. He married Lillie Asbury Wright (born June 11, 1864), the daughter of John Durrett and Virginia Ellen Henderson Wright. Their children: William Stuart ("Stan") Peatross was born January 27, 1894, married Lydia Remington in 1915 in Duchesne, Utah; he died August 7, 1980 in Orem, Utah. Virginia Josephine was born March 17, 1897. Lillie Henderson Peatross was born May 27, 1900 and married Phillip Brinkley, 1918. Willie died January 30, 1930 and his wife, Lillie died July 19, 1939, both of them in Richmond.[23] As an aside, this now explains the relationship of Phillip Brinkley, who was a baker in Richmond, and who made your author's wedding cake during World War II, when it was very hard to get enough sugar to make even a small cake.

James Odum Peatross

(153;125) James Odum Peatross, age 33 and a widower, married Minnie W. Campbell, age twenty-six and single on December 2, 1897. Her father was the brother of James Peatross' mother.[24]

Felix Zollicoffer Peatross

(153;126) correction: Felix Zollicoffer was born May 30, **1867**.[25]

Malcolm Ilus Peatross

(153;126) Malcolm Peatross and May Belle Duke were married October 15, 1901. Grace Peatross Hines was divorced in 1958. Her brother, Tazewell Peatross died May 25, 1974.[26]

PEATROSS FAMILY

Gen. 9 MATTHEW PEATROSS I	m	ELIZABETH MAYO	
Issue:	JOHN	m	ANN (—?—)
	Elizabeth	m	(p)John Hodgson
	Thomas	m	d.s.p.
Gen. 8 JOHN PEATROSS I	m	ANN (—?—)	
Issue:	Thomas	m	
	MATTHEW II	m	AMEY (—?—)
	John	m	Ann (—?—)
	Elizabeth	m	
Gen. 7 MATTHEW PEATROSS II	m	AMEY (—?—)	
Issue:	Rebecca	m	Thomas Terrell
	Anna	m	John Thompson
	Amey	m	James Gatewood
	ELIZABETH	m	JOSEPH CAMPBELL
	William	m	Amey Brame
	MATTHEW III	m	ANN HURT
	John	m	
	Sarah	m	(—?—) Hundley
	Mary	m	Joseph Haden
	Thomas	m	
	Richard	m	Agnes Hurt
	Joannah	m	
	James	m	
Gen. 6 MATTHEW PEATROSS III	m	ANN HURT	
Issue:	JOHN W.	m	MARY DEJARNATT
	son		
	daughters		
Gen. 5 JOHN W. PEATROSS	m	MARY DEJARNATT	
Issue:	FRANCES ANN	m	RICHARD WALLER HUTCHESON II
	Mary	m	George W. Peatross
	John Absolom	m	Suberta E. Saunders
	HENRY COOK	m	FRANCES ANN CAMPBELL
	Johanna	m	James F. Chiles
	Matthew		unmarried
	Joseph A.	m	unknown
	James	m	Virginia Ellen Hutcheson
Gen. 4 HENRY COOK PEATROSS	m	FRANCES ANN CAMPBELL	
Issue:	Katherine	m	Lewis Artemas Jacob
	Seth Campbell	m	Rozelle Burruss
	Mark 'Livia		died young
	DORA LIVINGSTON	m	RICHARD WALLER HUTCHESON III
	William Henry	m	Lillie Asbury Wright
	James Odum	m	Minnie Washington Campbell
	Felix Zollicoffer	m	(1) Julia Stuart Blanton
		m	(2) Myrtle Rea Carter
	Malcolm Ilus	m	May Belle Duke

Notes

1. Nell Marion Nugent, *Cavaliers and Pioneers*, vol. 1. 1934. (Baltimore: Genealogical Publishing, rep. 1991). 204, 245, 257 329.

2. National Society of Colonial Dames of America in the State of Virginia, *The Parish Register of Christ Church, Middlesex County, Virginia, 1653-1812*. 1897. (Richmond: NSCDA, rep. 1990). 15.

3. C.G. Chamberlayne, *The Vestry Book of Christ Church Parish, Middlesex County, Virginia, 1663-1767*. (Richmond: Old Dominion Press, 1927). x-xv, 5-6, 8-9.

4. George Carrington Mason, *Colonial Churches of Tidewater Virginia*. (Richmond: Whittet and Shepperson, 1945). 280.

5. It is believed that since this time Caroline County has instituted a plan of 911 street names and numbers to facilitate the location of homes in case of fire or other emergency.

6. George Carrington Mason, "*The Colonial Churches of Spotsylvania and Caroline Counties, Virginia, VMHB*. 58(1950): 468.

7. Ruth & Sam Sparacio, *Order Book Abstracts of Caroline County, Virginia, 1768-1770*. (McLean, VA: Antient Press, 1991). 73.

8. W. Mac. Jones, ed., *The Douglas Register*. 1928. (Baltimore: Genealogical Publishing, rep. 1985). 38.

9. Jones 106, 140, 205; Mrs. Ethel Haden White, 133 Southern Ave, Henderson, NC 27536.

10. He was 45 and a widower, and she was 32 and single. She was the daughter of Samuel D. and Sarah Peatross. Caroline County Marriage Register, 1842 and 1866; the papers of Max David Peatross (the son of William Stuart Peatross), 1680 South 2350 East, Price, UT 84501.

11. Caroline County Deed Book 49, 89.

12. Caroline County Marriage Register, 1912.

13. Lloyd and Helen Covington, *The Descendants of William Covington I, 1618-1696, "Bestland", Essex County, Virginia*. (privately printed, 1996). 25495 Ruther Glen Rd, Ruther Glen, VA 22546. 91, 114.

14. Correspondence (1998) with Herbert R. Collins, 3510 N Pershing Dr, Arlington, VA 22201.

15. Collins 2:115; *Caroline County Deed Book* 48 230; 51 189.

16. Lee A. Wallace, *A Guide to Virginia Military Organizations*. 1964 (Lynchburg, VA: H.E.Howard, rev 1986) 128-129.

17. From correspondence with Virginia Jacob Chiles, February 1998.

18. Brief prepared for the Department of Historic Resources, Commonwealth of Virginia, 1995.

19. *Richmond Times Dispatch*. September 14, 1995, B6.

20. Virginia L.H. Davis, *The Burruss Family of Caroline County, Virginia*. Unpublished Mss. 1990.

21. Letter from Jean Peatross Adams (daughter of Erin Peatross), 1994.

22. Collins 2:115.

23. Herbert Ridgeway Collins, Unpublished Mss., 1991.

24. The papers of Max Peatross, 1680 South 2350 East, Price, UT 84501.

25. Papers of Max Peatross.

26. Letter (1990) from Victor Leon Hines, Jr., 402 Walsing Dr, Richmond, VA 23229.

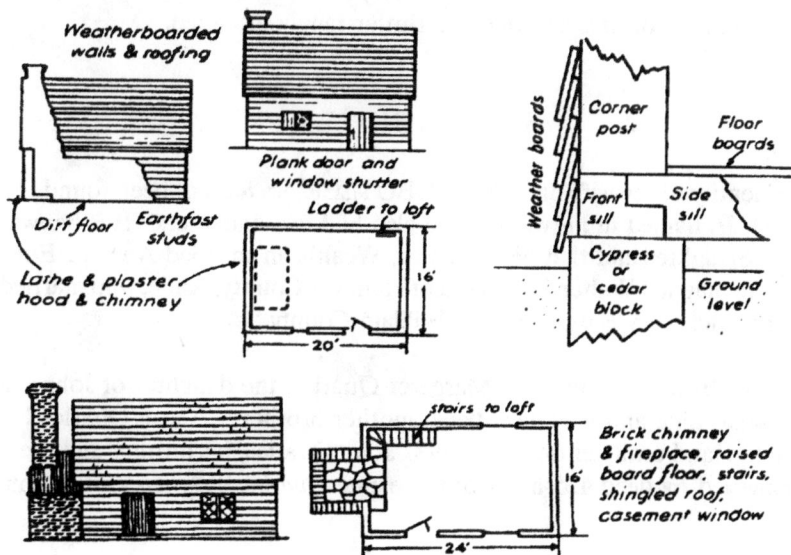

Construction of Early Homes

THOMAS BUTLER

Gen. 8

(158;130)   THOMAS BUTLER was living in the area that became King William County before its formation in 1701. He may well have been in the same area as early as 1685, when it was the county of New Kent. When one considers the entries in the St. Peter's Parish Register beginning in 1685 with the marriage of Thomas Butler and Margery Crue, this becomes a possibility. If one follows these entries and makes the assumption that they relate to the same Thomas Butler later found in King William County, then one would infer that Thomas married secondly, Mary. The Mary Butler who married Arthur Winchester, then may have been the same daughter of Thomas. By the time the name of his wife, ALICE appears with his name in the records, he was living in St. John's Parish, King William County.

(159-160;131) St. John's Parish was first formed in 1680 out of the northern section of Pamunkey Neck, and was ultimately coterminous with Pamunkey Neck and therefore with King William County, formed in 1701. There is evidence of extensive settlement in Pamunkey Neck by the end of the seventeenth century and there was, not only the old parish church in West Point, but an upper church and a frontier chapel. From extant land patents to William Maybank, it is believed that this frontier chapel was built on Acquinton Creek and was built before 1701.

Acquinton Church that now stands in neglected ruin is believed to have been built on the same site, near a headwater of the creek for which both the chapel and the church were named. It is located on the north side of the crossroads of CR 629 (one and one-half miles west of SR 30 and CR 681 (five and one-half miles south of US Route 360) in King William County, west of the old courthouse.

The part of Acquinton Church that now stands is the building presumed to have been completed about two years after the vestry order for construction in 1732.[1] At the time of Mr. Mason's writing, the north wing, added about 1760, was still standing, though abandoned. Today it has fallen into complete ruin, with only the side walls remaining and remnants of the church cemetery standing as memorials of an earlier time. It may well have been the first church on this site that the Butler family attended.

(162-167;134-138)
Gen. 7   SAMUEL BUTLER I

(162;134)   The identity of the wife of SAMUEL BUTLER, Sr. has not been found. It is known that with the brothers of Samuel, Jr. named in his will that he also had five daughters. It is known that his daughter, Sarah married Ezekiel Slaughter and that his daughter, Wealthean married Ambose Edwards. He also had daughters Elizabeth, who married Walter Grantland of Hanover County, Anne, who married Benjamin Bowles of King William County and Lucy Butler of King William County.[2]

James Butler The James Butler who married Margaret Quarles, the daughter of John and Frances Quarles appears to be of the same time and may have been another brother.[3] Aaron Quarles had left his estate to his wife, who lived on the land until her death in 1798. John Quarles, his brother and the executor of the will of Aaron Quarles conveyed by deed 135 acres of the estate *Quarles Warehouse* of Aaron Quarles to James Butler.

Wealthean Butler
(165-166;137-138) While circumstantial evidence indicated that Wealthean was a daughter of Samuel Butler, confirmation has been found in the form of a deposition given by James Edwards of King William County. He was called upon to testify as to the eligibility of Samuel Butler of Surry County for a military pension from

the Revolutionary War. James was the son of Wealthean Butler and Ambrose Edwards and he stated in a deposition in 1832, given in Surry County that Major Samuel Butler of Surry County was his **"own cousin"**. This was the Reverend Samuel Butler, rector of Southwark Parish, Surry County and the son of Thomas Butler II, and the first cousin of James Edwards.[4]

Cherry Grove, not far from the courthouse, was built by Ambrose Edwards about the middle of the eighteenth century on a grant of 4000 acres.[5] Tax records show that Ambrose was credited with 656 acres of land in 1782. The property passed to his son, Ambrose at his death.[6] Ambrose and Wealthean Edwards had the following children: Samuel, born c.1750, married (1) Jane Pemberton, daughter of John Pemberton and Jane Coleman, (2) Lavinia Lipscomb; James, born c.1752, married Mary Dunbar Dickey; Ambrose, born March 3, 1757, married Elizabeth Anne Slaughter, February 1775, she died July 16, 1829, three days before her husband; Thomas, married Mary Waller, daughter of John Waller; Butler, married Elizabeth Ellett, daughter of William Ellett; Wealthean, born c.1765, married Wilson Coleman Pemberton, the brother of Jane; Susannah, married Tunstall Quarles, the son of Aaron Quarles; Nancy, married Ambrose Pollard; Mary Elizabeth, married George Butler Pollard, probably the son of Robert Pollard, Sr., Clerk of Circuit Court, King William County and she died October 1837. Ambrose, Sr. married second, Barbara the widow of Henry Finch.[7] Ambrose Edwards, an old and respected inhabitant of King William County died **January 22, 1811**.[8]

(168-175;139-146)

Gen. 6   **THOMAS BUTLER II**

(168;139)   The additional information learned from documents concerning the heirs of THOMAS BUTLER and the settlement of his estate, the estate of his son, Samuel and the Revolutionary War service of Samuel has identified more accurately the children of Thomas and their ages. The order of birth, as inferred from the bill of complaint concerning the land in Granville County, North Carolina, appears to be as follows: Samuel, Thomas, John, **James**, Isaac, Reuben and Robert. The name of James having been added from the above named bill of complaint.[9] It also appears from the known activities of his son, Samuel that he was born earlier than had been originally thought, and Thomas the son, had been born later than thought, thus Judah may well have been the mother of Samuel and not of the other sons of Thomas.

(169;140)   It is now known that Thomas was active in the King William County militia during the Revolutionary War. In December 1776, Captain Thomas Butler was issued a warrant for the pay roll for his company of militia.[10] He was later to be styled "Colonel". In June 1778, Thomas was appointed to be among the commissioners named to hear petitions from persons damaged by destruction of King William records by fire. Thomas Butler was also a justice of the peace of King William County, listed as a gentleman and present and serving as a justice at the King William County Court held September 28, 1789.[11] Since so many of the records of this county have been destroyed, it is difficult to tell how long he served in that capacity.

(169;140)   As well as can be established, Thomas Butler lived between Judy Swamp and Mehixon Creek,[12] near Dabney's Mill, at least until 1784. The King William Land Tax Records credit him with 600 acres of land from 1782 until 1784. It is inferred that this land was the same land described earlier as adjoining the land of George Dabney and shown on a plat of the land of George Dabney.[13] The Dabney land lay at the forks of the roads to Manquin and Dabney's Mill, with the Pamunkey River nearby. All of the known activities of Thomas Butler during his adult life appear to have taken place in this general area, and with individuals who had associations in or near Aylett.

By the year 1787, Thomas was credited with 450 acres of land, along with the notation in the alterations that Thomas had never listed fifty acres. From 1787 until the year 1794, only the land transfers (alterations) were given in the King William Land Tax Records. In 1792 Thomas sold 458 acres to James Govan, along with this information was the notation that Thomas had gained eight acres by the survey of the land. It seems that Thomas had removed himself from the Mehixon Creek area and was living in the City of

Richmond/Henrico County area during the early 1790s. Several deeds are extant showing that he owned lots in Richmond and was identified as "of Richmond" in the deeds. In May of 1790 he purchased 115 acres in Henrico County and was identified as being "of King William County".[14] In November of 1792 Thomas executed a deed to Joseph Hillyard, of King William County, in which he was identified as "of Henrico County."

It is interesting that Thomas Butler was never credited with the 1030 acres of land belonging to *Tuckoman* until after his death. The land was listed in the name of Thomas Butler, Sen. in 1795 and in the name of John Butler in 1796, with the notation "Thomas' Est." following the name. This same year the land was sold to James Price.[15]

(170;141) *Butler, Col. Thomas, late of King William County, deceased, his executor, Thomas Butler, will sell his plantation called "Tuckoman" in King William County.*[16] This interesting notation was abstracted from the *Virginia Gazette and General Advertizer* for September 9, 1795. It provided the first definitive information as to the location of the plantation of Thomas Butler at the time of his death. The detailed advertisement reveals much about the life style of Thomas Butler and about his plantation:

"To Be Sold...

Agreeable to the last will and testament[17] *of Colonel Thomas Butler, deceased, on Wednesday the 30th day of September next on the premises. Agreeable to the last will and testament of Colonel Thomas Butler, deceased on Wednesday the 30th day of September next on the premesis. That well know Tract of land called Tuckoman lying in King William County pleasantly situated on the Pamunkey River twelve miles below the courthouse of the said county and eight miles above West Point; containing by a late survey Eleven hundred [sic] and Thirty acres, five hundred and thirty of which is high land and the balance marsh; about three hundred acres of the high land cleared and the residue in prime wood, on which is an excellent new two-story dwelling house, 36 by 34, a new kitchen, dairy, meat house, and corn house, all of which has been built within the last four years; there is also an excellent fishery, together with an abundance of wild fowl on the land. It is unnecessary to detail further particulars on the advantages of the seat Above described possesses as it is presumed that any person willing to become a purchaser will first view the premises. The land will be shewed by Thomas Butler who lives five miles above, to any person inclined to purchase. The terms of payment will be one third in one year one third in two years and the remaining in three years the purchaser giving bond and approved security to the executor.*

Also will be sold on the same place and day all the stock of horses cattle sheep and hogs, household and kitchen furniture and plantation utensils. Cash will be required on all sums not exceeding five pounds, nine months credit will be allowed on all sums above five pounds giving bond and approved security to the executor."

The first record of the marsh called Tococomans (sic) occurs in the land patent of William Claiborne in December 1657;[18] it was described as lying adjacent to his plantation[19]. It appears that it was, in fact, a part of the original grand patent of Claiborne for 5000 acres in 1653. This land was described as *lying on the north side of the Pamunkey River in the Narrows, adjoining the land of Captain John West, thence in a westerly direction to a point of land where the said Colonel Clayborne [sic] landed the Army under his command in 1644.* His plantation was called *Romancoke*. William Claiborne had been chosen by the Virginia Company as surveyor of the colony. He arrived in Jamestown in 1621 and was responsible for the laying out of the area known as New Towne. He was appointed to the Council in 1623, served as Secretary of the Colony (1625-1635, 1652-1660) and as Treasurer (1642-1660).

The plantation *Tuckoman* has survived today. It is located on the west side of present-day SR 30, east of Sweet Hall. It is a working farm, and while the present home dates back to the early 1800s, it is not the house in which Thomas Butler lived. It is set back from the highway, amid tall stately trees, magnolias and boxwoods and is clearly visible at the end of a long lane across cultivated fields. Tuckoman is privately owned and is not open to the public. The people in the area call it "Tuck'-o-mn", while those in the upper end of the county call it "Tuc-Kow'-mn".

Claiborne later gave the land of Tuckoman to his son, Captain Thomas Claiborne by deed of gift in 1673; it was a part of the original *Sweet Hall* dividend. After his death in 1732, the land passed to his son, Nathaniel Claiborne, who devised the land by will to his son, Thomas Claiborne. It seems that Thomas had continued financial problems and in 1772 offered the Tuckoman Tract for sale. Robert Ruffin, of the Surry County Ruffins, was living at Windsor by 1768, with land on the Pamunkey River just above Sweet Hall and

Tuckoman by Ruffin's Ferry.[20]

It was his son, Sterling who apparently purchased Tuckoman from Thomas Claiborne, for he was credited with 2000 acres of land in the land tax records of 1782. The loss of the deeds and other records of King William County make it very difficult to follow exactly what really happened with the land. It seems from a deed dated 1792 that Henry Young deeded to Sterling Ruffin, 2000 acres of land lying on the south side of the road to West Point, on the north side of the Pamunkey River.[21] In 1796 Sterling Ruffin and his wife, Alice conveyed to John Butler of the City of Richmond, a part of the large tract. The conveyance was for 530 acres of high land and 500 acres of marsh contiguous to, known by the name of Tuckoman. The record of this sale, as well as the sale by John Butler have survived.[22]

It is difficult to reconcile what has survived and is known from the county records with what is inferred from the description of the sale of the property of Thomas Butler. While it can be assumed that a deed to Tuckoman has not survived, no explanation can be found for the fact that land was deeded by Sterling Ruffin to John Butler in 1796, or that the Tuckoman acreage was not credited to Thomas Butler prior to his death. It would seem that he was in possession of the land and living on it from the year 1792. The date given for the construction of the home coincides with this date.

Dr. Harris related in his book that a cellar and some colonial-type bricks were found where the early house stood, near where the Southern Railway (now Norfolk Southern Railroad) crossed the back field. A description of this house was found in an insurance policy of 1805:[23] *William Ring, residing at Tuckoman, between the plantation of Robert Slaughter and G. W. P. Custis: Dwelling for $2500, Kitchen for $210, Dairy for $130. Wooden dwelling house 40 x 40 2 storeys underpinned with brick 3 ½ ft above ground; wooden kitchen 20 x 16 one storey.* This agrees with the description of the home of Thomas Butler, with perhaps an addition that increased the outside dimensions of the house. Dr. Harris further stated that this house burned during the occupancy of the Richards family, who acquired the plantation about 1828.

Dr. John Richards inherited the home from his sisters, Eliza and Penelope Richards and bequeathed it to his son, Dr. Buchan Richards. It was while he was living in the home that it burned and the dwelling was built that now faces the King William Road.[24] Tuckoman is just a short distance south of St. John's Church, west of SR 30 and would have been the church which Thomas Butler attended when he was at Tuckoman.

Samuel Butler

(171-173;142-143) From the documents that have come to light concerning the Revolutionary War service of Samuel Butler, and his obligation in the bond with his father for the purchase of the Granville County, North Carolina land in 1783, it is inferred that Samuel was born c.1755-1757.

Samuel was listed as a First Lieutenant in the Fifteenth Virginia Regiment, Continental Line in the Revolutionary War on March 21, 1777. He was retired, then listed as a Lieutenant of a State Regiment, and was later awarded 2666 acres of land for this service performed until the end of the war.[25] He was listed as a supernumerary in the Virginia State Artillery, 1782. One of the battles in which Samuel was engaged was fought at *Green Springs*. It was for this service, at half-pay that his brother Robert petitioned the US Government and received, after filing many documents and depositions, payment of $6360 to the estate of Samuel Butler.[26]

Samuel served as Brigade Inspector for General Bradley (probably the Capt. James A. Bradley of the State Artillery Regiment. John Roane of King William County confirmed this in his deposition of 1832 and that Samuel married the widow of General Bradley. It would appear that there were no children by this marriage.[27]

(171;142) Samuel Butler was ordained in May 1788 by Bishop White of Pennsylvania, then ordained to the diaconate on May 8, 1788, as listed in the records of the Virginia Episcopal Seminary. He served as the rector of Southwark Parish from 1789 until at least 1804.[28]

(172;143) Samuel Butler died August 31, 1812.[29] The children of the marriage of Samuel to Martha Newsum Cocke were still under age when he died: (listed in the order in which their names appear in the estate and guardian papers) Thomas, Samuel, Agnes and Lucy. The son Thomas instituted a suit against his uncle, Robert for his share of his father's estate in 1815, as he was approaching legal age. Samuel Butler, Jr. became a physician, living in Portsmouth. He married Catherine Wilson, December 15, 1825 and died September 12, 1833 in his thirty-third year. He left his wife and two young children, one of whom was William Wilson Samuel Butler.[30] Agnes Butler and Edmond Leneve were married by a justice of the peace in Hertford, North Carolina on July 25, 1819.[31] She died on December 20, 1825, leaving one child, Samuel B. Leneve.[32] Lucy married James Young on February 2, 1822.[33]

Thomas Butler
(171;142) The records that have come to light would indicate that Thomas was not the eldest son of Thomas Butler II, as originally inferred from the fact that he had been the executor of Thomas II's estate. Since the listing for Thomas, the son, did not appear in the King William Personal Property Tax Records until 1789 it would seem that he must have been born about 1767 or 1768. A Thomas Butler is found in Henrico County in the US Census for 1810.[34] It was thought in going over the available records that Thomas was married twice, but no conclusive record was found. The two marriages recorded to Thomas Butler in Henrico County are now believed to have been this Thomas Butler, since records have now come to light showing that his father owned land in Henrico County and apparently lived there, as Thomas, Jr. may have also. Thomas Butler and Susanna Carter were married September 14, 1791 in Henrico County. Thomas Butler was married February 7, 1803 to Nancy Grinstead, Nancy being the usual diminutive for the given name Ann.[35]

John Butler
(173;143) The name of John Butler first appeared in the King William County Personal Property Tax Records in 1790, identified as being over the age of sixteen. His name continued on the lists at least until the year 1811. It is believed that he lived in Mechanicsville, in Hanover County.

James Butler
(170,174;141,145) It was erroneously thought that the Lucy Butler who was referred to in the settlement of the Granville County land was the daughter of Thomas Butler. The name James Butler appeared in the King William County Personal Property Tax Records beginning in 1796, identifying him as being over the age of sixteen, but he could not be identified as a son of Thomas. The draft of the complaint filed by the Hillyards gives information about the heirs that had not been found elsewhere.[36] From the draft of the bill of complaint it is learned that Lucy Butler was the under-age daughter of James Butler, and thus the granddaughter of Thomas Butler. The King William tax lists show that James Butler died in 1801 or 1802, his estate was listed in 1803 through the year 1806. It is probably his daughter, Lucy that is recorded as having married Francis Row in 1817.[37]

Isaac Butler
(173;143-144) The name of Isaac Butler first appeared in the King William County Land Tax records in 1795. Isaac Butler was reported to be in Tennessee at the time of the draft of the bill of complaint drawn up for the case before the Court of Equity, 1810, Granville County, North Carolina concerning the land of Thomas Butler.

Robert Butler
(173-174;144-145) Since Robert was only ten years old when his father died, it is likely that he went to live with his brother, Samuel, who was well established in Surry County. Proof of the relationship can be found in the deposition (1832) given by Robert concerning the back pay of Samuel for service in the Revolutionary War. This also fully explain the role that Robert played of guardianship and in settling the estate of his brother, Samuel. It is because he was diligent in securing the payment for Samuel's military service that the descendants of Thomas Butler can now claim their relationship with the necessary documentation. As discussed originally, the great age difference between Samuel and Robert would indicate that they were, in fact, half-brothers.

(176-183;147-153)
Gen. 5   **REUBEN BUTLER**
(181;151)   Records for the interments in Shockoe Hill Cemetery have been found and the name of
ELIZABETH BUTLER, the mother of REUBEN BUTLER appears among those buried in the cemetery.[38]

(183a-200;154-166)
Gen. 4   **WILLIAM FLEMING BUTLER**

(186;155)   The area in which WILLIAM FLEMING BUTLER lived with his family overlooked *Rocketts*,
the thriving port of Richmond. It has been a source of frustration to the author that the origin of the busy
port on the James River at Chimborazo Bottom called *Rocketts* could not be identified. None of the accounts
of early Richmond history seem to have given more than a passing comment about this active port of entry
to Richmond. Richard Rockett was the clerk of the vestry of St. John's Church on Church Hill, Henrico
Parish, from November 13, 1749 to December 8, 1752. Chimborazo Bottom is at the foot of Church Hill,
where the City of Richmond Intermediate Terminal is now located. *Rocketts* is said to have been so known
from September 27, 1731.[39]

(187;156)   William's Company A of the Henrico Artillery was disbanded and became Company C, October
4, 1862 and was assigned to the Army of Northern Virginia. The captains were Johnson H. Sands and William
Bailey Ritter.[40]

(189;158)   William wrote to the father-in-law (Dr. W.J. Bates of Wheeling, West Virginia) of his son, William
just after the surrender of General Lee at Appomattox. This letter was found in a scrapbook of Louise Butler
Reed, the daughter of William, Jr. and has been preserved and copied by Dr. Andrew K. Butler, the grandson
of William, Jr. and the nephew of Louise.[41]
My Dear Sir
May 10, 1865, Richmond, Virginia
*Your highly esteemed favor of the 28th — reached me the day before yesterday & would have been promptly
replied to but being in daily expectation of seeing or hearing something of or from William, I decided to wait a day
or two, indulging the hope that we might in that time see him here; and I [would] have the great pleasure of
reporting to you his safe arrival. Although I cannot do this now, still I am not without hope, indeed confidently
believe that in a few days more and he will be with us — I have no apprehension about his safety, as he has not
been in the field since the fall of 1862 — and I cannot think he would be so indiscreet as to attach himself to the
desperate fortunes of Mr. Davis in his flight through No. Carolina.*

*The last letter I received from Wm was about six weeks since and dated it Salisbury, N.C. from which place
he expected to go the next to High Point, a Depot on the N.C.R. Road about 16 or 20 miles south west of
Greensboro and not between Danville and Greensboro as you suppose. It is possible that he may have been
subsequently farther south, say to Charlotte, N.C. or Columbia, S.C., indeed as far as Augusta, Ga. Now if it was
at High point or even Greensboro (which is nearer) when Genl. Johnston surrendered on the 29th, he could not
have reached here by this time for want of transportation on R Road facility for travel. The first train from Danville
to [t]his city since Genl. Lee's surrender came this last Saturday, and I saw a gentleman yesterday who got here
from Danville last Sunday after being detained three weeks. Sherman, I understand is using the road now to
transport a portion of his Army from N.C. to this city when that is accomplished we may expect to see the forces
under Johnston from Virginia brought forward — and I am confident William must have been embraced in that
General's surrender. Again, we have no mails to or from that section of the country.*

*These, my dear sir, are the reasons which have led me to believe that William is safe & relieves my mind
of anxiety on his account....*

*Thus my dear sir while God has laid his hand heavily upon me in a pecuniary sense, He has been
graciously pleased to bear safely through this bloody struggle my dear sons and to bless my family with almost
uninterrupted good health. Tell my dear Nannie [the younger William's wife, Marcia Bates] not to be uneasy or
disturbed in mind. A little more patient waiting and her prayers will be answered and then I trust to have all my
children once more together, with hearts uplifted to God in humble thanks for his goodness and sparing mercy to*

41

us all. I saw Lieut. B. Bates and his sister['s] wife Patty yesterday and all well. I will telegraph you as soon as William arrives — With affectionate love to you all, in which my family warmly unity, and our earnest desire to make your personal acquaintance.

I am, my dear Doctor, Yrs. Mo. truly and fraternally, W.F. Butler

P.S. Direct letters to me, Box 274 (P.O.)

(190;159) During all of William's struggles to revive his imported china and glassware business he kept his family poignantly in his heart. This letter to his granddaughter Mary Lou (Louise Butler Reed), found in the same scrapbook reveals his deep love for his family and his desire to keep in touch even though they were living in Wheeling at that time.   *Richmond, March 18th, 1868*

To Little Mary Lou Butler

My dear child   How glad it made my old heart to receive your letter and to learn from it that you and Jessee are so well, and having such a gay time of it since you left Richmond and returned home. I am almost tempted to wish I were a boy again, and to be <u>the one little boy</u> at just such a nice little party, and with just such nice little girls as Mary Lou, Jessee and their little companions in the memorable birthday celebration of Miss Jessee. Wouldn't I be a happy little boy — Why, to think of it makes me feel much younger....

Aunt Kate had a tree last Christmas. All of us spent a very quiet and sober time of it, the last season. But Aunt Cora and Aunt Kate are weekly enjoying themselves very much, attending the meetings of a sewing society, which meets at the house of first one neighbor and then another and at which, I believe, the old folks do all the sewing, while the little girls have fine fun playing games...Uncle Arthur says it is not much fun at a party when there is nothing handed around to eat, not even an apple....

Cow Mary is still filling Uncle Arthur's pail with nice rich milk every morning and evening — She is such a good cow, so gentle and minds every word Uncle Arthur speaks to her. As for Mr. Bow-wow, why he is just the same importunate little beggar around the breakfast, dinner and tea table, that he was when you were here....He keeps up a sharp lookout at night for such thieves as may be prowling about our back lot; and while I don't think he would do much biting, he never the less barks a great deal and thus frightens the rogues away....

Be a good child, as you are, study hard and write again to me soon — love and obey your father and mother and God will bless you and you will be happy.

Your affectionate GrandPapa Butler

William Fleming Butler, Jr.

(192-193;161) William Fleming and Marcia Bates Butler had two children: Mary Louise Butler, born February 24, 1861 and died June 11, 1939. She married Robert Jeffrey Reed, MD on November 30, 1887 in Wheeling, West Virginia. He was born May 6, 1859, the son of John and Jane Burns Reed. Their son, Arthur Bates Butler was born June 28, 1868 in Wheeling, West Virginia and married Mary Edna Kimmins, June 15, 1905 in Wheeling. Mary Edna was the daughter of John Luther and Louise Kersten Kimmins.[42]

BUTLER FAMILY

Gen. 8	THOMAS BUTLER I	m	ALICE (—?—)
Issue:	SAMUEL	m	UNKNOWN
	Sarah	m	(1) (—?—) Slaughter
		m	(2) Edward Harrison
	JOHN I (possibly)	m	(1) ANN
		m	(2) Susanna
		m	(3) Mary
Gen. 7	SAMUEL BUTLER	m	UNKNOWN
Issue:	THOMAS	m	(1) Judah (—?—)
		m	(2) UNKNOWN
	Samuel	m	Mary (—?—)
	Isaac	m	Mary Hunt
	Reuben	m	Anne Lisle Smelt

42

James (p)	m	Frances Quarles	
Sarah	m	Ezekiel Slaughter	
Wealthean	m	Ambrose Edwards	
Elizabeth	m	Walter Grantland	
Anne	m	Benjamin Bowles	
Lucy	m		

Gen. 6	**THOMAS BUTLER II**	m	(1) Judah	
Issue:	(1) Samuel	m	(1) Widow Bradley (Mrs. James)	
		m	(2) Martha Newsome Cocke	
	THOMAS BUTLER II	m	(2) <u>UNKNOWN</u>	
Issue:	Thomas	m	(1) Susanna Carter	
		m	(2) Nancy (Ann) Grinstead	
	John	m		
	Isaac	m	Maria Overton	
	James	m	unknown	
Issue:	REUBEN	m	ELIZABETH RUFFIN	
	Robert	m	(1) Sara (—?—)	
		m	(2) Otelia Voinard	

Gen. 5	<u>REUBEN BUTLER</u>	m	<u>ELIZABETH ANNE RUFFIN</u>
Issue:	Reuben	m	Martha Ann Deford
	Amanda R.	m	James Lefevre Dupuy
	WILLIAM FLEMING	m	VIRGINIA JUDITH WINSTON
	Thomas Francis	m	Virginia Laub

Gen. 4	<u>WILLIAM FLEMING BUTLER</u>	m	<u>VIRGINIA JUDITH WINSTON</u>
Issue:	Mary Ruffin		unmarried
	Virginia Elizabeth	m	James Clark Watson, M.D.
	William Fleming	m	Marcia Ann Bates
	Ada Clay		unmarried
	Harrison		died young
	Lucy Kyle	m	James Stewart McQueen
	ROBERT EMMET	m	ALICE MAUDE LEE
	Julia	m	John Winn
	Arthur St.Clair	m	Nannie Scott Betts
	Ann Winston	m	Lewis Andrews
	Cora Belle		unmarried
	Kate Bowling	m	Frank Scott Harker

Gen. 3	<u>ROBERT EMMET BUTLER</u>	m	<u>ALICE MAUDE LEE</u>
Issue:	Gertrude Lee	m	John William Clay
	Virginia Winston		unmarried
	Mary Elizabeth		unmarried
	Lucy Kyle	m	William John Groth
	Alfred Lee	m	Annabel Hardy
	Alice St.Clair		unmarried
	Ann Crawley	m	George Werter Sclater
	Grace Ruffin		unmarried
	NELLIE	m	WALLER BERNARD HUTCHESON

Notes

1. George Carrington Mason, *Colonial Churches of Tidewater Virginia*. (Richmond: Whittet and Shepperson,1945). 310-316.
2. Chesterfield County Deed Book 8 (1777), 183.
3. Malcolm Hart Harris, MD, *Old New Kent County History*. (West Point, VA: Privately printed, 1977) 763-764.

4. National Archives Register: Civil Reference Branch, RG 217 Accounting Officers of Treasury Department, Miscellaneous Treasury Account 62046, Loc: 9E3 16/35/1 and Treasury Warrant 6163 of 1832.

5. John H. Gwathmey, *Twelve Virginia Counties, Where the Western Migration Began*. 1937. (Baltimore: Genealogical Publishing, rep. 1997). 74.

6. Harris 764, 800, 990.

7. Harris 786; Peyton Neale Clarke, *Old King William Homes and Families*, 1897. (Baltimore: Clearfield, 1993). 109, 115, 116, 119, 124, 128, 130, 142, 155, 184.

8. *Virginia Gazette and General Advertiser*, January 1811.

9. Court of Equity, Granville County, North Carolina. 10 Jan. 1810. North Carolina State Archives.

10. H.R. McIlwaine, ed., *Journals of the Council of the State of Virginia*. vol.I, (Richmond: Division of Purchase & Printing, 1932). 279.

11. From the records of the Executive Department, Commonwealth of Virginia. Virginia State Library and Archives. Box 3, A-E. Pre-1790.

12. *Genealogies of Virginia Families: Virginia Magazine of History and Biography* vol II (Baltimore: Genealogical Publishing, 1981) 647-648.

13. Ibid.

14. Henrico County Deeds: Book 3, 591; Book 4, 312, 322, 424, 450, 574.

15. King William County Land Tax Records, 1782-1797.

16. Headley, Robert K., Jr. *Genealogical Abstracts from 18th-Century Virginia Newspapers*. (Baltimore: Genealogical Publishing, 1987). 51. *Virginia Gazette and General Advertizer*, 29 July, 9 Sept. 1795, 20 Jan. 1796. Film 44, Virginia State Library and Archives.

17. The will did not survive among the King William County records. It has been related that a copy of the will survived with his descendants in Granville County, NC; however, it seems to have disappeared and no record could be found among the court records relating to the disposition of his land in Granville County. In the suit concerning the land in Granville County the defendants were referred to as the "heirs-at-law".

18. Annie Lash Jester and Martha Woodroof Hiden, *Adventurers of Purse and Person*. 1956 (Richmond: Dietz, rev 1987) 184.

19. Nell Marion Nugent, *Cavaliers and Pioneers*. vol I 1934 (Baltimore: Genealogical Publishing, 1991). 244-245, 358-359; Harris 601-605.

20. Harris 601, 606-607.

21. King William County Records, 1700-1785, 143.

22. King William County Records, Book 3, 207, 140.

23. Harris 603; Mutual Assurance Society Policy 1805, No.529-770-648.

24. Harris 604.

25. John H. Gwathmey, *Historical Register of Virginians in the Revolution, 1775-1783*. 1938 (Baltimore: Genealogical Publishing, rep. 1996) 117.

26. National Archives, First Auditor: Miscellaneous Treasury Account 62045; National Register: Treasury Warrant 6163. of 1832.

27. Unpublished papers of John and Marianne Alcock, 1991. 3910 Lea Road, Marshall, VA 22125.

28. William S. Perry, *Journals of General Conventions of the Protestant Episcopal Church of the United States, 1785-1835*. vol.1. 179, 214, 256, 287, 332. No lists were returned from Virginia to the conventions of 1808, 1811, and 1814.

29. Alcock.

30. Alcock.

31. Isle of Wight Marriage Register, 1771-1853. 163.

32. Surry County Will Book F, 594.

33. Isle of Wight Marriage Register, 1771-1853. 470.

34. Elizabeth Petty Bentley, *Index to the 1810 Census of Virginia*. (Baltimore: Genealogical Publishing, 1980). 50.

35. Joyce H. Lindsay, *Marriages of Henrico County, Virginia, 1680-1808*. 1960 (Greenville, SC: Southern Historical Press, 1995). 14

36. Court of Equity, Granville County, North Carolina. 10 Jan. 1810. North Carolina State Archives.

37. Alcock.

38. A. Bohmer Rudd, *Shockoe Hill Cemetery, Richmond, Virginia: Register of Interments, April 10, 1822 - December 31, 1950*.

39. Rt. Rec. L.W. Burton, *Annuals of Henrico Parish*. 1904. (Bowie, MD: Heritage, rep. 1997). 19.

40. Wallace 2.

41. Charles Morrison Andrews, *Butler—Winston Our Early Parents and Their Descendants*. (Richmond: Privately printed, 1945). 41-43.

42. Andrews 41-42.

HUGH LEE I

Gen. 10

(201-202;167-168)   A number of researchers have pursued the origins of Hugh Lee who patented land in Charles City County in 1673 with no documented success. His origins can be related with greater assurance when one enumerates from whom he is not descended. The first misconception that should be put to rest is that he was the son of Hugh Lee of Northumberland County. Hugh Lee did not leave a will, his widow, Hannah is recorded as the administrator of his estate. The laws of the Colony of Virginia, as brought by the colonists from the common law of England, were such that had Hugh Lee of Northumberland County had a male heir, that person would have inherited his land. The land formerly owned by Hugh Lee went to Matthew Rodham, the husband of his wife, Hannah's daughter by her first husband, as was the law.[1] Hugh Lee of Northumberland County did not have a male heir; this specific relationship can be put to rest.

Extensive research has been conducted to establish the accurate origins of the immigrant Richard Lee (1618-1664). William Thorndale has analyzed the accepted genealogy and home of the Lee family of Shropshire, England and offered documented evidence of the descent and origin of Richard Lee that lays to rest the "Shropshire Lee" account.[2] He concludes with documented evidence from the parish registers and wills that Richard Lee, the immigrant, was the son of John Lee and Jane Hancock. John was buried February 23, 1629/30 in Worcester Saint Martin, Worcestershire, England; his wife was buried there after a second marriage. Their children, who were all christened there were: John, 1616; Richard, 1617/18; Edward, 1620; Thomas, 1622.

The fact that HUGH LEE named his plantation *Aberconnaway* provides a clue concerning his homeplace across the ocean. Over and over when one is able to trace families "across the waters", it is found that the name of their home in the colony of Virginia is the name that they remember nostalgically from an earlier time. Aberconway can be located on a map of the British Isles from 1690.[3] It is on the Irish Sea, a part of Wales, and in the modern county of Clywd. The town of Conwy on a modern map is close to the location of the earlier Aberconway, in fact, Conway is the official name for Aberconwy. Up the river from Conway is a National Trust Property called *Aberconwy House* that is preserved today.[4]

The parish records for Conway, Caernarvon, Wales have been searched, beginning in the 1500s and continuing to the mid-1700s. Because there is no reference date for the birth of Hugh Lee it is difficult to identify a possibility. The naming patterns of the Welsh require careful study to understand the evolution of names. A son was identified as the son of his father, using the given names of both, thus Hugh ap Hugh would indicate that Hugh was the son of Hugh. Later surnames evolved, using the given names in a surname context.[5] While Hugh is a Welsh name, the surname Lee apparently is English. The location of Aberconwy House may be the link to identifying the homeplace of Hugh Lee, but further study is necessary to understand the naming patterns and to develop a more definitive time frame. A great deal of effort and research by a number of people has gone into this quest and this information is recorded that future researchers may build on it.[6]

(202;168) There is still no definitive answer concerning the relationship of Hugh Lee of Northumberland County and Hugh Lee of Charles City County. It appears that the patent of 393 acres of land thought to have been inherited by Matthew Rodham, the son-in-law of Hannah Lee, the wife and widow of Hugh Lee of Northumberland County, was land assigned to Matthew Rodham by Hugh and Hannah Lee before his death.[7] The document executing this was signed by Hugh Lee, January 21, 1660. No record has been found that indicates that Hugh Lee of Charles City County inherited land owned by Hugh Lee of Northumberland County. Under the English law of primogeniture, the son of Hugh Lee would have inherited his land unless he had left a will that explicitly stated otherwise.

(205-211;171-176)
Gen. 9   **HUGH LEE II**

(212-219;177-183)
Gen. 8   **SAMUEL LEE I**

(212;177)   SAMUEL LEE married FRANCES EDWARDS, the daughter of THOMAS EDWARDS.
Thomas Edwards is found in the Rent Rolls of 1704-1705 and is credited with 250 acres of land in what was
then still listed as Charles City County.[8] Apparently the Tatums, Edwards and Lees all owned land in the
same area that became Prince George County. Samuel and Frances acknowledged the legacy from the estate
of her father in January 1713.[9]

Ann Lee
(217;182) The birth date of James, the son of William and Ann (Lee) Baughs is recorded in the *Bristol Parish
Register* as July 3, 1749 with his baptism on October 5, 1749.[10]

Mary Lee
(217;182) The birth of a son of Mary and Shands Raines is recorded in the *Bristol Parish Register*; however,
his given name is left blank in the transcription. He was born on September 12, 1731 and baptized on October
20, 1749.[11]

(220-221;184-185)
Gen. 7   **THOMAS LEE I**

(222-225a;186-189)
Gen. 6   **SAMUEL LEE II**

(225b-231;190-193)
Gen. 5   **LODOWICK LEE**

(231-246;194-205)
Gen. 4   **ALFRED STITH LEE**

        A letter written by ALFRED STITH LEE, Richmond, on February 19, 1866 expresses just
how hard pressed he, and most of the business men in Richmond and Virginia were, following the War
Between the States:[12] *To The Pres. of the Common Council of the City of Richmond, Dear Sir:*
        *After having paid a Class Tax of $25 for the privilege of transacting business in the City of Richmond.
I was presented a short time since With a bill for 75 cents additional assessment of which due notice had been given
in the papers.*
        *I do not recollect any such notice & even if I had noticed it I would no doubt been content for although
I was assessed higher than before the War & had not possession of my house but simply an office, I was led to
believe that I would soon get possession of it & expected to be able to pay my proportion of the increased taxation
which I thought very high ($25) for one in my situation. Contrary to all the promises made me since the 3rd May
last the Govt. still held my house & kept it until the 6th Febry. It is true I had the privilege of storing in one of the
lower rooms but the Govt. kept a magazine for powder & ammunition in the other hence I could get no insurance
on any stored & could put nothing in without taking the risk myself which I was not able to do.*
        *I had also every assurance that I would receive rent on my building but have been informed by Col. James
that the Secy. of War has orderd no rent to be paid.*
        *I now have possession of my house but it is too late as there is no business of that Kind offering, hence
under the circumstances I have no doubt you will agree with me that I am considerably overcharged in proportion
to others doing business in the City. I therefore trust it will be the pleasure of your honorable body to relieve me*

from the payment of any additional tax.

Very respectfully, Your Mo Obt Servt A S Lee

P.S. Without a great change for the better the additional tax will make about 10% on my gross profits, a percentage I do not suppose you have any idea of charging any one. ASL

(236;196) Prior to Alfred Lee's appointment in the Quartermaster's Department he organized at Springfield Hall, Church Hill the Henrico Liberty Guard (May 8, 1861) and served as captain in charge of the Guard[13] until he was relieved by Lieutenant Joseph J. English for larger duties. There were about forty volunteers enrolled in the Guard.

Gertrude Lee

(240;201) Gertrude Lee Mahood's husband, Fontaine Watts Mahood was born December 15, 1841 and died February 20, 1881. Their daughter, Elizabeth Lee Mahood was born February 14, 1874 and died September 11, 1894.[14]

Arthur Wellesley Lee I

Dallas Chesterman Lee married Peter P. Meclewski, first and then Mr. Franklin. Arthur Lee, Jr. married Marion Jordan. Cuthbert Lee married Logan Robins; Logan Robins Lee married and had a daughter, and William Davis Lee married and did not have children.[15]

LEE FAMILY

Gen. 10	HUGH LEE I	m	ANN (?BARNETT)
	Issue: HUGH	m	ANN TATUM
Gen. 9	HUGH LEE II	m	ANN TATUM
	Issue: SAMUEL	m	FRANCES EDWARDS
	Henry	m	Ann (—?—)
	Matthew (p)	m	Ann (—?—)
	Hugh	m	Mary (—?—)
	Thomas	m	Sarah (—?—)
	William	m	
	Nathaniel	m	(1) Elizabeth (—?—)
		m	(2) Rebecca (—?—)
Gen. 8	SAMUEL LEE	m	FRANCES EDWARDS
	Issue: Frances	m	(—?—) Williams
	William	m	died young
	Samuel	m	Mary (—?—)
	Ann	m	(—?—) Baugh
	Mary	m	Shands Raines
	Sarah	m	(—?—) Chambliss
	THOMAS	m	UNKNOWN
Gen. 7	THOMAS LEE	m	
Issue:	SAMUEL	m	(1) unknown
		m	(2) SUSANNA BONNER
Gen. 6	SAMUEL LEE	m	(1) unknown
Issue:	Littleberry	m	Elizabeth Temple
	Mary	m	Jeremiah Clements
	SAMUEL LEE	m	(2) SUSANNA BONNER
Issue:	Chappell	m	
	Richard	m	
	Thomas	m	Sarah Clements Lee

	LODOWICK	m	SARAH CLEMENTS
Gen. 5	**LODOWICK LEE**	m	**SARAH CLEMENTS**
Issue:	Susanna Bonner	m	Albert Gooch
	ALFRED STITH	m	**MARY ELIZABETH PETTYJOHN**

Gen. 4	**ALFRED STITH LEE**	m	**MARY ELIZABETH PETTYJOHN**
Issue:	**ALICE MAUDE**	m	**ROBERT EMMET BUTLER**
	Gertrude	m	(1) Fontaine Mahood
		m	(2) William Babcock
	William	m	Elizabeth Woodward
	Arthur	m	Cuthbert Chesterman
	Alfred Stith	m	Grace Greenwood
	Catherine		unmarried
	Mary Elizabeth	m	George Fleming
	Charles	m	Alice Hartwell
	Evelyn	m	Reuben Quinn
	Percy		died young

Notes

1. Northumberland County Record Book, 1658-1666. 32; Record Book 16, 22.
2. William Thorndale, AG, CG. "*The Parents of Colonel Richard Lee of Virginia*", *National Genealogical Society*. 76 (1988): 254-267).
3. From the papers of Dr. Benjamin B. Weisiger,III, Richmond, Virginia.
4. Robert Williams, *History and Antiquities of Aberconwy and its Neighborhood and Parish*. (Denbigh; T. Gee, 1835).
5. J. Rowlands, et al., eds., *Welsh Family History*. (Baltimore: Genealogical Publishing, 1984). 57-65.
6. Papers of Joseph Dean Lee, 5266 Cripple Creek Court, Houston, TX 77017.
7. *Northumberland County Record Book, 1658-1662* 51.
8. Louise Pledge Heath Foley, *Early Virginia Families Along the James River, Their Deep Roots and Tangled Branches, Charles City County, Prince George County, Virginia, vol II.* 1970. (Baltimore: Genealogical Publishing, rep. 1990). 194.
9. *Prince George County Deeds & Wills, Book B, 1710-1713* 269.
10. C.G. Chamberlayne, *The Vestry Book and Register of Bristol Parish, Virginia, 1720-1789* (Richmond: Privately printed, 1898) 291.
11. Chamberlayne 359.
12. *Richmond City Council Papers* 12 March 1866. Contributed by Minor Tompkins Weisiger.
13. Lee A. Wallace, Jr., *A Guide to Virginia Military Organizations.* 1964. (Lynchburg, VA: H.E.Howard, rev. 1986. 207, 305.
14. Benjamin B. Weisiger, III unpublished manuscript.
15. Weisiger.

SECTION III

THE HUTCHESON ANCESTORS

WALTER CHILES I

Gen. 10

(249-254;209-214) correction: It is upsetting enough to find transcription errors and misinformation when one writes a book and it is published. It is far more upsetting to have reconstructed several generations of a family based on inaccurate information, even after careful research and the use of well-documented information. Such was the case with the account of Walter Chiles I who patented 250 acres of land in Charles City County in 1638. The reader can accept the account of his life in Virginia as accurate, but **discount the English descent from William Childes of Wrington Parish, Somerset, England, without this researcher recounting the whole of the lives of the two Walter Chiles.** Following the explanation of the mistake and the correction thereof, is an accurate account of the lives of the two Walter Chiles in Virginia. These accounts are based on primary source records and correct earlier printed information that has been accepted since early in the 1900s.

The life of WALTER CHILES I as reconstructed in *Tidewater Virginia Families* as it was first published was based on work that had just been published (1987) by Arden H. Brame, Jr. II, a well-recognized genealogical researcher. It was well-documented and seemed to fit the persons and the times. It was with both chagrin and delight on both his and this researcher's part that new information quickly came to light negating the premises that had been developed from the earlier data. Mr. Brame published his second article *A Complete Revision of the Ancestry of Walter Chiles (1608-1653) of Bristol, England and Jamestown, Virginia*[1] shortly after *Tidewater Virginia Families* was published. Following is a revised and corrected reconstruction of the English ancestry of Walter Chiles I based on later information found by Mr. Cox in his research for Mr. Brame in the Society of Genealogists in London, England.

Mr. Cox discovered in the S.G. Great Card Index an entry referring to a Richard Childe, son of William Child and Margaret Payne.[2] This Richard Childe pedigree shows that Walter Childe, the son, and Walter Childe the grandson of William Childe of Wrington, Somerset were both dead by 1647. Thus Walter Chiles I of Jamestown could not be identified with the Walter Chiles of Wrington, Somerset England. Richard Childe had written in his will in 1647: *I give to Francis Childe my brother Walter Childe his sonne the 20th part...which fell to his after the death of Walter Childe, his brother, I being the said Walter Childe's administrator.* Thus Walter Chiles, Jr. christened 17 March 1608/9 and assumed to be Walter Chiles I of Jamestown, had died before 1647. The will went on to read *I give to William Childe sonne of my brother Walter Chiles, decd....*; thus both father and son had died by 1647. The records of the administration of the estate of Walter Child, Jr. of Wrington and St. Mary's Parish have been found, and indicate that he died unmarried. Walter Child, Sr. was deceased by April 1624 as found in the will of William Payne.[3]

Further research uncovered an entry in the **Bristol Burgess Book:**[4] *1632/3 April 1st. Walter Chiles is admitted to the liberties of this cittie for that he was the sonne of JOHN CHILES and hath paid 4 shillings & 6 pence.* The July 24, 1637 deposition of *Walter Chiles of Bristol, clothworker, aged 29 or thereabouts...was given* in connection with his voyage on the *Blessing*, when he served as assistant purser under Henry Tutton, the purser, from September 27 to June 24, 1637. His reported age would mean that he was born about 1608 and would probably be about one year or so older than the Walter Childe of St. Mary Redcliff, Bristol[5] (as reported in the original article by Mr. Brame).

While it has not been the practice of this researcher to continue the generations of tidewater Virginia families into the British records, it seems appropriate to do so in this case, if for no other reason than to clarify and correct the record. From the extant records of Crowle, Worcestershire and Bristol, England it appears that the great-grandfather of Walter Chiles of Virginia was likely RICHARD CHILDE, who was buried at Crowle, Worcestershire on May 6, 1540. The great-grandmother of Walter was possibly either Isabel Childes who was buried on February 10, 1545/6 or Margaret Childes, listed as deceased in October 1547 at Crowle.[6]

William Childes, the son of Richard married at Crowle on January 31 1543/4, probably Alice. He was buried May 24, 1583 at Crowle and Ales Childes, widow was buried January 7 1598/9 at Crowle. William and Alice had three sons baptized at Crowle: Richard Childs on March 10, 1547/8; William Childs on February 5, 1551; and John Childs on October 20, 1555. John was later identified as the son of William *put to David Oldfield, sherman, and Alice his wife for 8 years.*

Temple Parish, Bristol records show that John Childe married first Katherine Johnes on January 12, 1582 and second Alice Wellstedd on February 6, 1603. They had a daughter, Margaret baptized October 30, 1605, and probably at least two sons: William Child, the mariner of Christchurch Parish, Bristol, who married Joane Elkington on May 8, 1631 and had probably died by late 1634; and it is believed, Walter Chiles of Bristol, England and Jamestown, Virginia. While there is no baptismal record for WALTER CHILES, his identification as the son of JOHN CHILES in the Bristol Burgess Book would so indicate. There are a number of records of John Chiles in the British Apprenticeship Books, clearly identifying him as "sherman' and his wife as Alice. His name also came to be recorded as "Chiles". He was known to be alive in February 1628/9.

This information changes the account of the probable aged of both Walter Chiles I and II as presented in *Tidewater Virginia Families*. Walter Chiles who gave his age as "29 or thereabouts" in 1637, was Walter Chiles I and he would have been forty-seven or forty-eight years old when he died in 1653.

There are many theories about the lives of the two Walter Chiles, father and son, of Jamestown and about their wives and children.[7] It is very difficult to identify the two men in relation to their individual activities, and even more difficult to be sure of who they married and accurately identify their children. This further account is an attempt to bring together information that has been gathered from primary sources and to present a documented account of the two men. While it is tempting to resort to earlier printed material and the inferences drawn by earlier researchers, and to accept the earlier accounts of their lives, this is an effort to rectify some of these misconceptions. While this may not be the final answer with regard to these two men, it is felt that it presents a more accurate picture than most that have been drawn in the past.

It would be simple to go to the records of England and resolve the issues of the identity of Walter Chiles, who patented land in Charles City County; when he was born and who he married. While work has been conducted among the English records, definitive inferences cannot at this time be drawn. Many of the parish records of the period in question simply are not extant. Marriage and baptismal records that might identify Walter and his wife and children do not seem to be available. This makes it even more difficult to follow the continuity of his life in Virginia. With the further loss of the early records of the counties of residence of the two Walter Chiles in the colony of Virginia, it makes it almost impossible to be certain of conclusions that are drawn.

Of all the families that this researcher has studied, the Chiles family has prompted the most discussion and provoked the most questions. There seem to be descendants of Walter Chiles in every corner of the United States and they all would like to be able to reconstruct the lives of the father and son in Virginia. So would this humble descendant, and the following is an attempt to do so.

Walter Chiles of Charles City and James City Counties

It would appear that the identification of WALTER CHILES of Charles City County with the apprentice and earlier parish records of Bristol, England would indicate in so far as can be determined, that he was the son of John and Alice Wellstedd Chiles of Temple Parish, Bristol, England.[8] Walter Chiles served on *The Blessing* from September 1636 to June 1637, spending fourteen weeks in Virginia.[9] This information has been found in a deposition given by him on July 24, 1637. He identified himself as Walter Chiles of Bristol, a cloth worker, aged 29, or thereabouts. He served as an assistant to Henry Tutton, then the purser of *The Blessing*.

Two Walter Chiles (Chides) of that period have been discovered in the Bristol area records:
* Walter Chide son of Walter Chide of St. Mary Redcliff Parish was born March 20, 1608/9.[10]
* On April 1, 1632 WALTER CHILES was recorded as *admitted to the liberties of this city [Bristol] for that he was the son of JOHN CHILES.*[11]

It appears that Walter Chide of St. Mary Redcliff Parish died prior to 1647, from the will that has been found of Richard Chide of Poddington, Bedfordshire.[12] No birth record has been found for the Walter Chiles of Bristol, the son of John Chiles. The entry of the marriage of a John Chiles of Temple Parish, Bristol on February 6, 1603/4 is found in those parish records, but not the birth record of Walter Chiles presumed to be his son, and born in 1608/9.

The land patents indicate that Walter Chiles, merchant patented land on May 2, 1638, on the Appomattox River in Charles City County.[13] He claimed as headrights, Henry Tutton, Jon. Gerry, Jon. Shaw and Sarah Cole. On March 1, 1638/9 he repatented the 200 acres and an additional 200 acres for the personal adventure of himself, his wife, Elizabeth Chiles, and his sons, William and Walter (so identified in the patent).[14]

Just as no documentation has been found to conclusively identify Walter Chiles of Charles City County with those found in the records of Bristol, England, of the approximate same time; no records have been found to positively identify the Walter Chiles of the deposition as the same person who executed the land patent of 1638 in Charles City County. While the proximity of the dates has led researchers to assume they were one and the same person; this cannot be definitively established.

Henry Tutton was named in both court records associated with Walter Chiles. In the deposition, Walter Chiles was hired to serve under Henry Tutton, the purser of *The Blessing*; however, in the land patent, it is implied that Walter Chiles paid the passage of Henry Tutton and claimed him as a headright.

(251;211) It is known that Walter Chiles I owned the land called *Black Point* at the tip of Jamestown Island, from a later patent by *his son and heir* in a patent of May 20, 1670.[15] What follows is a very personal account by your author of identifying this site.

What came to be known as Black Point, Jamestown Island, Virginia was the first land of that island the settlers saw as they searched for a place to land in 1607. It was on this island they landed, and it became the site of the first permanent English settlement in North America. I have stood at the edge of the James River at Black Point, knowing it to have been owned by my ancestor before 1653. He came to Virginia quite early and also owned a house in James Towne (c.1640). It is a moving experience to look across the same river he must have gazed across, to feel a part of this person who dared to cross the Atlantic into the unknown, and to accept the challenge of being a part of building a new country.

Through intensive and innovation research in the extant records of the colony of Virginia, I have been able to walk where he walked and where each successive generation of his descendants lived and walked. His grandsons must have been imbued with the same independent adventuresome spirit, for they settled at the edge of the civilization in Hanover County. Their sons moved on into land still under attack by Indians; in the wilderness and isolation of Caroline County in the colony of Virginia.

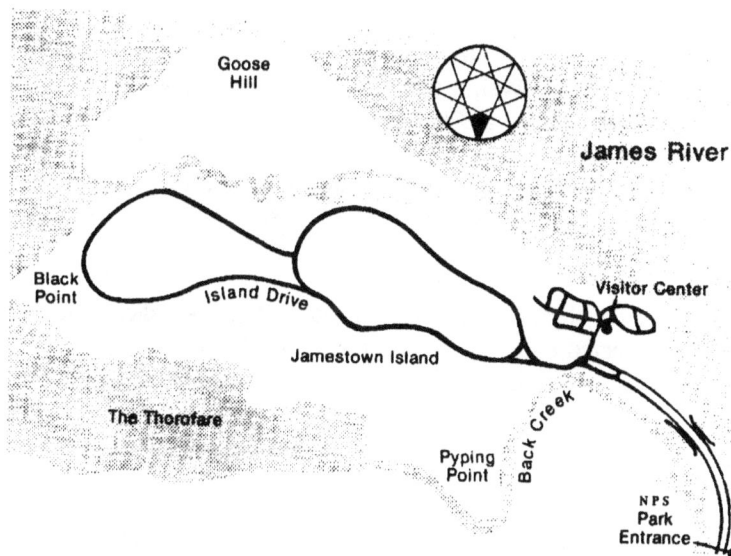

It was this family that first gave me my true sense of identity and continuity as a Virginian. It was this family that piqued my curiosity, challenged my research skills, and caused me to learn about the surviving records of colonial Virginia. It also became necessary to learn about the laws and customs of tidewater Virginia families in order to understand these records. A number of the earliest counties have had all or many their early records destroyed by the three wars fought on their soil (and by courthouse fires). There are few counties in colonial Virginia where one can follow the continuity of the usual record search for successive generations. The search of the identity of early Virginia ancestors and connecting generations is frustrating and difficult; but not impossible.

The date has not been found of when WALTER CHILES first patented the land at Black Point, but apparently the first land that he patented was in Charles City County on the Appomattox River on May 2, 1638 and on March 1, 1638/9. This inference is based upon the date of his arrival on the ship *The Blessing* and the fact that he first represented Charles City County as a Burgess. He brought to the colony of Virginia with him, his wife, ELIZABETH and his sons, William and WALTER (so identified in the land patent).[16]

New information is continually unfolding; a house site on Black Point has been found and identified as belonging to Walter Chiles. Dennis B. Blanton, Director of the Center for Archaeological Research for the College of William and Mary spoke to the *Jamestown Rediscovery* group of his archaeological research under the auspices of the US National Park Service. What is known as test shovel holes have been dug at predetermined sites, from a carefully drawn grid design, extending from the New Town area of Jamestown to the eastern extremities of the island. The house site has been located, plotted and identified, with a number of significant artifacts recovered.

Your author and Fay Parrish Wade (also a Chiles descendant) visited this site in March 1998 with Mr. Blanton. He described the site with expert knowledge and enthusiasm and feels that a complete survey of the site would yield valuable information about how the early settlers lived. One can only make assumptions at this time; perhaps it was the first home of Walter Chiles on Jamestown Island or perhaps it was the first home of his son. It is likely that the house would have been a post-supported, wattle and daub house, perhaps sixteen feet long, with a wooden chimney, and earthen floor. It may have been the home of the overseer of his land on the island where he would have had enough land to produce tobacco. Mr. Blanton noted that the original patents for land on the island were for twelve acres each, but ownership may have expanded as individuals purchased land from others.

The continuum of history is fascinating beyond description. Mr. Blanton and his associates have found artifacts dating back to the Woodland Indians of 12,000 years ago. These artifacts are of the same nature and time frame as of those who arrived in the North American continent across the land bridge from Asia. With Mr. Blanton's expertise, Mrs. Wade was able to find a number of stone chips from weapons produced on the site some 6000 years ago.

(250;210.255;215) It would have been Walter Chiles I who petitioned the General Assembly in 1640 for permission to explore the west. By 1645 Walter Chiles represented James City County as a Burgess, and again in 1646 and 1649.[17] He purchased the Kemp House in Jamestown on March 23, 1648.[18]

(251;211.255;215) Walter Chiles served as a Burgess from Charles City County for the Assembly terms, 1641, 1642 and 1643.[19] Lef't Colonel Walter Chiles, member of the House of Burgesses was elected Speaker of the House, July 5, 1653.[20]

(255;215) The bill of sale for the ship, *Leopoldus*, to Walter Chiles was dated July 12, 1653. There is every reason to believe with the corrected dates for Walter Chiles I, who had just been elected the Speaker of the Assembly, that it was he, in fact, to whom the events occurred following concerning the seizure of the vessel.[21]

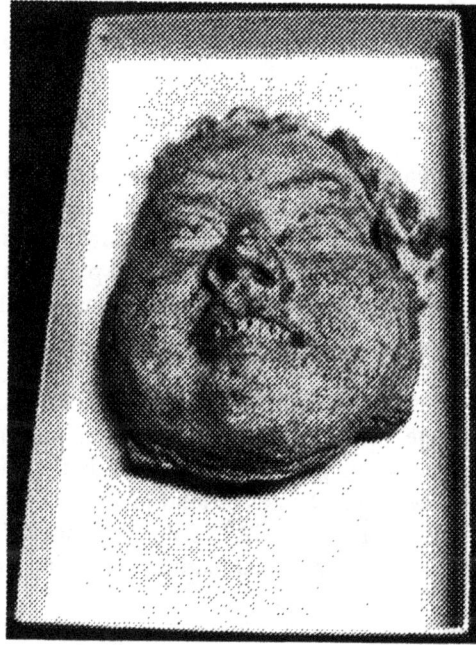

Wall Ornamentation Found in
Excavation of Chiles' House NPS

(253;213) Walter Chiles (I) died in 1653, as stated in the deed signed by Susanna Chiles, widow and executrix of Walter Chiles (II), deceased and identified as the son of Walter Chiles. There are researchers who have questioned the implications (and relationship of the persons involved) of the sale of the Kemp House by Susanna Chiles Wadding to John Page. The deed clearly states that Susanna was acting as the executrix of her husband's estate, and it was his wish, as stated in his will, that his property be sold. This deed was dated November 20, 1673.[22]

It appears that the above sequence of events all relate to the same Walter Chiles, since land was patented and repatented (1638, 1639, 1642, 1649)[23] in Charles City County in his name, and in each case, it was additional acreage with the same identification. He later served as a Burgess from that county. He also later purchased land and a home in Jamestown and served as a Burgess from James City County. He was identified as father to Walter Chiles in both a land grant (dated 20 May 1670),[24] in which Walter Chiles was identified as the son and heir, and the deed conveying the (Richard) *Kemp House* property (November 20, 1673).[25]

The son, Walter Chiles (II) was evidently the son of Elizabeth. There is no further record of the son, William. No surviving records have been found to indicate when Elizabeth Chiles died. As stated before, no records have been found among the parish records of England that have been examined, that give the marriage date of Walter and Elizabeth; or the birth dates of Walter and Elizabeth, the parents, or Walter and William, the sons. While both a maiden name for Elizabeth has been suggested by earlier researchers, and the source as a parish register, there does not seem to be a parish register extant for that time period, for the parish of their residence. Until definitive evidence is found, conjecture on this point should be set aside.

It has been said that Walter Chiles I may have married a second time and his wife may have been Alice Lukin. No concrete evidence has been found to document this, but as existing information is evaluated this possibility does exist. Keep in mind though, the year of John Page's patent in which he included Alice Page as a headright was 1653; the same year that Walter Chiles died. This is cutting it a little close to believe that Alice Lukin, the widow of Walter Chiles would have already become the wife of John Page before the patent date. Although most researchers have concluded that the daughter of John Page was Mary Page, and that she married Walter Chiles, the son; this is not supported in the evidence at hand. It is believed that those researchers may have misinterpreted the identification by John Page of John Chiles and Elizabeth (Chiles)

Tyler, as grandson and granddaughter, and taken these relationships literally, when in fact they were relationships that, today would be designated as step-grandchildren. Alice Lukin may have, then, married John Page as her second husband.

Colonel John Page

(256,260;218-219) The following information about the life of John Page is presented to further elucidate his relationship with the Chiles family. John Page patented land on the south side of the York River and named, among others, Alice Page, Eliza. Page and Mary Page (without further identification) as headrights.[26] No date was included in the patent. The preceding patent on the same page was dated September 11, 1653. The inscription of John Page's gravestone gave his death date as January 23, 1692, aged sixty-five.[27] Thus he would have been born in 1627.

John Page of Middle Plantation made his will on March 5, 1686/7. He named his wife, Alice Page and his sons, Francis and Matthew, to whom he left his substantial holdings.[28] John Tyler identified himself as the grandson of Colonel John Page when he claimed his inheritance on August 19, 1706. John Page identified him as his grandson, the son of his granddaughter, Elizabeth Tyler, and left him the sum of £50 sterling.[29] John Tyler was contingent heir to 200 acres of land in James City County, which he received after the death of Francis Page (son of John Page) in 1692.[30] John Page identified John Chiles as his grandson when he bequeathed him a mourning ring. He also bequeathed mourning rings *to his coz. Henry Tyler and his wife, and to his sister, Eliz: Diggs.*

Alice Page made her will on November 12, 1696 and died on June 22, 1698.[31] She left her estate to her son, Matthew Page and his children: Mann, Alice and Mary Page. She did not name any Chiles connections as legatees in her will. The inscription of Alice Page's gravestone gave her death date as June 22, 1698, aged seventy-three. Thus she would have been born in 1625.[32] Alice Page has been identified with the maiden name of Alice Lukin because of the facsimile of the Lukin family arms cut into her tombstone.[33]

Francis Page, the son of Colonel John Page, made his will on April 23, 1692[34] and died on May 10, 1692 at the age of thirty-five. His wife had already died, and he left one child, Elizabeth Page. In his will, he bequeathed mourning rings to his *cussen Tyler and his wife*, among a number of other persons.

John Page was twenty-six years old in 1653 when he named Alice Page, Elizabeth Page and Mary Page as headrights in a land patent. Alice seems to have been his wife and Elizabeth was evidently his sister, as he later identified Elizabeth Diggs (the wife of Edward Diggs)[35] as his sister. The identity of Mary Page is not clear. Some have thought she may have been the wife of John's brother, Matthew. She could have been an early wife; however, in a land patent of Matthew Pagge (sic) on March 19, 1662, the patent identified his wife at that time as Elizabeth Crump, the widow of John Crump.[36]

Since John Chiles served as a witness to a deed involving John Page in 1673/74 it would appear that he was close to being of age at that time. Under those circumstances he would have probably been born about the year 1655. John Chiles may be considered to have been above the age of sixteen he time he witnessed the document. While he may not have been legally of age, there are instances where those of maturity did perform this service before legal age.[37] At this time, John Page, himself, would have been only about twenty-eight years old. Chronologically, Mary Page as a daughter of John Page, could not have married Walter Chiles, and be the mother of John Chiles. Given the known information about Walter Chiles (II), and about John Page, the legend that Walter Chiles (II) married, first, a daughter of John Page can be dispelled.

John Page's identification in his will of John Tyler, grandson, Elizabeth Tyler and John Chiles as granddaughter and grandson respectively, seems indicative of kinship of a different nature. Later York County records indicate a continuing relationship between the Tyler family and the Page family. Henry Tyler's mother requested the favor of John Page as her *well-beloved friend* in a document dated 1672.[38]

Henry Tyler and wife were named as *cousins* in both the wills of John and Francis Page, and it would seem that this may have been more related to their associations with Henry Tyler, than with his wife. The legacy left John Tyler may have been for the same reasons. As a number of researchers have observed, it may have been the namesake connection that prompted the above legacy, as well as that of the mourning ring to John Chiles, to the exclusion of his brother, Henry. The term grandson may have been used, as it was in that time, to designate a step-child relationship. Alice Page did not identify any Chiles grandchildren, nor name any of the Chiles family in her will.

It appears that John Page may possibly have married Alice Lukin, the widow of Walter Chiles (I). Dr. Lyon G. Tyler wrote of his conviction that this was the only logical explanation for the relationship[39] and further stated that Edward Neill in *Virginia Carolorum* erred in his identification of Captain John Page.[40] "*He meant to say that Captain John Page was the father-in-law of Walter Chiles, son of Colonel [Walter] Chiles. Father-in-law then meant stepfather and John Page's wife, Alice, was doubtless the widow of Colonel Walter Chiles.*"[41]

Dr. Tyler's assertion that John Page married the widow of Walter Chiles I does not seem realistic upon closer analysis. Perhaps it should just be assumed that Edward Neill made a mistake and leave it at that. The observations of Dr. Tyler not withstanding, there appears to be no completely satisfactory explanation to the nature of John Page's will; his consideration of his collateral relatives of the Page blood and his scant recognition of the Chiles "grandchildren". Dr. Tyler further observed that Alice Page did not mention the Chiles children in her will.

(255-263b;215-223)
Gen. 9   **WALTER CHILES II**

Documentation that WALTER CHILES (II) was the son of Walter Chiles (I) can be found in the transfer of the land *Black Poynt*, on May 20, 1670, granted Walter Chiles, father, by right of descent to Walter Chiles, son and heir.[42] Mr. Walter Chiles represented James City County as Burgess in 1658.[43] He was appointed to a committee to proportion the levy in March 1660.[44] He continued to represent James City County in 1663 and 1664.[45]

An inspection of the original patent confirmed the name of Susanna Chiles as correct; she was listed as a headright in the land patent of William Drummond for land in James City County, dated March 26, 1662.[46] William Drummond owned land adjoining land of Walter Chiles. An earlier patent by William and George Worsnam for land in Henrico County at Old Town on the Appomattox River named Sarah and Susan Chiles as headrights. It was dated February 15, 1652.[47] An inspection of the original patent on microfilm confirmed the name Chiles (for each person) and the name Sarah; the name Susan was not legible.

(257;217) Walter Chiles of Jamestown added to the *Kemp House* property in August 1658, when he bought a brick house from Edward Hill.[48] The house adjoined the one his father had bought. It had long been the intent of this researcher to view the artifact collection from the excavations made by the National Park Service under the direction of John L. Cotter between 1954 and 1956. David Riggs, Curator of the NPS Collection met with Mrs. Wade and your researcher in March 1998 and shared his enthusiasm and expertise about the variety of artifacts found at the site of the *Kemp House*, during the time that the two Walter Chiles lived in the house.

As seen on the drawing, the three structures that made up the Chiles' house are designated as Structures 44, 53 and 138, with Structure 44 making up the north wing, Structure 53 the center, and Structure 138 the south wing. It was a large house with two wings situated on either side of a central square room. The central part was built above a six-foot, brick-paved cellar.[49] It has been learned that this home was one of only two brick houses in the colony at the time that it was built. Which is not to imply that all three sections were constructed at the same time, it may well have grown as the needs of the occupants grew.

Many pieces of ornate plaster were found; indicating a home of lavish decoration for the time. One cannot help but compare this with the description of the wattle and daub house of Black Point. Of particular note is the intact, highly decorative, ornamental bust of a cherub taken from the Structure 53 house, and believed to be a wall ornamentation (see page 55). It is believed to be associated with the *Order of the Garter*, which fraternal society dates from the fourteenth century. Also found were other pieces of ornate plaster and pieces of glassware, goblets, storage jugs, spoons, pipes, roof tiles and bricks. An intact padlock was also found.[50]

Walter Chiles patented land April 4, 1671 in Westmoreland County on behalf of his sons, John and HENRY CHILES.[51] Walter Chiles died between November 15, 1671,[52] when he made his will and

November 25, 1671 when an order of the Council, through William Berkeley, granted SUSANNA Giles (CHILES), relict and executrix of Walter Childs 200 acres of land for ninety-nine years. *"This land to remain with John Giles [later in the document identified as John Child] the eldest son of the said Walter Giles, deceased and ye said Susanna his wife."*[53]

John Chiles witnessed a deed from George Bates to Mr. John Page on March 16, 1673/4.[54] Francis Page also witnessed the deed. Elizabeth Chiles witnessed a deed to John Page on February 4, 1673/4, also in York County.[55] John Chiles and Mary, his wife deeded the lease from William Berkeley to Sir Edmond Andros on September 29, 1693, on account of moving. The land was not described in detail, but was identified for the remainder of the term of ninety-nine years, and in the same manner as that granted by William Berkeley to Susanna Chiles.[56]

An entry dated June 25, 1684, in the York County records identified Henry Tyler as having married Elizabeth Chiles.[57]

No conclusive evidence has been found as to the birth date of Walter Chiles II. It would seem from subsequent court documents that it is likely that he may have been married before the mid-1650s. From the deed witnessed by John Chiles in 1673/4, he would have been of competent age at that time. It appears that he must not have been of age in 1671, when William Berkeley and the Council granted Susanna Chiles a lease for 200 acres of land in her name (as executrix of the will of Walter Chiles) and in the name John Chiles. It appears the land would have gone directly to John, as son and heir, had he been of age at that time.

Contrary to most of what has been written about the Page-Chiles connection, this same document clearly identified John Chiles as the son of Susanna and Walter Chiles. From this it would appear that she was his only wife. **The quote from the grant from Lord Berkeley is an original court document, a primary source record as it were; and should be accepted as evidence that both John and Henry were sons of Walter and his wife Susanna Chiles.**

It seems likely that the Susanna Chiles claimed as headright by William Drummond (1662) was the wife of Walter Chiles, given the known associations of Drummond. The headright purported to be Susan Chiles in 1652 by John Worsnan is less certain, but given the variations in names recorded in the extant records of the time, it may well have been, in fact, Susanna Chiles, in which case the date that she was recorded as a headright is significant.

No information has been found to validate the claim by Mr. Lanciano[58] that the maiden name of Susanna Chiles was Page. The same chronologies of age exist in this instance that exist in relationship to Mary Page (see John Page preceding). Further, there is no mention in any of the court documents or history concerning the Page family, that has been found, to identify a daughter named Susanna.

It has been suggested that Susanna may well have been a Brooks. Walter Brooks is known to have had association with Walter Chiles I in the purchase of land and perhaps living on adjoining lands in Charles City County. The land that Walter Chiles patented in 1649 was assigned to Walter Brooks, then later repurchased by Walter Chiles. Walter Brooks additionally patented several parcels of land from 1653 to 1663 in the same area.[59] From what is known of the patterns of marriages of the colonial period, it would make the daughter of Walter Brooks a less than likely candidate; Walter Chiles and Walter Brooks may well not have been from the same social and political milieu.[60] There is little hope of finding the names of Walter Brooks children in that time period with the paucity of extant records.

(259;219) It is evident, from existing records that Susanna Chiles was the mother of the three children identified as the children of Walter Chiles (II) of Jamestown: John Chiles, Elizabeth Chiles and Henry Chiles. It is further believed that these three children were all born at an earlier date than has heretofore been considered. Susanna Chiles apparently did marry the Reverend James Wadding between the date she sold Black Point August 7, 1672 and November 1673 when the deed to the Kemp house was executed.

The Reverend James Wadding had created an M.A. at Oxford on December 20, 1670 and was the minister at Jamestown in 1672. He was identified in a deed of sale, 25 May 1672, in Middlesex County, of plantations (200 and 600 acres respectively) that he sold to Henry Whiting, as being "of Ware Parish, Gloucester County".[61] He was the rector of Petsworth Parish in Gloucester at the time of Bacon's Rebellion but was succeeded by the Reverend Thomas Vicars in 1677.[62]

As a final statement concerning the lives of Walter Chiles I and Walter Chiles II, the data presented

in the first editions of *TIDEWATER VIRGINIA FAMILIES* are accurate, with the exceptions noted here. One must sort out the relevant dates and reconstruct the ages and the lives of the two men accordingly. It would be impossible within the intent of this supplement to rewrite the two biographical accounts in their entirety.

John Chiles

(260-261;219-220) correction: John Chiles was the son of Walter Chiles II and his wife Susanna, and was born sometime around the date of 1655, in as far as can be determined. It is known from the records that his first wife was named Mary. Her maiden name is not known. He married second, Eleanor, who is identified in printed accounts to be a Webber. This is based on the deed executed by Henry and his wife Jane Webber to the two sons of John Chiles, Henry and John.[63] When one reads the deed carefully one determines that, not only does Henry not identify the two Chiles sons, as his grandsons, but he states explicitly that the deed is in consideration of £100 of current money already paid him by John Chiles, deceased. Thus Henry Webber was fulfilling a contract that included the lease of the land to Eleanor Chiles until her death, made with John Chiles before his death.[64] When Eleanor Chiles petitioned the Council (May 16, 1723) to stop the land patent to Henry Chiles or any other children of John Chiles, deceased, she did not identify herself as the mother of any of John Chiles' children, only that she was his widow.

(260-261;220-221) The following relates to the children of John and Mary Chiles the following elaborating on the two daughters who married respectively a Carr and a Southerland.[65] William Carr of Spotsylvania County wrote his will on 2 August 1760.[66] He named his wife, Susannah, and eleven children. Those who received land (which was in both Spotsylvania and Louisa counties) were Thomas Carr, William Carr, Ann Carr, Elizabeth Carr, Phoebe Carr, Walter Chiles Carr, Charles Brooks Carr and Agnes Brooks Carr.[67] Daughters Susanna Carr, Sarah Carr and Mary Carr each received a cow and calf.[68] In respect to the remainder of his estate, he said in a clause that was later to figure in litigation, *I give all the rest of my estate both real and personal not herein particularly mentioned to be equally divided between my wife and children (William, Ann, Elizabeth, Charles, Agnes, Walter, Phoebe and Thomas), and I do hereby give the estate by this clause of my will devised to my said wife and children respectively and to their heirs forever, provided nevertheless that [should] either of my said children die before they arrive to the age of twenty-one or marry that their share or part given by this clause be sold by my executors and the money arising by such sale be equally divided between my wife (if living) and all my children and their legal representatives.* His wife was named an executor, along with Edward Herndon and Joseph Brock. Witnesses to the will were Anthony Foster, William Ellis and John Gordon.

A codicil to his will annexed, was written ten days later on 12 August 1760; he empowered his executors, of whom Fendall Southerland was named as one, to divide his personal estate according to his will. The will was admitted for probate 4 November 1760.[69]

Within a few days of William Carr's having written his will, Walter Chiles died intestate in Amelia County.[70] A record of the chancery suit which followed the death of Walter Chiles is found in a published work by Thomas Jefferson, *Reports of Cases Determined in the General Court of Virginia.*[71] It is through this litigation that family relationships are revealed.

correction: It is now known that it was this Walter Chiles who patented land in Prince George County, in an area that later became Amelia County. He did not have a son, Peter Chiles. This was a misinterpretation of the entry in the *Bristol Parish Register*; the entry is, in fact, *Peter M S [male slave] of Walter Chiles, born 14th January 1727*; a later entry is for *Jenne female Slave of Walter Childs Born Decr 1732.*[72]

Walter Chiles' only heirs were the children of his two sisters, the elder of whom married a Mr. Carr, father of the above William Carr, and the younger of whom married a Mr. Southerland. The estate of Walter Chiles was large, and included slaves. It was stated that William Carr had notice of this accession to his estate, and died without having altered or republished his will. The question then arose as to whether the slaves which William Carr acquired from Walter Chiles after his will was written but before it was probated, should be distributed in accordance with the provisions of the will or not. Because of the court case to determine the distribution of the slaves of Walter Chiles to the heirs of William Carr, the mother of William Carr has been identified as a Miss Chiles.

According to a manuscript in the collections of The Virginia Historical Society, the Mr. Southerland who married the younger sister (possibly named Elizabeth) of Walter Chiles was Joseph Southerland, and their son was Fendell Southerland.[73] Walter Chiles and his two sisters were children of John Chiles and his first wife, Mary. John Chiles, in turn, was a son of Walter Chiles II, the son of Walter Chiles, the immigrant.[74]

The suit proves that the William Carr who died in Spotsylvania County in 1760 was a nephew of the Walter Chiles who died the same year in Amelia County. Although there was another contemporary Walter Chiles, who lived in Caroline County and was a cousin of the one who died in 1760, that Walter Chiles had brothers, and his heirs would have included children of his brothers (had he not had children of his own as heirs). The Walter Chiles who died in Amelia County had only sisters, which accords with known records of John Chiles.[75]

What are the implications for the Carr family genealogy? Thomas Carr, gentleman, is assumed to be the immigrant. He was granted a patent for 546 acres of land in St. John's Parish in Pamunkey Neck, King William County on 25 April 1701, for the importation of eleven persons into the colony. He was a Justice of the Peace for that county as early as 1702 and High Sheriff in 1708-9.[76] His son was Major Thomas Carr of Caroline County, who was born in 1678; this relationship is proven by a King William County deed of 1705, from Thomas Carr, Sr., gentleman, to his son, Thomas Carr, Jr., witnessed by William Carr.[77]

Captain William Carr of Spotsylvania County has long been believed to have been another son of Thomas Carr, Sr.[78] We now know that William's mother was a daughter of John Chiles.[79] This John Chiles was born before 1660[80] and married by 1693. It was his daughter, born about 1692, who became the mother of the William Carr who died in 1760. If the reasoning of the above cited manuscript is correct, then William Carr would have been born about 1710 or earlier. He clearly was not the William Carr who witnessed the deed of Thomas Carr in 1705.[81]

All that is proven by the 1760 court case is that the Thomas Carr who was born in 1678 and died in 1737 and the William Carr who died in 1760 did not have the same mother. Although Thomas Carr was dead by the time of the court case he had at least one son, John Carr, who was still alive in 1760 and would have been a heir to the estate of Walter Chiles, had he been a grandson of the latter's sister.[82] Perhaps further investigation will determine that the William Carr who died in 1760 was grandson to Thomas Carr, Sr., and son of the William Carr who witnessed the deed of 1705. This seems a logical conclusion, but evidence has not been found to verify this.[83]

Elizabeth Chiles

(261-262;221-222) correction The revised dates and relationships heretofore presented would indicate that Elizabeth was the daughter of Walter and Susanna Chiles. While John Page referred to Elizabeth Tyler as his grand daughter, the exact terminology and nature of this relationship has not been determined.

Of interest to Tyler descendants is the will of Anne Tyler, relict of Henry Tyler (Sr.), deceased, late of Middletowne Parish, York County (as abstracted).[84]... as well as out of affection I owe to my well-beloved sons, Henry, John and Daniel Tyler, sons of my well-beloved husband, and for other good and valuable considerations, give and grant to my sons at their several ages; viz., to my son Henry, a tract of land whereon I now live, a young mare, featherbed and furniture to value of £10, 4 pewter dishes and one mulatto servant named John Williams; and to my two sons John and Daniel, a tract in the forest on branches on Nominy Creek between the Potomac and Rappahannock Rivers, 1200 acres as according to patent, to be equally divided between them at their several ages. To each of them 4 cows, 1 featherbed and furniture to value of £10, 4 pewter dishes and to each servants. To John a negro called Lucy and to Daniel a negro called Black Tom at 21; but if I am living when they come of age, I may make use of above. I put in trust my friend Mr. Martin Gardner, feoffee in trust, to see this deed performed, and in case of his decease, I request Major Robert Baldrey, Mr. John Page, and Mr. Daniel Wyld. Will dated 29 June 1672. Witnesses: John Baskervyle, Fran. Mathews. Signed by Anne Tyler with her mark A. Recorded 4 January 1672.

It was the son, Henry Tyler who married Elizabeth Chiles and was a justice, the coroner and sheriff of York County. In 1699 he was appointed one of the directors for building Williamsburg, the new capital city. As senior warden of Bruton Church in Williamsburg, he headed the petition of the vestry in 1710 to the General Assembly for a new brick building. This was finished in 1715 and is still standing. He was the ancestor of John Tyler, President of the United States in 1841-1845.[85]

Notes

1. Arden H. Brame, Jr., II, "*A Complete Revision of the Ancestry of Walter Chiles (1608-1653) of Bristol, England and Jamestown, Virginia*", *The Augustan Society Omnibus*, 12:110-111. (Torrance, CA, privately printed, n.d.) address: PO Box P, Torrance, CA 90507-0210.

2. Mrs. V.T.C. Smith, *West Indies: Smith Collection*. 15: 110-111.

3. PCC Wills — 211 Fines of Richard Childe of Poddington, Bedfordshire.; Adm. dated 13 May 1626 granted Richard Child, the uncle. Research by Dr. Paul Child, Ogden, UT and letter from Arden H. Brame, Rosemead, CA 1993.

4. *Bristol Burgess Book, 1632/3*. 221.

5. Arden H. Brame, Jr., II, "*The English Birth and Ancestry of Walter Chiles (1609-1653) of Jamestowne, Virginia*", *The Augustan Society Omnibus*. 7(n.d.):102-109.

6. This lineage of Walter Chiles of Virginia (taken from *The Augustan Society Omnibus, 12: 110-111*) is used with the kind permission of Arden H. Brame, Jr., II, who has contributed his articles with the intent of correcting the record for readers of both his works and *Tidewater Virginia Families*.

7. See *Tidewater Virginia Families, A Magazine of History and Genealogy* 1 (1992): 67-72, 120-126 for articles relating to the Chiles and Page families.

8. Brame, *Omnibus* 12 110-111.

9. *High Court of Admiralty Libels and Depositions*, (PRO Class HA 13, 24 & 30), Public Record Office, London.

10. Brame 103; St. Mary Redcliff Parish Records. For documentation for the earlier account (now inaccurate) see the book *Tidewater Virginia Families* 215-233.

11. Brame; *Bristol Burgess Book, 1632-1633* 221.

12. Brame, *Omnibus* 12 110; Smith Collection 15 110-111.

13. Nugent I:87.

14. Nugent I: 103-104; L P Bk 1 P II 625.

15. Nugent II: 112.

16. L P Bk 1 II: 551, 625.

17. William Waller Hening, *Statutes at Large vol 1* (Richmond: Pleasants, 1807) 322, 358.

18. *The Virginia Papers*, Ambler Mss #4, Library of Congress; Lindsay O. Duvall, *Virginia Colonial Abstracts*, Series 2, vol 4, (Easley: Southern Press, 1979) 3.

19. Hening 1(1807) 239; William Glover Stanard, *Colonial Virginia Register* (Baltimore: Clearfield, rep 1989) 61.

20. Duvall 4:377-379.

21. Duvall 4:382-383.

22. Ambler Mss 24.

23. L P Bk 1 II: 551, 625, 859; Bk 2 193.

24. L P Bk 6 413; Nugent II: 112.

25. Ambler Mss 24.

26. L P Bk 3 212; Nugent I: 279.

27. Richard C.M. Page, *Genealogy of the Page Family* (New York: Jenkins, 1893) 16; Gravestone, Bruton Parish Church Cemetery; Annie Lash Jester & Martha Woodroof Hiden, *Adventurers of Purse and Person* (Princeton, NJ, 1956) 231.

28. *York County Will Book 9* 103-106.

29. *York County Court Records*, June 2, 1707; Lyon Gardiner Tyler, *The Letters and Times of the Tylers* vol 1 (New York: DeCapo, 1970) 49.

30. *York County 9* 127-129.

31. *York County Record Book 11* 85-86; Gravestone; George Harrison Sanford King (G.H.S. King) Papers, Page Folder. Mss1K5823. Virginia Historical Society, Richmond, VA.

32. Jester & Hiden 231.

33. Jester & Hiden 231.

34. King Papers; York County 11 127-128.

35. Nugent I:279.

36. L P Bk 6 298; Nugent II: 76.

37. See as to age of competency: *National Genealogical Society Quarterly*. 79(1991): 203.

38. Benjamin B. Weisiger, III, *York County Records, 1672-1676* (Richmond: privately printed, 1991) 20.

39. Lyon Gardiner Tyler, ed., *William & Mary Quarterly (W&M Q)*, Series 1, vol VI 146-147.

40. Edward D. Neill, *Virginia Carolorum* (NY: Munsell's, 1886) 232.

41. *W&M Q* 1 VI 146-147.

42. L P Bk 6 413; Nugent II: 112.

43. Hening 1: 506.

44. Hening 2: 31.

45. Hening 2: 198,211.

46. L P Bk 4 12; Nugent I: 400.

47. L P Bk 3 23; Nugent I: 238-239.

48. Ambler Mss 24; Duvall 4:4.

49. John L. Cotter, *Archaeological Excavations at Jamestown, Virginia*, 2nd ed. (Courtland, VA: The Archaeological Society of Virginia, 1994) 74-75.

50. Artifacts from Lot B68, coordinates 96:108. National Park Service Archaeological Survey, 1954-1956.

51. H.R. McIlwaine, ed., *Minutes of the Council and General Court of Colonial Virginia*. (Richmond: Virginia State Library, 1979) 245.

52. Ambler Mss 24.

53. Lee Papers, Mss1L51f673. Virginia Historical Society, Richmond, VA.

54. *York County Record Book 5* 65.

55. York Book 5 64-65.

56. Lee Papers.

57. *York County Deeds, Orders, Wills, Etc. VI* 499.

58. Claude Lanciano, *Rosewell, Garland of Virginia*. (Gloucester: Gloucester Historical Comm.,1978) 15.

59. Nugent I 186-7, 281, 298, 469, 505.

60. See *TVF* 5(1997): 71--82, 211-220; 6(1997): 5-16).

61. Recorded 11 Feb. 1673/74; *Essex County Court Order Book, 1673-1680*, Pt 1 40.

62. Edward Lewis Goodwin, *The Colonial Church in Virginia* (Milwaukee: More House, 1927) 313, 326.

63. *Spotsylvania County, Virginia Deed Book A, 1722-1729* 88-91.

64. Arden H. Brame, Jr., II, "Thomas Jefferson Reveals Three More Children of John Chiles", *Omnibus* 14(n.d.): 71-72.

65. Jeanne Brooks Gart, 2126 Connecticut Ave NW, Washington, DC 20008. "Thomas and William Carr and the Chiles Connection", *TVF* 4 (1995) 80-83). Mrs. Gart is a Certified Genealogist and author. She has researched extensively in the Middle Peninsula, and is the author of *The Two Ralph Sheltons* TVF 3 (1994): 220. Since this article was published she has learned that Joseph Bickley died in King William County.

66. *Spotsylvania County Will Book B*: 497-501.

67. Although Thomas was the first son named in the will, he apparently was a minor at the time. The widow, Susannah was appointed guardian to Charles Brooks Carr, Agnes Brooks Carr, Walter Chiles Carr, Phoebe Carr and Thomas Carr, orphans of William Carr. William Armstrong Crozier, ed. *Virginia County Records: Spotsylvania County, 1721-1800.* vol I 1905 (Baltimore: Genealogical Publishing Co, rep. 1990) 73.

68. These three daughters had already been given land: Susanna and her husband, William Crenshaw in 1751; Sarah and her husband, Mordecai Hord in 1752; and Mary and her husband, Nicholas Crenshaw in 1755. *W&M Q* ser.1 8(1899): 132.

69. The codicil signed 12 August 1760 gave his wife, Susannah use of a "mulatto girl named Flora" during her natural life. On 4 September 1792, the executors "received of Walter Chiles Carr of Fayette County, Kentucky, certain slaves, descendants of a mulatto girl lent to Susannah, the wife of William Carr, decd., by will...which said Susannah is lately dead...". Crozier 454.

70. It seems likely that the codicil to William Carr's will was added when he received news of the death of Walter Chiles, and of his inheritance from him.

71. Thomas Jefferson, *Reports of Cases Determined in the General Court of Virginia, 1730-1740 and 1768-1772.* (Buffalo: William S. Hein & Co., 1981) 132-133.

72. C.G. Chamberlayne, *The Vestry Book and Register of Bristol Parish, Virginia, 1720-1789* (Richmond: privately printed, 1898) 297, 299.

73. Chiles Folder, G.H.S. King Papers, Mss1K58239Fa1. Virginia Historical Society, Richmond, Virginia.

74. V.L.H. Davis, "Walter Chiles, Father and Son" *Tidewater Virginia Families: A Magazine of History and Genealogy*, 1 (1992): 67-69, 120-122.

75. King Papers; Gart.

76. *W&M Q* 1 8(1899): 106.

77. *Virginia Land Records.* (Baltimore: Genealogical Publishing Co, 1982) 304, Gart.

78. *VMHB* II(1895): 225.

79. Gart.

80. *TVF* 1:121.

81. Brame 14(n.d.): 67-73.

82. *W&M Q* 1 8(1899): 107.

83. Brame 14(n.d.): 69-73.

84. Benjamin B. Weisiger, III, *York County, Virginia, Records, 1672-1676* (Richmond: privately printed, 1991) 20.

85. Lyon Gardiner Tyler, LLD, ed., *Encyclopedia of Virginia Biography, vol I* 1915 (Baltimore: Genealogical Publishing Co, 1998) 346.

HENRY CHILES

(264;224) correction: As has now been seen, HENRY CHILES was the son of Walter and his wife, Susanna Chiles, and would have been a full brother of John Chiles. There is no evidence that Walter Chiles II was married twice.

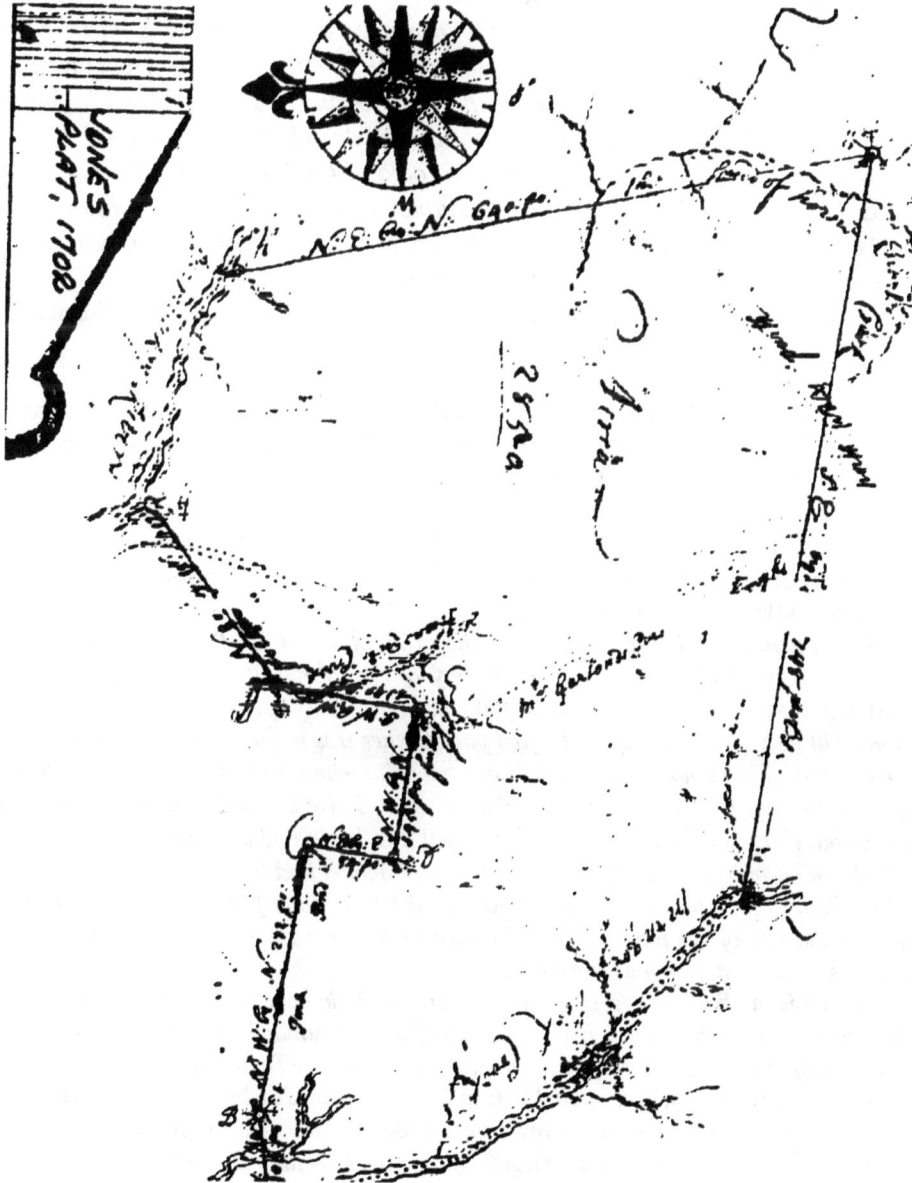

    While this is not a land plat of land of Henry Chiles, he is noted as an adjoining land owner of land surveyed for Frederick and Thomas Jones in King William County in 1702.[1] The land in all probability lay across the Pamunkey River from land on which Henry Chiles lived in Hanover County.[2]
December the 2ᵈ 1702. Then measured for Mʳ Frederick and Thomas Jones Two Thousand Eight hundred and fifty acres of Land Bought of Mʳ Richd Littlepage part of a greater patt[ent] of fower Thousand Eight hundred Eighty Six acres divided Aprill the Last 1702. Lying in Sᵗ Johns Psh in King

William Cty upon ye North Side of Purmunkey [Pamunkey] River above Mangohick Creek Being:
bounded as followeth, Beginning at a Sma[ll] Reade Oake in Mangohick Creek in Col. Parkes Line
t^h[us] a long ye s^d Parkes Line No: l halfe west one hund^d & six poles to the Collidge Corner a Stake by
fower hicorys & two oake sapIns T^h a Long ye Collidge Line No:West By North two hundred Seventy two
poles t[o] a corner maple of Mr Henry Chiles standing in a pond t^h a Long ye s^d Chiles Line N:E: by E:
Eighty fower poles To a stake by a Read Oak on a hill another Cor[ner] of ye s^d Chiles t^h keeping ye s^d
Chiles Line N:W: by N: one hundred & fortey five poles to fower slooping white oakes anothe[r] Corner
of ye s^d Chiles Standing in Horne Quarter furlong˙ t^h downe ye s^d Chiles Line S:W: by N: one hundred
& forty poles to a Read Oake Standing in Horn Quarter Creek t^h No: Eighty deg:[rees] west Two hundred
& Twelve poles to two Brushes Standing one [on] the River bank t^h up ye River two hundred forty fower
poles to an old dead Spanish oake Just below the mouth of a deep branch Running t^h No:Ea: by No: Six
hundred & forty poles to a Stake by two pines and two oakes Standing one [on] a hill t^h So:Ea: by No:
Seaven hundred & forty Eight poles to three small Maples Just by ye mouth of a branch in Mangohick
Creek t^h downe ye s^d Severall Courses five hundred Eighty two poles to the first Station wch s^d Land was
Layd out p^r ye Consent of both partys ye day & year above Written.
'(a furlong was a division of an unenclosed corn-field)³   [As] P^r Me [Signed] James Taylor

Walter Chiles

(268;228) correction: This Walter Chiles did not live in Prince George County, and did not have a son Peter as was related earlier. This was a case of mistaken identity, as is now realized from the chancery suit related earlier involving Walter Chiles (the son of John Chiles) of Amelia County.

(269-229) The following will confirms the relationship of Benjamin Faulkner, his daughter Esther and Walter Chiles IV, the grandson of Henry Chiles.⁴ The names of the two men were often linked in the county court records and they apparently were close neighbors.
In the Name of God Amen. I Benjamin Faulkner Senr of Halifax County Planter being of sound mind and disposing mind and memory yet considering the uncertainty of this mortal life do think it necessary to make and ordain this my last Will and Testament which is as follows.
Imprimeus It is my will that all my just debts be first paid further it is my will that my son Jacob Faulkner have the lent of the fourth part of my land to be laid off convenient to where he now lives for his life and his heirs m [sic] present wifes widowhood If he leaves her behind after which I give the said land to his son Benjamin to him and his heirs forever but if my son Jacob should want to sell it in his life he is at liberty so to do provided he give his son Benjamin the value of it at his Death likewise Negroe Rachael and her future increase. I lend him during his life only the first from now to be Benjamins his Sons or the first of her future increase that lives to the age of twenty one. She and the rest of her future increase I have at my sons Death to be equally divided amongst the children he has by his present wife or may have hereafter.
Item the rest as follows it is my Will my two Daughters Sarah and Jane have the labors of negroes Harry for twenty years directly after my Death the rest of my Estate both Real and Personal I leave to my wife Frances to dispose to the children she has by me at her discresion for twenty years after my Death and at the end of the said period I give Dennis, Davey — Harry, Minny, Coss and Buck to be equally divided between the children of my son John and Jacobs and my daughter Chiles the rest of my Estate I leave to my wife to give to her Children as she sees cause this will revoking all other wills by me made not forgetting lend my little Daughter Killay the negroe child Matt so called till he is forty years old after that period to Benjamin, son of Jacob all things given or lent to any of my children I now forever give I constitute my sons John and Jacob Execrs of this my last Will and my wife Exectrix given under my hand this 20th Day of October 1783.Signed and Published in presense of
John Meacham Joseph West   [signed] *Benjamin Faulkner*

[added] *In the name of God Amen it is my will and desire to give and bequeath to give to my dater Ester Chiles one hundred acres of land on the Rock spring brance duing life this 20th November 1783.*
Test: John Pillman John Markams   [signed] *Benjm Faulkner⁵*

From a Faulkner/ Thomas Family Bible the following were recorded:[6] John Montford Thomas, son of Belle Faulkner Thomas, who was the daughter of John H. Faulkner and Helen Hall Faulkner (the owner of the Bible). Benjamin Faulkner (the second son by that name) was the son of Thomas and Mary Faulkner and was born Tuesday, 7 December 1714; Thomas Faulkner died 15th November 1736. The births of other children of Thomas and Mary Faulkner recorded in the family Bible: Henry, 20 Oct 1689; Sarah, 9 Jan 1691; Thomas, 11 July 1695; Mary, 3 Nov 1698; Anne, 3 Jan 1699; William, 3 Nov 1702; John, 9 March 1704; Jacob, 3 July 1707; Robert, 2 Nov [---]; and Benjamin, 1 Nov 1711; Benjamin, 7 Dec 1714.

James Chiles

(270;229) From work presented by Maurine Childs Parker it is known that this James Chiles is in fact the James Chiles of Spotsylvania County who married Elizabeth Durrett and had three children: Elizabeth, Harry and James.[7] James later became a Baptist minister and died in Ninety-six District, South Caroline in 1784.[8]

William Chiles

(270;230) A connection between William Chiles and the Dabney and Overton families of Hanover County was suggested, but this researcher was unable to find proof. The journal kept by Henry Burruss in 1823 (with his added notes) of his trip to Kentucky and Tennessee may provide that link in his notes about his family relationships.[9] He wrote at the end of his trip: *Not to know what happened before you were born, is to be always a child.*

May the 27th 1832 It came into my mind to some memorandums of my Ancestors from the Most Authentic sourse in my power. My Grand father on my fathers side was JACOB BURRUSS and was born October the 14th 1714 of his Father or Mother I have no tradition. He had several brothers and sisters but I never knew but Charles his youngest brother who married Sally Woolfolk moved to Amherst county Virginia, where [he] lived until his death and had sons and daughters. My Grandfather married Martha Harris[10] about the year 1739 or 1740 she was the daughter of Overton Harris [actually, if Jacob did marry Martha Harris she would have been the daughter of William Harris][11] and her Mothers maiden name was [Elizabeth] Burnet she [Martha Harris] had one brother by the name of Overton that I knew and a number of sisters. One married William Chiles[12] one John Day one Edward Nelson one James Nelson one a Davis one a [Samuel] Baker beside my Grandmother already mentioned[13]. My Grandfather on my Mothers side was David Terrell and the tradition is that he was born about the year 1705 and was married to Agatha Chiles in the year 1729 or 1730 Agatha was born on the 14th Oct 1714 the day on which my Grandfather Burruss was born being about 9 years younger than her husband [sic]. They had twelve children 7 sons and 5 daughters (Viz) David, Henry, Micajah, Pleasant, Chiles, Christopher, & Jonathan; daughters Mildred, Mary, Anna, Rachel (my Mother) and Susanna--My Grand father died in the year 1753 and his widow in the year 1768. I think the twelve children (all of whom I knew) If they had been weighed in their best or Fleshiest time that the agregate weight would have been at least 3000 lbs and altho one had no Child and one other had but one.

The journal included entries from the Burruss Family Bible added by Henry Burruss, the son:

Married: Henry Burruss & Elizabeth Johnson, October 9, 1794

        Henry Burruss & Sally T Wortham, November 14, 1805

Born: Henry Burruss, December 23, 1769; Sally T Wortham, November 28, 1782;

        Grand Father Charles Wortham, July 13, 1759; Grandfather John Burruss, 1745

        Children: Sally T Burruss, March 25, 1797; Nancy Burruss, August 18, 1798

        Rachel Burruss, July 27, 1800; Elizabeth G Burruss, September 25, 1802

        Margaret Burruss, April 10, 1804; John Burruss, September 21, 1806

        A Daughter, March 11, 1809; Mary Jane Burruss, April 4, 1810

        Charles C P Burruss, September 18, 1812; Elliott W Burruss, January 13, 1815

Died   Grand Father Jacob Burruss April 8 1778

        Grandfather Wortham 7 ½ O'Clock PM June 4 1818

        Henry Burruss, My father ½ 12 night December 6 1839

Sep 5 1859 Will of Henry Burruss (I) of Caroline County:

Lend to my wife Sally T Burruss, tract I live on for life, and one-half my mill, choice of stock and household items.

Negroes to be divided between my wife and her four children and my four children and two grandchildren by my first wife; except those given my two daughters at marriage. To wife, negro woman Maria and her son Spencer. To my daughter Rachel, negro girl Isabella. To my daughter Eliza[beth] G Burruss, negro Lucy Ann. To my daughter Mary Jane Burruss, negro Kitty. To my two grandchildren, negro Alice. Balance to be divided into five parts, with one-fifth to my daughter Mary Jane, one-fifth to my wife and three-fifths to my sons: John, Charles C P, and Elliott W Burruss. Other one-half of my negroes divided equally among my first four daughters and my two grandchildren James T Burruss and Elizabeth M Johnson Burruss to have one fifth part of the half of my negroes assigned my first children. Four oldest daughters to take into consideration legacies specified and advance made, to wit: Sally T Terrell, Nancy Burruss, Rachel Burruss and Elizabeth G Burruss. Unmarried daughters, Nancy, Rachel, Elizabeth G and Mary Jane Burruss a feather bed and furniture. One-half of mill and 94½ acres called Locust Hill be held in trust for Nancy's share during her life. John Burruss and Chas C P Burruss Executors Dated 24 Feb 1836 Signed: Henry Burruss. Wm Dickinson and Aaron C White deposed that they were well acquainted with the testators hand writing and believe the writing and name to be wholly written by testator. Writing [will] ordered recorded 13 January 1840[14]   *Teste John L Pendleton*

(274-278;234-238)
Gen. 7   **MICAJAH CHILES**

The plat of Micajah's first land patent in Caroline County has survived. It shows the metes and bounds but does not give the orientation or show any of the adjoining land owners. The rolling road and Martin's new road intersect in the middle, but that is the only land mark evident.

Survey'd for MICAJAH CHILES three hundred seventy nine acres of King's land in ye Parish of St. Margaret's in ye County of Caroline. Beginning at William Terrell's two corner red and two corner white Oaks in [William] Conner's Line and runing thence West with Terrell's line 150 pole to a corner red and white Oak of Joel Terrell's thence with his line South 26 West 224 pole to [Richard] Mauldin's corner red Oak and Pine, thence along his line North 72 East 161 pole to a corner Pine and white Oak; thence along his line south 82 East 168 pole to a corner Pine, thence East 90 pole to a corner Pine, thence North 66 East 112 pole to [Thomas] Carr's corner Pine, thence North 74 pole to Conner's white Oak, thence West 263 pole along his line to his corner white Oak, thence North 60 pole to ye beginning. This 10th day of December 1729.[15]

Henry Chiles
(276;236) Henry Chiles was the brother of William Chiles and died before July 6, 1756 when his will was recorded in Lunenburg County. Henry left two daughters, Mary and Elizabeth Chiles.[16] His widow, Elizabeth Woolfolk Chiles married second, Charles Bibb of Louisa and Caroline County.[17] Her life as the wife of Charles Bibb will be presented with the Bibb family account.

John Chiles
(276-277;236) John Chiles learned the carpentry trade from Mourning Richards and by 1759 was living on Ducking Hole Creek in Fredericksville Parish (in 1763 to become Trinity Parish) in Louisa County, when he became the guardian of his half-brother, Matthew Mills. James and John probably decided together about moving to North Carolina. John went to Anson County in 1772, and James moved his family there in 1773.[18] John received a 640 acre grant which included the island Fish Trap and Ferry Place on the PeeDee River, and in 1775 he received a grant for an additional 503 acres including the Grassy Island Ford on the river.

John was a carpenter, a blacksmith, operated a ferry on the river, owned an ordinary and also was a justice of the peace. He took an active part in establishing the government of Anson County and later was elected a State Senator from Anson County; later when Richmond County was cut off, he represented Richmond County in the House of Commons in North Carolina.[19]

James Chiles
(277;237) Many records confuse Micajah's son, James, with a cousin, the Reverend James Chiles of

Spotsylvania County. Maurine Childs Parker has written that she is descended from Micajah's son, James, brother to Senator John Chiles of Anson and Richmond counties, North Carolina.[20] This James had three children, **two daughters and one son**: Elizabeth, Lydia (who married James Lyles, Jr., the son of James and the grandson of Ephraim Lyles) and James, Jr. (born about 1771 and married Sarah, he died between 1830-40) named in the will of Senator John Chiles.[21] The Reverend James Chiles married Elizabeth Durrett and had three children, **two sons and one daughter**: James, Elizabeth and Harry, named in their grandfather's will.[22] The Reverend James Chiles died in Ninety-six District, South Carolina in 1784.[23]

James, the son of Micajah, died in Anson County a year earlier, in 1783, before April 8, as his daughter, Elizabeth, referred to as, "Miss Chiles" furnished an inventory of his estate on April 8, 1783.[24] James and his wife, Elizabeth lived on Ducking Hole Creek in Fredericksville Parish (in 1761 this became Trinity Parish), Louisa County. James owned at least 100 acres of inherited land and bought another 867 acres. He owned eleven slaves, two of whom were named Adam and Ben. He and his family moved to Anson County, North Carolina in 1773 and he bought 300 acres on the PeeDee River. James died before April 8, 1783, the date of the record of the inventory of his estate. His wife Elizabeth had probably died earlier as it was his daughter, Elizabeth referred to as "Miss Chiles" who furnished the inventory. The two slaves named above were listed by name in estate papers after his death in Anson County, which proves that the James who lived near Ducking Hole Creek in Louisa County was the same man that died in Anson County in 1783.

James Chiles had a cousin with the same name, and apparently about the same age. Both of their wives were named Elizabeth. Many printed accounts show that researchers have confused these two. Both lived in Louisa County at one time, and both lived in Anson County. The James Chiles of Spotsylvania County and Anson County was a Baptist minister who married Elizabeth Durrett and later lived in Ninety-six, South Carolina.[25]

(279-286;239-245)

Gen. 6   **WILLIAM CHILES**

(279;240)   Since it appears that WILLIAM CHILES was born about 1730, and there is no record of his marriage until the late 1770s or early 1780s, it has been of interest to know of his endeavors in the intervening time. An entry of a William Chiles is found among the records of the Virginia Navy during the Revolutionary War.[26] William Chiles was assigned to the *Dragon* in September 1779; however, this does not indicate the full term of his service. The *Dragon* was the inspiration of Colonel Fielding Lewis of Fredericksburg, and her keel was laid in that town in late 1776. Along with the *Tartar* and the *Tempest*, the three vessels were dispatched to the Chesapeake Bay in 1778, with increased munitions. After engaging in warfare with the British they were assigned to the Bay, "often chasing, oftener being chased by the enemy", but in the position of protecting the Bay.[27]

It was reported in the *The Kentucky Historical Register* (1918) that William Chiles had married a Miss Bent. Every effort was made to find this information elsewhere, but no connection could be found, thus it was included with the hope that it may provide a clue for further research. What has been found instead provides greater insight as to the wife of William Chiles. Few records for Caroline County have survived for the period in which William would have been married, and the following conclusions are based on circumstantial evidence and the customs of the times. It is known that the wife of William was Sarah, or Sally as she was also called. It is known that Charles Bibb, who lived at Oxford, in the general area of William, had a daughter named Sally (Sarah) Bibb. It is believed that WILLIAM CHILES married SARAH BIBB. See also account of the Bibb and Woolfolk families.

Circumstantial evidence includes a number of associations, among them the fact that the father of SARAH BIBB married ELIZABETH WOOLFOLK Chiles, the widow of William's brother, Henry. William Chiles was appointed the guardian of Eleanor and Anne Bibb, the orphans of Charles Bibb, in 1785.[28] David Bibb, the brother of Sarah, was associated with William and Sarah Chiles, while John Bibb, landowner, also a brother, was listed to help maintain the road next to the name of William Chiles.[29] Elliott Chiles named a daughter Sarah Bibb Chiles, and it just may be that the middle name of John B. Chiles was in fact Bibb.[30]

Thomas Chiles

(282;242) Lucy F. Hargraves Chiles, was born in Caroline County, February 2, 1797. She joined Burruss Church in 1827. Thomas and Lucy moved to Alabama in 1831 and died in 1859, leaving Thomas and six children. One of these was Thomas C. Chiles, who was born October 6, 1829, married Katherine C. Huff, August 16, 1849 and died October 15, 1850.[31]

Samuel Chiles

(242;282) A deed from Samuel and Frances Chiles dated the fourth day of October, in which they sell to Lewis W. Garrett, 138 acres of land in Caroline County would indicate that it was about this time that they moved to Franklin County, Alabama. It seems that several of the Chiles family moved to Alabama during the time between 1831 and 1838, with a number of dismissals from Carmel Baptist Church in 1837. The records of the family of Samuel Chiles of Caroline County show that all of his children were born in Caroline County, and died in Franklin County, Alabama, except where noted:[32]

Samuel Chiles was born February 10, 1785 and died September 15, 1818.

Frances L.B. Hewlett was born January 15, 1793 and died June 17, 1858.

Samuel Chiles and Frances Hewlett were married March 10, 1808. Their children:

Amanda Fitzallen Chiles, born February 18, 1808, died in February, year was illegible;
married James McCluskey, August 9, 1830, in Virginia.

William I. Chiles, born May 12, 1801, died April 1874 in Maryland;
married Mrs. Jane Barnes, February 9, 1838 in Virginia.

Robert R. Chiles, born December 19, 1811, died October 29, 1860;
married (1) Lucy Cleer, (2) Molly Ann Fry in Alabama.

Sarah F. Chiles, born March 28, 1814, died 1862; married Gregory Rogannia of Richmond, Virginia.

Selina G. Chiles, born February 9, 1816, died January 20, 1888;
married Jesse Richeson, 18 February 1835 in Caroline Co.

Caroline S.J. Chiles, born November 22, 1817; married Martin N. Spears.

Mary E. Chiles, born August 1, 1819; married (1) James Wallace, (2) James Hooker in Alabama.

John L.H. Chiles, born November 13, 1821, died December 10, 1850;
married Catherine Hurst in Alabama.

Thomas H. Chiles, born August 22, 1823, died August 23, 1823.

Susan M.C. Chiles, born July 21, 1825; married William M. Kent, September 13, 1849 in Alabama.

Thomas B. Chiles, born February 14, 1827, died June 6, 1869; married Mary E. Counts in Alabama.

Elliott W. Chiles, born February 9, 1829;
married (1) Catherine Kirkland, (2) Matilda Holliman in Alabama.

Pamela A. Chiles, born May 10, 1831, died June 27 (year missing).

Clementina D.A. Chiles, born March 29, 1832, died September 1, 1856;
married William C. Bradfoot in Alabama.

Lucy C. Chiles, born August 12, 1834, died August 1865; married James M. Corsby in Alabama.

Obituary of Samuel Chiles

At his residence in Franklin County, Alabama, Samuel Chiles died on 15th September after a short but severe illness of eight hours. He was formerly a deacon of Burris Church, Caroline County, Virginia. After removing to Alabama he became a member and deacon of the Bethel Baptist Church, Franklin County. He "used the office of deacon well", "purchasing himself a good degree and a great boldness in the faith which is in Jesus Christ. He died as he lived, a happy Christian.

John B. Chiles

(283;242) In light of circumstantial information now gathered, it would seem that the middle name of John B. Chiles was probably Bibb. His wife, Mary Ann Hewlett was the daughter of William and Sarah Hewlett of King George County. John B. purchased land in Fluvanna County in the area that came to be known as Chiles' Cross Roads. This was the junction of the Stage Coach Road and the Courthouse Road. Their children: (to add to information already given) Alfred H. Chiles, born 1811 and died September 23 1880, his wife Susan was born April 2 1811, the daughter of James and Ann Richardson; Cordelia married a second time, Albert Gentry, the son of John and Mary Gentry, November 10, 1859; Mary, who was born in 1829; Pamelia married Elias King and died March 12, 1882; and Angelina, married Edwin Thacker, both of whom died young, leaving a daughter Wilhemina in her grandparents care.[33]

Elliott Chiles
(283-284;242) William Andrew Chiles died July 6, 1851, in the 22nd year of life, in Chesterfield County; he was a merchant in the City of Richmond.[34]

(287-294;246-253)
Gen. 8 (7)   **MANOAH CHILES**

(287;246)   It is believed that MANOAH CHILES married first, Elizabeth, the widow of Peter Garland.[35]

(291;249)   Agnes Chiles married Peter Hubbard and moved to Cherow District, South Carolina, where they both died after 1773. Their daughter, Elizabeth Hubbard married William Stubbs.[36]

Thomas Chiles
(292-292;250,252) correction: The Thomas Chiles who was listed on the rolls of Carmel Baptist Church is now believed to the Thomas who was the son of William Chiles.

Henry Chiles
(292-293;250-251) A complete listing of the children of Henry and Sarah Cheadle Chiles was found among the G.H.S. King Papers[37] and is as follows: Tarleton Woodson Chiles married his cousin Nancy (Ann) Chiles, May 14, 1796; Henry Chiles, who lived and died in Caroline County; Fleming Chiles married a Miss Winn, who also lived and died in Caroline; Judith Woodson Chiles married Meriwether Smith and moved to Kentucky in 1809; Nancy Chiles married George Coleman and moved to Kentucky; Sarah H. Chiles moved to Kentucky in 1809; Lucy Woodson Chiles married John W. Laughlin, January 25, 1805; Elizabeth Chiles married William Hawes Blaydes; Mary Chiles married Judge William Mercer Samuel; and Edna Fawney married Dr. David McFall (died c.1831).

Samuel Chiles
(293-294;252) Because Samuel Chiles, the son of Manoah lived during a part of the same time period as Samuel Chiles, the son of John, it has been difficult to separate the lives and activities of the two men in Caroline County. It is believed that Samuel Chiles, the son of Manoah was the Samuel who was dismissed from the Society of Friends for marrying contrary to discipline, as recorded in the Cedar Creek Monthly Meeting Minutes of October 11, 1788. It is further believed that he married Sarah Rogers of Spotsylvania County. She was the daughter of Lucy and William Rogers. Samuel and Sarah, his wife and Catharine Rogers of Caroline County conveyed land to John Rogers of Fayette County, Kentucky, June 26, 1789. They are identified as the daughters of William Rogers, deceased, and John Rogers is concluded to be their brother, since the three shared an interest in the land, and they conveyed it *with the love and affection they bear*.[38]

(295-301;254-259)
Gen. 7 (6)   **JOHN CHILES**

(296;255) correction: While the description of "the Old Chandler Place" is correct, this is not the house in which John or Samuel Chiles lived. The Chiles land, and homeplace is adjoining the Charles Burton Collins property and south of it (behind), as the old house now faces CR 601. It is believed that the Chiles house was similar in construction to the Hugh Chandler place, and the chimney was standing until a few years ago. The road to Chesterfield (Ruther Glen) passed in front of the house, with the Chiles cemetery on the east side of the road and the home on the west side of the road. It seems that John and Mary Winston Chiles were both buried in this cemetery, as there is evidence of a large number of grave sites. It was this house in which Susanna Chiles and Seth Campbell lived, and Seth operated his ordinary.[39]

(297;256) John Chiles married Lucy Coleman, the daughter of Richard Coleman and his wife, Lucy. Lucy was the daughter of Ann Covington and the granddaughter of Richard and Sarah Covington. Richard and Ann were married in August 1748 and lived in St. George Parish, Spotsylvania County. Richard Coleman died September 29, 1788, leaving Ann, his wife and children: Lucy, Molly, Richard, Robert G. and Nanny.[40]

(302-309;260-266)

Gen. 6 (5)   **SAMUEL CHILES**

The title page of the book of Henry Burruss gives the date, April 11th 1826, in his handwriting, under his title, *Henry Burruss's Book*. The actual departure date, and the date that he entered as he began his account of his journey, is recorded as August 27th, 1823. *Henry Burruss's Book* is a handwritten journal of his trip west on horseback. His traveling companions were Captain SAMUEL CHILES[41] and George Burruss of Caroline County.

Henry Burruss, who kept this journal, was the son of John and Rachel Terrell Burruss. It is of special interest that Henry Burruss was the son of the well-known John Burruss of Caroline County, the dissenting Baptist minister. John Burruss was instrumental in the organization of Polecat Church, later to become Burruss Baptist Church in his honor, then still later, Carmel Baptist Church. He was the grandson of David Terrell, an active member of the Society of Friends in Caroline County.

Henry Burruss was born on December 23, 1769 in Caroline County. He married first, Elizabeth Johnson on October 9, 1794, and second, Sally T. Wortham (born November 28, 1782) on November 14, 1805. Henry Burruss died on 6th December, ½ 12 night, 1839. These dates were inscribed in the Burruss Family Bible by his son (sic), Henry Burruss (II) on September 5, 1859. Notations from the Burruss Family Bible were written by Henry Burruss at the end of his book. They will follow the last journal entry.

Henry Burruss was fifty-three years old when he made his trip to western Virginia, Kentucky, and Tennessee. He traveled a total of 1655 miles during the course of slightly over two months. Captain Samuel Chiles was about fifty-two years old, and was at the time of his trip a member of the House of Delegates of the Virginia General Assembly.[42] He died in Caroline County in 1829.[43]

While Henry Burruss alluded to the purpose of his journey, he never really stated the purpose. The reader is left to wonder at his brief entry, upon meeting with Doctor John Shelby: *Here I cannot deny but what I was somewhat disappointed. He was measureably the cause of my western trip....The information I received was but little....* Both Mr. Burruss and Captain Chiles had a number of relatives, and many acquaintances in Kentucky and his account is filled with meeting and enjoying the hospitality of these people. The journal is a treasure trove of who lived where, and who was kin to whom. Many of the citizens of Caroline County migrated west when the lands in Kentucky opened up to settlement. Henry Burruss wrote in his journal:

August 27th 1823 I started to the westward met with Capt Samuel Chiles at Chilesburge and rode to Mr. Geo Tylers where we met with George Burruss who was also on his way westward and Tarried all night.

28th Started at 1/2 past 8 o'clock and rode to Pleasant Hacketts in the neighborhood of the Green Springs Louisa county where we tarried all night.

Sept 3rd Capt Chiles got his horse shod this morning which put us back a little rode 9 miles to Mr. Percys to breakfast in passing from the White Sulphur Springs to Lewisburg you pass Howards Creek 6 times and Greenbrier river once 100 yds wide

Respecting my western trip and appeared in good health 11th rode to Winchester to breakfast we now approach a highly improved country of rich land generally but all more broken than I had any Idea of from thence to Mr. Richard Chile's where we were cordially received and kindly treated where we staid 4 days visiting in the neighbourhood around this place the people live very near mostly old Virginians in riding right across the country 5 miles I counted 27 different settlements amongst them 6 0r 7 Ellegant brick houses Richd Chiles has 94 acres which he has located at $10,000 expense it has 17 corners and cut at right angles with the road; gave the washer woman and Horseler 1/6 brot forward $ 20.22   Miles 497

Sept 15 we set out after dinner in company with Richd Chiles & Lindsey Coleman and rode to Lexington in Fayatte county & put up for the night, here we were introduced to a number of old Virginians had several invitations to Sup & stay went to the Theatre. Here Cap' Chiles [Richard Chiles was his half-brother]⁴⁴ and myself parted he had not gotten up when I left town 16th rode to the halfway house to breakfast excellent fare then on to Frankford where we made but little stay Frankford stands under a high hill on Kentucky river has some excellent building but does not show to any advantage on account of its situation in getting from Lexington to Frankford you pass through part of Scott & Woodford countys into Franklin from thence to Overtons through a broken poor country the land becomes poorer 2 or 2 1/2 miles before you reach Frankford...

(304;262) It is believed that Samuel and Martha Bell Chiles were both buried in the cemetery of the Chiles homeplace, that is south of the Chandler place.

Hiram Chiles
(305;262-263) Hiram and Elizabeth Rebecca Allen Chiles moved to Sumpter County, Alabama about 1839. He and Rebecca had three children, born in Caroline County: Mary Champ Chiles, born January 1, 1829, married Jordan Short, January 4, 1846 in Livingston, Alabama and died there August 19, 1897; Sarah Chiles, who married a Mr. Stark and lived in Mobile, Alabama; and Samuel H. Chiles, born June 1837, married M.B., and died in January 1866 in Livingston, leaving a wife and two small sons (one named Hiram).⁴⁵

Eldred Chiles
(305;263) The grandfather of Isabell A. Chiles, John Gray died about 1807, naming his children in his will: Peggy Gray, John Morgan Gray, Fanny Gray and Phoebe Gray, and his widow, Phoebe Gray (who died about 1830). Phoebe Gray left heirs: Joseph Sale for his wife, Peggy; Reuben Saunders for his wife, Fanny; the heirs of John Morgan Gray, deceased, who were Eldred Chiles in the right of his wife, Isabella Chiles, Joseph Jesse in right of his wife Mary M. Jesse, and the heirs of Phoebe Gray, deceased, who were Sarah Gray, Frances Gray and Elizabeth Gray (the name of their father is not given in the suit). This suit was recorded in chancery January 10, 1831.⁴⁶

John M. Chiles
(306;263) John M. Chiles was born in 1796 and went to live in Mississippi as an adult. He married Martha Caroline Hirons Lafarge, daughter of Dr. John Lafarge. Their children were: James Chiles, a lawyer in Starksville, Mississippi; John Samuel Chiles, married (2) Harriet Hatcher Maxedy of Brandon, Mississippi; William Hirons Chiles, died in Starkville in 1913; Grace Ann Chiles, born 1828, died 1905 and married Morris Randolph Mitchell (1820-1883); Virginia Caroline Chiles, married (1) Dr. William Watt, (2) R.P. Curry; Clementina Chiles, married Mr. Hogan and lived in Durant, Oklahoma; and Martha Bell Chiles, married (1) Mr. Stratton and (2) Mr. Stancell.⁴⁷

CHILES FAMILY

Gen. 12 <u>WILLIAM CHILDES</u>		m	<u>ALICE (—?—)</u>
as taken from *The Omnibus 12:11-12:*			
Issue:	Richard		
	William		
	JOHN	m	(1) Katherine Johns
		m	(2) ALICE WELLSTEDD
Gen. 11 <u>JOHN CHILDE</u>		m	(1) Katherine Johns
		m	(2) <u>ALICE WELLSTEDD</u>
Issue (2):	Margarett		
	William		
	WALTER	m	ELIZABETH (—?—)
Gen. 10 <u>WALTER CHILES I</u>		m	<u>ELIZABETH (—?—)</u>
Issue:	WALTER	m	SUSANNA (—?—)

71

	William		died young

Gen. 9 WALTER CHILES II		m	SUSANNA (—?—)
Issue:	Elizabeth	m	Henry Tyler
	John	m	(1) Mary (—?—)
		m	(2) Eleanor (—?—)
Issue:	HENRY	m	(1) unknown
		m	(2) MARY (—?—)

Gen. 8 HENRY CHILES		m	(1) unknown
Issue:	Henry	m	Anne Harrelson
	Walter	m	Mary (—?—)
	James	m	Elizabeth Durrett
	William	m	

HENRY CHILES		m	(2) MARY
Issue:	MICAJAH	m	MARY TERRELL
	MANOAH	m	(1) Elizabeth Garland (widow)
		m	(2) ANNE CHEADLE
	Malachi	m	Frances (—?—)
	Ann	m	Henry Terrell
	Agatha	m	David Terrell

Gen. 7 MICAJAH CHILES		m	MARY TERRELL
Issue:	Henry	m	Elizabeth Woolfolk
	WILLIAM	m	SARAH BIBB
	John	m	d.s.p.
	Micajah	m	
	James	m	Elizabeth (—?—)

Gen. 6 WILLIAM CHILES		m	SARAH BIBB
Issue:	Thomas	m	(1) Polly Wright
		m	(2) Lucy Hargraves
	Samuel	m	Fanny Hewlett
	John	m	Mary Ann Hewlett
	Elliott	m	Elizabeth Broaddus
	Sarah	m	Thomas Burruss
	MARY	m	RICHARD WALLER HUTCHESON
	Edmund	m	(1) Elizabeth Hargraves
		m	(2) Lucy Ann Bowers
	Elizabeth	m	Peter Everett
	Pamelia	m	William Mallory

Manoah is the eighth generation from the writer in his line of ascent. The generations of ascent from Bernard Hutcheson make it the seventh generation to Micajah, through William and the eighth to Manoah, through John.

Gen. 8 MANOAH CHILES		m	(1) Elizabeth Garland
Issue:	Joseph	m	Agnes Stone
	Agnes	m	Peter Hubbard
	Elizabeth	m	dis mou
	Manoah, Jr.	m	Mary (—?—)
	Susanna	m	Micajah Moorman
	Mary	m	Joseph McGehee
MANOAH CHILES		m	(2) ANNE CHEADLE
Issue:	JOHN	m	(1) MARY WINSTON
			(2) Lucy Coleman

Anne	m	Jeremiah Harris
Henry	m	Sarah Cheadle
Patty	m	Thomas Hutchins
Samuel	m	Sarah Rogers
Thomas	m	Susanna Kimbrow

Gen. 7 <u>JOHN CHILES</u>		m	(1) <u>MARY WINSTON</u>
Issue:	SAMUEL	m	MARTHA BELL
	Ann (Nancy)	m	Tarleton Woodson Chiles
	Lucy	m	John Coleman
John Chiles		m	(2) Lucy Coleman
Issue:	Richard	m	Sarah Johnson
	John G.	m	Miss Morgan

Gen. 6 <u>SAMUEL CHILES</u>		m	<u>MARTHA BELL (Patsy)</u>
Issue:	Clementine	m	William Dickinson
	Hiram	m	Elizabeth Rebecca Allen
	Cheadle	m	Patsy Stevens
	SUSANNAH D.	m	SETH CAMPBELL
	Eldred	m	Isabel Gray
	Caroline Ann H.	m	Littleton Goodwin, Jr.
	Louisa Anna		unmarried
	John M.	m	Caroline Lafarge

Notes

1. See *TVF* 3(1994): 13.
2. Roger Jones Family Papers, Reel 1; *TVF* 3:11-12..
3. James Orchard, *A Dictionary of Archaic and Provincial Words, vol 1.* 1872. Transcribed by R.Y.Clay and VLHD.
4. Contributed by Mary McClune, 6130 Belpree Road, Amarillo, TX 79106; *TVF* 5(1996): 100-101.
5. *Halifax County Will Book 2, 1784.* 73.
6. From Ms. McClune, copy of Family Bible given her by John Montford Thomas.
7. Spotsylvania County Will Book E, 1775 107.
8. In letter (1996) Maurine Childs Parker, 1704 Cedar Bend, Luftin, TX 75904, letter (1996) relates the account of James Chiles and his descendants, *Anson County Heritage, North Carolina*, (NC: Walsworth Publishing Co, 1995) 119-121; Also see *TVF* 5 (1996):102-103).
9. See *TVF* 2(1994): 226-232; 3(1995) 39-45, 103-110).
10. The Caroline County Court Order Book entries give the name of the wife of Jacob Burruss as Susanna in a suit recorded in 1763 (CCCOB 1763 423) and as Diana, widow of Jacob Burruss, in 1778 in a renunciation of her husband's bequests in lieu of her dower (CCCOB 1778 134).
11. See Malcolm H. Harris, "Three William Harrises in Hanover County", *The Virginia Genealogist.* 22 (1978): 3-15,99-104.
12. This appears to been the William Chiles who lived on the road from Chesterfield to Needwood in Caroline County (1750).
13. These names do not agree with those in the Harris article, nor is Martha named as a daughter. Harris 104.
14. Will abstracted by Benjamin B. Weisiger, *Burned County Data, 1809-1848, As Found in the Virginia Contested Election Files.* (Richmond: privately printed, 1986). Caroline County Contested Election Papers, 1843, Box 14. Archives and Records Division, The Library of Virginia, Richmond, VA.
15. Ruth and Sam Sparacio, *Caroline County, Virginia County Surveys (1729-1762) and Proceedings of Committee of Safety (1774-1776)* (McLean, VA; Antient Press, 1997) 15.; referred to as the *New Wales* tract of land.
16. Davis *TVF* 2nd ed 236; *Lunenburg County Will Book 1*, 158-160.
17. From the unpublished manuscript of Fay Parrish Wade, 8703 Ewes Court, Richmond, VA 23236.
18. *Anson County Heritage, North Carolina* (NC: Walsworth Publishing Co, 1995) 120.4
19. Ibid.
20. Parker; *Anson County Heritage 119-121; TVF* 5 (1996):102-103).
21. Anson Co. Wills, 1786, 51.
22. John Durrett, Spotsylvania County Will Book E, 1775 107.
23. Parker.
24. Parker.
25. Parker's sources: *VMHB*; Virginia County Court Order Books; Virginia and North Carolina wills; North Carolina land records and other public records.
26. Robert Armistead Stewart, *The History of Virginia's Navy of the Revolution* 1934 (Baltimore: Genealogical Publishing Co, rep 1993) 168.

27. Stewart 57-60.
28. *Caroline County Court Order Book, 1785* 206.
29. *Caroline County Land Tax Records, 1789-1799; Surveyors' List, 1804*, Caroline County Historical Papers, Box 4, Archives and Records Division, Virginia State Library and Archives, Richmond, VA.
30. Alfred Brian Chiles, a descendant of John B. Chiles was never able to determine the middle name of his ancestor. See his family history of the Chiles family in Fluvanna County, privately printed, 1992, for the family.
31. Correspondence and Bible Records, Mary Richeson McAllister Ingram, 2512 Avenue I, Bay City, Texas 77414 (1996) is the daughter of Watkins I. Richeson, born September 8, 1887 in Franklin County, Alabama. He was the son of William Elliott Richeson, who was the son of Jesse Richeson and Selina Chiles.
32. Ingram.
33. Alfred B. Chiles, Jr., *The Chiles in Fluvanna County* (Richmond, VA: privately printed, 1984). Distributed only to family members.
34. Obituary, *Religious Herald*, 1828-1838.
35. Correspondence with Waverly Barbe (1997), 800 Rice Valley Rd N #A7, Tuscaloosa, AL 35406.
36. Barbe.
37. G.H.S. King Papers, Mss1K58239FA1, Chiles Folder, No.2, Virginia Historical Society, Richmond, VA.
38. William Armstrong Crozier, *Virginia County Records, Spotsylvania County, 1721-1800, vol 1* 1905 (Baltimore: Genealogical Publishing Co, rep 1990) 426.
39. Herbert R. Collins, 3510 Pershing Dr., Arlington, VA 22201. Unpublished Manuscript, 1995.
40. Lloyd and Helen Covington, *The Descendants of William Covington I, 1618-1696, "Bestland", Essex County, Virginia* (Ruther Glen, VA: privately printed, 1996) 49.
41. "Henry Burruss's Book, 1823, Caroline County", *TVF* 2(1994): 226-232; 3(1995): 39-45, 103-110). Contributed by Alexander Burruss, Gloucester, Va, a descendant of Henry Burruss.
42. Marshall Wingfield, *A History of Caroline County* 1924 (Baltimore: Clearfield, rep 1991) 40 316-317.
43. Caroline County Land Tax Records, 1828, 1829.
44. V.L.H. Davis, *Tidewater Virginia Families (TVF)* 2nd ed 258.
45. US Census, Caroline County, 1830, Livingston Co, AL, 1850, 1860. Correspondence with Waverly Barbe (1997) and Ruth Jenkins Curley (1992), 2633 Ensenado Way, San Mateo, CA 94403.
46. William Lindsay Hopkins, *Caroline County Court Records and Marriages, 1787-1810* (Richmond, VA: privately printed, 1987) 97.
47. Barbe.

insert after these pages:
(309;266)

BIBB FAMILY

Gen. 7-10

The Bibb family came into the colony of Virginia early, it was some three hundred years later before it came into this author's life through the WILLIAM CHILES family. The evidence is circumstantial, but its associations continue to mount, and as in many of the burned records counties, relationships are difficult to document. None the less, there seems little doubt that it was SARAH BIBB who married William Chiles, the son of MICAJAH and MARY TERRELL CHILES, and who were the parents of MARY CHILES HUTCHESON. Fay Parrish Wade[1] is a descendant of Eleanor Bibb, the daughter of CHARLES BIBB, the father of Sarah Bibb. She is therefore a fifth cousin and her line is documented. Mrs. Wade has done extensive and well-documented research on the Bibb family (as extensive as the gaps in the records of Caroline County allow).

As far as can be determined BENJAMIN BIBB (I) was in King William County well before its inception in 1702. He probably lived in what was before that King and Queen County, and may have been there before its inception, in what was New Kent County. Benjamin's wife was MARY, beyond that there is nothing known of her. They had sons, BENJAMIN (II), William, James and Thomas, but the names of their daughters are not known.[2] James appeared to have died young as there seem to be no further records of his life.[3]

On July 9th, 1720, Benjamin Bibb III, the son of Benjamin Bibb, of Hanover County sold to William Fairfield a parcel of land in King William County, which land was said to have been deeded by James Bibber on May 10th, 1685 to Benjamin Bibb (I) and by him deeded on May 12th, 1702 to his son Benjamin Bibb (II).[4] Benjamin Bibb was charged with 100 acres of land in the King William County Quit Rents of 1704. This may have been the son, as it seems that Benjamin, Sr. had died in 1702.[5]

BENJAMIN BIBB II had bequeathed the land to his son, Benjamin III, described as 100 acres and being the land on which he lived. If he died without issue it was to go to his son William and if he died without issue, to the surviving heirs. The land was in St. John's Parish, King William County.[6] The land that Benjamin bequeathed to his son, Benjamin was bounded by the lands of William Alvise, John Mallory, Martin Palmer and Humphrey Brooks. Benjamin made his will on June 16, 1720.[7]

Benjamin's wife was NANCY, but her maiden name has not been found. They had sons, Benjamin, William, HENRY and Thomas, but the names of their daughters are not known. William migrated to Georgia, Alabama and Kentucky.[8]

It was Benjamin (III) and his descendants who remained in the King William, Hanover, Caroline, Louisa and Spotsylvania counties area. He married Mary Arnett, became a Hanover County merchant and died in Louisa County, where his will (1768) and that of his wife, Mary (1791) are on file.[9] They had children: William, married Elizabeth Bigger, 1767; John, married Margaret Todd, 1776; Benjamin, married Agnes Tate, 1790; a daughter who married Edward Corry; David; Thomas, married Elizabeth Philipps, 1797; James, married Nancy Walker, 1783; Ann; Henry, who went to Kentucky; Susanna, married Robert Tate, 1780; Mary, married Joseph Edwards, 1790; Oney, married Joseph Sheperdson, 1799; Elizabeth, married Robert Groom, 1788; and Martha, married John Durrett, 1788.[10]

HENRY BIBB, the son of Benjamin II was born in 1690, in King William County or in Hanover County, he died about 1750. He married ELEANOR FLEMING (1714), the daughter of WILLIAM FLEMING, the sheriff of Hanover County (at least for the years 1727-1728). Henry and Eleanor had the following children: Benjamin (IV), 1715-1768, married Ann Fleming, daughter of William Fleming; Robert Fleming, 1719-1811, married Justina Burruss, the daughter of Jacob Burruss; CHARLES, c.1720-1768, married ELIZABETH WOOLFOLK Chiles, daughter of JOSEPH WOOLFOLK; Henry, 1722-1750, died without issue; John, 1725-1750, died without issue; Thomas, 1728-1761; Elizabeth, 1730-(?), married Nathaniel Garland; Ann, 1734-1798, married Anthony Thompson and moved to Kentucky; Christiana, 1736-(?), married Joseph

Woolfolk, Jr. and David, 1842-1850, died young.[11]

It is interesting that the will of William Fleming has survived in a county where few records are available for that time period; his will was dated September 13, 1742 and relates the legacies to his daughter and all of his grandchildren. It is of further interest to this researcher that the will had been read and re-read with the hopes of establishing a relationship with William Fleming Butler, and was filed when this was not accomplished. It has now become an important documentation of the relationship of William Fleming to the Bibb family and thus to the author.

Little is known of William Fleming's earlier life. He lived in an area where few to no records have survived. It is thought that he may have been a brother of Charles Fleming, and suggested that he was the son of John Fleming. It is thought that he was the father of Robert Fleming who was a Burgess for Caroline County, *who died at his father's home in Hanover County*.[12] William lived in St. Paul's Parish; had been overseer of the road in his precinct and later was a vestryman of St. Paul's Parish.

Uppowac Plantation in King William County, dating back to the early 1700s was named in the will of William Fleming. It was part of the land leased and known as *the College Lands*. William did not name his son, but stated his desire *That my body may be interred on my plantation on ye college land where my first wife and eldest son were buried.*[13] William Fleming had a grandson named Robert Fleming Bibb. He named three granddaughters bearing the maiden name of Fleming: Mary Fleming, Martha Fleming and Elizabeth Fleming. It is practically certain that William Fleming did not leave any male descendants bearing his family name (Dr. Harris).

To quote the text of the body of the will William Fleming gives not only the names of his daughter, but of both daughters husbands, and his grandchildren and their husbands, as well as the name of his second wife, Elizabeth.[14]

I give and bequeath to my son-in-law Henry Bibb and my beloved daughter Eleanor the wife of the said Henry the use of two hundred and fifty acres of land Beginning at the main road on the north side of sedgy creek...to Mr. John Poindexters line...being part of a tract of one thousand acres of land whereon they now live...and after their decease I give...the same to their son Benjamin Bibb...I give and devise unto William Pollard [whose father married a daughter of William Fleming][15] the son of Richard Pollard, dec'd two hundred acres of land beginning at the mouth of Sedgy Creek, and running up the north side of the creek...Item I give and devise to my grandson Henry Bibb son of the said Henry and Eleanor his wife three hundred fifty acres of land including the old plantation part of the above said one thousand acres...Item I give and devise unto my grandson Robert Fleming Bibb my new quarter with two hundred and fifty acres part of the tract aforesaid (the dividing line of Henry and Robert land is beginning at a great hickory in Mr. John Carrs line...on sedgy creek...if any of the said legatees should happen to die before they do attain to twenty one years of age then...land left him shall revert to their younger brother John Bibb...Item I give and bequeath unto my dear and well beloved wife Elizabeth Fleming six negro slaves...the use of my plantation in King William County on the college land and the land belonging to it during her natural life she paying the yearly rent of the same and that she do petition the masters of the College for a new lease within six months after my decease...I give and bequeath unto William Fleming Cocke [great grandson] the son of Pleasant Cocke a legacy of forty pounds current money...if any of my relations should come out of England...they may have the tract of land I purchased of Ambrose Joshua Smith Gent...I give and bequeath all the rest of my estate in Virginia, England or else where...equally divided among all my grandchildren hereinafter named, that is to say William Pollard, Benjamin Bibb, Henry Bibb, Robert Fleming Bibb, CHARLES BIBB, John Bibb, Thomas Bibb, Mary Pollard (who married [George] Thomason), Mary Fleming (who married Pleasant Cocke), Martha Pollard (who married Biggars), Elizabeth Fleming (who married [John] Wily), Martha Fleming (who married Gaines), Elizabeth Bibb, Ann Bibb, Christian[a] Bibb to them to share and share alike...If Henry Bibb shall...keep my plantation and land which I bought of John Brown junr for a halfway house and resting place then he shall pay twenty pounds for the same to the legatees.... He appointed his son-in-law Henry Bibb and his trusted friends Mr. John Carr and Barttelott Anderson the executors of his estate. He further gave his wife Elizabeth and his daughter, Eleanor any ready money found in the house at the time of his death and his daughter, Eleanor his chaise and two horses, and Henry Bibb, his wearing clothes. His will was witnessed by Eliza Anderson, W. Ford and Robert Netherland.

It is believed that William Fleming was married twice, the first time c.1680, and that he had by his first wife, a son Robert Fleming and a daughter, who married Richard Pollard. He married second, Elizabeth and

Eleanor Fleming was the daughter of William and Elizabeth Fleming; the only surviving child of William.[16]

The will of William Fleming was presented by Barttelott Anderson and Henry Bibb, two of the executors, for probate. Harry Gaines and John Wily, who married two of the co-heirs and Mary Cocke, the widow of Pleasant Cocke, the other co-heiress declared they had no objection and the will was so recorded on October 4, 1744. The chancery suit of *McAllister vs Bibb* found in the papers of Louisa County Circuit Court provide the information and the documentation of the wife and children of Henry Bibb. An authentic copy of the will of William Fleming was included in the suit papers as a part of the necessary evidence, the Hanover County records for this period do not contain a reference to the will.

CHARLES BIBB, the son of HENRY and ELEANOR FLEMING BIBB married the widow of Henry Chiles of Lunenburg County, Elizabeth Woolfolk Chiles. Henry Chiles was the brother of William Chiles and died before July 6, 1756 when his will was recorded in Lunenburg County. Henry left two daughters, Mary and Elizabeth Chiles.[17]

Elizabeth Woolfolk was the daughter of JOSEPH and ELIZABETH BULLARD WOOLFOLK of Caroline County. This is known from a deed of gift from Joseph Woolfolk of St. Margaret's Parish, Caroline County to David Bibb, Thomas Bibb, SALLY BIBB and Lucy Bibb and daughter Elizabeth Bibb, the Negroes Dianh and Hannah. The said Negroes given to my daughter and granddaughters (sic) towards their livelihood and no other purpose. Charles Bibb is to have no property in the said gift. This was dated April 18, 1768.[18]

Charles Bibb and Elizabeth, his wife had just a few years earlier (May 13, 1765), sold 250 acres of land bequeathed him by William Fleming (September 13, 1742) to his brother, Benjamin Bibb.[19] Over a period of several years a number of Louisa County court order entries chronicle the activities of Charles Bibb. He had been the defendant in several suits concerning debts, some judgements against him and some dismissed, some brought by his brother, Robert Fleming Bibb and some not; he had been brought before the court for non-attendance at church and swearing and Thomas Craighill testified at one time that Charles Bibb was "in liquor". Charles was later appointed constable of Louisa County.[20]

The children of Charles and Elizabeth Woolfolk Bibb, as reconstructed from various records are as follows:

David Bibb, born 1758[21] and died before April 8, 1826; married first, Mary Chandler, (the daughter of Robert Chandler and Suzannah Robinson) October 16, 1789.[22] He married second, Rachel Terrell Hargrave the daughter of Pleasant Terrell and Catherine Farish, and the widow of Joseph Hargrave) December 8, 1814.[23] David owned 139 acres of land in Caroline County before 1782[24] and is listed in the Land Tax Records (1787) as adjoining the land of William Chiles. He later added to his land holdings and owned some 300 acres of land, and at the time of his death he owned 373 acres.[25] The children of David Bibb and Mary Chandler were: Ann Bibb, born about 1790 and married John Trainham, 1805 in Caroline County; George Garrett Bibb, born about 1791 and married Mary Cobbs, December 2, 1808; Fleming Bibb, born about 1793 and died before August 1864 in Caroline County; and Lucy Woolfolk Bibb, born May 1, 1798 and died December 7, 1855 in Caroline County.[26]

Thomas Bibb, born c.1760, married Sarah Brockman, September 14, 1785 in Orange County. William Chiles witnessed the marriage bond of Thomas Bibb, and Joseph Woolfolk, Jr. provided the security.

SARAH (Sally), born c.1764[27] and died in 1828, married WILLIAM CHILES.

Lucy, born c.1770, died young 1785, in Caroline County.

Eleanor (Knelly) Bibb, born about 1772, married Thomas Burruss, the son of John Burruss the Baptist minister and founder of Burruss Church, and his wife Rachel Terrell. She died before December 1818. Their children were: Charles Burruss, born August 23, 1795; Rachel Terrell Burruss, born about 1798, died November 1876 in Caroline County; Lucy Burruss, born about 1800 and married George Robinson, March 1824 in Caroline County; John Burruss, born December 15, 1802; Mary Burruss, born September 3, 1804 and married John Boulware, December 25, 1823 in Caroline County; Thomas J. Burruss, born February 19, 1807; Frances C. Burruss, born December 21, 1808 and married Mr. Henly; Agnes Burruss, born 20 March, 1811 and married Mr. Bryan; and Samuel O. Burruss, born January 2, 1816. Thomas Burruss married second, Sarah Chiles the daughter of William and Sarah Chiles.[28]

Ann (Nancy) Bibb, born about 1774 and died in Caroline County.

John was born about 1775, but it is not known who he married, he died about 1851 in Caroline County. He left children: Mary Ann Bibb, born about 1802 married Robert H. Martin, 1822, Caroline

County; Eliza P. Bibb, born about 1804, married Reuben Pemberton, 1823; Lavinia C. Bibb, born about 1806 and married James Southworth, 1831, Caroline County; and William Bibb, born about 1808, married Sarah Ann Quarles in Caroline County.[29] John Bibb was listed next to William Chiles as being responsible for keeping the road maintained, along with the other property owners on that road.[30]

No will has been found for Charles Bibb, and it is believed that he later lived at Oxford, a community near the North Anna River, in Caroline County. Charles evidently did move to Caroline County and died there because a court order book entry first in 1783 shows that Lucy Bibb, orphan of Charles Bibb, made choice of Julius Coleman as her guardian;[31] in February 1785; an entry refers to the appointment of William Chiles as the guardian of Eleanor and Ann Bibb, children of Charles Bibb, deceased.[32] It is believed that he died just before Lucy chose her guardian in February 1783.[33] In 1786 David Bibb was appointed the guardian of John Bibb.[34]

After reconstructing the lives of Charles Bibb and his children and their spouses, there are so many associations, both familial and legal, that there seems enough circumstantial evidence to accept the marriage of SARAH BIBB with WILLIAM CHILES, the son of Micajah Chiles.

JOSEPH WOOLFOLK is said to have been the son of RICHARD WOOLFOLK of Abingdon Parish, Gloucester County (1678-1761).[35] Richard Woodfolk was listed as paying quit rent on 125 acres of land in 1704.[36] The full name of his wife is not included, but her given name was ELIZABETH. Joseph Woolfolk, born 1696 is believed to be his son. Joseph Woolfolk of King William County patented 1000 acres of land in 1728 on the North Anna River in St. George Parish, Spotsylvania County. Richard Woolfolk, the brother, also owned land on the North Anna River in Spotsylvania County at this time.[37] He is later identified as living in St. Margaret's Parish, Caroline County. It is believed that JOSEPH married ELIZABETH BULLARD, the sister of Ambrose Bullard, who married Joseph's older sister, Betty. Joseph and Elizabeth had children: John, married Elizabeth Wigglesworth; Elizabeth, married (1) Henry Chiles (2) Charles Bibb; Augustine, married Anne Harris; Joseph, Jr., married Christiana Bibb; Thomas, married Miss Southerland; and Robert, married Mary Hackett.[38] There is a court entry that refers to a suit against the executors of the estate of Joseph Woolfolk, deceased dated July 11, 1771.[39] Elizabeth Woolfolk, John Woolfolk and Robert Chandler, were the executors and executrix of his estate.[40] An account of the executorship of the estate of Joseph Woolfolk, deceased was returned and recorded June 10, 1773.[41]

Elizabeth Woolfolk died before March 10 1785, as her will was presented into court and proved by the witnesses, Augustine Woolfolk and John Woolfolk and certificate of probate was granted. Joseph Campbell, Joseph Jones, William Chiles and James Gatewood were appointed to appraise her estate.[42]

BIBB FAMILY

Gen.10 BENJAMIN BIBB I	m	MARY (—?—)
Issue:	BENJAMIN II	m	NANCY
	William	m	
	James	m	
	Thomas	m	

Gen. 9 BENJAMIN BIBB II	m	NANCY (—?—)
Issue:	Benjamin III	m	Mary Arnett
	HENRY	m	ELEANOR FLEMING
	William	m	
	Thomas	m	

Gen. 8 HENRY BIBB	m	ELEANOR FLEMING
	Benjamin IV	m	Ann Fleming
	Robert Fleming	m	Justina Burruss
	CHARLES	m	ELIZABETH WOOLFOLK CHILES widow
	Henry		unmarried d.s.p.
	John	m	unmarried d.s.p.
	Thomas	m	(1) Elizabeth Phillips

		(2) Sarah Martin
Elizabeth	m	Nathaniel Garland
Ann	m	Anthony Thompson
Christiana	m	(1) Joseph Woolfolk, Jr.
		(2) Samuel Brockman
David		died young

Gen. 7	CHARLES BIBB	m	ELIZABETH WOOLFOLK CHILES widow
	David	m	(1) Mary Chandler
			(2) Rachel Terrell Hargrave widow
	Thomas	m	Sarah Brockman
	SARAH	m	WILLIAM CHILES
	Lucy		unmarried
	Eleanor	m	Thomas Burruss
	Ann	m	
	John	m	unknown

Notes

1. Fay Parrish Wade, 8703 Ewes Court, Richmond, VA 23236 has done extensive research on the Bibb family and has documented the information of the descendants of Charles Bibb thoroughly.

2. Charles William Bibb, *The Bibb Family in America, 1640-1940* (Baltimore: privately printed, 1941) 5-7.

3. Bibb.

4. *King William County Deed Book A.*

5. Annie Laurie Wright Smith, *The Quit Rents of Virginia, 1704* 1957 (Baltimore: Genealogical Publishing Co, rep 1987) 8.

6. Bibb 5-6.

7. Bibb 6.

8. Bibb 6.

9. Wade, Uunpublished Manuscript (1998); Clayton Torrence, *Virginia Wills and Administrations, 1632-1800* 1930 (Baltimore: Genealogical Publishing Co, 1990) 34.

10. Bibb 7.

11. Wade.

12. *Genealogies of Virginia Families, Virginia Magazine of History and Biography vol V* (Baltimore: Genealogical Publishing Co, 1981) 235.

13. Malcolm Hart Harris, MD, *Old New Kent County, some Account of The Planters, Plantations and Places in New Kent County vol II* (West Point, VA: privately printed, 1977) 810, 811.

14. *Virginia Will Records* (Baltimore: Genealogical Publishing Co, 1993) 723-726.

15. G.H.S. King Papers, Mss1K5823a, Bibb Folder, Virginia Historical Society, Richmond, VA.

16. G.H.S. King Papers.

17. *Tidewater Virginia Families, 2nd ed.* 236.; Lunenburg County Will Book 1, 158-160.

18. *Louisa County Deed Book C & D, 1759-1774* 99-100 (original).

19. Ibid. 86-88.

20. *Louisa County Minute or Order Book, 1760-1764.*

21. Ruth and Sam Sparacio, *Caroline County, Virginia Appeals and Land Causes, 1787-1794* 87.

22. William L. Hopkins, *Caroline County Court Records and Marriages, 1787-1810* 134, 175, 212. David gave deposition at John Chiles store on July 8 1788 that he was 30 years old. Wade, Chandler will on file.

23. *Caroline County, Virginia, Marriages Part 1* 72; LVA microfilm Reel 59.

24. Hopkins 134.

25. *Caroline County Land Tax Records* 1782-1826, listed as his estate in 1826.

26. Wade.

27. Smith 100; This information comes from the chart compiled by Mrs. James Claiborne Pollard, Assistant State Archivist, Virginia State Archives, from the Woolfolk Papers, The Virginia Historical Society, Richmond, VA.

28. Caroline County Marriage Bond, 1818.

29. Bibb 58.

30. *Caroline County Surveyors List* 1804, Caroline County Historical Papers, Library of Virginia, Richmond, VA.

31. Ruth and Sam Sparacio, *Caroline County Court Order Book, 1718-1783* 88.

32. Sparacio, *Caroline County Court Orders, 1785-1787* 45.

33. Wade.

34. Sparacio *CCCOB 1785-1787* 51.

35. Smith 100; The name is listed as Richard Woodfolk. Pollard, the Woolfolk Papers.

36. Smith 100.

37. Nell Marion Nugent, *Cavaliers and Pioneers vol III* 1979 (Richmond: Virginia State Library, 1986) 349, 368.

38. Wade.
39. Sparacio, *CCCOB, 1771-1772* 18.
40. Sparacio *CCCOB, 1771-1772* 18, 47.
41. Sparacio *CCCOB, 1772-1776* 46.
42. Sparacio *CCCOB, 1781-1785* 10.

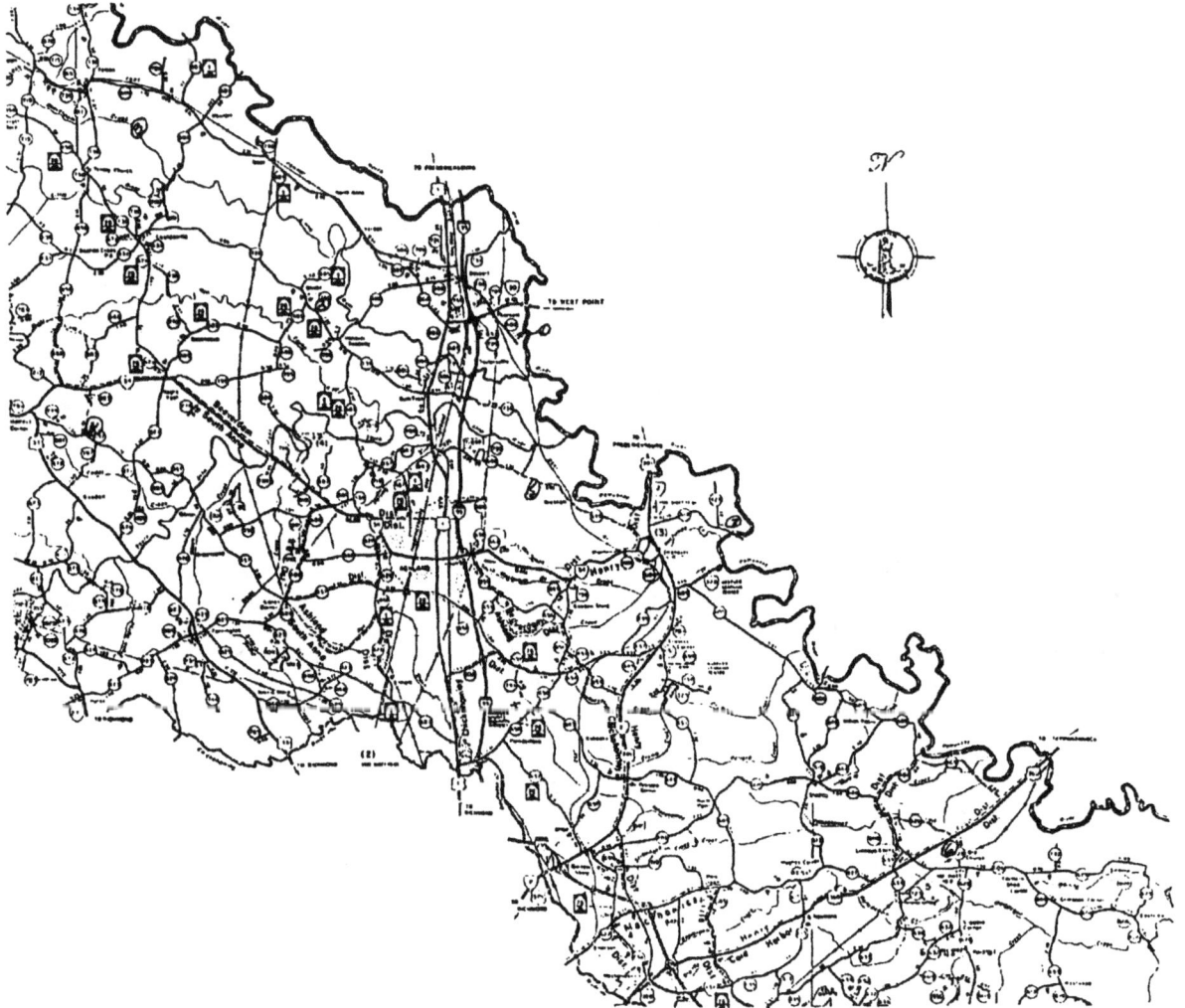

HANOVER COUNTY

insert before these pages:
(310-318;267-274)

ROBERT TERRELL

Gen. 10

The Terrell family is so rich in history that numerous books have been written to illuminate the family exploits from the time of William the Conqueror to the present. Richmond Terrell is of particular interest to Americans because of his role in establishing the Terrell name in Virginia. Many variants of the name have been used in America and England throughout their respective histories, and that will not be expounded here. We will use the most popular form of the name in America — Terrell — except when quoting from specific sources which use a different spelling.[1]

The focus here is on the brief period from 1616, just before Richmond Terrell was born, to 1677, when he was well-settled in Virginia. Richmond was apparently very close to two of his brothers. Together, they endured war, plague, fire and the rigors of life in the colony. In retrospect, we might observe that life was not easy in the seventeenth century, no matter where one lived, and perhaps life on the frontier, surrounded by hostile Indians, did not seem so extraordinary to the early colonists.

By June 29 1617, ROBERT TYRRELL and JOANNE BALDWIN were married in the parish of St. Giles in Reading, a large town in Berkshire, just west of London.[2] Robert had probably been born in West Hagbourne in Oxfordshire, and had come to Reading to establish himself as a clothier.[3] The wool and cloth trade was discussed in some detail and RICHMOND TERRELL settled within twenty miles of William Hockaday when he came to Virginia[4]. Earlier associations open the possibility that the Terrells and Hockadays had coordinated their moves to Virginia through prior contacts made in their activities in the cloth trade.

Robert had already served as Councilor and Borough Guardian of Reading in 1616, and was apparently a man of respect and stature. In the year after his marriage, he was "Overseer of the Poor," a parish duty frequently assigned to newly-wed young men. He served again as Overseer of the Poor in 1626 and 1637 and was a Church Warden in 1631 and 1632.[5] Further entries in the Reading, St. Giles Parish Register document the birth of nine children to Robert and Joanne, and the early death of two of them.[6]

John Tyrrell	*bapt*	*15 Jun 1618*	
Robert Tyrrell	*bapt*	*14 Nov 1619*	
Mary Tyrrell	*bapt*	*2 Oct 1621*	
Margaret Tyrrell	*bapt*	*7 Aug 1623*	
Richmond Terrell	*bapt*	*17 Oct 1624*	
Joanne Tyrrell	*bapt*	*5 Apr 1626*	*buried 15 Apr 1626*
Charles Tyrrell	*bapt*	*9 Nov 1627*	*buried 28 Sep 1629*
William Terrell	*bapt*	*22 Jun 1629*	
Timothy Tyrrell	*bapt*	*24 Jan 1632*	

Robert Terrell's widow submitted his will, dated 8 July 1643 (?June) for probate at Oxford on 27 Sep 1643.[7] Reading would not normally be under jurisdiction of the court at Oxford, and it is not certain whether conditions of war caused this irregularity. Perhaps Mrs. Terrell had moved to Oxford on account of Royalist sympathies and succeeded in presenting the will in a more friendly venue. In his will, Robert Terrell made bequests to his wife and children: Robert, Richmond, William, Timothy, John, Mary and Margaret. At the time of his death, four of his children were minors. Unmarried daughters, whether minors or not, probably remained with their mother.

Richmond and William almost certainly joined their older brother Robert, in London. They may have gone to London even before their father's death, as it was the custom to start apprenticeship in the mid-teens.

Robert is shown as an apprentice to the Company of Fishmongers in 1634, when he was about fourteen.[8] William was a member of the Company of Grocers, but the record does not show when he was accepted as an apprentice.[9] It should be pointed out that Fishmongers and Grocers were but two of the dozens of "Livery Companies," so-called because of the elaborate uniforms which they wore on ceremonial occasions. Members occupied the top level of London's political and social hierarchy. The mayor was always chosen from among members of the companies; not surprising, since only members were considered citizens of London and qualified to vote. Richmond, though not a member of a Livery Company, no doubt enjoyed some of their privileges by association.

Robert Terrell engaged in trade with Virginia merchants and made several voyages to conduct his business in person. There are entries in York County records which document his presence there in 1647, 1650 and 1662. He is also mentioned in two notices of "Passenger Arrivals From Virginia."[10] Further evidence that Robert Terrell made numerous trips to Virginia is contained in the patent to Richmond Terrell on 28 Nov 1656.[11] Richmond claimed 640 acres for transportation of thirteen persons, including ...*the trans. of Robert Terrell 3 severall tymes*.

It appears that his travels kept him away from London so much that he did not maintain a residence in London, but made a practice of staying with his brother, William. The will of Robert Terrell, dated 26 Oct 1677, was recorded in the Probate Act Book of the Parish of St. Nicholas, Cole Abbey, in London.[12] He left his estate to brothers, sisters, nieces, nephews and lesser kin; and from this we may infer that he had no wife or children. One peculiar aspect of Robert's will was the provision that his executors deliver *to brother Richmond Terrell the small cup and three silver spoons I now have of his*. It is likely that these were among the items mentioned in his father's will, to be delivered to Richmond after he reached the age of twenty-one years, and were held by Robert for some thirty-four years.

William Terrell is mentioned several times in Virginia records. He was a headright of George Morris and George Long in their patent of 29 Sep 1667.[13] This same patent also lists Robert Tirrell and Henry Tirrell (twice). We would assume that this Robert and William were brothers of Richmond. William Tirrell is named as a headright of Richmond Tirrell in a patent dated 8 Feb 1670.[14] The most conclusive evidence that William and Richmond were partners in business is a deed dated 29 Apr 1672.[15] By this deed, Richmond Terrell sold the 600 acres which he had patented on 8 Feb 1670 to Henry Wyatt. The deed specified that *Reserved out of this I will sell or grant to Francis Waring, his heirs, etc., 100 acres of land, part of the above six hundred, formerly by me given unto my Brother William Terrell, and since by him sold unto said Francis Waring by sale bearing date 26th day of December, 1665, being bounded as in the said sale, is mentioned at, in and by the record of the said New Kent County*. The above activities indicate that the brothers, Robert, Richmond and William maintained their contact and offered each other support and encouragement, bound by those strongest of ties — family, business, politics and religion.

Gen. 9   **RICHMOND TERRELL**

Of the three brothers Robert, RICHMOND and William, Robert was definitely a merchant, rarely leaving his place of business in London. William was also a merchant, but made a number of voyages to Virginia, even owning land there for a time. Richmond was the only one to leave his progeny in Virginia.[16] Richmond Terrell had settled in New Kent County, Parish of Blisland, by 28 Nov 1656, when his first patent for land was granted. He was thirty-two years old, and apparently unmarried. On his patents, the list of headrights includes himself and his brother Robert (three times), but no female Terrells, and no other headright list mentions any female Terrell who might have been his wife. He probably married in Virginia, but his wife is unknown.

Richmond appears later as a headright of Charles Edmonds, his neighbor, who was granted a patent for 2750 acres of land on 28 Feb 1658/9.[17] Also on that list was Edward Terrell, whose connection to Richmond can only be speculated.

Adding to the difficulty in researching the history of New Kent County and the genealogy of its people is the fact that the population was living in a time of political and religious turmoil. No doubt there were competing factions at all levels of society, and the animosity eventually led to Bacon's Rebellion in 1676. Governor Berkeley crushed the rebellion in the traditional way. Hang the leaders and impose even more restrictive regulations on survivors. Since most of the people had supported Bacon — *de facto* treason — many prominent men knew they might be arrested anytime. Property was confiscated and families thrust into the wilderness.[18]

In this atmosphere of fear and suspicion, it was important to have neighbors you could trust. Politics and religion were inseparable. Courtship and marriage could be a life and death matter for the whole family. Those with the most rebellious inclinations tended to move as far from the center of government as possible. Suspected rebels knew they were being watched and became very cautious in the conduct of their affairs.

When going through the land patent records, one notices that some land owners submitted new headrights to renew a patent for land which they already owned. Why? One answer may be that they were being harassed about real or imagined legal defects in their old patent. One also notices that some patents are very vague in describing bounds, while others have great detail in the length and bearing of bounds and identification of landmarks. Perhaps these differences in the records may have been a safeguard in that a person had no friends in high places, he had to be more rigorous in the conduct of his business. If he was an "outsider" he would be careful to get an accurate and certified survey, and he would try to avoid having a neighbor whose influence at a corrupt court might ruin him in a boundary dispute.

RICHMOND TERRELL's first patent for land was for "...640 acres in New Kent County on the west side of York River...*bounded from a Marked Corner spanish Oake on y*[e][19] *North Side of Cattaile Swampe & Running thence south East 320 pches to three Marked Trees by A Branch of Tiascun Swamp Thence North East Three Hundred Twenty poles More to a Marked Corner Chesnut neare Rickahock path thence south by y*[e] *s*[d] *path N:W:W:N:W & N:W; by W: 344 pches to a Mk*[d] *Corner red oake att y*[e] *Head of a Valley Descended Into Cattaile Swampe Soe downe That Valley & Swampe & by Charles Edmonds Lyne of Marked Trees To y*[e] *place it began....*[20] At the time he acquired his land, Richmond Terrell's only close neighbors were Charles Edmonds and John Pouncey. It appears that Richmond made a subsequent trip back to England, as his name once again appears as a headright in a patent for 2750 acres to Charles Edmonds on 28 Feb 1658.[21] Neighbors naturally engaged in a businesslike trading of resources, and Edmonds probably bought Terrell's headright and merged it with others to claim this large tract of land.

John Pouncey's land was a tract of 900 acres including 300 acres called *Hogg Pen Neck*, granted on 8 Dec 1652.[22] This land was apparently acquired by William Bassett, who bequeathed it to his nephew, Joseph Foster in 1671.[23] Bassett's will described it as ...*all the lands I purchased of John Pouncey Scituate and being a Neck of land between Diascon & Mr Richmond Terrill in the County of New Kent....*

This Pouncey land is located in about the right place to correspond with the place called *Basset's Landing* in the description of the line between Blisland Parish and St. Peter's Parish. The parish boundary, as laid down by order of the Governor and General Council at Jamestown on 18 Oct 1689 was: *The line dividing y*[e] *Parish of St. Peter's and Blisland as follows, Viz: Beginning at Pamunkey River side — at Basset's landing where there is a small wt: oake markt, thence by a line of markt trees, south seven degrees and ½ west over severall poynts and bottoms until you come to y*[e] *maine Rhode to a markt Corner Red oake of y*[e] *lands of Richmond Turrell, thence by y*[e] *lines of y*[e] *s*[d] *Turrells land leaving all y*[e] *s*[d] *Turrells land in Blisland Parish, thence by y*[e] *lines of y*[e] *s*[d] *Turrells land and Capt. Joseph Fosters land including y*[e] *s*[d] *Joseph Fosters in St. Peter's Parish.*[24] Bassett's landing is still a good place to pull up a boat, though it is now called Cook Landing. A small snip of the tract map of this area is presented on the next page to give a picture of how these tracts and parish lines relate to each other and the geography. It is not practical to display other lands owned by Richmond Terrell on this map because of the great area they encompassed. Suffice to say that he was granted a patent for 600 acres in New Kent County 8 Feb 1670.[25]

Richmond Terrell apparently had yet another tract of land on or near Toe Ink Swamp. This can be inferred from the patent for 800 acres to Thomas Mimes (or Mines) 3 Feb 1662, which names Meredith, Smith and Terrell as owning adjoining lands.[26] Mimes' land can be placed on Toe Ink Swamp, and there is no patent to Terrell which can be located in this area. Terrell must have bought this land, and only by plotting all the patents in this area could one decide which adjoining patent was sold to Terrell. Again, we have the same three men as neighbors.

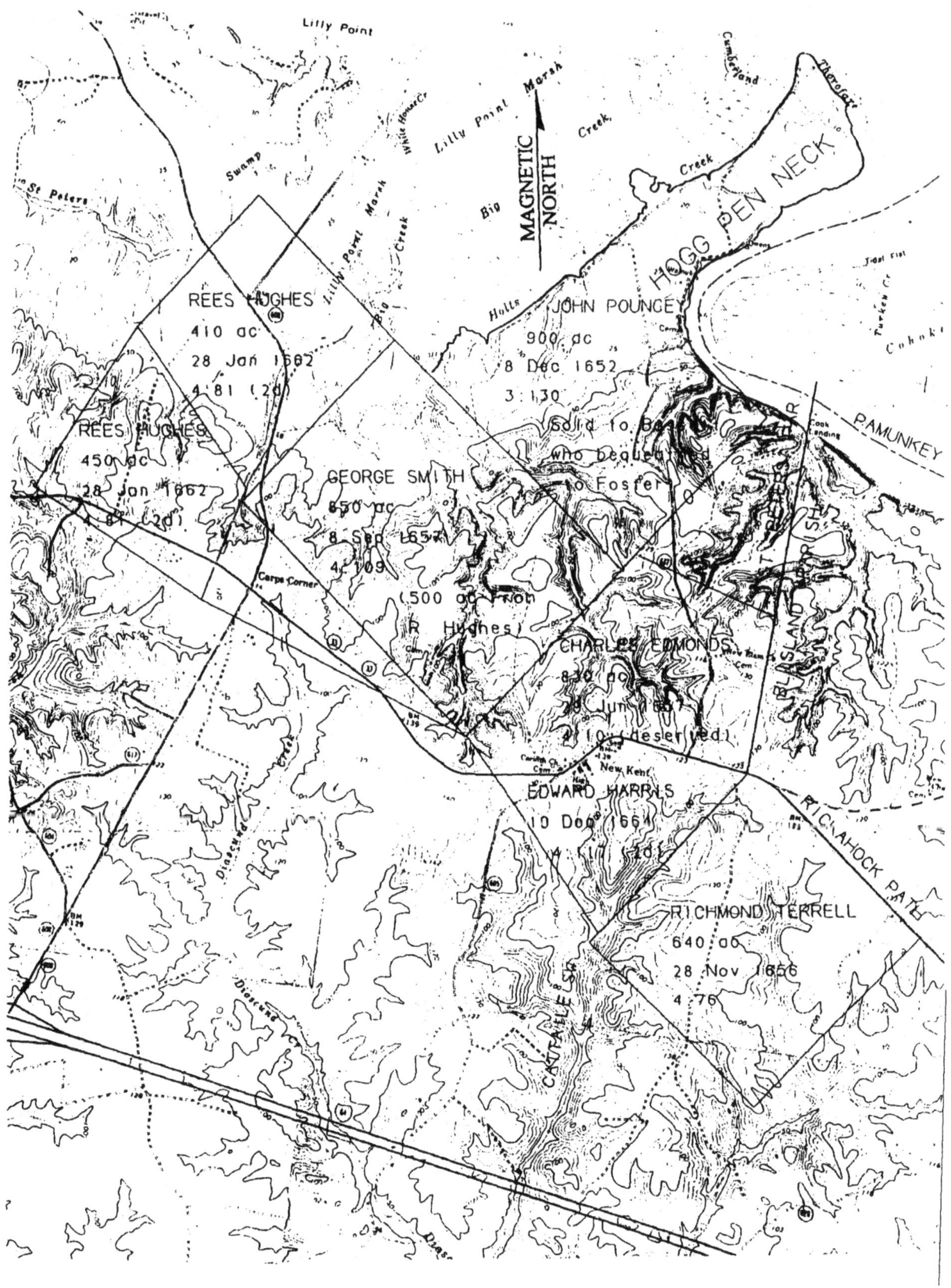

Tract Map, Richmond Terrell and Neighbors, Blisland Parish, New Kent County

84

There is certainly a fourth tract of land which must be considered when assessing the situation of Richmond Terrell in New Kent County. There is a record of a patent for 720 acres of land, granted to Elizabeth Terrell and Thomas Correll on 20 Nov 1683.[27] The land is located some six miles east of Richmond Terrell's 640 acres, with the northern tip just touching the village of Talleysville. This patent poses several questions, and answers none. Who was Elizabeth Terrell? Who was Thomas Correll? What brought them together? Neither is mentioned elsewhere in the land patent books, and neither is mentioned in the St. Peter's Parish Register or Vestry Book. It could be speculated that Elizabeth was the widow of Richmond; but why would she have moved? Business partnerships between a man and woman were rare. For the woman to be named first in a partnership certainly signals that something very unusual was going on.

In trying to figure what might have been the motivation for this odd couple to patent a significant tract of land, one must keep in mind that Bacon's Rebellion was only six years in the past. As detailed above, Berkeley grabbed as many of the leaders as he could and hanged some as examples. Some wealthy rebels probably bought their way back into society. But for most, it was a matter of lying low until things cooled down. One by one, they quietly came home, and as long as they kept out of trouble and paid their taxes, it was an uneasy situation of live and let live. Among the fugitives, there must have been some who were named in specific warrants for arrest. For them, there was no coming back — unless it was under false identity. Of course, nobody was really fooled, but the officials could conveniently overlook the little deceit in order to get the fugitive back to work and out in the open where he could be watched more easily. We imagine a clerk solemnly accepting the tax payment of one Tom Correll, while sliding a warrant for the arrest of Tim Terrell into his bottom drawer, knowing full well that they were one and the same. In this regard, note that Timothy Terrell had three children baptized in St. Peter's Parish between 1689 and 1699.[28] Emma Dicken has inferred that the wife of Timothy Terrell was Elizabeth Foster.[29]

Among the eighty-eight signatures on the petition from Blisland Parish were Rees Hughes, Roger Pouncie, Richmond Terrell (Junr.), George Smith and Nicholas Barnhouse.[30] Four of these surnames appear on the map above, and Barnhouse had land immediately east of Richmond Terrell. Bacon's rebels were truly fired by the spirit of '76; but the year was 1676, a century before the Revolution that won our liberty. One can also relate these activities to those of Stephen Tarleton of Bacon's Rebellion and the *Blisland Parish Grievances*.[31]

(310-318;267-274)
Gen. 8   **WILLIAM TERRELL**

The accounts of the lives of ROBERT TERRELL, the grandfather of WILLIAM TERRELL, and of the father, RICHMOND TERRELL and his brothers, Robert and William offer documented evidence of the two earlier generations and the relationships of the individuals. Much has been written about the Terrells, and many confusing accounts have been presented. The work of LtCol. James Doyle is well-researched and well-documented, and establishes relationships clearly. The account of William Terrell, the son of Richmond Terrell should be read with the proper relationships established, and in the correct time frame.

James Terrell
(315;271) The will of James Terrell was found among the Miscellaneous Papers of Cumberland County. It provides proof of the sons of James Terrell and for the first time identifies his daughters.[32] James identified himself as of St. Margaret's Parish, Caroline County and wrote his will on October 18, 1766. He named his wife, Margaret and first, his five oldest children: sons, William Terrill and James Terrill (to receive the land on which his father lived), daughters, Betty Newton and Patty Hord and son, John Terrill. He then gave land to his sons, Dudley Terrill and Jonathan Terrill. He then named two daughters, Neffe and Mary Herndon. He named his son-in-law, Thomas Hord and his son, James Terrill, the executors of his estate. Apparently the estate settlement was under question for a notation attached when a suit was brought in 1778, that stated: *I cannot think that Dudley Terrill can take under this will Lands lying on the north side of Muddy Creek when Lands on the south side of the Creek only are devised to him: But Lands not within the Description of the Devise*

must descend to the Heir at Law. This was signed by Th: Willes, 13 December 1778.

John Terrell

(315;271) A copy of the will of John Terrell is of interest, identifying himself as John Terrell of Franklin County, North Carolina, he bequeathed to his *reputed wife Elizabeth who is called and known by the name of Elizabeth Terrell with whom I have cohabited,* furniture, etc. He named the following children, and in the same manner: *my reputed daughter, Loruhimah born of the body of Elizabeth Harrison aforesaid reputed wife; my reputed son Jeptha called and known by the name of Jeptha Terrell born of the body of the aforesaid Elizabeth; my reputed daughter Anne...; my reputed son Joel...; my reputed son Timothy's children, that is his daughter Elizabeth, his son Richard and his daughter Susannah.* He disposed of his mill on Sandy Creek by dividing it in six parts among his four children, to wit. Jeptha, Joel, Lorihuma and Anne and the orphans of his two deceased sons, Timothy and John. The will was written September 20, 1783.[33]

His family Bible records as given below were taken from the original papers by Mrs. Anne William (Smith) Smith (1830-1871) with the permission of the present owner Miss Martha Amis, Fordyce, Arkansas.[34] The entries do not quite agree with the work of Emma Dicken[35], nor does he name all of his children in his will.

Lomhannah Terrell born January 18th 1731 (Lorihannah?)
Jeptha Terrell born October 29th 1733
Hezkiah Terrell born August 15th 1735
John Terrell born November 15th 1737
Ann Terrell born July 10th 1741 (sic)
Timothy Terrell born June 22th 1741 (sic)
James Terrell born December 9th 1743
Agnes Terrell born October 25 1746
Betsey Terrell born June 15th 1749
Joel Terrell born December 5th 1751

TERRELL FAMILY

Gen.10 ROBERT TERRELL	m	JOANNE BALDWIN
Issue:	John	m	d.s.p.
	Robert	m	d.s.p.
	Mary	m	Thomas Warner
	Margaret	m	
	RICHMOND	m	UNKNOWN
	Joanne		died in infancy
	Charles		died young
	William	m	
	Timothy	m	
	Thomas		died young

2
Gen.9 RICHMOND TERRELL	m	UNKNOWN
Issue:	Richmond	m	
	Timothy	m	(—?—)
	WILLIAM	m	SUSANNAH WATERS

GEN.8 WILLIAM TERRELL	m	SUSANNAH WATERS
Issue:	William	m	
	Joel	m	Elizabeth Oxford
	MARY	m	(1) MICAJAH CHILES
			(2) Matthew Mills
	Anne	m	David Lewis
	David	m	Agatha Chiles
	Henry	m	Ann Chiles
	Timothy	m	Mary Martin
	James	m	Margaret (—?—)

| John | m | Sarah (—?—) |
| | reputed wife | Elizabeth Harrison |

Notes

1. LtCol James W Doyle, Jr, 2923 Tara Trail, Beavercreek, OH 45434. From the article *"The Terrells of Reading, London and Virginia"*, *TVF* 6(1997): 144-153.

2. *Register of the Parish of St. Giles*, Reading, Berkshire, England.

3. *Terrell Trails*, vol.XII, No.2, 1012. *Terrell Trails* is published quarterly by The Terrell Society of America, 128 20th Ave. NW, Cairo, GA 31728-1017.)

4. *TVF* 3:222.

5. *Churchwardens' Account Book of the Parish of St. Giles*, Reading, Berkshire, England.

6. *The Parish Register of St. Giles*.

7. Emma Dicken, *Terrell Genealogy*, (San Antonio, TX: Naylor Co, c.1952). Copies may be rented or purchased from The Terrell Society of America. See address above.)

8. Percival Boyd, *Pedigrees of London Citizens*. Mss. p.28239. Film #0094587, LDS Family History Library.

9. Ibid., 28240.

10. *W&M Q*, (1) 21:262; (1) 22:53.

11. Nugent I:342.

12. *VMHB* XVI(1910):190.

13. Nugent II:42.

14. Nugent II:96.

15. Manuscript in Library of the Virginia Historical Society.

16. James W. Doyle, Jr., *"Richmond Terrell, New Kent County"*, *TVF* 6 (1998) 213-218.

17. Land Patent Book 4, 254.

18. Thomas J. Wertenbaker, *Bacon's Rebellion*. (Baltimore: Clearfield, 1957).

19. Readers should note that the word yᵉ as used here was not meant to be "ye" as we know the archaic form of "you". It is an even more archaic Saxon form of the word "the" using a letter called the *thorn*, written much like a "y" and pronounced as "th".

20. Land Patent Book 4, 76.

21. Land Patent Book 4, 254.

22. Land Patent Book 3, 130.

23. Will of William Bassett, signed 28 Aug 1671, proved 4 Jan 1671/2.

24. C.G. Chamberlayne, ed., *Vestry Book and Register of St. Peter's Parish*. (Richmond: VA State Library, 1937). 29.

25. Land Patent Book 6, 369.

26. Land Patent Book 5, 218.

27. Land Patent Book 7, 333.

28. Chamberlayne, 392,397.

29. Dicken; *TVF* 6(1997): 151.

30. C.G.Chamberlayne, ed., *The Vestry Book of Blisland Parish*, (Richmond: VA State Library, 1935). xliv-xlvii.

31. V.L.H. Davis, *Tidewater Virginia Families, 2nd ed* 424.

32. Lyndon H. Hart, *"Will of James Terrill, Planter"*, *Magazine of Virginia Genealogy* 33 (1995) 231-232.

33. *Terrell Trails* XIII(1997): 1076-1081.

34. *Terrell Trails* II(1986): 64.

35. Dicken 263.

36. Knee Buckle of Richmond Tyrrell; Born 1624 Reading, Eng.; Died c.1680 Virginia - From Lake E. Terrell, Columbia, SC

JAMES TAYLOR

James Taylor, Clerk of St. Peter's Parish, New Kent County[1] between 1707-1720, is an ancestor of James Williams Davis. It was Susanna Taylor, the daughter of James Taylor, who married James Watts, who later migrated to Ninety-six District, South Carolina.[2] It is believed that the parents of James Watts (born January 6, 1729) were John Watts who married Elizabeth Foster, the daughter of Joseph Foster.[3] This does not agree with the marriage of the daughter of Joseph Foster as inferred by Dicken.[4] James Watts is found in St. Paul's Parish in the processioning returns as a land owner until 1767. It is assumed that he left for South Carolina a short time after this.[5] It is interesting that he migrated to the same area as James Chiles, and that there are other names in the records of South Carolina of this time that can be associated with Caroline and Hanover counties.

The account of James Taylor and his sons is included because it clarifies the early generations of this James Taylor, the clerk of St. Peter's Parish, his family in Virginia and where the Taylor sons lived. It is also because of the relationship with Joseph Foster, and his land ownership in New Kent County that the following is included.

An agreement was made between Daniel Taylor, minister, and the vestry of St. Peter's Parish, New Kent County on December 30th 1707. It was agreed that Mr Taylor officiate as minister of the parish for three months.[6] A relationship between Daniel Taylor and James Taylor, appointed clerk cannot be established.

At the vestry meeting of St. Peter's Parish at the brick church on February 4th, 1707/8 it was ordered that James Taylor officiate as clerk of the vestry and reader (at divine services), and that he be paid at the usual rate, 1200 pounds of tobacco for 12 months, excepting cask.[7] From that time forward, until September 29, 1719, when he signed, for the last time, the minutes of the vestry meeting of St. Peter's Parish, held at the brick church; he served as clerk of the vestry and reader.[8] The November 18th, 1719 meeting was held in his home, but the minutes were not signed by a clerk. The minutes of the meeting of July 11, 1720 were signed by Charles Gore, Clerk.[9]

St. Paul's Parish was created in 1704 in what was to become Hanover County (1720)[10] While John Shelton signed the earliest minutes of the vestry meetings, apparently, James Taylor served as clerk of the vestry and reader from at least 1706.[11] He must have continued in this role, as reader and clerk of both churches in St. Paul's Parish until John Hopkins was appointed in February 14, 1707/8[12]. No explanation is given in the minutes for the removal of James Taylor, and the request that he relinquish the parish register and the papers belonging to the vestry to John Hopkins.

One of the churches of St. Paul's Parish was located on Mechamps Creek, and St Peter's Church of New Kent County was on the north side of the Pamunkey River while St Paul's Parish was on the south side of the Pamunkey River. As far as can be determined, James Taylor continued to live in New Kent County. There is no doubt that James had to travel some distance to serve as clerk and reader of both parishes.

James Taylor may have been in poor health when he was replaced as clerk of St. Peter's Parish vestry in July 1720. It seems probable that he died in 1720; however, his death is not recorded in the parish register. Widow Taylor was paid for two delinquents in 1720, evidently payments from the parish vestry by the vestry of St. Peter's Parish on September 29, 1722. A subsequent meeting of the St. Peter's Parish Vestry was held on November 19, 1722 at the home of Mrs. Taylor.[13]

The names of James Taylor and Elizabeth his wife are entered in the St. Peter's Parish Register with the birth of each of their children. The maiden name of Elizabeth, and the names of her parents has not been found. Listing them in chronological order, the names of the children recorded in the church register are as follows:

Mary Taylor, born August 11, 1705
William Taylor, born March 7, 1707/8
George Taylor, born March 20, 1709/10

Elizabeth Taylor, born September 26, 1712
Christian Taylor, (daughter), born June 10, 1715
Francis Taylor, (daughter), born January 26, 1716
Susanna Taylor, born November 8, 1719[14]

The names of some of the children of George and Lucy Taylor are entered in the St. Peter's Parish Register. The maiden name of Lucy has not been identified, nor have the names of her parents. Apparently George was married before 1731, as his daughter Susanna was born on February 26th of that year.[15] It was Susanna, the daughter of George Taylor[16] who married James Watts of Hanover County about 1755.[17] It is not known whether Lucy was her mother or not, as Susanna's birth has not been found in the parish register; however, one would assume so, since the birth of a daughter of George and Lucy Taylor was recorded in 1733. These later births of children of George and Lucy Taylor entered in the St. Peter's Parish Register are:[18]

Frances, daughter, born December 8, 1733, baptized January 20, 1733
James, son, born May 1, 1736, baptized June 6, 1736
George, son, born December 11, 1737, baptized January 7, 1737
William, son, born May 1, 1739, baptized June 17, 1739

It is difficult to follow the life of George Taylor because of the complete destruction of the early county court records of New Kent County, and the almost complete destruction of the early records of Hanover County. The register of St. Paul's Parish has not survived, so that early vital records from Hanover County are also not available. The fact that the births of George's children are recorded in the St. Peter's Parish Register would indicate that he may have continued to live in New Kent County in the 1730-1740 period. Family tradition holds that Susanna Taylor was born in New Kent County. Two entries in the parish vestry book relate to payments to George Taylor in 1739 and 1744 for keeping two indigent persons.[19]

A notation found among the Davis papers[20] identified George Taylor of Newcastle, Hanover County as the father of Susanna Taylor. His name has not been found as an owner of a lot in the town of Newcastle, but the name of William Taylor has been found as the owner of two lots, and occupant of one, as shown on a plat of the town dated 1744. Newcastle was laid off by William Meriwether on the south side of the Pamunkey River in 1730 as a tobacco port.[21]

No further mention was found of George in the St. Peter's Parish Vestry Book or Register; however, his name was entered in the records of the St. Paul's Parish Vestry Book as early as 1751,[22] when he was ordered to keep Mary Kenny and Margaret Thomson at the October 15th vestry meeting. He was paid annually for this for several years. Later the names of both James and George Taylor appeared in the accounts of the parish vestry. Without any further identification it is difficult, after the time that George's son would have come of age (1758) to be sure of the identification of George Taylor, the elder.

The name of George Taylor appeared in the processioning returns of St. Paul's Parish as early as 1759,[23] along with the name of William Taylor. The land owners listed were not the same as those owning lots in Newcastle, thus this would have been a more substantial land holding. It would seem that these were brothers, and the older generation. In 1763 the names of George Taylor and William Taylor appeared in one precinct and the names of George Taylor and James Taylor appeared in another precinct as land owners.[24] George's name continued to appear until 1767. This year George was appointed one of the processioners, to oversee the processioning and to make the return to the vestry.[25]

When the name of George Taylor had first appeared on the processioning lists his land was listed in the same precinct as William Taylor. At the time of his death the name of George Taylor appeared only in the precinct in which his name had appeared with that of James Taylor; however, the name of James Taylor did not appear.[26]

When the processioning order was given at the vestry meeting on November 12, 1771, the lands of George Taylor were identified as those of George Taylor, deceased.[27] It would appear that this was the elder George Taylor, and he died between September 1760 and November 1771.

James Taylor

Notes

1. *TVF* 2(1994) 238-240.
2. Dudley Cozby Davis and Martha Davis Abernethy, *Sketches of the John Davis-Anne Byrd Descendants* (Phenix City, AL: The Herald Press, 1969) 68. From the unpublished manuscripts of Thomas Wier Davis, Genealogist, South Carolinana Library, Columbia, SC.
3. C.G. Chamberlayne, *The Vestry Book and Register of St Peter's Parish*, 1937 (Richmond: Virginia State Library Board, rep 1989) 355.
4. Emma Dicken, *Terrell Genealogy*, (San Antonio: Naylor Company, 1952) 38, 41.
5. C.G. Chamberlayne, *The Vestry Book of St. Paul's Parish, Hanover County, Virgina, 1706-1786* (Richmond: Virginia State Library Board, 1940) 467.
6. Chamberlayne 125.
7. Chamberlayne 125-126.
8. Chamberlayne 171-173.
9. Chamberlayne 185, 176.
10. C.G. Chamberlayne, *The Vestry Book of St Paul's Parish, Hanover County, 1706-1786* (Richmond: Virginia State Library, 1940) xii.
11. Chamberlayne 7, 10.
12. Chamberlayne 25.
13. Chamberlayne 185, 186.
14. Chamberlayne 398, 399.
15. Davis and Abernethy 68.
16. Manuscript, Mrs Sara Davis Ackerman, State Regent, DAR, 1922, Macon, Georgia.
17. Davis and Abernethy 68.
18. Chamberlayne 514, 529, 542, 552.
19. Chamberlayne 260, 281.
20. Akerman.
21. Hanover County Historical Society, *Old Homes of Hanover County, Virginia* (Summersville: Walsworth, 1989) 35.
22. Chamberlayne 328.
23. Chamberlayne 383-384.
24. Chamberlayne 419-421.
25. Chamberlayne 459-460.
26. Chamberlayne 482.
27. Chamberlayne 482.

St. Peter's Church c. 1985

Chapter 10

JOHN BUTLER I

Gen. 7

(319;275) An interesting piece of information has come to light concerning *Aspen Hill*, thought to have been built much later than the early 1700s. Virginia C. Jarrel had in her possession a brick from the original chimney with the initials and date "I.B. 1739". If this in fact relates to Isaac Butler's family, it could mean that an Isaac Butler was living in 1739. The name Isaac carried through many generations and members of the Thomas Butler family that originated in New Kent and then King William County from the late 1600s.

If this is in fact evidence of an earlier Isaac Butler, this may establish a further link between JOHN BUTLER of Caroline and the THOMAS BUTLER of King William County. This also raises the question of whether this may have been a brother or another son of John Butler I.[1]

(323-332;275-277)
Gen. 6

JOHN BUTLER II

Isaac Butler

(328-329,282-283) Judge Leon Bazille collected information about a number of Hanover and Caroline county residents. Along with the Butler Family Bible records already published, he also made further notes from the records of Isaac's family.[2] Isaac Butler, the son of JOHN BUTLER II married Anne P., as noted by Judge Bazille. This does not necessarily conflict with previously recorded information, as Nancy Cobbs may well have been named Anne and the P. was her middle name, as was so often used in lieu of the maiden name, during that time. Their children were: John Dabney; Leland W. (born August 19, 1822); Isaac O.; Martha Anne (born December 6, 1827); and Patrick H. Butler.

Leland Butler married October 15, 1857, Martha Virginia Gentry, the daughter of Austin Gentry and his first wife, Sarah Winn Burruss(? difficult to read), born March 10, 1843. Their children: Valentine Caroline, born July 9, 1858, died May 9, 1862; Frederick Austin, born December 11, 1859; Virginia Leland, born April 5, 1863; and Isaac, born April 22, 1865. Leland died at *Humanity Hall*, Hanover County on January 19, 1883.

Martha Anne Butler married Austin Gentry as his second wife, their children: John W. Gentry, Charles W. Gentry and Isaac A. Gentry. Martha died before her father. Isaac O. Butler had children: Thomas T. Butler, Edward Butler and Elizabeth O. Butler. Isaac died in Loda, Illinois in 1857. Patrick Butler had children: Celia Butler, Mary Butler, Nancy J. Butler, Franklin Butler, William Butler and Otho S. Butler. Patrick Butler died April 9, 1877, before his father's will was probated.

Isaac Butler made his will April 9, 1875 and it was probated on July 18, 1877 in Hanover County.[3] He appointed his sons, John D. and Leland W. Butler the executors. In his will he named his grandson, Thomas T. Butler; his son, Leland Butler; his grandsons Isaac A. Gentry and Isaac Butler. He named his daughter, Martha A. Gentry, who had died and his sons, John D. Butler, Isaac O. Butler, who had died, Leland W. Butler and Patrick H. Butler. Isaac's estate was valued at $11,789.57. He had advanced something over $5000 to each of his children, amounting to a sum total of over $32,000.

BUTLER FAMILY

Gen. 8 THOMAS BUTLER	m	ALICE (—?—)	
Issue: SAMUEL	m	UNKNOWN	
Sarah	m	(1) (—?—) Slaughter	
	m	(2) Edward Harrison	

	JOHN (possibly)		m	(1) ANN (—?—)
			m	(2) Susanna
			m	(3) Mary

Gen. 7	JOHN BUTLER I		m	(1) ANN (—?—)
Issue:	JOHN II		m	(1) JANE ANDERSON
			m	(2) Mary Boughton
	Samuel		m	
	John Butler I	m	(2) Susanna (—?—)	
	John Butler I	m	(3) Mary (—?—)	
Issue:	children (unidentified)			

Gen. 6	JOHN BUTLER II		m	(1) JANE ANDERSON
Issue:	Anderson		m	
	John			(p) died young
	Samuel		m	Patty Douglas
	Thomas		m	Elizabeth Southworth widow
	Ann			died young
	SARAH		m	JOHN AMBROSE HUTCHESON
	Lucy			died young
	William		m	
	Edward Gee		m	

	John Butler II	m	(2) Mary Boughton	
Issue:	Joseph			died young
	Nancy			died in infancy
	John		m	Mary Southworth
	Mary			died in infancy
	Elizabeth		m	(—?—) Southworth
	Polly		m	John Southworth
	James			died young
	Isaac		m	Nancy Cobbs Chiles widow
	Lucy		m	James Eubank

Notes

1. Correspondence with Herbert R. Collins, Arlington, VA (1995).
2. Butler Family and Gentry-Butler Family Bibles, Frederick A. Butler, Richmond, VA. Mss1B3483aFA2, Virginia Historical Society, Richmond, VA; Collins, 2:34. There are additional papers of Isaac and Leland Butler at the Duke University Archives.
3. *Hanover County Will Book 4* 136-138; 560.

JEAN de JARNAT

Gen. 9

The surname DeJarnette will be used consistently throughout this account, since it is the present-day spelling of the name.

(333,341;286,294) A granite memorial to the DeJarnette family has been erected on the present US Route 301 on the road frontage of the original *Spring Grove* land. This gives the various French Huguenot spellings of the name that later became John DeJarnette: deJarnat, deJaournette and Dejeurner. Mr. Walter Martin, a contributor and a Norfolk attorney has written that JEAN de JARNAT was originally from LaRocelle, France from the town of Jarmac. This has not been confirmed. The generations of DeJarnettes who occupied the Caroline County land are listed on the marker, along with dates, and these have been incorporated in the accounts of each generation of the family.

MUMFORD FAMILY

Gen.10	EDWARD MUMFORD	m	MARY WATKINS
Issue:	MARY	m	JEAN deJARNAT
	Joseph	m	
	Edward	m	
	Daniel	m	

WATKINS FAMILY

Gen.12	RICHARD WATKINS	m	ELIZABETH
Issue:	JOSEPH	m	ELIZABETH PURNELL widow
Gen.11	JOSEPH WATKINS	m	ELIZABETH PURNELL widow
Issue:	MARY	m	EDWARD MUMFORD

(340-348;293-301)
Gen. 8

JOSEPH DEJARNETTE I

The accounts of the children of JOSEPH DEJARNETTE provide corrected information about their ages, marriages and offsprings. Dorothy Granholm Hankins[1] has done extensive research in correcting the relationships of these DeJarnette children.

Mary DeJarnette
(346-347;299) Mary DeJarnette was probably the firstborn of the seven children of Joseph DeJarnette and his wife Mary Pemberton. An affidavit with the Revolutionary War pension application filed by her daughter Sarah (Wright) Moore in 1847 indicates that Mary was born August 8, 1739.[2] In the same pension application; however, a family Bible record gives her birth year as 1744. She married first Richard Price, son of John Price and Ann Younger of Essex County.[3] Until Richard's death in 1781, he and Mary kept an ordinary and lived on the Cumberland County plantation he bought from his brother-in-law, Stark Boulware. Richard and Mary had two children, Mary (Polley) and William Price.[4]

About twelve years after Polley Price's 1788 marriage to Abner Watson, they moved to Prince Edward

County. Although he was the youngest son, Abner inherited the plantation of his father, John Watson.[5] The ten children born to Polley and Abner Watson were: Richard Price, Mary P., John A., William P., Abner Y., Sarah A., Benjamin B., Joseph D., Frederick W. and Susan E. Watson.[6]

In 1797 Mary's son William Price married Mary (Polly) Richardson, daughter of John Richardson, BH (Black Head)[6] and Rebeckah Davis of Charlotte County. William and Polly Price had four daughters: Sarah (Sally) Price who married George R. Jeffries in 1825; Mary D. Price who married Thomas Terry Totty in 1831; Martha Price who married Fitzhugh Lipscomb in 1832; and Lennis Wade Price who married Joseph W. Vaughan in 1837.[7] They also had sons, not yet identified.[8] By 1820 schoolmaster William Price was a widower. His late-life marriage in 1839 to the daughter of Alexander and Jane Trent of Prince Edward County — Mary (Polly) Trent Faris, widow of Benjamin Faris of Campbell County — left William widowed again by 1842.[9]

Archibald Wright of Cumberland County became Mary DeJarnette Price's second husband circa 1782. The Wrights were neighbors and friends of the Price family and had also come to Cumberland from Essex County.[10] Archibald's father, George Wright, died in 1774, having apprenticed Peter Francisco for two years[11] — the hero whose fame spread as the "Hercules of the Revolution." Archibald and his brother, William Wright served during the war in Capt. John Morton's company, Fourth Virginia Regiment.[12] Mary and Archibald Wright's children were Sarah (Sally) Wright, Archibald D. Wright, and possibly the unidentified Mary Wright Jr. whose death was recorded in the family Bible.

Sarah Wright and William Jones Moore, who married in 1813, had six children: Mary (Marie) Archer, Archibald W., Frederick Bradley, Martha H., Sarah Elizabeth and William Anthony Moore.[13]

Archibald D. Wright, called Archer, began medical studies at the University of Pennsylvania in 1810,[14] the year his father died. Mary probably needed her son at home in Buckingham County after her husband's death; Archer did not return to Philadelphia for a medical degree. Perhaps he "read medicine" with Dr. John Peter Mettauer of Prince Edward, an 1809 graduate of the University's Medical School, and well known for the number of students he taught throughout his life. By 1815 Archer was one of seven physicians and surgeons practicing for fees in the County of Buckingham,[15] and later consulted by Dr. Mettauer.[16] Archibald D. Wright married two Cumberland County women, Mary Raine who died in 1815,[17] and Martha Isbell who survived him. He died without issue in 1819 at age 30.[18]

Mary DeJarnette Price Wright and her children Sally Wright Moore and Archer Wright moved from Buckingham County to Prince Edward County in 1818, where for more than two decades she lived near her many Price and Wright descendants. She died there January 11, 1840.[19]

Elizabeth DeJarnette

(346;298) Elizabeth DeJarnette may have been younger than her brothers James Pemberton and Joseph DeJarnette, but she was probably second eldest daughter. Her father, Joseph DeJarnette's deed of gift to her and her three sisters in 1778 likely was made soon after her marriage to George Richeson. It is their children, Mary (Polly) and Rebecca Richeson, who were thought to have been the children of Elizabeth's father because of the deed of gift he made to them in 1783. In 1785 Joseph DeJarnette was appointed guardian of Polly and Rebecca Richeson, children of George Richeson.[20] Perhaps this guardianship was a result of Elizabeth DeJarnette Richardson's recent death and George's remarriage. The "Richeson" spelling was preferred in Caroline County, but in Mecklenburg County where the family resided after 1791, the name was alternately written "Richardson." Mary and Rebecca were old enough then to choose their guardians. Joseph DeJarnette had died in 1790, and George had children by his second wife. In 1791, *Mary and Beckey Richardson made choice of their father George Richardson for their guardian.*[21]

After relocating in Mecklenburg, George Richeson transferred 194 acres of land in Caroline County to Giles Richeson in 1793.[22] Giles must have been a close relative, as George named one of his sons Giles. A family relationship between the elder Joseph and Thomas Richeson of Caroline, and George and Giles Richeson of Caroline, has not been established. Their properties were not in the same district.

George Richardson died six or seven years after moving to Mecklenburg County. An account of the estate of *George Richeson deceased* begins *1797 Octo. 26   To Cash paid Doct: Webb per receipt. . £8-16-0.*[23] He died intestate, but the guardians' accounts in the loose papers of Mecklenburg[24][24] are a source for determining how many of George's eight children were Elizabeth DeJarnette's children.

In Obediance to an Order of the Worshipfull Court of Mecklenburg County to us directed we have examined Stated & Settled the Account of George Richardson lately deced & find that in the year 1791 that a Negroe Moses was Sold under the direction of the late will of Joseph Degarnett Sen'. deced in the County of Caroline for the sum of Eighty five pounds on the 12th day of April 1792. We find the said George Richardson, late Guardian of Mary, Rebeccah & Joseph Richardson Stands Justly Indebted to them the sum of One Hundred & Nine pounds 8/9 — Including Interest to this 8th day of January 1798. Given under our hands the day & year above. [signed] Thomas Burnett, John Holmes, Swepson Jeffries.[25]

Mary, Rebecca and Joseph were the oldest of George Richardson's children and the only three mentioned in the above settlement of his estate linked to Joseph DeJarnette's estate. Elizabeth DeJarnette Richardson's son Joseph Richardson may be the "Joseph Richeson" who by tradition went to Kentucky through the Cumberland Gap, and settled in Green County with a wife Mary.

George Richardson's other five children were: Elizabeth (Betsy), Giles, Frances "Fanny," Sarah P. (Sally) and George.[26] Guardians accounts by Nathaniel Moss in 1800 for Elizabeth, Fanny, Giles, George and Sally P. list payments to *your mother for board*.[27] In 1802 and 1803, the estate of Sarah Richardson, deceased, was appraised and sold.[28] Among the buyers were Elizabeth Richardson (both spellings) and Nathaniel Moss, giving reason to believe that this Sarah Richardson was George's widow and the mother of his five youngest children.

Elizabeth DeJarnette and George Richardson's daughter Mary married Thomas Jeffries in 1798.[29] In 1802 Mary and Thomas Jeffries relinquished any further claim to her father George Richardson's estate, having been granted some advances by the administrator, Nathaniel Moss.[30] Apparently Mary and Thomas Jeffries left Mecklenburg soon afterward. One other marriage of this family appears in Mecklenburg records: Elizabeth Richardson and Wilson Bottom on December 20, 1806; the bondsman was Nathaniel Moss.[31] Possibly some of the Richardson children returned to their Caroline roots. Others undoubtedly migrated westward.

Daniel DeJarnette

(345-346;298) Joseph and Mary Pemberton DeJarnette's son Daniel married twice, leading to the earlier conclusion that his wife was Mary Elizabeth Davis, the combined names of his two wives. Daniel's first wife was Mary Young, and his second wife was Elizabeth Davis. The complexity of family relationships in Daniel's marriages is more readily seen by referring to the following chart:

1)George Davis = Mary Young = 2)Daniel DeJarnette = 2)Elizabeth Davis (daughter of George & Mary Young Davis)

Williamson David	Nancy DeJarnette	William Young DeJarnette
Elizabeth Davis		Mary DeJarnette
Catharine Davis		Elizabeth DeJarnette
Mary Davis		Catherine DeJarnette
		Daniel DeJarnette

Mary Young was the daughter of Williamson and Mary Young of Essex County. A number of years after her father's death, the sale of a slave from his estate to Daniel DeJarnette, reveals that Mary and her brothers William, Jr. and Williamson Young were the only surviving children in November 1776. At that time, she was *Mary the now wife of Daniel DeJarnette*.[32] When she married Daniel on February 12, 1775,[33] she was Mary Davis, widow of George Davis, who died between September 1772 and April 1773.[34]

George Davis and Mary Young married before September 1764.[35] George was a family friend of the Youngs, and the guardian of Mary's brother Williamson Young.[36] In the eight to ten years of their marriage, George and Mary had four children — Elizabeth, Catharine, Mary and Williamson Davis. Williamson inherited his father's plantation. In 1782 seven years after Mary Young Davis and Daniel DeJarnette's marriage, George Davis' estate was divided among his children, each receiving a portion of equal value in slaves and pounds (current money).[37] As their guardian, Daniel DeJarnette managed the estates of his stepchildren.[38]

Daniel and Mary had one child, Nancy DeJarnette, who was under ten years of age when Mary died about 1785.[39] Within the next two years, Daniel married Elizabeth Davis, his late wife's daughter by her first husband, George, and moved his family to Hanover County. They were in Hanover County when Daniel and Elizabeth sold their Middlesex County property in 1788.[40]

Elizabeth Davis' sister Catharine married John Jackson, the friend named as the executor in George Davis' will.[41] The other two Davis children, Williamson and Mary, died about 1792, possibly at the same time in Hanover County, as inventories of their estates were recorded on the same date.[42] Not long before he died intestate, Williamson's sale of twenty-five acres of land (yet to be conveyed) to Cheslee Daniel in 1791, indicates he had recently come of age.[43] This indenture names the heirs of Williamson: *Catharine and Elizabeth the wifes of the said Dejarnett and Jackson being his Sisters of the whole blood and Nancy being a sister of the half blood and also being the only next of kindred....*

Daniel DeJarnette died almost five years after he wrote his will in Hanover County in April 1790; his will was recorded in Hanover County on February 5, 1795. His witnesses were his first wife's two brothers, William and Williamson Young, and his second wife, Elizabeth's brother Williamson Davis, who did not survive him. Besides his wife, Daniel's heirs were his eldest daughter, Nancy and the five children he had by Elizabeth: William Young DeJarnette, Mary DeJarnette, Elizabeth DeJarnette, Catherine DeJarnette and Daniel DeJarnette.[44]

Susanna DeJarnette

(346;298-299) Susanna DeJarnette not only remained at home to be with her parents, but was the one who went to help with other members of the family who were sick. She helped tend the family of her sister, Ann Price when a smallpox epidemic struck. Susanna DeJarnette gave a deposition in a suit brought by Dr. Lynn, the attending physician against John Price for under payment of his fees. She was questioned at Chesterfield in Caroline County, on November 15, 1790 about the care that little Susanna Price had not received from Dr. Lynn when she was ill with smallpox. Susanna DeJarnette stated that she was thirty-three years old at the time of the deposition, and that Dr. Lynn had made only brief calls to the family while the whole family was ill with smallpox, and that he denied the administration of some medicine they believed would have been helpful. Little Susanna died after several days illness. From this deposition, Susanna DeJarnette is known to have been born in 1757.[45]

Ann DeJarnette

(346;299) Ann DeJarnette, known as Anna, was perhaps even younger than her sister Susanna, for she was usually mentioned after her sisters in her father, Joseph DeJarnette's deeds of gifts. She married John Price, brother of her sister Mary's husband Richard Price.[46] The 1737 marriage of the Price brothers' parents, John Price and Ann Younger, was recorded in the Middlesex County Christ Church Parish Register. The register also notes the births of John and Ann's first two sons: Thomas Price on March 13, 1738, and John Price on March 11, 1740.[47] This researcher questions whether the John Price born in 1740 is the same John L. Price who died in Cumberland County seventy-seven years later, leaving a widow and six children.[48] The hypothesis that a later-born son of John Price and Ann Younger may have been given the name John L. Price after the death of his brother John, born in 1740, seems reasonable. Supporting this is the 1771 will of John Price of Essex naming his son John last of four sons, but naming firstborn Thomas first.[49] Anna would have been about twenty years younger than her husband had he been born in 1740.

In Essex County the Prices were of the Parish of St. Ann, for which there are no surviving registers to make known either the birth dates for the children born after Thomas and John, or any death dates. In 1769 John Price of Essex purchased 416 acres in Cumberland County from Ambrose and Elizabeth Wright.[50] John's will directed that this land be equally divided between his wife during her life or widowhood, and his son-in-law Stark Boulware. After his wife's decease, her interest was to go to their four sons, Thomas, Richard, William and John;[51] but only John was still living at the settlement of the elder John Price's estate in 1792.[52] Ann Younger Price had died sometime after giving her interest in her husband's estate to her son John in 1778.[53] At the time of the gift, she was in Halifax County, Virginia, where Younger relatives from Essex County were living.

John L. and Anna DeJarnette Price remained in Cumberland on the property received from his parents. In 1787 the entire family of four suffered through a smallpox epidemic. John and their little daughter

Susanna were "dangerously sick," Susanna succumbing several days after being nursed by her Aunt Susanna DeJarnette of Caroline.[54]   John L. died intestate in 1817.[55] In 1820 Anna and her children, Elizabeth Williams, Mary DeJarnette, Sophia Price and John P. Price sold their shares of John L. Price's estate to Anna's sons William DeJarnette Price and Warner Williams Price.[56] Anna lived for the next twenty-two years with her son William who wrote in an 1842 letter to Robert M. Burton of Tennessee, *My mother Anna Price is living and confined to her bed the greater part of her time. Her deposition was taken two or three years past...*[57] Late in the year 1842, a Cumberland County court order directed an inventory and appraisement be made of the estate of Anna Price, deceased.

Except for Susanna who died young, the Cumberland estate records of John L. and Anna DeJarnette Price identify their children. Elizabeth Price married Warner Williams and resided in Buckingham County. Mary Pemberton Price (also known as Polly and Marie) married her cousin, James DeJarnette, and resided in Pittsylvania County before moving to Rockingham County, North Carolina. Sophia W. Price and her husband, John Smith migrated to Wilson County, Tennessee. Warner W. Price and his wife Susan E. Walke lived in Cumberland until two years before he died, when he moved to Prince Edward. William DeJarnette Price married Mary A. Wright and continued to live in Cumberland. John P. Price and his wife Amelia Young had several children who went to Kentucky and urged others in the family to come west. Their letters reveal the hardships of those who sought a "better life" west of their origins and believed they had found it.[58]

(349-356;302-308)
Gen. 7   **JOSEPH DEJARNETTE II**

(352;305)   The cemeteries on the lands of *Poplar Grove* and of *Spring Grove* have been identified in Mr. Collins' book, *Cemeteries of Caroline County, vol 2.*[59] *Poplar Grove* was known as the "old DeJarnette homeplace", the home having burned in the 1940s and a new home now occupies the site. This home was located on CR 664, the Balty Road, just off CR 601, the road to Golansville and Cedar Fork Road. The graves in this cemetery date from birth dates in the mid-1800s to death dates in the late 1800s. The *Spring Grove* cemeteries are located on what has been identified as Cox's Flats, originally a part of the DeJarnette lands and also a more recent one at the present *Spring Grove* home, some 200 yards north of the house.

(357-362;309-312)
Gen. 6   **JOHN DEJARNETTE**

No gravestones have been found for JOHN DEJARNETTE and his wife, FRANCES FAVOR DEJARNETTE.

DEJARNETTE FAMILY

Gen. 9 <u>JEAN deJARNAT</u>	m	<u>MARY MUMFORD</u>
Issue: Elias	m	Elizabeth (—?—)
John	m	
Elizabeth	m	Edward McGehee
Mary	m	
Daniel	m	Martha Ford
JOSEPH	m	MARY PEMBERTON
Ellenor	m	Jacob McGehee
Mumford (p)	m	
Gen. 8 <u>JOSEPH DEJARNETTE I</u>	m	<u>MARY PEMBERTON</u>
Issue: Mary	m	(1) Richard Price
	m	(2) Archibald Wright
James Pemberton	m	(1) Edna George
	m	(2) Mary Saunders, widow
	m	(3) Elizabeth Pillow
JOSEPH II	m	MARY HAMPTON

97

Elizabeth		m	George Richardson
Daniel		m	(1) Mary Young Davis widow
		m	(2) Elizabeth Davis
Susanna		m	William Bourne
Ann		m	John Price
Rebecca		m	Thomas Richardson

Gen. 7 JOSEPH DEJARNETTE II		m	MARY HAMPTON
Issue: JOHN		m	FRANCES FAVOR
Joseph III		m	Phoebe Sale
Mary		m	Edward Weathers
Daniel		m	(1) Jane Coleman
		m	(2) Hulda Coleman
Elliott		m	Elizabeth Coleman
Ann		m	Samuel Coleman, Jr.

Gen. 6 JOHN DEJARNETTE		m	FRANCES FAVOR
Issue: Joseph IV			d.s.p.
MARY		m	JOHN W. PEATROSS
Frances		m	Richard Norment

Notes

1. The research and articles of Dorothy Granholm Hankins, 101 Holsworth Rd, Williamsburg, VA 23185 is presented for these children of Joseph DeJarnette I; Earl C. and May Miller Frost, *DeJarnette and Allied Families in America, 1699-1954* (San Bernardino, CA: privately printed, 1954) 186; see also *"Finding Mary's Lost Identity," Magazine of Virginia Genealogy* 29(1991): 79-91.

2. Affidavit of James McDearmon, *Revolutionary War Pension File VA* W18460, The National Archives, Washington, D.C.

3. Dorothy Granholm Hankins, *"Finding Mary's Lost Identity," Magazine of Virginia Genealogy* 29 (1991): 79-91.

4. *Cumberland County Will Book 2* 280.

5. *Prince Edward County Will Book 3* 403-405.

6. Abner and Mary Watson,*Rockingham County, North Carolina Wills and Estate Settlements,* North Carolina State Archives, Raleigh, NC.

7. Marriage Bonds of Prince Edward and Cumberland counties.

8. *Charlotte County US Census 1810;* William Price listed with two white males under 10; *Prince Edward County US Census 1820,* William Price listed with one white male under 10.

9. *Campbell County Marriage Register #1* 130; *Campbell County Deed Book 22* 255; *Deed Book 23* 125; *Campbell County Land Tax Records:* 1830s and 1840s.

10. *Cumberland County Deed Book 4* 415,416.

11. *Cumberland County Loose Suit Papers, 1770s* Library of Virginia, Richmond, VA.

12. *Virginia Military Records* (Baltimore: Genealogical Publishing Co, 1983) 677-679.

13. *Revolutionary War Pension File VA* W18460; Family Bible Record; Hankins 91.

14. *Microfilm Attendance Record,* University of Pennsylvania Archives, Philadelphia, PA.

15. *Buckingham County Personal Property Tax, 1815, District 2,* Library of Virginia, Richmond, VA.

16. *Account Book of Dr. John P. Mettauer* Sec. 2 77, Mss1 M5677a 50, Virginia Historical Society, Richmond, VA.

17. Obituary for Mrs. Mary Wright, *Richmond Enquirer,* December 9, 1815 3.

18. *Revolutionary War Pension File VA* W18460.

19. Ibid.

20. *Caroline County Court Order Book, 1785-1787* 162.

21. *Mecklenburg County Court Order Book 7* 652.

22. *Caroline County, Virginia Land Tax Lists 1787-1799* (Miami Beach, FL: TLC Genealogy, 1991) 115.

23. *Mecklenburg County Guardians Accounts* Box 1, Library of Virginia, Richmond, VA.

24. Ibid.

25. Ibid.

26. *Mecklenburg County Court Order Book 12* 262.

27. *Mecklenburg County Guardians Accounts.*

28. *Mecklenburg County Will Book 5* 62-64.

29. John Vogt and T. William Kethley, Jr., *Mecklenburg County Marriages 1765-1853* (Athens, GA: Iberian Publishing Co, 1989) 78, 261.

30. *Mecklenburg County Deed Book 11* 356.

31. Vogt and Kethley 260, 261.

32. *Essex County Deed Book 31* 322.

33. National Society of Colonial Dames of America in the State of Virginia, *The Parish Register of Christ Church, Middlesex County, Va. from 1653 to 1812.* 1897 (Baltimore: Clearfield, rep. 1990) 201.
34. *Middlesex County Will Book F* 2-3.
35. *Middlesex County Court Order Book, 1758-1767* 465.
36. *Essex County Guardian Book 2* 45-46.
37. *Middlesex County Will Book F* 271-272.
38. *Middlesex County Orphans Book A-1* 170-171.
39. *Middlesex County Court Order Book 1784-1786* 268.
40. *Middlesex County Deed Book 10* 82-83.
41. *Middlesex County Will Book F* 271-272.
42. *Middlesex County Will Book G* 290.
43. *MIddlesex County Deed Book 11* 126-129.
44. Will of Daniel DeJarnette, Accession Number 24838, Library of Virginia, Richmond, VA.
45. Deposition of Susanna DeJarnette, suit *Lynn vs Price*, Prince Edward County Court Papers, Box 4, Library of Virginia, Richmond, VA.
32. Hankins 80.
47. Chamberlayne 170, 146, 150.
48. *Cumberland County Will Book 5* 1, 2; *Cumberland County Will Book 8* 688, 689; *Cumberland County Deed Book 16* 135-138.
49. *Essex County Will Book 12* 448, 449.
50. *Cumberland County Deed Book 4* 415, 416.
51. *Essex County Will Book 12* 448, 449.
52. *Cumberland County Court Order Book 16* 62, 63; *Cumberland County Loose Suit Papers* Library of Virginia, Richmond, VA.
53. *Cumberland County Deed Book 5* 554.
54. Deposition of Susanna Dejarnette, suit *Lynn vs Price*, Prince Edward County Court Papers, Box 4, Library of Virginia, Ricmond, VA.
55. *Cumberland County Will Book 8* 688,689.
56. *Cumberland County Deed Book 16* 135-137.
57. Copy of letter in possession of Gustine Agee in the papers of Reta C. Kirk, "*John L. Price and Anna DeJarnette*".
58. *Edwin Y. Price Papers*, Special Collections, Perkins Library, Duke University, Durham, NC.
59. Collins 48-53.

Lynn vs Price, 1787

JOHN FAVOR

Gen. 9

It took a great deal of research to identify the wife of JOHN DEJARNETTE, and she was known only as Fanny F. at first; finally her full name emerged, FRANCES FAVOR. It seemed that the Theophilus Favor who was appeared in the Caroline County records for a brief time must have been her brother, but this was the extent of the information concerning the Favor family. It came as a pleasant revelation to discover that they had roots in nearby St. Ann's Parish, Essex County.

A John Favor, age eighteen, is listed as having arrived in Virginia from London on the *Bonaventure* on January 2, 1635. He would have been a generation earlier than the JOHN FAVOR of Essex County, and he cannot be found in other early records. A Luke Favor witnessed a deed in Essex County in March 1661.[1] It can be seen that the records of Essex County need to be researched more exhaustively, but several generations of the Favor family can be reconstructed from the wills executed by each generation.

John Favor executed his will on the 24th of December 1722 and signed it John Faver. It read as follows:[2]

In the name of God Amen I John ffavor of the County of Essex being sick and weak of body but good sound disposing memory praise be given to God for the same do make this my Last Will & Testament in manner and form following that is to say first and principally I resign my Soul into the mercyfull hands of Almighty God my Creator assuredly hoping through the merits of my blessed Savior to obtain remission of all my Sins and my body I commit to the Earth whence it was taken to be buryed without any issue by my Exec. herein after named & as for my worldly goods & Estate the Lord hath lent me I dispose of as followth, Imprimis
Item I give unto my wife Suzana ffavor additon & her oldest Son John ffavor the plantation called porige pot and all the Land belonging to it to him & his heirs & the rest and residue of my Estate after my debts & funeral expenses discharged to be equally divided amongst my wife and all my Children & I do give this Lease of Land during the time to my wife during her widowhood & to my Eldest Sons John ffavor Winifret and THEOPHILUS ffAVOR my three Children born of Mary ffavor I do make Executs. of this my Last Will & Testament revoquin all other wills heretofore by me made and in case my wife Suzana will not stand to this my Will and Testament not withstanding what is given above I cut of all her Children with a English Shelin from any part or parasell of any of my Estate
Witness my hand & Seal this 24th of Xber 1722.   *[signed] John Faver*
Signed Sealed and delivered in presence of Philip [his P mark] Coupeland and John Baxter
At a court held for Essex County on Tuesday ye 21st day of Jany 1723. The within last Will & Testament of John ffavor was presented in court by Susanna ffavor his relict who made oath thereto as adminix. with the will annext & being proved by ye oath of Philip Copeland & John Baxter witnesses thereto was admitted to record.
       Test [signed] W[illiam] Beverley

The bond signed by Susanna Favor, with Henry Oswald and John Motley as her securities was acknowledged by John Lomax, William Daingerfield, Thomas Waring and Francis Thornton in the amount of £100. Susanna signed with her mark, as did John Motley, while Henry Oswald signed his name. It was noted that Theophilus Favor was a minor and the goods and chattels due him would be turned over to him when he came of age.

The will is confusing in that John identified John as the oldest son of Susanna Favor when he bequeathed him the plantation *Porige Pot*. Further on in the will he identified his eldest sons, John Favor, Winifred and Theophilus Favor as being three children born of Mary Favor. He then referred to "all of Susanna's children".

The name of John Motley appears as security for Susanna's bond, and the names of Motley men appear in deeds for land on Occupacia Creek adjoining Theophilus Favor at a later time (1754). Apparently the land on which John lived remained with the two generations of Theophilus Favor. The inventory of John

Favor's estate is recorded with a total value of £69/5/9. He owned a number of head of cattle, hogs, sheep and a horse and a mare, along with all of the necessities of maintaining his plantation and a comfortable home.

addition
Gen. 8

THEOPHILUS FAVOR I

THEOPHILUS FAVOR inherited the plantation of his father. From selected deeds it is learned that he purchased thirty acres of additional land from John and Tabitha Motley on October 11, 1754.[3] He purchased an additional eighty-one acres from James and Sarah Charles, also land that had been owned by John Motley, in January 1757.[4] Theophilus is identified as living in St. Ann's Parish, which is the area through which Occupacia Creek flows.

The maiden name of the wife of Theophilus Favor has not been found; however, her given name was ESTHER, as evidenced from a deed executed July 25, 1740 to Edward Rowzee.[5] She must have died before Theophilus made his will as she is not mentioned and he asked that Theophilus, Jr. bring up his two daughters Rosemond and Betty Favor.[6] Theophilus wrote his will on January 27, 1758. It was recorded at Tappahannock on February 18, 1760. Theophilus signed his will himself and identified himself as Senior. Caleb Lindsey, Henry Motley and John Mitchell witnessed the will. While his two sons, Theophilus and Thomas were appointed executors of the will, only Theophilus qualified.

Theophilus left the plantation where he lived to his son, THEOPHILUS and to his son, Thomas the lands at his quarter amounting to 162 acres. His son Caleb was to have the land if either of them died without heirs, in lieu of that Caleb was to have £50 current money to buy land. His Negroes were to be equally divided with the rest of his estate to all of his children, whom he named as follows: Theophilus, Thomas, Caleb, Rosemond and Betty Favor. He also made a bequest to Elizabeth Keelling's child called Mary, thirty pounds current money to be paid at the age of her marriage, he further gave Elizabeth Keelling *the bed and furniture she now lives in.* There is no further explanation of this bequest.

The slaves of Theophilus were divided and set apart according to his will for the use of his children, in each case with an equitable valuation of between £140 and £150:[7]

> To Theophilus Favor: Lucy, a woman and Annaky, a girl.
> To Thomas Favor: Phillis, a woman and Nan, a girl.
> To Caleb Favor: Tom, a man; Jenny, a girl; and Ben, a boy.
> To Rosemond Favor: Bristol, a man; July, a woman; and Betty, a girl.
> To Betty Favor: Billy, a boy; Dinah, a woman; and Letty, a girl.

The son, Thomas Favor died between March 1, 1786 when he wrote his will and April 18, 1786 when his will was recorded.[8] He named his wife Susanna and his children: John, Clara, Mary, Thomas, Susanna, George, Elizabeth and Ann. His land was to be sold at the death of his wife. He named his wife and his sons John, Thomas and George the executors of his estate. He signed his name to his will.

addition
Gen. 7

THEOPHILUS FAVOR II

By the time THEOPHILUS FAVOR inherited his father's plantation in St. Ann's Parish, it consisted of 244½ acres. His brother, Thomas owned an additional 162 acres bequeathed him by his father.[9] Little is known of the life of Theophilus, but his will reveals much about his family.

...Item I lend unto my Loving wife ELIZABETH FAVOR the one Third part of my Estate During her natural life and after my wifes Decease I give the Negros and Personal Estate lent to be Equally Divided amongst my seven Children William, Richard, James, Theophilus, Jenny, Elizabeth and Fanny Favor....Item I give my Son William all the Lands I purchased of Edwin Motley and Thomas Callis...if he departs this life before becoming of age I give

the said Lands...to my son James...Item I give unto my son Richard the Land whereon I now live...if he dies before he comes of age I give the land to my son Theophilus...I give my wearing apparel to be equally divided between my two sons James and Theophilus...Item I give the remainder of my Estate to be Equally divided between my five children Hereafter named...James, Theophilus, Jenney, Elizabeth and Fanney Favor...I nominate my brother Thomas Favor and my son William Favor my executors.   *[signed]   Theophilus Favor*

John Rouzee, Lewis Thomas and John Favor witnessed the will. It was presented to the court on December 15, 1783 and Thomas Favor and William Favor offered proof and it was so recorded. It should be noted that the entry of the will in the will book consistently showed the name Favor as spelled Faver. Hancock Lee signed the recordation as Clerk of Court. It would seem that the Favors were from the same cultural background as the DeJarnettes, as each generation of men signed their wills.

An entry in the order book provides further insight concerning the daughter, Frances (Fanny) Favor.[10] On the motion of JOHN DEJARNETTE and Fanny his wife, who was FANNY FAVOR, orphan of Theophilus Favor, it was ordered that Janey Sale, the administratrix of Joseph Sale account for the guardianship of Fanny before the Justices: Major William Saunders, Thomas Burke, John Sutton, William Jones and James Garnett, or any of the three of them in attendance at court July 21, 1800. This confirms the information inferred from the Chancery Court suit in Caroline County, where the letter of cousin Fanny Abbott to her parents had provided the only information about Fanny and John's marriage. Fanny must not have been of age when she and John married.

The son Theophilus was in Caroline County briefly. It is known from the records of Culpeper County that several of the Favor family migrated west by the late 1700s.

FAVOR FAMILY

Gen.10	JOHN FAVOR	m	(1) MARY (—?—)
Issue:	John	m	
	Winifred	m	
	THEOPHILUS	m	ESTHER (—?—)
	John Favor	m	(2) Susanna (—?—)
Gen. 9	THEOPHILUS FAVOR I	m	ESTHER (—?—)
	THEOPHILUS	m	ELIZABETH (—?—)
	Thomas	m	Susanna (—?—)
	Caleb	m	
	Rosemond	m	
	Betty	m	
Gen. 8	THEOPHILUS FAVOR II	m	ELIZABETH (—?—)
	William	m	
	Richard	m	
	James	m	
	Theophilus	m	
	Jenney	m	
	Elizabeth	m	
	FRANCES	m	JOHN DEJARNETTE

Notes

1. *Essex County Deed Book 2 230.*
2. *Essex County Will Book 4 43-46.*
3. *Essex County Deed Book 27 71.*
4. Ibid., 253.
5. *Essex County Deed Book 22 157.*
6. *Essex County Will Book 11 243-244.*
7. *Essex County Will Book 11 262.*

8. *Essex County Will Book 22 157.*
9. *Essex County Land Tax Records, 1782.*
10. *Essex County Court Order Book 35 416.*

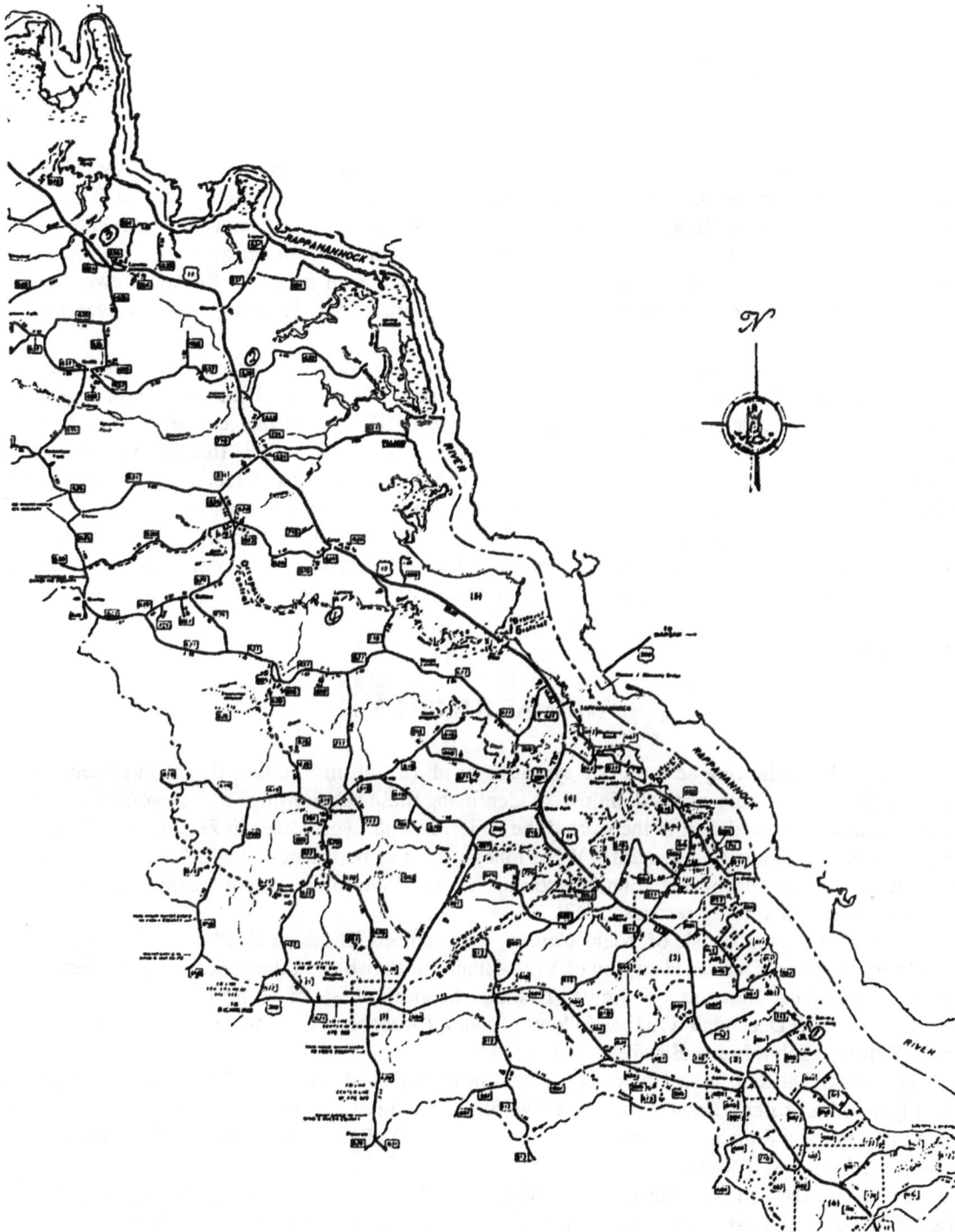

ESSEX COUNTY

WILLIAM HAMPTON

Gen. 13

(365;315)   No further information has been searched concerning WILLIAM HAMPTON; however, some clarification of the life of the Reverend Thomas Hampton, a contemporary of William's seems appropriate. This Thomas Hampton came to Kecoughtan Parish as its minister. He later moved to Nansemond in Upper Norfolk County. As has been stated in the account of the life of William Hampton, there seems to have been a family connection, but this has not been defined. Edward Lewis Goodwin in writing of the Colonel Church in Virginia[1] appears to have confused this Thomas with the Reverend Thomas Hampton, the son of William.

      Mr. Goodwin's background account of the Reverend Hampton of Nansemond Parish does seem to establish the fact that William and Thomas were not brothers. He identified this first Thomas as being the son of William Hampton, clerk of Reigate, Surry. He matriculated at New College, Oxford March 11, 1624/25 at the age of sixteen, attaining a B.A. from Corpus Christi College, January 3, 1626/27 (he was once called Morris Hampton). As has been related, he became the rector of James City Parish and moved to Jamestown Island by 1639. The further account of this Reverend Thomas Hampton has been confused by Mr. Goodwin in extending his activities to those of the Reverend THOMAS HAMPTON, who served parishes in York and New Kent counties and was the son of William Hampton of Elizabeth City County and later, Gloucester County.

(369-372;319-322)
Gen. 12

THOMAS HAMPTON I

      The following account is a synthesis of all of the information that it has been possible to gather. The court records are not as definitive in identifying these relationships as one would like. There are apparently misconceptions drawn in the work done by Dr. Joseph Lyon Miller in The Virginia Hamptons[2] and in The Venturers by Virginia G. Meynard.[3] What follows seem to be the most logical conclusions that can be reached without positive proof that John, the son of Francis Hampton of Isle of Wight County, was the one found in the Frederick County records, 1747[4].

      Thomas Hampton of Isle of Wight County, who married Elizabeth Bridle[5] is believed to have been the son of the Reverend Thomas Hampton of York-Hampton Parish , and the grandson of William and Joane Hampton of Hampfield, Gloucester County.[6] Thomas Hampton of Isle of Wight County named his children in his will (recorded 9 December 1703) as follows: Francis (probably named for Francis Biddle, the father of Elizabeth Biddle),[7] John, Mary, Elizabeth and Sarah.[8]

      The will of the son, John Hampton, of the Lower Parish of Isle of Wight County (son of the above Thomas) named his brother, Francis and John Hampton, the son of Francis.[9] The will of Elizabeth Hampton Neville named her son Francis as an executor of her will (1747). Dr. Miller wrote that Francis Hampton had sons: Andrew, John and Thomas Hampton.

      It is John, the son of Francis, who is believed to be found in Frederick County in 1747 when he executed a deed of gift, as "John Hampton the Elder" to his two sons, George Hampton and Thomas Hampton.[10] He gave them "all and singular of my estate real and personal that I now am possessed with.....It was signed by John Hampton Sener and recorded 3 November 1747.

      The will of John Hampton was recorded August 15, 1751[11] in Frederick County; in it he named his wife, Lydia and sons: William, John, Andrew and David. He referred to his six children. Dr. Miller named additionally, George and Thomas and stated that John had no daughters. John named his brother, Thomas

Hampton as the executor of his estate. While it has not been possible to conclusively identify John as having migrated from Isle of Wight County, there are enough references linking the families that it provides good evidence that it is this John Hampton who was the father of George Hampton.

An article in *Tidewater Virginia Families, A Magazine of History and Genealogy*[12] by Frank Corum,[13] entitled *"The Benefit of an Unusual Name: Charles Chester Colson Hampton"*, chronicles the life and descendants of the son of George Hampton. This account also helps identify the earlier generations and their migration to the north and west in Virginia.

(373-380;323-329)
Gen. 11

JOHN HAMPTON I

John Hampton (the son)
(377-378;327) Anthony Hampton, the son of John and Margaret Wade Hampton, died June 30, 1776 in Spartenburg District, South Carolina. He married Elizabeth Preston, the daughter of Edward Preston on March 10, 1741. She was born March 10, 1720 and died June 30, 1776. Both she and her husband were massacred by Indians, along with their son, Preston and their grandchild, the son of their daughter, Elizabeth Hampton Harrison. There is a Daughters of the American Revolution Historical Marker memorializing the site of the massacre and their graves near SR 29 at Greer, South Carolina.[14]

Anthony and Elizabeth were the great-grandparents of General Wade Hampton of the Civil War reputation. As a personal aside, the grandparents of James W. Davis were living during the Civil War in South Carolina, and were ardent admirers of General Wade Hampton. This carried down to Jim's childhood when his grandfather, John Calhoun Davis and grandmother, Emily Watts Davis related accounts of General Hampton. In honor of his grandmother and General Hampton, he taught his horse to kneel when he gave the command "Salute General Hampton", much to the delight of his grandmother.

(381-382;330-331)
Gen. 10

THOMAS HAMPTON II

(383-384;332-333)
Gen. 9

JOHN HAMPTON II

Jacob Hampton
(383;332) Correspondence with Dr. M. Bruce Sullivan[15] provides information about Jacob Hampton, the possible son of John Hampton II. Reuben Hampton owned land on Hickory Creek in Warren County, Tennessee in 1808; he migrated from Wilkes County, North Carolina by way of Kentucky. In the process of searching for the father of Reuben, Jacob Hampton and his associations with the Hampton family of Wilkes County became the likely candidate. Jacob Hampton of Caroline County deeded land to John Hampton III in 1777 and deeded additional land to James Shelton in 1778. He disappeared from the Caroline County records after 1778. He may well have been the Jacob Hampton who later lived in Wilkes County, North Carolina.

(385-390;334-338)
Gen. 8

JOHN HAMPTON III

HAMPTON FAMILY

Gen.14	LAURENCE HAMPTON	m	(1) unknown
		m	(2) unknown
Issue:	WILLIAM	m	JOANE (—?—)
	Richard	m	

Ann	m	Henry Rand
Elizabeth	m	
Laurence	m	(—?—) Garrett
Philadelphia	m	

Gen. 13 <u>WILLIAM HAMPTON</u>   m   <u>JOANE (—?—)</u>

Issue:		
William	m	
Grace	m	
Elizabeth	m	
THOMAS	m	UNKNOWN

Gen. 12 <u>THOMAS HAMPTON I</u>   m   <u>UNKNOWN</u>

Issue:		
JOHN	m	(1) MARY MANN
	m	(2) (—?—) Cary
Mary	m	(1) (—?—) Duke
	m	(2) (—?—) Wade
Thomas	m	Elizabeth Bridle

Gen. 11 <u>JOHN HAMPTON I</u>   m   <u>(1) MARY MANN</u>

Issue:		
THOMAS	m	MARY (—?—)
John	m	Margaret Wade
William	m	Martha Catlett widow
Richard	m	Martha (—?—)
John Hampton	m	(2) (—?—) Cary

Issue:		
Cary	m	

Gen. 10 <u>THOMAS HAMPTON II</u>   m   <u>UNKNOWN</u>

Issue:		
JOHN	m	UNKNOWN
Jacob (p)	m	

Gen. 9 <u>JOHN HAMPTON II</u>   m   <u>UNKNOWN</u>

Issue:		
JOHN	m	ELIZABETH (—?—)

Gen. 8 <u>JOHN HAMPTON III</u>   m   <u>ELIZABETH (—?—)</u>

Issue:		
George	m	Mary (—?—)
Anna	m	(1) (—?—) Collins
	m	(2) (—?—) Northrup
MARY	m	JOSEPH DEJARNETTE II
Frances	m	Edmund Jones
Sarah	m	Edwin Gibson
Jane	m	William Ball

Notes

1. Edward Lewis Goodwin, *The Colonial Church in Virginia* (1927) 276.

2. Miller, Dr. Joseph Lyon, *The Virginia Hamptons.* Howard Hampton Papers, Mss. Southwest Collection, Texas Tech University, Lubbock, TX.

3. Virginia G. Meynard, *The Venturers* (Greenville: Southern Historical Press,1981). (see Ms Meynard in the 1991 reprint 344) further identified a George Hampton as the son of William Hampton, (descended from John Hampton of Gloucester County) who died in Stafford County in 1749/50, from his will. Inspection of his will, recorded 13 March 1749/50, shows that William left his wife Martha Catlett Hampton "all my estate" with no mention of any of his children. *Stafford County Deed Book* Liber O: 85-86. See this book for a generally good account of the early Hampton family, and descendants of William.

4. *Frederick County Deed Book 1* 323.

5. V.L.H.D., *Tidewater Virginia Families.* 321. See account of the early Hampton family and through John to Mary Hampton who married John DeJarnette.

6. Davis 315, 321.

7. Davis 321; *Isle of Wight County Record of Wills, Deeds, Etc 2*, 1689.

8. *Isle of Wight County Will & Deed Book 2*, 1661-1719: 459-460.

9. Isle of Wight County Will Book 5 79.

10. *Frederick County Deeds 1* 323.

11. *Frederick County Will Book 1, 1743-1751* 488-489.

12. *TVF* 4 (1995): 3-11.

13. Frank Corum is an accomplished researcher and lives at 750 Oakwood Lane, Madisonville, KY 42431-8638. This genealogical study was made in 1991.

14. Correspondence with Chris Adams, 3146 Maryola Ct, Lafayette, CA 94549, from material given her by Mary Hardy Merritt, 825 Bayshore Dr, #202, Pensacola, FL 32507.

15. M. Bruce Sullivan, MD, 84 Cross Creek Park, Birmingham, AL 35213.

KING WILLIAM COUNTY

SECTION IV

THE PEATROSS ANCESTORS

CAMPBELL

Gen. 9,8

(396-404;344-352)
Gen. 7

JOSEPH CAMPBELL

(394-395;342-343)   Further investigation of the land holdings of James Campbell provide greater confirmation of the fact that he was likely a contemporary of JOSEPH CAMPBELL, and very likely his brother. Through tracing the deeds first from the Land Tax Record alternation entries where James' land was sold, to the present deeds following the progression through sales and land transactions, his land has been located.[1] Seventy-five acres of his land was sold in 1787 to Moses Standley and the remainder, 535 acres were sold in 1789 to William Dabney. The records seem to confirm the fact that James did not leave a widow or children.

The land of James Campbell has been located just off CR 632 and in the triangle of CR 633 and CR 626, south of the intersection called Welchs and east of US Route 1 and Interstate 95. GEORGE CAMPBELL apparently lived in the area of Ginney Bridge, now known as Guinea. This area is north and west of Welch and in the same general area. There is no direct relationship between the land holdings of James and Joseph, nor in the area in which they lived; nor is there any evidence of any distribution of land or estate between the two.

(396;344) A great deal of time was spent trying to locate the homesite of Joseph Campbell from the less-than-helpful land tax records, there being no surviving deeds. Information has come to light, with the help of Herbert Collins and many trips driving through the roads of Caroline County. *Poplar Grove* has been identified as the homeplace of JOSEPH and ELIZABETH CAMPBELL. The farm still exists, with a white farmhouse at the end of a lane on the west side of SR 207 southwest of the intersection with CR 601. The original part of the house goes back to about 1788, which is in keeping with the time that Joseph would have built a substantial house for his family. The initials of Zaccheus Campbell are carved in a mantel in the home. It has now been learned that there is a family burying ground on the property, and since no gravestones have survived, one would be inclined to think it dates back to the time of Joseph and Elizabeth.

Matthew Campbell
(400;338) The daughter of Matthew and Margaret Campbell who married Ira Dickinson has been identified.[2] Ira was born c.1803 and died between April and August 1860, when his will was probated in Caroline County. He married on January 9, 1826 Jane Campbell; they had no children.

Elizabeth Campbell
(400;348) correction: Elizabeth Campbell married Reuben Mitchell. **Reuben Mitchell died in 1796** in Caroline County.[3]

Elliott Campbell
(402;350) Of the children of Elliott and Elizabeth (in what is believed to be the order of their birth):
(1) Joseph W., born March 23, 1811, died unmarried, drowning in a swollen river on a trip to visit his brother William in Arkansas.
(2) William Hugh Campbell, formerly of Caroline County, Virginia married in Washington County, Arkansas Miss Julia Rutherford, the daughter of Captain John Rutherford, on March 21, 1843.[4] William Hugh was

born July 6, 1813 and went to Washington County (1840) after he finished his enlisted time in the army. He served in the War Between the States, became ill and was sent home, where he died December 18, 1861, just one month after his enlistment. He left Julia with nine young children and the tenth on the way. Their children were: John Elliott, James Bayless, William Hugh, Joseph Wilson, Winnie Elizabeth, Julia, Thomas Harrison, Mary Henderson, Noel Graves and Richard Dye. Julia Rutherford Campbell died December 30, 1885.

(3) James Campbell married and lived in Powhatan County.

(4) Mary L.(Elizabeth) Campbell correction, 2nd edition: was the daughter of Elliott and Elizabeth Wilson Campbell. She married her cousin, John Henderson on October 21, 1828. They had five daughters and one son: Elizabeth, born December 22, 1829; Sarah, born c.1830; Lucy Ann, born February 25, 1831; Mary Elizabeth, born February 5, 1833; Thaddeus, born c.1834; and Virginia Ellen Henderson, born c.1836.[5]

(5) Elizabeth Peatross Campbell married William Burruss, June 2, 1846.

(6) Dorothy, born January 3, 1823, married Edward Swann on October 26, 1841;

(7) Atwell Elliott, born August 13, 1819, never married and was killed during the Civil War (1863) in Caroline County.

(8) Sarah Jane married Phillip Sidney Rennolds May 20, 1850 and lived in Richmond.[6]

(9) Mannaseh, born April 22, 1828, married in 1866 and took his wife, Emma Allen to live at *Poplar Grove* and lived there until their deaths, he died in 1918.

Note: It can be seen that this listing does not agree with the previous account of the children of Elliott and Elizabeth Campbell.[7]

(405-408;353-356)
Gen. 6   **ZACCHEUS CAMPBELL**

While many landmarks and names from the earlier days of Caroline County have remained the same, the roads have changed and it was a continued challenge to identify just where these people lived. Herbert Collins has a better knowledge of the people of Caroline County, their homesites and their associations than any other person. It was he who finally put it all together for this researcher. ZACCHEUS and SARAH ANN TURNER CAMPBELL lived at *Poplar Grove*. Whether his initials carved into the mantle embellished the mantle from his childhood mischief, or whether he carved them as an adult, this was his homeplace. It is believed that he and Sarah Ann, or Sally as she was also called were both buried in the family graveyard on the homeplace. No other children have been identified as being children of Zaccheus and Sally than those already entered in his biographical account.

Zaccheus had regularly exercised his civic duty in casting his vote in the election of representatives to the General Assembly. He was probably upset that he was called upon to give a deposition concerning his activities when the election of delegates in 1822 was contested.[8]

Pursuant to the annexed order & notice We the Subscribers have met this 27th April 1822 at the Bull Church and after being duly sworn do proceed to take the depositions of the following Gentlemen To wit Zacharias [Zaccheus] Campbell being duly sworn saith that he should have gone to the last elections of delegates for the County of Caroline, that he was fixed to start, but the rain prevented him, that he had for ten years past not missed an election in the County and that he expected the polls would be kept open and he should attend the next day. [signed] Zach Campbell

His neighbor Patrick Carnal (Carneal) agreed, and further observed that had the polls stayed open the next day as he believed they would, he too would have voted. Isaac Butler went to great lengths to explain where he lived, how far it was to Chesterfield and to the courthouse, and how it had rained early in the day, stopped then rained a little later in the day. He must have felt righteous about braving the weather.

The site of Bull Church can be identified today as being east of US Route 1 near the intersection of CR 633 and 639. It was probably some three miles or more from where Zaccheus lived and he would probably have ridden horseback to the voting polls.

(407;355) The will of John R. Turner, the husband of Elizabeth Turner (the sister of Sarah Ann Campbell) has survived, naming the children of Elizabeth Turner. John Turner wrote his will on July 23, 1855 and it was recorded in Caroline County on February 8, 1858. He named four sons: Richardson, John William, Eldred and James Watkins Turner. He did not name his wife Elizabeth in his will, and he appointed his son, Richardson his executor. Witnesses to his will were; Richard W. Hutcheson, John W. Peatross and Matthew Peatross.[9]

The Turner family cemetery is believed to be located on the old Turner homeplace, that of Richard and Frances Turner. It is east of SR 2, turning south on SR 30, past Bethel Church almost to the King William County line. Richard Turner died in 1807 and his wife, Frances in 1834 and are believed to be buried in the family cemetery. Their daughters, Sarah married Zaccheus Campbell and Elizabeth married John R. Turner. The place passed to John William Turner, the son of John R. and Elizabeth Turner. The graves are unmarked, but Mr. Collins has identified the names of some of those interred there: John R. Turner, born 1790 and died 1865/6; Elizabeth W. Turner, his wife, born 1790 and died January 13, 1862; John William Turner; Eldred Turner, born 1822 and died July 28, 1894; James Watkins Turner, born 1826 and died August 2, 1857.[10]

(409-417b;357-365)
Gen. 5   SETH CAMPBELL

CAMPBELL FAMILY

Gen. 9 JOHN CAMPBELL	m	(1)Mary Killman
	m	(2)SARAH KILLMAN CAMPBELL
Issue: GEORGE (p)	m	ELIZABETH (—?—)
James	m	

Gen. 8 GEORGE CAMPBELL	m	ELIZABETH (—?—)
Issue: George	m	Caty (—?—
James	m	
William	m	Elizabeth (—?—)
(p) JOSEPH	m	ELIZABETH PEATROSS

Generations 8 and 9 are given with the understanding that, although there is circumstantial evidence to substantiate the relationship, it cannot be documented that George was the son of John and Sarah Campbell. Further, the relationship between these two generations and Joseph Campbell cannot be documented. It is conjectural that George was the father of Joseph.

Gen. 7 JOSEPH CAMPBELL	m	ELIZABETH PEATROSS
Issue: Elizabeth	m	Reuben Mitchell
Matthew	m	Margaret Haley
Jane	m	Caleb Mitchell
Amey	m	Meriday Haley
Joseph, Jr.	m	Rosy Sale
Sarah (Sally)	m	Jeremiah Yarbrough
William	m	Susanna Burruss
Nancy	m	Carter Marshall
ZACCHEUS	m	SARAH ANN TURNER
Dorothea	m	Samuel Alsop
Elliott Peatross	m	Elizabeth Willson

Gen. 6 ZACCHEUS CAMPBELL	m	SARAH ANN TURNER
Issue: SETH	m	SUSANNAH D. CHILES
sons (possibly 3)		
a daughter		

Gen. 5 SETH CAMPBELL	m	SUSANNAH D. CHILES
Issue: FRANCES ANN	m	HENRY COOK PEATROSS
James F.	m	Emuella Wright
Felix Winston	m	Ogenia Burk Collins
Martha	m	William Kelly
Sarah Winston	m	John W. Collins
Henrietta	m	Richard H. Chiles
John W. (Henry)		d.s.p.

Notes

1. *Caroline County Land Tax Records*, 1787-1789; *Caroline County Deed Books*; 49:535; 60:361; 61:26; 65:50, 248; 73:209; 75:67, 136; 86:176; 87:284; 95:190; 97:172; 100:318, 319; 282:6; 364:362. These records have been traced by Ray Campbell, Clerk, Circuit Court, Caroline County.

2. Correspondence with William Dickinson, 312 Twin Bridge Circle, Pleasant Hill, CA 94523.

3. *Caroline County Minute Book*, 1796.

4. Ibid.; *The Arkansas Intelligencer*, Van Buren, AR, March 25. 1843.

5. Mrs. L W Ledgerwood, Jr P O Box 8081, Hot Springs Village, AR 71910.

6. Ledgerwood, unpublished manuscript. The numbers in parentheses indicate the order of birth as given by Mrs. Ledgerwood. The names of the children do not agree with the listing in *Tidewater Virginia Families*.

7. Campbell Family Bible records contributed by Mrs. Ledgerwood.

8. Caroline County Contested Elections, 1822, Box 3, Library of Virginia, Richmond, VA.

9. *Caroline County Will Book, 1858* 637.

10. Herbert R. Collins, *Private Cemeteries, Caroline County, Virginia vol 3 Private Cemeteries* (Westminster, MD: Family Line Publishers, 1998). to be publishied.

JOHN HURT

WILLIAM HURT

TITUS HURT

BENJAMIN HURT

It appears that the Hurt family lived in the same area for all of the early period in Caroline County. Their home place and land was adjoining the Matthew Peatross home place and land, as evidenced by the extended court case concerning the construction of the mill of Matthew Peatross. The home site can be identified today from the location of Matthew Peatross' home site. This site is located in the woods on the east side of SR 2 (US 301), just south of where CR 653 intersects SR 2 on the west side of the highway. There is evidence of the foundations of two house sites and two cemetery sites. the graveyards covered with periwinkle, but with no visible gravestones (1995). The wooded area is located off a dirt road behind the Thomas home (on the east side of SR 2), designated as #28179 for emergency identification. The Hurt land is separated from the Peatross land today by US 301, as it lies on the west side of the highway. There is a family cemetery on the land and evidence of a house site. The cemetery is known to be the Hurt family graveyard, but the grave stones all date from the mid-1800s.

HURT FAMILY

Generations eleven through eight are presented with the understanding that complete documentation of these relationships has not been found. Where documentation has not been available the relationships have been assumed on the basis of court record entries of associations and of land holdings.

Gen.11 WILLIAM HURT		m	(p)MARGARET (—?—)
Issue:	(p) William	m	
	(p) JOHN	m	SARAH (—?—
Gen.10 JOHN HURT		m	SARAH (—?—)
Issue:	WILLIAM	m	ANN (—?—)
	(p) Philemon	m	Elizabeth (—?—)
	(p) John	m	
Gen. 9 WILLIAM HURT		m	ANN (—?—)
Issue:	James	m	Clara (—?—)
	(p) TITUS	m	UNKNOWN
	William	m	
	(p) Moses	m	Ann (—?—)
Gen. 8 TITUS HURT		m	UNKNOWN
Issue:	Titus, Jr.	m	
	BENJAMIN	m	ANN (—?—)
Gen. 7 BENJAMIN HURT		m	ANN (—?—)
Issue:	William	m	Ann Hundley
	Benjamin	m	(1) Frances Richeson
		m	(2) Mary Sutton

ANN	m	MATTHEW PEATROSS
John	m	
Rebecca	m	William Venable
Titus	m	
Molly	m	Willson Turner
Frances	m	
James	m	

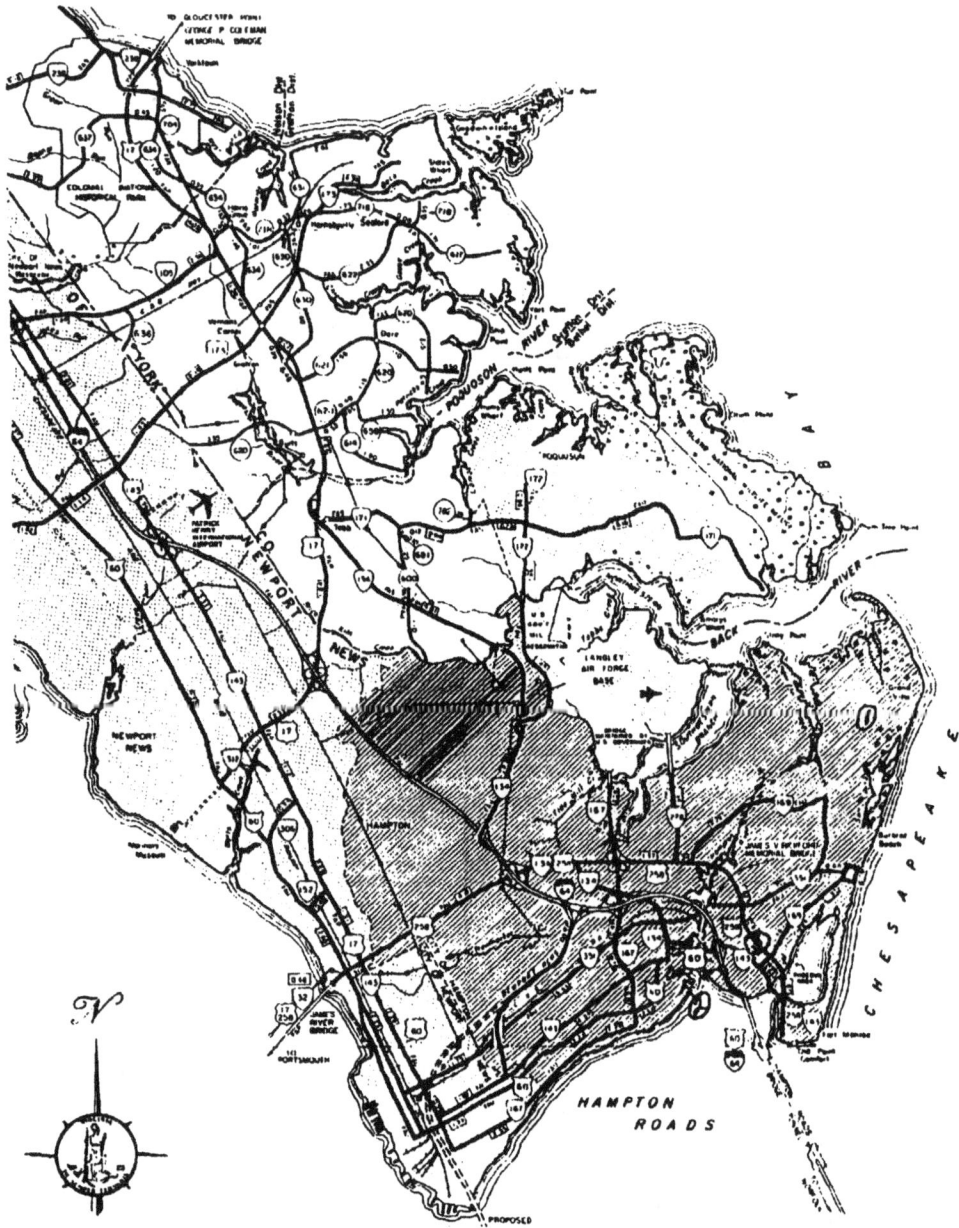

JAMES CITY COUNTY

116

DAVID BELL

Gen. 10,9 (8)

(430-432;376-378)
Gen. 9,8 (7)   **GEORGE BELL**

So often more information has come to light about where the early families lived, than have records of their marriages, their children and their deaths. Within the Quaker community this has been less a problem than in many other families; however, even these records are not complete. A further complication is the fact that geographic names may be repeated within a county, or within two adjoining counties. It has been difficult to visualize where GEORGE BELL lived because this researcher's knowledge of Hanover County placed Beaverdam Creek near the community of Beaverdam in northwestern Hanover County. Only recently has it all come together with regard to where the Bells lived and conducted business.

Beaverdam Creek is in the area of Cold Harbor, in eastern Henrico County, and in fact, one crosses Bell Creek on US Route 360 just east of Mechanicsville, before one reaches Richmond.[1] *Walnut Lane*, owned by Anthony Winston is described as located on Cold Harbor Road near Beaverdam Creek and the old Ellerson's Mill site. The land (1812) was described as being south by Chickahominy Swamp and north of Nathan Bell, the son of George. When George Bell was identified with the Henrico Friends Meetings, it was in this area that he lived.

George Bell, II
(431-432;377) George Bell, Jr. married (1)Elizabeth Woodson in the Friends Meeting House. He married second, in 1763, Cecilia Johnson, daughter of Ashley and Martha Wooday Johnson, the son of John and Lucretia Massie Johnson of St. Peter's Parish, New Kent County.[2] Even with the knowledge that Cecilia and George were first cousins, it has not been possible to confirm the maiden name of George's mother.[3]

Nathan Bell
(432;378) Additional research has not uncovered the maiden name of Sarah Bell. Since Nathan was dismissed from the Society of Friends at the time of his marriage for marrying out of unity, her name was not recorded in the Monthly Meeting Minutes. When they were reinstated as a couple only her married name was recorded.

Nathan Bell was active in the affairs of what is now the City of Richmond. He was the owner of *Bell Tavern*, a well-known Richmond landmark. It was located at what was then Main Street just below Fifteenth Street on the northeast corner; remember the street numbers were not the same at that time as they are now. He also owned a "meal house" on the southeast corner of Main and Fifteenth streets. Bell Tavern replaced Bowler's Tavern about 1802.[4]

The tavern was the gathering place of many of the local folks and was noted as the scene of recruiting in the War of 1812 and also of countless slave auctions. It is interesting that both of these activities were in opposition to the firm beliefs of the Friends. All of the early taverns were crude places, intended primarily for men. Their later replacement by hotels with greater comfort, catering to women, is a telling statement about the changes in the ways of the traveling public. George and James Winston erected four buildings just west of the tavern and rented them as stores with dwelling or boarding houses above. Nathan had leased Bell Tavern to Robert and George Turner before his death.[5]

Nathan had extensive land holdings, as evidenced from his will.[6] He directed his executors to sell the seven tracts of land in Grayson County containing 1425 acres. He loaned his wife the tract of land where William Wood was living, containing 250 acres, reserving 20 acres adjoining *Brandy Mills* for his son, John's use. He apparently had only one son, John and he left him the plantation on which Nathan lived called *Brandy*

Mills[7] and containing 400 acres, also a tract called Sheppersons, containing 120 acres, together with the mill called *Beaverdam Mills*. He further left him a tract of land called Young's containing 128 acres and a piece of meadow ground adjoining that contained twenty-eight acres as well as two one-half acre lots in Hanover Town.

Nathan left his wife and his two unmarried minor daughters, Mary and Rebecca, well provided for, with a horse and chair, the use of a plantation and the freedom to live on the homeplace with a liberal allowance. Were she to remarry she would receive an annual allowance of one hundred-thirty-three and one-third dollars. He appointed Sarah the executrix of his estate, along with his son, John Bell, son-in-law Thomas Ladd, friend George Winston and James D. Ladd the executors.

It was Sarah, the wife of Nathan Bell who inherited from seventy-five to one hundred slaves and freed them legally then sent them north in wagons to settle near the Quaker settlement of Wright's Ferry, Pennsylvania on the Susquehanna River. Soon after this it was rumored that slaves were escaping from Virginia to Wright's Ferry; it was true, as William Wright was a leader among the Quakers there in helping the slaves relocate.[8]

Thomas Ladd, acting as the agent for John Bell, on the first day of the fifth month (May) of 1813 executed a deed with Wilson Allen, William Hoomes and Richard C. Wortham (the former of the county of Caroline and the latter the county of Henrico) to lease Bell Tavern. They were to maintain the building in good repair and also support the reputation of the tavern. In turn Thomas Ladd agreed to erect a small brick building to serve as a stage office and a three-story brick building on the southeast end of Bell Tavern, for which the lessees were to pay the cost of construction and the rent specified.[9]

(433-436;378-381)
Gen. 8,7 (6)

MOORE BELL

BELL FAMILY

DAVID BELL would be the ninth generation from Bernard Hutcheson through Moore Bell and the tenth generation through Jemima Bell Winston. He would be the eighth generation from Nellie Butler through Jemima Bell Winston.

Gen. 9 DAVID BELL	m	BETHIA (—?—)
Issue:	a daughter	m	
	David	m	Mary (—?—)
	GEORGE	m	REBECCA MOORE

Gen. 8 GEORGE BELL	m	REBECCA MOORE
Issue:	JEMIMA	m	NATHANIEL WINSTON
	George, Jr.	m	(1) Elizabeth Woodson
		m	(2) Cecilia Johnson
	Bersheba	m	dis mcd
	MOORE	m	AGNES ELLYSON
	Nathan	m	Sarah (—?—)

Gen. 7 MOORE BELL	m	AGNES ELLYSON
Issue:	MARTHA	m	SAMUEL CHILES
	Rebecca	m	(—?—) Clark dis mou

Notes

1. Hanover County Historical Society, *Old Homes of Hanover County, Virginia* 1983 (Richmond: Walsworth Publishing Co, 1989) 58.
2. William Wade Hinshaw, *Encyclopedia of American Quaker Genealogy, vol VI* 1950 (Baltimore: Genealogical Publishing Co, rep 1993) 251.
3. Hinshaw 6: 157, 251.
4. Mary Wingfield Scott, *Old Richmond Nieghborhoods* 1950 (Richmond: William Byrd Press, rep 1984) 131-132.

5. Wingfield 134-135.
6. Fiduciary Records, Guardian Bonds and Wills and Deeds, Box 11-D-11-5-3, Library of Virginia, Richmond, VA.
7. Branch Mill survives today, it stopped operation in 1941 and stood idle until 1963 when it was purchased and restored as a residence. The water wheel was retained as an adjunct to the patio. *Old Homes of Hanover County* 12.
8. Jay Worrall, Jr., *The Friendly Virginians* (Athens, GA: Iberian Publishing Co, 1994) 294-295.
9. Fiduciary Papers.

NEW KENT AND CHARLES CITY COUNTIES

ROBERT ELLYSON I
Gen. 12

       Records have been searched whenever the opportunity has arisen and information gathered earlier has been reassessed. Several readers have corresponded with this researcher, but still there does not seem to be a definitive answer as to the relationship of the wife of ROBERT ELLYSON to the Gerrard family. Circumstantial evidence has been presented in earlier editions of *Tidewater Virginia Families*, and this seems to be applicable. It does not provide documented evidence of the relationships. The wording of the entry concerning the baptism of Thomas, the infant son of Robert and Susanna Slye seems to be the most definitive information that has been found. The entry reads *Baptized on ye 1st day of December, 1666 A.D., Thomas, infant son of Robert and Susanna Slye. The sponsors being his uncle Justinian Gerrard and aunt Elizabeth Ellyson.*[1] This apparently came from Slye family papers and may have been recorded in a Slye Family Bible. Elizabeth Gerrard's sister Susannah Gerrard married Robert Slye. It has been further stated in correspondence that ELIZABETH GERRARD did not marry Nehemiah Blackiston on May 6, 1659, but on **May 6, 1669**.[2] This is probably the most definitive information to date.

       The Erwin Family Bible, dated 1613, imprinted in London by Robert Barker, and owned by Elizabeth Allison Ervin yields the following information, recorded on blank pages: *My father, Robert Allison, passed in 1772. (the name during long years has been spelt, Allyson, Ellison, Elison, Allison, etc.). My mother was Mary Lide or Lloyd, (dtr. to Robt. Lloyd from Wales to Penn. abt. 1683). My grparents were John Allison & Elizabeth Matthews of Va. He being son of Robt and Ann Myhill. He being son of Capt. Robt Allison & Hannah Gerard of Maryland & Va....*[3]

       The above information has been presented, not to be accepted as authoritative, but only to be used to further the quest to find documented information concerning the parents of Elizabeth Ellyson, the wife of Robert Ellyson.

Gen. 11   **GERRARD ROBERT ELLYSON I**

MYHILL FAMILY

Gen.12 JOHN MYHILL		m	MARY LOCKEY
Issue:	Joshua		d.s.p.
	ANNE	m	GERRARD ROBERT ELLYSON
	Judith	m	Charles Collier

Gen. 10   **GERRARD ROBERT ELLYSON II**

       John Johnson, son of John of Hanover County married in the Friends Meeting House, New Kent County, Elizabeth Ellyson, daughter of GERRARD ROBERT ELLYSON, New Kent County. Four of their sons married daughters of Benjamin and Jane (Watkins) Watkins (c.1698-1753). Jane, the daughter of Thomas Watkins, was born in 1708 in Henrico County, married in 1726 to Benjamin and died December 2, 1777 in Goochland County. Benjamin, the son of Henry Watkins, Jr. had married the daughter of his father's brother.[4]

Gen. 9

ROBERT ELLYSON II

CREW FAMILY

Gen.11 JOHN CREW	m	SARAH GATLEY	
Issue:	John, Jr.	m	Agatha Ellyson
	SARAH	m	ROBERT ELLYSON
	Andrew	m	Hannah Ellyson
	Mary	m	John Ladd

GATLEY FAMILY

Gen.12 NICHOLAS GATLEY	m	SARAH (—?—)	
Issue:	SARAH	m	ROBERT ELLYSON
	Lockey	m	Sarah (—?—)
	Joseph	m	Massey Johnson

Gen. 8

JOSEPH ELLYSON

BINFORD FAMILY

Gen.11 ANTHONY BINFORD	m	UNKNOWN	
Issue:	JAMES	m	UNKNOWN
	Hulda	m	William Ladd

Gen.10 JAMES BINFORD	m	UNKNOWN	
Issue:	JOHN	m	AGNES MOSBY
	Thomas	m	Elizabeth (—?—)
	Peter	m	Rebecca Chappell

Gen. 9 JOHN BINFORD	m	AGNES MOSBY	
Issue:	MARY	m	JOSEPH ELLYSON
	James	m	Martha Chappell
	Agnes	m	Benjamin Chappell
	John	m	dis mou

ELLYSON FAMILY

Gen.12 ROBERT ELLYSON I	m	ELIZABETH (?)GERRARD	
Issue:	GERRARD ROBERT	m	ANNE MYHILL
	Hannah	m	Anthony Armistead

Gen.11 GERRARD ROBERT ELLYSON	m	ANNE MYHILL	
Issue:	GERRARD ROBERT	m	SARAH (—?—)
	John	m	(—?—)
	Thomas	m	(—?—)

Gen.10 GERRARD ROBERT ELLYSON	m	SARAH (—?—)	
Issue:	ROBERT	m	SARAH CREW
	Agatha	m	John Crew, Jr.
	Hannah	m	Andrew Crew
	William	m	Agnes Johnson
	Elizabeth	m	John Johnson

Judith	m	James Ladd	
Cecelia	m	Thomas Elmore, Jr.	
Ursula	m	William Ladd, Jr.	
Thomas	m	Elizabeth Crew	

Gen. 9 ROBERT ELLYSON	m	SARAH CREW	
Issue:	Matthew	m	Elizabeth Ladd
	JOSEPH	m	MARY BINFORD
	Susanna	m	John Binford
	John	m	Agnes Woodson

Gen. 8 JOSEPH ELLYSON	m	MARY BINFORD	
Issue:	AGNES	m	MOORE BELL
	Mary	m	Robert Jordan
	Susanna	m	Thomas Jordan

(449-454;394-398)

Gen. 10

EDWARD MOSBY

EDWARD MOSBY's wife SARAH died and Edward married a second time, the widow Mary Watkins. Mary was the wife of Henry Watkins, Jr. There is no entry in the Henrico Monthly Meeting Minutes of the death date of Sarah Mosby, but the will Henry Watkins was probated on February 7, 1714/15. Mary Watkins and Edward Mosby were married on November 15, 1716 in the Henrico Quaker Meeting House.[5]

Benjamin Mosby

(452;397) Poindexter Mosby, the son of Benjamin and Mary Poindexter Mosby married Mary Woodson the daughter of Joseph and Susanna Watkins Woodson.[6]

MOSBY FAMILY

Gen.11 EDWARD MOSBY	m	(1)SARAH WOODSON	
Issue:	John	m	Martha Womack
	AGNES	m	JOHN BINFORD
	Richard	m	Hannah (—?—)
	Robert	m	Agnes Watson widow
	Joseph	m	Sabrina (—?—)
	Hezekiah	m	Elizabeth Cox
	Jacob	m	Susanna Cox
	Benjamin	m	Mary Poindexter
Edward Mosby		m	(2) Mary Watkins widow

Notes

1. Notes of Mrs. Wirt Johnson Carrington, correspondence (1976) from Lorand V. Johnson, MD, 10515 Carnegie Ave, Cleveland, OH 44106 to Brother Ambrose, Mount Angel Abbey, St. Benedict, 97373.
2. Correspondence of Brother Ambrose with Sharon J. Doliante author of *Maryland and Virginia Colonials*, (Baltimore: Genealogical Publishing Co 1991), in which he stated that records in the Maryland Hall of Records yield the date of 1669.
3. Correspondence with Barbara Petty, 3107 Quail Hunt Ct, Midlothian, VA 23112. From the book *A South Carolina Family: Mills-Smith and Related Families*, Laurens Tenney Mills, 1960 by Lilla Mills Hawes and Sarah Mills Norton.
4. Hinshaw, 6:185; John Hale Stutesman, *Some Watkins Families of Virginia and their Kin* (Baltimore: Gateway Press, 1989) 49, 66.
5. John Hale Stutesman, *Some Watkins Families of Virginia and their Kin* (Baltimore: Gateway Press, 1989) 3-64.
6. Stutesman 49.

JOHN WOODSON I

Gen. 12 (11)

It was certainly fortuitous that JOHN WOODSON chose to settle at Flower de Hundred after their arrival in the colony of Virginia and were living at Piersey's Hundred nearby in 1624.[1] Having arrived in Virginia in 1619, they may well have decided to move further up the river and become a part of the new Henricus Cittie. They would have been present at the time of the first Indian massacre of 1622. They may not have survived. It was miraculous that Sarah survived the later massacre of 1644.

The story of the Woodson gun has been interesting to recount. It does not detract from this heroic act of SARAH WOODSON and their indentured servant, Ligon that time has altered the gun and shaded the story. The gun has been taken out of its seclusion at the Virginia Historical Society and placed in a display case for public viewing. Accompanying it is a placard with an explanation:

By traditional explanation, the Ligon name was carved on the stock —However the gun has been restocked several times over the years which explains the absence of the Ligon name. This 7'4" weapon —best described as an English fowler, designed for shooting birds —largely dates to 1740 and after, but it is just possible that the barrel only may coincide with the earlier Woodson Ligon date. The barrel is approximately 80 caliber or 12 gauge and has a slight swell at the breech and also a slight flare at the muzzle. Proof marks appear on the barrel near the break and the flint lock is marked "Collicot", the name of a locksmith in Bristol, England about 1750. The brass furniture consists of a cast butt plate with a graduated four-step tang, a convex side plate with tail, an unmarked escutcheon plate at the wrist, a trigger guard and three ram rod pipes of equal length with a fourth possessing a tail when the ramrod enters the lower stock.
Deposited by Charles Granville Scott

Questions have been raised concerning the various dates that appear in the records concerning John and Sarah Woodson. Assumptions have been made that have continued to raise questions because of the length of time between their arrival in the Colony of Virginia and the inferred dates of birth of their children. It should be considered that John and Sarah may not have been husband and wife at the time of their arrival in the colony, Sarah may well have been younger than has been supposed. It has generally been accepted that Deborah was a later child and was under age at the time of Sarah's death. With this inferred time span one would wonder whether accurate conclusions had been drawn. Just as Sarah may have been younger than previously thought at her time of arrival in the colony, so might Deborah Woodson been older than thought. She may well have been of age and Sarah was concerned about her maintenance because she was unmarried. All of which is to say, the relationships may have been interpreted correctly, just the chronology may have been misinterpreted.

It has been further questioned as to why during this lengthy period of time there were only three children of John and Sarah that have been identified. Researchers should be ever reminded that one can only interpret records that have survived. When it is stated that there were two, three, five or however many children of a particular husband and wife, it actually means that these are the only ones identified in the records. The mortality rate of infants and young children was quite high. No one knows how many wives and children are relegated to obscurity because of the records that have been lost or burned. Or because the names of wives and daughters simply did not appear in the extant records.

Descendants still identify with the two sons and the purported ingenuity of their mother in the encounter with the Indians. Today they will ask whether one is descendant of "Tub" Woodson (that is, John) or "Potato Hole" Woodson (that is, Robert). This is in spite of the fact that potatoes had not found their way to the New World at that time, and that the Woodsons would probably not have had a wash tub.

Proceedings of the Virginia Council for 1629 record that Dr. Pott was pardoned after Sir John Harvey had superseded him as President of the Council on the grounds that he was the only physician in the colony. Dr. Bohune the company surgeon had been killed in an engagement with a Spanish vessel in March 1621.

Thus Dr. Woodson would not have had the medical training attributed to him.[2]

(459-464;403-408)

Gen. 11 (10)   **ROBERT WOODSON**

(459;403)   The settlement of the Citie of Henrico in 1611 was a significant event in our American heritage, but for reasons which are not clear, disappeared from our history books until recently....This city, founded by Sir Thomas Dale, in response to a directive from the Virginia Company of London, was named Henrico, but like many cities its name changed with time...many twentieth century historians have adopted the name Henricus in their descriptions of this settlement....The story begins at Jamestown, which was an important beginning to the colonization of North America....[3]

Misled by the Spanish experience to the south, a prime objective of the Virginia Company was the discovery of the "royal mines", a source of gold, silver and precious gems. They also anticipated that the large estuaries of our rivers would provide a shortcut to the Orient, and the highly remunerative China trade. Needless to say, neither of these objectives was achieved.

Further objectives of the Virginia Company were to establish a permanent colony, become self-sufficient and to establish a rewarding trade with the Indians.[4] While the project seemed to be based on the knowledge at hand, it was unfortunate that the venture was essentially a military operation, with persons of military experience constituting a significant portion of the early settlers, along with some artisans and craftsmen. None were experienced in surviving in the new land called Virginia.

The story of the choice of Jamestown as the site of the first settlement can be found in the words of Captain John Smith and in the history written by Warren M. Billings.[5] In meeting some of the directives of the Virginia Company, the colonists found other circumstances to be significant in making their choice of that settlement site. The disastrous consequences of the choice of site are well known in retrospect.

Sir Thomas Gates realized the colony at Jamestown was demoralized and in despair in the spring of 1610. It was the peak of the "starving time" when the colonists had been reduced in number from 500 in the fall of 1609 to sixty the spring of 1610. The decimated group set sail for England, only to meet Lord De La Warr as he sailed up the Chesapeake Bay, arriving just in time to save the colony. Sir Thomas Dale relieved Lord De la Warr (Thomas West) in 1611, serving as Deputy Governor of the colony. He and Sir Thomas Gates complemented each other in leadership capabilities during their five-year administration. Dale reestablished the colony's defense, restored Jamestown, and led two punitive expeditions against the Indians.

Seek to the sun than from it, which is under God the first cause both of health and riches. And that such places which you resolve to build and inhabit upon, have at least one good outlet to sea and fresh water to the land, that it be a dry and wholesome seat.[6] So advised the officials of the Virginia Company in their instructions to Gates. In 1611 when Dale assumed leadership of the colony he set out to explore the James River to build a new settlement in what he considered a safe and healthful setting.

Dale found the site east of the fall line of the James River on the north side of the river.[7] The site he chose was a high bluff, forming a peninsula and set between loops of the James on its north side. This setting met the requirements of being on high, well-drained land, with a good supply of fresh water available. The peninsula jutted into the river in such as way that it provided an excellent view of river approaches, and was easily defensible because of its narrow connection to the mainland.

In September 1611, Dale established Henricus, the colony's second settlement. As commander of this new town, Dale was responsible for overseeing the construction and defense of the city. Men were assigned specific tasks; clearing the land, constructing the palisade and buildings, digging a ditch across the narrow neck of the peninsula, and keeping watch against the hostile Indians. Under his direction and strong authoritarian rule, a city was carved out of the wilderness.[8]

Dale confidently expected the new city to replace Jamestown as the principal seat of the colony. The location upriver provided security from possible Spanish attack, as well as protection from Indian attacks and the high bluffs provided a healthier environment than the swamps at Jamestown. A fence was constructed around the townsite, watchtowers were built at each of four corners and a storehouse and church were built first. Lodgings were then built and each man was allotted sufficient land for his own orchard and garden.

Dale saw a town arise out of the wilderness, and his visions for the colony of Virginia become reality. The Citie of Henricus became distinctive as a city of "firsts":

◻ The first attempt to extend the settlement in Virginia into the continent, beyond the foothold at Jamestown.
◻ The first hospital in British North America (1612), built to house eighty patients, with forty beds, named *Mount Malady*.
◻ The first university to be chartered in the New World, *Henricus Colledge*, with 10,000 acres set aside as college land.
◻ A library donated by an unknown Englishman to the university, known to contain a copy of St. Augustine's *De Civitatis Dei* (The City of God).
◻ The first college for the education of Indian youth, with an additional 1000 acres so designated; and the award of the first scholarship given to an Indian youth to attend the college.
◻ The first Indian convert to Christianity; Pocahontas was baptized by the Reverend Alexander Whitaker.
◻ The economic salvation of the Virginia Company, achieved by John Rolfe with his commercially acceptable tobacco variety called *Varina*.
◻ The initiation of a capitalistic system with the private ownership of land; instituted by Dale in lieu of the ineffective communal system of ownership.

Also significant was the establishment of Henrico Parish, and the church that was built in 1611 at Henricus. This was a frame structure; the brick foundation was laid for a later church shortly after 1616, but was never completed. The Reverend Alexander Whitaker, the first minister, built a frame parsonage known as *Rock Hall* on the south side of the James (in what later became Chesterfield County).

The warriors of the Powhatan Chiefdom, upset by the increasing numbers and aggressive expansion of English settlements, made plans to extinguish all traces of the European presence upon their land. On March 22, 1622, they swept down upon the small settlements along the banks of the James River, killing the inhabitants and destroying their homes. At Henricus five men lay dead; the surviving colonists fled down river to the safety of Jamestown.

Out of fear of another Indian attack, the settlers did not return. The Citie of Henricus was no more. It was destined to exist as a functional town for only a few brief years, but it had an unprecedented impact on the growth and destiny of America. It has not been forgotten.

The site was visited by boat in November 1984 by a group of executives of Henrico Doctors' Hospital, and a loosely organized meeting of interested direct descendants, local historians, scholars and government officials came together. From this The Henricus Foundation was formed to acquire additional land at Farrar's Island (site of Henricus) and the site of the Henrico monuments at Dutch Gap.[9] The goals of The Henricus Foundation were to rebuild the Citie of Henricus, its structures, the first college and Mt. Malady, the first hospital in America. Under the auspices and direction of The Henricus Foundation, with the cooperation of foundations, private enterprise and local government agencies, this exciting venture is becoming a reality. An 805-acre Dutch Gap Conservation Area adjoining Henricus has been set aside and will be open for public use. All persons with an interest in the early history of Virginia and America should share in this vision and reconstruction.

When JOHN WOODSON's descendants moved up the river to Curles and to White Oak Swamp they walked the same land that is today being restored for their later descendants.

Robert Woodson, Jr.
(462;405) Robert Woodson, Jr. married first, Elizabeth Lewis, the daughter of John Lewis and they had one son, Stephen. He then married Sarah Lewis, the sister of Elizabeth Lewis and they had children. His third marriage was to Rachel Watkins, it is not certain which children were hers and Robert's. Mr. Stutesman believes that Rachel was the daughter of Henry Watkins, Sr., and not the son, Henry.[10]

Richard Woodson
(462;406) Obadiah, the son of Richard and Ann Woodson married **Constant** Watkins. She was mistakenly called Constance, but her name appears in the Watkins family records as Constant.[11]

Gen.12 RICHARD FERRIS	m	UNKNOWN
Issue: Richard	m	
ELIZABETH	m	ROBERT WOODSON

(465-469;409-413)

Gen. 10 (9)   JOHN WOODSON II

(466;409)   A great deal of effort went into trying to identify what was called "the Quaker Road". Having traveled over all of the roads in New Kent County, especially with a son who lived there for several years, it was still impossible to establish its route. It was not until the introduction of the emergency 911 telephone service that counties began to identify roads by name rather than county route number, thus making it easier for emergency personnel to find the homes of residents quickly. The Quaker Road was thus named and identified. It lies to the north of SR 249; one turns north on CR 613 at Quinton, then northeasterly on CR 611. It may have continued westerly across Chickahominy Swamp somewhere close to where CR 613 enters Hanover County and into the White Oak area.

(470-476;414-419)

Gen. 9 (8)   TARLETON WOODSON

(472;415-416)   On the way to Henricus an exciting discover was made. After inaccurate directions to Henricus Historical Park, and a long drive on CR 618 (one proceeds west from Hopewell on SR 10, to reach CR 618, north), a fork in the road appeared. The left fork was identified with a sign and arrow, *Meadowville Farm*. As curious travellers, we followed the beckoning road. The woods opened into a large farm and cultivated fields. The James River appeared at the end of the road, along with all of the farm buildings that lined the river. It was especially interesting to see a very large and architecturally unusual house with many large dependencies. A modern house brought contrast to the scene. There was a sweeping view of the James, with no industrial intrusions; unusual for the area. Later, to gain insight concerning the farm, the authoritative, *Chesterfield County, Early Architecture and Historic Sites,*[12] was consulted. The old *Meadowville* home dates back to c.1888, and was built by Edward Barney. When Mr. Barney bought the farm it contained 2,200 acres, and was one of the two largest farms in Chesterfield County at that time. The original name for this tract appears to have been *Woodsons.* TARLETON WOODSON's plantation has been identified as lying between Hopewell and Dutch Gap. He was living there before 1750 and died there in 1771. This further information definitively places the plantation of Tarleton Woodson, first known as *Neck of Land*, across the river from Varina, and with a magnificent view of the James. It was here that he was able to load his tobacco for transportation by the river, and was also able to receive goods from distant ports. He left the plantation to his son, Charles Woodson.[13]

One of the reasons it has been so difficult to correctly identify where Tarleton lived was the fact that he was engaged in so many land transactions involving his father, then CHARLES FLEMING, and later land that he patented himself. For several years there were many records of sale, lease and release of land signed by Tarleton, as eldest son and heir of JOHN WOODSON, deceased, in settling the estate of his father. He inherited 1000 acres at Dover on the north side of the James; he patented 3080 adjoining acres of land in Henrico County on Beaverdam Creek, then 300 acres on Jenitoe Creek on the south side of the river. He patented 2307 acres known as Bear Forest near the Pamunkey River in 1717 and bought 200 acres in 1727 on the south side of the James. He was, during this time also selling small parcels of land. He inherited the tract of land called *Neck-of-Land* from his father.[14]

Tarleton's plantation is just a few miles down river from the Citie of Henricus; it having been moved to the south side of the James with the canal built during the Civil War by the Union Army, and by later dredging by the Corps of Engineers to provide a more direct shipping lane to the Richmond terminal.

WOODSON FAMILY

ROBERT WOODSON would have been the eleventh generation from Bernard Hutcheson, through SARAH WOODSON MOSBY. In the line of descent of Nellie Butler, JUDITH WOODSON CHEADLE would have been generation seven and thus ROBERT WOODSON, the tenth generation.

Gen.12	JOHN WOODSON I	m		SARAH (—?—)
Issue:	John	m		(1)
		m		(2) Sarah Browne widow
	ROBERT	m		ELIZABETH FERRIS
	Deborah			

Gen.11	ROBERT WOODSON	m		ELIZABETH FERRIS
Issue:	JOHN	m		JUDITH TARLETON
	Elizabeth	m		William Lewis
	SARAH	m		EDWARD MOSBY
	Robert	m		(1) Sarah Lewis
		m		(2) Rachel Watkins
	Richard	m		Ann Smith
	Joseph	m		Jane Woodson
	Benjamin	m		Sarah Porter
	Judith	m		William Cannon
	Mary	m		George Payne

Gen.10	JOHN WOODSON II	m		JUDITH TARLETON
Issue:	TARLETON	m		URSULA FLEMING
	John	m	d.s.p.	Susanna Bates widow
	Robert	m		Sarah Womack d.s.p.
	Josiah	m		Mary Royall
	Jacob			d.s.p.
	Judith	m		Stephen Cox
	Elizabeth	m		Joseph Pleasants
	Stephen	m		Elizabeth Branch

Gen. 9	TARLETON WOODSON	m		URSULA FLEMING
Issue:	Charles	m		(1)Mary Pleasants
		m		(2)Agnes Richardson widow
	Tarleton			unmarried
	Jacob			unmarried
	Susanna	m		John Pleasants
	Sarah	m		Henry Terrell
	Mary	m		John Pleasants
	JUDITH	m		THOMAS CHEADLE

Notes

1. John Camden Hotten, *Original Lists of Persons of Quality, 1600-1700* 1874 (Baltimore: Genealogical Publishing Co, 1986) 172.
2. *Proceedings of the Virginia Council*, Virginia Historical Society Collections vol 1 19, 139. From notes made by Allen Howard Godby in H.M. Woodson's *Woodson Book*, St. Louis Public Library.
3. *The Citie of Henricus, 1611, TVF* 6(1997): 71-75.
4. Dennis A.J. Morey, M.D., F.A.C.P., Chairman, Historical Research, The Henricus Foundation. He has done extensive research concerning the founding, development and inhabitants of the Citie of Henrico and has written a number of monographs about this early settlement. He has also spoken widely on these subjects. His address is 2870 Braidwood Rd, Richmond, VA 23226.
5. Warren M. Billings, *Jamestown and the Founding of the Nation.* (Gettysburg: Colonial National Historical Park and Eastern National Parks and Monument Association, 1991). Mr. Billings is a Virginian who once lived at Jamestown. A specialist in the study of seventeenth-century Virginia, he is the author of six books and numerous articles for scholarly journals. He is Professor of History at the University of New Orleans and Historian of the Supreme Court of Louisiana.

6. The Virginia Company of London, 1609. From The Henricus Foundation brochure, 1992.

7. Today Henricus lies east of the City of Richmond and the James River flows in a shorter and straighter course than its natural course of the 1600s. Dale began to transform the land in 1611 at the settlement of Henricus. The town was located on a peninsula connected to the mainland by a 174-yard neck of land. Dale employed a tactic used by the Dutch in the lowlands; a ditch was dug and a paled fence constructed behind it. The land masses on each side of the ditch took on separate identities. A later canal (1864) dug by the Union Army during the Civil War effectively moved the peninsula (by then known as Farrar's Island) from Henrico County to Chesterfield County on the south side of the river. This same canal and a later shipping channel probably destroyed any remnants of Henricus, and there remains little of the original site of Henricus for archaeological exploration. The Citie of Henricus site is now under the governmental jurisdiction of Chesterfield County.

8. The Henricus Foundation brochure prepared by the Historic Committee of the Henricus Foundation; Dr. Louis H. Manarin, Chairman, Susan Hanson, Emily Kimball, Dr. Henry Nelson, Sandra V. Parker and Paul Hunter Shelton.

9. Calder Loth, ed., *The Virginia Landmarks Register*. (Charlottesville: University Press of VA, 1987). 199-200.

10. Stutesman 79, 80; Margaret Lotterhos Smith, 3209 Reba Dr, Houston, TX 77019.

11. Correspondence with John Hale Stutesman.

12. Jeffery M. Odell (Chesterfield County, Virginia: privately printed, 1983), 260-261.

13. *Henricus Historical Park* lies at the end of CR 732/615 at Dutch Gap. After proceeding west from Hopewell on SR 10, one turns north on CR 732. Traveling south on US Route 1, Dutch Gap and Henricus can be reached by turning east on CR 615. *Southside Virginian* X(1992):22.

14. From the unpublished manuscript of Margaret Lotterhos Smith, 3209 Reba Dr, Houston, TX 77019.

MT. MALADY 1611
(Courtesy of the Henricus Foundataion)

Gen. 10   **CHARLES FLEMING**

      Following the oft read statement that CHARLES FLEMING was descended from Sir Thomas Fleming, second son of the Earl of Wigdon, a number of serious researchers have attempted to verify this relationship. It has been well established that there was no Sir Thomas who was the 2nd son of the Earl of Wigdon. Attempts have been made to carry the heritage of Charles Fleming back to John Fleming 6th Lord, 1st Earl as presented in *Scots Peerage*, 8: 545-549. It is through this line descending to Captain Alexander Fleming, born in Lanarak, Scotland that the association is made with John Fleming of New Kent County in Virginia. No such relationship can be documented. There is a reference to the marriage of an Alexander Fleming to Elspet Anderson December 6, 1643, Lanark, Glasgow. No direct connection has been found between this Alexander and the Alexander Fleming of the Virginia records.[1]

      An Alexander Fleming appears first in the Virginia records when he patented 250 acres of land on the north side of the Rappahannock river in 1658.[2] He married three times in Virginia and there is no record of a son named John. He appears to have spent his life largely as a land owner[3] in the Northern Neck, with a number of other patents under the title of Captain Alexander Fleming.[4]

      What is known is that John Fleming was named as a headright in 1653 in a patent of Joseph Crowshaw. He patented 250 acres land in his own right in New Kent County in 1658, and an additional 493 acres in 1661.[5] He additionally patented 900 acres with Thomas Glass in New Kent County between Totopotomoy and Matadequain creeks in 1670, and 1000 acres with Andrew Davies on a branch of Mechamps Creek.[6]

      In 1688 Charles Fleming patented 1070 acres of land in New Kent County between Matadequain and Totopotomoy creeks adjoining the land of John Fleming, deceased on Whiting Swamp. In 1690 he patented the 1000 acres that had been granted John Fleming and Andrew Davies and deserted by them, this land was on the south side of Totopotomoy Creek.[7]

      A Charles Fleming was a headright in 1653. Thirty-five years later in 1688, a Charles Fleming appears again in the records when he patented land in New Kent County adjacent to the land of John Fleming. No direct connection was stated in the records, nor has any been found; however, the fact that their land was adjacent and that Charles repatented land of John Fleming just after the death of John Fleming of St. Peter's Parish indicates a strong likelihood of the relationship of father and son. It is reassuring to find that independent work done by a careful researcher has yielded the same conclusions concerning father and son, as first presented by this author.

      It is known that Charles Fleming and John Woodson were associated, not only through the marriage of their children, but in land transactions, and then in the settlement of the estate and large land holdings of John Woodson. This does not negate the fact that Charles Fleming was in his own right a large land owner, buying and selling land, but also at times the owner of large acreages of land.

FLEMING FAMILY

Gen.11 CHARLES FLEMING		m	SUSANNA TARLETON
Issue:	Elizabeth	m	Samuel Jordan
	URSULA	m	TARLETON WOODSON
	Grace	m	George Bates
	Judith	m	(1) Thomas Randolph
		m	(2) Nicholas Davies
	Susanna	m	(1) John Bates, Jr.
		m	(2) John Woodson
	Tarleton	m	Hannah Bates
	John	m	Mary Bolling

BATES FAMILY

Gen.12 JOHN BATES	m	ELIZABETH (—?—)
Issue: George	m	Mary (—?—)
John	m	
Anne	m	(—?—) (?)Bellbee
Alse (Alice)	m	William Deane
SUSANNA	m	STEPHEN TARLETON

These two generations of the Bates family are not direct ancestors, but are included because of the later connection with the Fleming and Woodson families.

Gen.11 George Bates	m	Mary (—?—)
Issue: James	m	Sarah (—?—)
John	m	(1) Elizabeth Daniel
	m	(2) Hannah Trudall
George	m	(1) Elizabeth Crispe
	m	(2) Grace Fleming
Mary	m	

Gen.10 John Bates	m	Elizabeth Daniel
Issue: John	m	Susanna Fleming
Isaac	m	Elizabeth (—?—)
Hannah	m	Tarleton Fleming
Ann	m	John Daniel
George	m	
James	m	Sarah (—?—)

(481-484;424-426)

Gen. 11,10

STEPHEN TARLETON

TARLETON FAMILY

Gen.11 STEPHEN TARLETON	m	SUSANNA BATES
Issue: SUSANNA	m	CHARLES FLEMING
JUDITH	m	JOHN WOODSON II
Stephen	m	
John	m	Susanna Fleming
Charles	m	
Elizabeth	m	Stephen Hughes

Notes

1. From research and correspondence with Mary Elizabeth Stewart, PO Box 485, Irvington, VA 22480. Information following comes from her documented research.
2. Nugent vols 1-2, *passim*.References refer to volume and page number.
3. Nugent 1:424, 1:503, 1:419.
4. Nugent 1:518, 519. 2:18, 47.
5. Nugent 1:386; 1:397.
6. Nugent 2:77, 207.
7. Nugent 2:324, 354.

SECTION V

THE BUTLER ANCESTORS

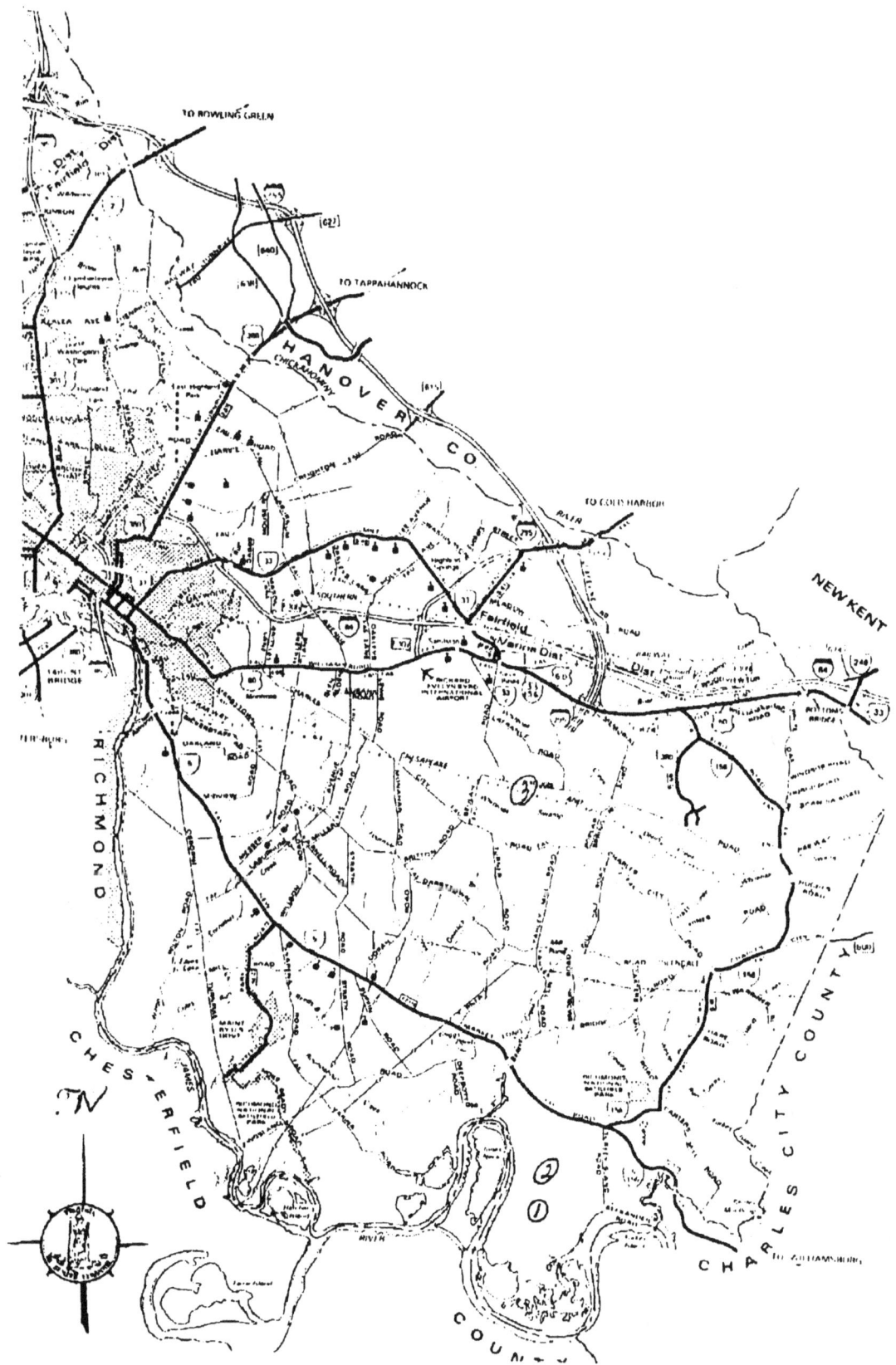

HENRICO COUNTY

WILLIAM WINSTON

Gen. 11 (9)

(491-493;433-435)
Gen. 10 (8)   **ANTHONY WINSTON I**

(494-495;436-437)
Gen. 9 (7)   **ANTHONY WINSTON II**

(496-502;438-443)
Gen. 8 (6)   **NATHANIEL WINSTON**

(499;440)   A great deal of research went in to understanding the part that JEMIMA played in the settlement of NATHANIEL WINSTON's estate and the ownership of his slaves. The suit in chancery court was brought by the slaves (plaintiffs): Jacob, Frank, Esther and her children, Fanny and her children, Sarah and her children, and the children of Kate who are infants and represented by Micajah Crew and Samuel Parsons as their next friends against the children of Nathaniel and Jemima Winston.[1] The suit stated that Nathaniel, about 1786, gave the slaves to his wife Jemima for life and after her death he gave them their freedom (the boys at twenty-one and the girls at eighteen). The will was given to Thomas Terrell, who was a witness, for safe keeping. Nathaniel died sometime in 1787 without altering the will. It was stated that the will was surreptitiously taken by someone after his death, wishing to unjustly detain the slaves in bondage, and the will was destroyed. The plaintiffs believed that some of the children of Nathaniel had a copy of the will. When Jemima died in 1794 a number of the plaintiffs had become of age but were still held in slavery.

JOHN CHILES the husband of MARY WINSTON, deceased, testified *a certain group of people calling themselves Quakers had made it their business to go from house to house for the purpose of persuading the heads of families to free their negroes to the utter confusion and discontent of wifes and children, and the said Nathaniel had told this defendant that it was not worth their while to trouble him on that subject for it was confidently his opinion, that those negroes that had good masters and mistresses were in a better situation than those that were freed, and that he should never free his.*

One of these troublesome companies visited the mother of this defendant for the purpose of persuading her to emancipate the negroes left her by the defendant's father as her dower and after a long and tedious harrangue of persuasions, threats of excommunication and even horrors of everlasting perdition (if she did not come into the measure) they prevailed on her to sign an instrument of writing for that purpose. At the completion of which one of the company huzza's with a "Glory be to God", the intent was to scatter the negroes held by his mother for life and thereby put it out of the power of those holding them in reversion ever collecting them again. A combination appears to have been carried on to defraud this defendant and his brethern of the small patrimony intended for them by their father.

The day succeeding those transactions this defendant's mother reflecting on the matter and getting much dissatisfied at what was done, requested this defendant to go with her to the place where the said company was assembled and request them in the presence of this defendant and others that they would give her back the writing they had extorted from her. Her request was positively refused, with an intent to admit the same to record...and that she had no power over the same.

John went on to say that he felt it was his duty to oppose the practice as it had happened to others, and he no longer felt safe without putting his property under lock and bolt. He further stated that Nathaniel died leaving a number of debts, some still unpaid and that his estate should be used to pay his debts. John Chiles was at that time a justice of the peace for Caroline County, and also a delegate to the General Assembly. The suit was abated in March 1796 due to the death of John Chiles.

When the suit was reinstated Pleasant Winston, the son of Nathaniel testified that he had seen his father's will and believed it was extorted from him by persuasions and threats of excommunication and the eternal loss of his soul by a set of people called Quakers. He further said that he remembers writing a will for his father which he believed to be his last except the one that Pleasant Terrell said he wrote. In the will written by himself, his father had given his slaves amongst his children, and since he was under age he could hardly have influenced his father.

Thomas Terrell testified to the later will, saying that he left a tract of land in Fluvanna County to John Chiles, the plantation on which he lived to his wife during her lifetime and after her death to be divided among his four youngest sons. The negroes mentioned were to be freed at his wife's death. He left Jemima Winston, John Chiles, George Winston and Edmund Winston his executors.

Subsequently the defendants were questioned, and it was learned that Nathaniel Winston was not a Quaker at the time that he made his will. Thomas Terrell testified that Nathaniel had told him he had a will that he had made at home to satisfy his family, but it was not his will and he asked Thomas to keep the will a secret or he could not live in peace. After Nathaniel's death Jemima had gone to Thomas Terrell's home and asked for the will; his wife Rebecca gave it to her to look at but Jemima took it home with her, against Rebecca's protests.

Nathan Bell testified that Nathaniel had him write the will freeing his slaves and asked him to keep it. Later he returned and asked for it, not wanting to cause hard feelings between Nathan and his sister Jemima. He then gave it to Thomas Terrell to keep. Pleasant Terrell testified that he had seen the will freeing the slaves, and verified the entire contents of that will.

The decree was handed down on September 20, 1799 with the court adjudging, ordering and decreeing that the defendants liberate the plaintiffs from servitude. And for all of the confusing entries read from the records earlier, the mystery of the will of Nathaniel Winston and the behavior of Jemima Winston is finally understood.

Rebecca Winston
(500;441) Rebecca and George Harwood had children: Winston Harwood; Besha Harwood who married John Carter; and Polly who married Benjamin Hilliard.[2]

Anthony Winston
(500;441) Anthony Winston married Nancy Haley, the daughter of John and Mary Haley. They had children: John Winston, Patsy Winston, who married Edmund Collins, Polly Winston, who married Frederick Hart, Samuel Winston, George Winston (who was in North Carolina in 1817) and Betsy Winston.[3]

Pleasant Winston
(501;442) Pleasant Winston married Jane Quarles, the daughter of Roger and Mary Goodloe Quarles.[4]

Nathan Winston
(501;442) Nathan Winston and Ann Yarbrough Winston had the following children: Eliza Winston, Patty Winston, Sally Winston, Jefferson Winston, William Winston and Jane Winston.[5]

Edmund Winston
(501;442) The will of Edmund Winston has been found and it seems certain that Edmund did not marry as he left his personal property to James Young. He left his share of the wheat, corn and fodder that may be on the land to James Young also; there was no mention of owning a home or the land.

Sarah Winston
(501;442) married Stephen Haley of Richmond, c.1816.[6]

GEORGE WINSTON

So much has been learned about the life of GEORGE WINSTON since the research of the book that it is difficult to condense it. While he touched many lives in the area of the City of Richmond, so have many lives touched the life of your author in the quest for information to save one of the last examples of his construction of buildings in Richmond. Charles Pool of the Oregon Hill Home Improvement Council (OHHIC)[7] called to thank your author for the extensive research and biography of George Winston and the Society of Friends. He related the part that this account had played in their efforts to save a house built by George Winston from demolition by Virginia Commonwealth University to make room for their new School of Engineering building. Extensive documentation of the "Jacob House" has been presented by the OHHIC to the Department of Historic Resources. Following is a condensation of their report (1995).

George Winston was known as the Quaker master builder/developer and partner in the development of the Town of Sydney, consisting of 500 acres of the *Belvidere* estate, to be divided into two acre squares, each with four lots. This was to be a suburban community on the western edge of Richmond, along the Westham Turnpike.[8] He was clearly one of the most important figures on the Richmond scene in the areas of construction and real estate development from about 1787 until his death in 1826. He constructed at least 100 major buildings in the Shockoe Bottom and thirty on Church Hill, as well as others throughout the area. His activity as a builder-developer constitutes one of the greatest contributions to the community made by any of his contemporaries.

He was also a leading Quaker, and played an important leadership role in the Quaker movement to free slaves and to prepare slaves and freedmen for citizenship through education and apprenticeship. While the Society of Friends simply required the elimination of slavery for continued fellowship in the Society, George dealt with the situation creatively. He took on young free black men as apprentices, and in the year 1820, alone, twenty young free blacks were living in his household on Church Hill. He was able to move dozens of these young men into a position of earning a living for themselves. This may have been the most important accomplishment of his life.

Some of the impressive homes, now gone from the Richmond scene, were built by George Winston: *Moldavia*, for David and Molly Randolph Meade; the home of William Marshall, the brother of Chief Justice John Marshall; the Thomas Rutherfoord House; *Clifton*, the home of Benjamin J. Harris and *Bellville*, the home of John Bell (the son of Nathan Bell).[9]

The last known house associated with the founding Quaker community of Richmond was threatened with being moved or demolished by Virginia Commonwealth University for parking space for their proposed engineering school. A coalition of twenty-five organizations, including the Friends Historical Association, the National Trust for Historic Preservation, the Victorian Society in America, the Colonial Williamsburg Foundation, the William Byrd Branch of the Association for the Preservation of Virginia Antiquities (APVA), the Historic Resources Committee of the Virginia Architectural Institute of America (AIA), and the Richmond Chapter of the National Association for the Advancement of Colored People (NAACP) all asked the University to leave the historic house undisturbed on its authentic site.[10]

The State Review Board of the Virginia Department of Historic Resources determined at its meeting on April 18 that the Jacob House appeared to be eligible for individual listing on the National Register of Historic Places; the house was already listed on the state and National Register as a contributing structure to the Oregon Hill Historic District. A principal reference for the successful nomination report was *Tidewater Virginia Families: A Social History* by Virginia Lee Hutcheson Davis (1989).

Professor Arnold Ricks, of the Department of History at Bennington College, and a birthright Quaker, wrote the following concerning the historic Jacob House and its builder, George Winston:

We know that this house was constructed about 1817, the first improvement in the ambitious 500 acre 'development' project undertaken by Jacqueline Harvie, Benjamin J. Harris, and George Winston know as the 'Town of Sydney', encompassing what is today the Fan District as well as Oregon Hill. Winston was the builder among the partners; it was he who erected the original Friends Meeting House at 19th and Cary Streets in 1797, the first house of worship built in Richmond after St. John's Church. Himself a prominent Friend, he like other Friends of the period had manumitted his slaves, and — as has been detailed especially in a recent study by Gregg Kimball of the Valentine Museum[11] — he made a practice of training and employing free Black apprentices in his extensive building operations, which included work on Jefferson's Capitol and Virginia's pioneering Penitentiary. Benjamin Harris, brother of Winston's wife, a major entrepreneur of the times as a cotton and tobacco manufacturer, was also from a Quaker family; his father, JAMES HARRIS, was the first General Manager of the James River Navigation Company (George Washington, President), and as a Friend served as a member of the executive committee of the rather short-lived Virginia Abolition Society founded in 1790. Benjamin Harris himself owned the house for a few years in the 1820s. John Jacob, a Friend whose house it was for more than twenty years, expressed a characteristic Quaker concern for penal reform in serving as Assistant Superintendent of the penitentiary under Samuel Parsons (another Friend) as Superintendent.

The William Byrd Branch of the APVA offered to cover any costs the University might incur in redesigning the proposed engineering school to accommodate the historic house. The Oregon Hill Home Improvement Council and the Central Virginia Business and Construction Association offered to renovate the Jacob House at no cost to the University. The latter proposed utilizing the house as a facility for training young blacks in the building trades, a use that would be in keeping with the history of the house, built by the free black apprentices of George Winston 178 years ago. It is significant that this house provides one of the last physical links to the rich social history of, not only the early Quakers, but also the free black community of Richmond. The house would be a representation of the building trades of the 19th century as well as the building skills of free black apprentices and craftsmen.

As President Kenneth Carroll, of the Friends Historical Association wrote regarding VCU's threats to move or demolish the Jacob House: *Built circa 1817, the Jacob House is probably the last physical link that we have to this important early Quaker heritage of Richmond. There may be no other historic resource surviving from this period of Richmond that can be used for interpreting the notable contributions of these courageous Quakers. On this, the 200th anniversary of the Richmond Friends Meeting it would be sad indeed for the Jacob House to be demolished or moved from its historic site.*[12]

It would have been a magnificent gesture of recognition of the heritage of both groups had the Board of Virginia Commonwealth University (VCU) capitulated and allowed the building to stand in its original location, on the corner of 610 West Cary Street, taking up probably four spaces in the projected parking lot for the projected School of Engineering of VCU. The juxtaposition would have been especially meaningful as the Black Contractors Association (BCA) had proposed using it as a training facility for teaching young blacks as apprentices in the building trades, in keeping with the history of the house and the future of the Engineering School. This was not to be, the house was moved across the street to an inappropriate site and incongruous, declining surroundings.[13] VCU had circumvented normal state reviews (Virginia's Art and Architectural Review Board) to accomplish this move; especially upsetting in an institution of higher learning with a fine architectural history program.[14]

(508;449) Through this effort it was learned that the year 1995 was the Bicentennial Celebration of The Richmond Society of Friends. Two hundred years ago six Richmond families founded the Richmond Friends Meeting. The group was an offshoot of the White Oak Swamp Monthly Meeting. Founding families included Samuel and Sarah Parsons, George and Judith Winston, Thomas Ladd, Nathan and Sarah Bell, James and Sarah Lownes, and brothers, Thomas and Ebenezer Maule. Robert Pleasants was also among those of the first meetings in 1795.

Jay Worrall, the author of *The Friendly Virginians*[15] and R. Arnold Ricks, III, Professor of History Emeritus of Bennington College in Vermont both spoke of their heritage. Many Friends descendants from a distance gathered for worship, lunch and fellowship. Not only were acquaintances renewed, but cousins met cousins for the first time. It was a celebration of faith, unity and friendship.

The Richmond Society of Friends Meeting House, on Kensington Avenue, is a simple, small frame building that had been the old Battery Park Disciples of Christ Church. It is the only meeting in the entire Richmond area. The only known surviving rendition of the original Richmond Friends Meeting House is the background of a family portrait of Hannah Watts Clarke painted with her sitting at a window, with the Meeting House (c.1840) seen through the window.[16] The Henrico Monthly Meeting Minutes give the specifications of the Richmond Meeting House to be *a good brick house of about Thirty by Forty feet in the upper part of the*

Town, with the convenience of one acre of Ground. 4th da.: 2 mo.: 1797.[17]

(510;450) Depositions of the authenticity of the will and codicil of Judith Harris Winston were taken in Louisville, Kentucky of witnesses to the will: Nathaniel Charles and Pleasant Winston and to the codicil: George Winston (Jr.), Pleasant Winston and Thomas B. Winston. **Eight** of the children of George and Judith Winston had moved west.

The following accounts (except where otherwise indicated) have come from correspondence with Dr. Lindley M. Winston, MD,[18] and Mary Elizabeth Stewart[19], both of whom are descendants of Pleasant Winston.

James Winston
(511-512;451-452) James Winston's son William was born in 1835 and died in 1852; Virginia Henry was born in 1832, a son James, Jr. is also named. From family accounts both James and his son, James traveled to the west to Ohio and Indiana to visit relatives a number of times.

   Note: When the account of the murder of the Joseph P. Winston family was given it was not the intent of this author to state what he was a son of James Winston. His parents had not been identified beyond the newspaper article, and the account was meant to be a commentary on the culture of the times. It appears that Joseph Pendleton Winston, born April 5, 1825, was the son of Philip Bickerton Winston and Sarah Madison Pendleton. Joseph married Virginia Bell Pankey and they had a daughter Virginia. Joseph, who recovered from the bludgeoning by the servant, married a second time Lelia Saunders. Joseph died July 3, 1880.[20]

Pleasant Winston, M.D.
(512-513;452) Pleasant's wife, Elizabeth Cheadle Clark was the first cousin of Judith Winston through the Cheadles, which apparently was considered to be "too closely related by the Friends". Pleasant studied medicine in Philadelphia and in Indiana he practiced medicine and farmed, being less than successful at either. Elizabeth Winston's life in Darlington, Indiana was difficult. She was frightened of the wolves, and felt strongly the absence of her relatives. Her health was poor very early, and she probably suffered from a slowly developing tuberculosis, which she passed on in a more rapid fatal form to several of her children. She came home to die in the old Clark plantation, *Hill's Creek*, in Campbell County.

   To add to the information about the children of Pleasant and Elizabeth Winston: Bowling Henry married second, Julia Ricks the daughter of Alfred Ricks and Mary Ann Terrell, July 11, 1866 in Montgomery County, Indiana; Pleasant, Jr. married Chloe Ann Sleeper (born January 7, 1834), September 20, 1854; Ambrose married first, Lucy Eldridge Davis, May 20, 1863, she died c.1865, he married second, Lelia Lee Rucker, (born April 12, 1848) September 2, 1873; Charles Jones married Mary Elizabeth Alexander (born January 17, 1839?) December 24, 1868, she died February 1, 1923; and William Henry married Nancy Powell Moorman (born January 1, 1841) February 28, 1866, he died March 14, 1934.

Mary H. Winston
(513;452-453) Mary married Arnold W. Ricks, son of Richard and Julia Ricks of Southampton County. Mary's first husband, Arnold Ricks died in 1817, shortly after their marriage, their young daughter Julia Ann, born August 3, 1813 had died in infancy. Their second daughter, Deborah Ann was born February 8, 1816. Mary Ricks married a second time to Thomas Terrell who had come to the large Quaker community near Mt. Pleasant, Ohio.

Nathaniel Winston
(513;453) Further research into the Quaker records indicates that Nathaniel and Zalinda were in Louisville, Kentucky in 1835 and had not decided where to settle; it was not until 1842 that they moved to Ohio and in 1848 were accepted into the Short Creek Monthly Meeting at Mt. Pleasant, Ohio. He traveled on the river when he was in Louisville, owned a ferry and was clerk of the Mississippi steam boat, the *Hail Columbia* for a time. The only daughter recorded is known by her initials, ML, from family letters.

Elizabeth H. Winston

(513;453) From family correspondence it appears that Elizabeth lived for a time in Campbell County, moving to Mt. Pleasant by 1840.

Lucy Ann Winston

(513;453) Lucy Winston Kyle was married for thirteen years, apparently suffering with an "intemperate" husband; however, he died leaving her financially independent. She had a daughter, Virginia who married in 1840 in St. Louis.

George Winston, Jr.

(514;453) **correction:** George Winston, Jr. was mistakenly confused with his nephew, the son of Pleasant Winston. The son of George Winston, Sr. did marry, but his wife has still not been identified, and later lived in Illinois. His oldest son Nathaniel died in 1847 and George was reported in Lebanon, Ohio in 1861.

Amelia Winston

(514;453) It appears that Amelia and her husband, George Simpson lived in Covington, Kentucky and continued to live there after her husband became an invalid. They had five children, whom she supported. During the Civil War she served as an intermediary for mail between her Southern and Northern nephews. She was a strong Unionist. In 1861 her adult children were listed as Annie, Virginia and John.

Thomas B. Winston

(514;454) Thomas Winston traded on the Mississippi River, became wealthy and had homes in St. Louis and in New Orleans, Louisiana. He was reported to the family as living in great style. In 1836 he married Margaret Shall of New Orleans and intended to give up the river, but he died on a steamboat enroute to New Orleans in 1860.

WINSTON FAMILY

MARY WINSTON was the seventh generation in ascent from BERNARD HUTCNESON, through JOHN CHILES. GEORGE WINSTON was the fifth generation in ascent from NELLIE BUTLER. This is explained in the Winston family sketch.

Gen. 9 WILLIAM WINSTON		m	SARAH (—?—)
Issue:	ANTHONY	m	UNKNOWN
	William	m	(1)Sarah Jennings Dabney
		m	(2)Martha Tomlin Gouldman
			(3)Barbara Overton
Gen. 8 ANTHONY WINSTON		m	UNKNOWN
Issue:	Isaac	m	Mary (—?—)
	ANTHONY	m	UNKNOWN
Gen. 7 ANTHONY WINSTON		m	UNKNOWN
Issue:	Isaac	m	Sarah (—?—)
	NATHANIEL	m	JEMIMA BELL
Gen. 6 NATHANIEL WINSTON		m	JEMIMA BELL
Issue:	MARY	m	JOHN CHILES
	Samuel	m	Elizabeth Bates
	Rebecca	m	George Harwood
	Anthony	m	Nancy Haley
	GEORGE	m	JUDITH HARRIS
	Martha	m	Edmund Collins
	Sarah	m	Stephen Haley

138

	Pleasant	m	dis mcd
	Nathan	m	Ann Yarbrough
	Edmund		unmarried

Gen. 5	GEORGE WINSTON	m	JUDITH HARRIS
issue:	James	m	Ann R. Ricks
	Pleasant	m	Elizabeth Clark
	George	m	died in infancy
	Mary H.	m	(1) Arnold W. Ricks
		m	(2) Thomas Terrell
	Nathaniel	m	Zalinda Lynch
	Elizabeth H.	m	William Clark
	Lucy Ann	m	Hazlett Kyle
	Ann		died in infancy
	George	m	unknown
	Amelia H.	m	George Simpson
	Benjamin Thomas		died in infancy
	Thomas B.	m	Margaret Shall
	Benjamin		died in infancy
	VIRGINIA JUDITH	m	WILLIAM FLEMING BUTLER

Notes

1. Suit Jacob et al vs Winston et al, at High Court of Chancery, Richmond, Virginia. G.H.S. King Papers Mss1K5823a, Winston #3. Virginia Historical Society, Richmond, VA.
2. G.H.S. King Papers.
3. G.H.S. King Papers.
4. Lloyd and Helen Covington, *The Descendants of William Covington I, 1618-1696, "Bestland" Essex County, Virginia* (privately printed, 1996) 114. 25495 Ruther Glen Rd, Ruther Glen, VA 22546.
5. G.H.S. King Papers.
6. G.H.S. King Papers.
7. Charles Pool, 421½ S Laurel St, Richmond, VA 23220, a member of the Oregon Hill Home Improvement Council, has worked tirelessly to save their historic community.
8. Beginning at what is now Belvidere Street and extending westward along Cary Street and Three Chopt Road.
9. See Mary Wingfield Scott, *Houses of Old Richmond* (New York: Bonanza Books, MCMXLI).
10. From correspondence with Charles Pool 1995.
11. Gregg D. Kimball, "*African-Virginians and the Vernacular Building Tradition in Richmond City, 1790-1860*", *Valentine Museum Publication* (Richmond: Valentine Museum, c.1990) 121-129, 226-229.
12. Charles Pool.
13. *Richmond Times Dispatch*, July 11, 1995 and September 14, 1995.
14. Kelly Lane, SOHO Committee Chairman, August 9, 1995.
15. Jay Worrall, Jr., *The Friendly Virginians*, (Athens, GA: Iberian Publishing Co, 1994).
16. Hannah Watts Clarke (Mrs. John Clarke) lived at 19th and Cary streets apparently across the street from the Meeting House. The portrait is in the possession of Ms. Eda Martin, Williamsburg, VA. The artist was Charles Burton.
17. Clayton Torrence, ed., *Edward Pleasants Valentine Papers, vol III* 1927 (Baltimore: Genealogical Publishing Co rep 1979) 1753.
18. Dr. Lindley Winston, 619 S Warren Ave, Malvern, PA 19355.
19. Mary Elizabeth Stewart, P.O. Box 485, Irvington, VA 22480.
20. Alfred Sumner Winston, III, *The Winstons of Hanover County, Virginia and Related Families, 1666-1992* (Baltimore: Gateway Press, 1992) 746, 776.

Richmond Friends Meeting House, Sketched from Portrait of Hannah Watts Clark c.1840

ROBERT HARRIS

Gen. 9

No further information has been found to verify the descendants of this ROBERT HARRIS. As more has been learned of the customs of the people and the migration patterns it seems more likely that the relationship has been inferred accurately. Further research on the William Claiborne family has not confirmed the assertion that Robert Harris married Mary Claiborne Rice, the daughter of William Claiborne, the Secretary of the Colony.[1] It is felt that the second daughter of William Claiborne was named Elizabeth, previously based on the land patent references. The name of the wife of William Claiborne II was Katherine, which removes the probability that the Elizabeth, Jr. referred to his wife. Perhaps some day old records will be found that clarify these relationships.

The following is taken from the work of David Gaddy for *Tidewater Virginia Families,* and appeared in the magazine.[2] From what is known of the land holdings of Robert Harris it is believed that he would have attended the first church on the site of the "Upper Church" of Blisland Parish. Since Blisland Parish was established before 1653, it would seem likely that there was a church on the site before the Warranigh Church here described, was built. It was also probably this church that Robert Harris attended.

The church was apparently named for Wahrani Creek (as spelled on a modern map), because of its location in close proximity to the creek. Warranigh Church is known by many variant spellings of the creek name. It is spelled Warranigh in the Vestry Book of St. Peter's Parish.[3] Dr. Malcolm Harris used the name Warreneye[4], as did the Chesapeake Corporation in its account in their Nature Trail Guide[5]. Early land patents describe land as bordering Warrany Creek[6].

The church was erected at the head of what is today, Wahrani Swamp, shown on a modern map to flow in a southerly direction into Diascund Creek Reservoir and the Chickahominy River (US Route 60). Wahrani Creek emerges between SR 30 and SR 33 on the south side of the York River. This is just a few miles from West Point on the north side of the Pamunkey River, and Eltham on the south side. The confluence of the Pamunkey and the Mattaponi at West Point make up the York River. The site of Warreneye Church can be located as stop number 48 on the nature trail map.

Little has been written about the Upper Church of Blisland Parish, and yet it held a prominent place in the lives of New Kent County residents. It was certainly in this church that Colonel George Washington worshipped when he visited the family of Colonel Burwell Bassett of Eltham. Mrs. Bassett, Anna Marie Dandridge, was a sister of Martha Washington. Some names that have been found in the records concerning the Upper Church[7] are those of John Gaddey, sexton, at the time of his death in 1753,[8] and ministers, Daniel Taylor (1721), David Mossom (1729), William LeNeve (1729), Chicheley Thacker (1730-1763), and Price Davies (1763). Only the vestry book of Blisland Parish has survived, and it is interesting to note that all of the references to the church are to "the Upper Church", with only one reference to Warrany Creek as being that from which the church took its name[9].

Since the vestry book entries begin in 1721, there is no reference to the details of the construction of the Upper Church. Its appearance must be inferred from the later entries that have survived. An entry in the vestry minutes for September 1745 ordering a public notice of the repairs to the Upper Church described the nature of the repairs, and thus the construction of the building, as follows: *to be new cover'd with Cypres Shingles & a new floor laid, whitewash'd & painted inside and out, the Church yard wall repair'd & new gates made.*[10] It is revealing to note the agreement reached in 1746[11] by the vestry as to the addition for the church: *Thirty three feet long from outside to outside, and twenty three feet wide from outside to outside, and two sash windows on each side the S^d Addition, and a folding door at the end of the addition made of brick, (and the Isle laid with brick,) and cover'd with Cypres Shingles, and plaister'd and whitewash'd.*

Most of what is known about the church has been preserved in the letter of Samuel Mordecai written to his sister Rachel while he was with the Richmond militia during the War of 1812. The militia was dispatched to New Kent County in an effort to repel a threatened invasion of the British who were expected to come up the York River to attack Richmond. His letter was dated "Camp Warranigh Church, 11 September 1814". It is this letter that furnished the first-hand evidence of the date of erection of the Upper Church of Blisland Parish [12]. He wrote of his encampment in the ruins of the old church. The church was set on a high elevation overlooking the junction of the Pamunkey and Mattaponi rivers at the formation of the York. It was by the old road, the colonial highway, that ran from Eltham to Williamsburg. In 1814 only the walls and a part of the roof remained, the floors, doors, windows, and all the timber apparently had been used by "the pious parishioners". An inscription over one of the doors survived, with the inscription "Blisland Parish" and "1703". The walls were in good condition and a few pieces of timber were sound. Two ancient tombstones identified the churchyard. Today, a few broken bricks remain; English-size, with some of the blue-purple coloring of the salt glaze.[13] It is said that the remaining bricks were sold to a local landowner for use on his plantation.

At present two graves, placed side by side, are visible in the graveyard, having been enclosed in a white picket fence by its caretakers, the Chesapeake Corporation. Interred are the bodies of Dr. Thomas Arnott (died 1745) and Mr. John Long (died 1736).[14] The last entry in the vestry minutes for a vestry meeting of the Upper Church is dated October 11th 1786. The meeting was held at the Upper Church. Following the official record entries these lines were added later: John Taylor, January; John Augustine Taylor 1816. Warrany Church, the Upper Church of Blisland Parish, was reportedly razed not long after this.

(521-527;461-466)
Gen. 8   WILLIAM HARRIS

The father of TEMPERANCE OVERTON HARRIS, WILLIAM OVERTON arrived in Virginia before 1670. The Land Patent Book shows that William Overton patented over 4600 acres of land on the south side of the Pamunkey River, on Falling Creek, which was in New Kent County on 23 April 1681, having claimed transport for ninety-two persons, included among them, his wife ELIZABETH OVERTON.[15] He had paid the passage of his bride who arrived in November 1670 after his arrival. It is known that he later lived near WILLIAM HARRIS on the North Anna River. Elizabeth's mother, ANN WATERS died in England and her will was dated September 29, 1697 and recorded on July 4, 1670. In it she named sons: John, "gone to Virginia"; Samuel and Margaret Waters, his wife; Elizabeth Overton, now in Virginia and her husband William; son-in-law William Goodwin; with son Thomas as the residuary legatee.[16]

Robert Harris
(525;464) Of the children of Robert Harris and Mourning Glenn further information has been received concerning the son, Christopher. Dr. Benjamin L. Harris has an extensive collection of Harris genealogy and has shared the following:[17] Christopher Harris was born February 3, 1725 and died in Kentucky in 1794; he emigrated from Albemarle County to Kentucky between 1780 and 1790 and settled in Madison County. He and his son were confused in accounts of their lives probably because they were both Baptist ministers. He married first on February 22, 1745, Mary Dabney. Their children were (named in his will)[18]: Dabney Harris; Sarah Harris married James Martin; Robert Harris married Nancy Grubbs; Tyree Harris; Elizabeth Harris; Mourning Harris married Foster Jones; Christopher Harris married Elizabeth Grubbs; and Mary Harris. He married a second time and had the following children: Jane Harris married Richard Gentry; John Harris married Margaret Maupin; Benjamin Harris married (1) Frances Jones and (2) Nancy Burgin; William Harris married (1) Ann Oldham and (2) Jessie Oldham; James Harris; Margaret Harris; Isabel Harris married John Bennett; Samuel Harris married Nancy Wilkerson; Barnabas Harris married Elizabeth Oldham; and Overton Harris married Nancy Oldham. While he differentiates between the children of his first wife and those of his second he does not give the name of his second wife in his will.[19]

OVERTON FAMILY

Gen. 9 WILLIAM OVERTON	m	ELIZABETH WATERS
Issue: Elizabeth	m	Robert Anderson
William	m	Peggy Garland

TEMPERANCE	m	CAPT. WILLIAM HARRIS
Samuel	m	(—?—) Carr
James	m	Elizabeth Truehart widow
Barbara	m	William Winston II

(528-531;467-470)
Gen. 7   BENJAMIN HARRIS

Because of the Quakers noncompliance with the laws of the colony, there were many instances of their possessions being confiscated for their unwillingness to "take the oath". This author was unable at the time the book was written to define this, but has since come across a definition, and explanation. It was frequently required by the court that citizens take an Oath or Affirmation of Allegiance to the State in the Revolutionary period. A number of lists of those who "took the oath" have survived in county court papers. It was this Oath of Allegiance that many Quakers refused to take.

The deed has survived where in 1780, SARAH DUMAS HARRIS of Hanover County, bought 472 acres of land from Joseph Richeson. The land was formerly the property of Thomas Todd of Gloucester County and lay on the Mattapony River and adjoining the land of John Baylor and Joseph DeJarnette.[20]

Judith Harris
(529;468) Judith married James Crew who was the son of Andrew Crew of Charles City County.[21]

(532-539;471-477)
Gen. 6   JAMES HARRIS

When the life of JAMES HARRIS was researched initially your author had no understanding of the many and varied business interests of James and his sons and son-in-law. Much of this information has now come to light because of the documentation of the work of George Winston and the development of the Town of Sydney. The following is from the documented report to the Virginia Department of Historic Resources.

James Harris was the manager of the James River Canal and was named General Manager of the James River Company. He was a part of the creation of the first canal system in the North American continent. It was this canal system that made possible the honeymoon trip to Lynchburg by ROBERT and ALICE LEE BUTLER in 1868. James Harris must have been in Henrico County/Richmond prior to 1789. It is thought that the great Richmond fire of 1787 opened areas of opportunity in rebuilding the area decimated by the fire. It was also a period of great expansion following the creation of a new nation upon new and exciting principles. By 1790 James and Mary had sold to George Woolfolk a 472 acre tract of land in Caroline County on the Mattaponi River adjoining Joseph DeJarnette for £1000.[22]

Benjamin James Harris
(553;474) James Harris brought his son, Benjamin J. Harris to work with him in developing the James River Company. He later established one of the first tobacco factories in Richmond, from which he became quite wealthy. His home *Clifton* was insured for the enormous sum (for that time) of $20,000. Benjamin went on to work with his brother-in-law, George Winston and Jacquelin Harvey (who married the only daughter of Justice John Marshall) on a number of business ventures in Richmond including the Town of Sydney.

Benjamin spent a life-time of involvement with the civil and mechanical engineering problems associated with canal building and with tobacco, flour and cotton manufacture. The venture into real estate with regard to the Town of Sydney was less than as successful as the three partners had hoped. The economic boom from the 1790s had collapsed by 1817 and building was in a decline until the 1830s. All three men, Benjamin, George and Jacquelin suffered losses but were financially secure enough to weather the storm.

A brochure (c.1996) printed by Reynolds Metals Company describes the history of the James River Canal and the present effort to preserve parts of it through the Historic Places and Virginia Historic Landmarks. The sole remaining stone locks on the James River and Kanawha Canal Tidewater Connection at 12th and Byrd Sreets (the double locks, numbers 4 and 5) are preserved by the Reynolds Metal Company. The canal was conceived by George Washington as a key part of a *Great Central American Waterway* to stretch from the Atlantic to the Rockies. The James River Company created the first canal system on the North American continent. The eastern terminus, completed in 1800, was known as the *Great Basin* and was located in the center of the City of Richmond between 8th, 12th, Canal and Cary Streets. By 1854 this was enlarged with five granite locks, allowed boats to navigate between the tidewater of the James River and the eastern terminus of the canal.

From 1820 to 1835 the canal was extended west from Westham to Maidens Adventure, where the James drops through the Blue Ridge Mountains. Improvements to navigation were made in the Great Kanawha River and a road built from Covington to the Ohio River. By 1840 the canal had been extended west to Lexington and eleven years later it was completed to Buchanan. With the 1854 turning basin in Richmond, the canal was complete and boats could navigate from the harbors of the Atlantic Coast to Buchanan, a distance of 197½ miles.[23]

Elizabeth Harris
(536;475)

It was later that the old home, *Prospect Hill* assumed the name of *Shannon Mills*, and was offered for sale by W.P. Patterson in the 1920s, styled as *An Old Virginia Country Estate*.[24] All of this property is now known as *Caroline Pines*, the intent having been to develop and style as a resort. The graves of Alfred Ricks (died 1858, age 58), the son of Richard and Julia Wilkinson Ricks of Southampton County and Mary Ricks, his wife, (died 1869 **(1870)**, age sixty-eight), the daughter of Samuel and Elizabeth Terrell are just to the front and left of the house beside the road leading to the North Anna River. They are enclosed in a fence of iron piping.[25]

Elizabeth Harris inherited the property that was later to be known as *Prospect Hill* from her father, James Harris. As was the law of the time, the land then became the property of her husband, Samuel Terrell. Elizabeth and her husband, Samuel Terrell both named their surviving children in their wills. (20 da: 9 mo: 1842 and 7th mo: 1852, respectively).[26] The Terrell Family Bible of Pleasant Terrell and his wife Caty the parents of Samuel, born January 8, 1770), and of Samuel Terrell and his wife, Elizabeth Harris has survived.[27] The births, marriages and deaths of their children are recorded, and also the fact that several members of the family are interred in the Caroline-Golansville Friends Meeting House cemetery. The children: Mary Ann, born November 3, 1801, married Alfred Ricks, April 14, 1822 and died October 18, 1870 **(the date on the gravestone is incorrect)**; Samuel, born December 29, 1802, died October 19, 1826, unmarried, it is believed; Walter, born April 15, 1805, married (1) Talitha (sic) Crew (2) her sister Jane; James Pleasants, born December 2, 1808, died October 14, 1867, unmarried; Henry O., born March 2, 1815, unmarried, said to have been killed by Indians on his way from Louisiana to California; and George Fox Terrell, M.D., born October 16, 1817, died May 28, 1855, unmarried. He was buried at the Golansville Meeting House cemetery beside his mother. George Fox Terrell was one of the last members of the Golansville Quaker Meeting.

A moiety of the land had been given to Mary Ann Ricks from the will of Samuel Terrell, with the other given to the son George Fox Terrell, who left his share to Mary Ann. Richard, the son of Mary Ann and her husband, Alfred, ultimately owned the farm *Prospect Hill* and Ricks' Mill. Richard was born in 1831, married first Martha Whitlock and second Eliza Crenshaw, the daughter of John and Rachel Crenshaw. It was their son who became Judge J. Hoge Ricks (born 1886) of the Richmond Juvenile Court and who was the well-respected defender of youths in the criminal court system. R. Arnold Ricks, who has continued his family Quaker traditions, is the son of Judge Ricks. He graduated from Haverford College and from Harvard University with a background in history and a great appreciation for the preservation of his Quaker heritage.[28]

While this account of the Ricks family is only one branch of the family of Elizabeth Harris Terrell, it seems important to the author to present it. The Ricks and Butler/Winston families were inextricably interwoven through marriages in the late 1700s and 1800s. Arnold and the author have been actively involved in the effort to save the Jacob House and presently (1996-1998) the Golansville Meeting House site and cemetery. As cousins who had "heard of each other" for some years through their parents, it was at the Friends Bicentennial celebration that they finally met.

Elizabeth Harris Terrell left an allowance, with the legacy held in trust by her trustee or caretaker, to be paid annually to her sister, Lucy. It seems that Lucy Harris was not capable of looking after herself.

Mary Harris
(536;475) Mary Harris did not marry and lived with her sister, Elizabeth. When she petitioned the court concerning the mill it may have been another mill on the property, rather than what became known as Ricks' Mill. She apparently suffered from periods of disability as did her sister Lucy.

HARRIS FAMILY

Gen. 9 <u>MAJ. ROBERT HARRIS</u>		m	<u>UNKNOWN</u>
Issue:	WILLIAM	m	TEMPERANCE OVERTON
	Robert	m	Elizabeth Turner
	John	m	Anne (—?—)
	Richard	m	
Gen. 8 <u>CAPT. WILLIAM HARRIS</u>		m	<u>TEMPERANCE OVERTON</u>
Issue:	Robert	m	Mourning Glenn
	BENJAMIN	m	SARAH DUMAS
	William	m	Elizabeth Burnett
	John	m	
	James	m	
	Jemima	m	William Overton
Gen. 7 <u>BENJAMIN HARRIS</u>		m	<u>SARAH DUMAS</u>
Issue:	Judith	m	James Crew
	Obediah	m	Rebecca Johnson
	Jeremiah	m	Ann Chiles
	JAMES	m	MARY CHEADLE
	Unity	m	John Ladd
	Rachel	m	Clark Moorman
	Thomas	m	Chlotilda Ladd
Gen. 6 <u>JAMES HARRIS</u>		m	<u>MARY CHEADLE</u>
Issue:	JUDITH	m	GEORGE WINSTON
	Benjamin James	m	(1) Sarah Ellyson
		m	(2) Flora Wyatt
	Elizabeth	m	Samuel Terrell
	Mary		unmarried
	Thomas	m	Unity Ladd
	Lucy		unmarried
	James	m	

Notes

1. John Frederick Dorman and Claiborne T. Smith, Jr., M.D., *Claiborne of Virginia, Descendants of Colonel William Claiborne* (Baltimore: Gateway Press, 1995). 1-6.
2. David Winfred Gaddy, PO Box 46, Tappahannock, VA 22560. "*Warranigh Church, Upper Church, Blisland Parish, New Kent County, TVF* 3:83-85.
3. See Mordecai's account: C. G. Chamberlayne, *The Vestry Book and Register of St Peter's Parish.* (Richmond: VSLA, 1989) 684,689.
4. Malcolm H. Harris, *Old New Kent County Some Account of the Planters, Plantations and Places of New Kent County.* vol.1 (Privately printed, 1977) 2, 26,40,41,77.
5. Chesapeake Corporation, *New Kent Nature Trail Guide.* (West Point VA 23181, n.d.) 21.
6. Nugent I: 318,376,390.
7. C. G. Chamberlayne, *The Vestry Book of Blisland Parish.* (Richmond: VSLA, 1979) xiv.
8. *Gaddy Newsletter.*
9. Chamberlayne, *VBBP* xiv.
10. Chamberlayne, *VBBP* 90.

11. Chamberlayne, *VBBP* 94.

12. Chamberlayne, *SPPVB&R* 684-685.

13. *Gaddy Newsletter.*

14. Both are marked with table top gravestones, on one is written: *Here lyeth interr'd the body of Doctor Thomas Arnott who departed this life 29 January 1745 aged 38 years.* The second reads: *Here lies interr'd the body of Mr. John Long of Ramsgate in the County of Kent in Great Britain late commander of the Ship The John and Mary who departed this life the 24th of July 1736 aged 25 years.* [An inscription follows]: *Sobriety justice and truth: adorn'd the Soul: of this sweet Youth. but that soul we hope is gone: unto a better State and home. and when the last loud trump shall Sound: and wake the Nations underground. he shall we hope then live and stand amongst the Sheep and Christ right hand.*

15. Nugent II:218.

16. W.E. Dickenson, *"The Overton Family"*, *Richmond Times Dispatch*, September 5, 1915. contributed by Marian Brigham. Williamsburg, VA.

17. Benjamin L. Harris, M.D., *"The Case of Confused Identity: Two Christopher Harrises"*, *Bluegrass Roots* 22(1995): 140.

18. *Madison County, Kentucky Will Book A-1*: Richmond County Courthouse 54-55.

19. Harris, unpublished manuscript.

20. The Woolfolk Papers, Mss1W8844a, 61-65, Virginia Historical Society, Richmond, VA.

21. Judge Leon Bazille Papers, Mss1B348aFA2, Virginia Historical Society, Richmond, VA.

22. Woolfolk Family Papers.

23. From the brochure, Reynolds Metals Co.

24. Papers of Arnold R. Ricks, Professor Emeritus, Bennington College, 370 Elm Street, Bennington, VT 05201. Sales brochure of *Shannon Mills Farm*, (Richmond: Whittet & Shepperson, 1926). Also deed, 1887 conveys mill to R.A. Ricks, Caroline County Deed Book 61, 412. See also account of James Harris' land in Caroline County.

25. Collins 1:123.

26. Copy of will in possession of R. Arnold Ricks, 370 Elm St, Bennington, VT, handwritten by M.A. Ricks.

27. Bible Philadelphia, 1808-1809, Family Record of Samuel and Elizabeth Harris Terrell of "Prospect Hill", on the north side of the North Anna River, near Ruther Glen, Caroline County, VA Bible in possession of (1998) R. Arnold Ricks, Bennington, VT

28. Hinshaw 6:265-266; 274.

Fork Church, Hanover County c.1985

JOHN CHEADLE I

Gen. 10 (9)

On January 29, 1666, a General Vestry meeting was held at the house of Sir Henry Chichley (Rosegill).

We doe accord and agree that ye two parishes formerly call Lancaster and Peanckatanck from hense forth be united as one and called Christ Church parish.

"Item. That a Mother Church be built in ye small Indian field next ye head of Capt. Brocas his ground. It being adjudged by us to be about ye middle of ye p'ish.

"Item. That ye Mother church be called by name of Christ Church...building the Mother Church, in every respect to be done and finished according to the Middle Plantacon Church [in Williamsburg], to be finished in six months, glass and iron worke convenient time to be given for its transportation out of England.[1]

This first building appears to have been of clapboard construction. It was used until 1712, when at the vestry meeting of June 9, a new church was ordered built of brick. The work was to have been completed by June 10, 1714, and we have every reason to believe it was completed by that date. The clapboard church was the nucleus of the Christ Church Parish in Middlesex County. It became the "Mother Church", but the "Upper Church" followed closely in 1667, and was ordered to be of the same design. It would have been this church that JOHN CHEADLE and his family attended regularly, going to the mother church on rare occasions.

Without question, the present Christ Church building occupies the identical ground of the original 1666 "Mother Church", for when the new church was ordered built, directions were given also for an "arbor", in which services might be held during construction.

There are seven graves under the church. Sir Henry Chichley, Deputy Governor of Virginia, was buried near the present Communion Table on February 9, 1682. Another of the graves is that of the Reverend John Sheppard, rector of Christ Church from 1668 until his death in 1683. The others are: Madam Catherine Wormley, Aylmer Wormley, Edward Thompson and Mary Reeves and her son. The Thompson slab, now set in the aisle flagstones, was found under the floor of the church when the building was renovated in the 1920s.

The Communion Plate of Christ Church consists of some modern pieces given as memorials and three ancient pieces that are believed to remain from the set presented by the Honorable Ralph Wormley of Rosegill in 1687. During the Revolution the Communion Silver was placed in a bank vault in Fredericksburg where it remained for more than thirty years. On being returned to the parish, it was partially destroyed by fire. It was restored by S. Kirk and Son of Baltimore in 1855. There were originally five pieces, but after the fire they were only able to gather up enough silver to restore three pieces: a chalice, a paten and an alms plate.

The parish is most fortunate in the possession of historic records in the form of two printed volumes, *The Vestry Book of Christ Church, 1663-1767*, compiled by Dr. Chamberlayne from documents stored at the (Episcopal) Seminary at Alexandria, shows the early social service entrusted to vestries, and expenditures in pounds of tobacco. The other, *The Parish Register, 1653-1812*, lists births, baptisms, marriages and deaths. This may be seen in the Urbanna Library. The graveyard contains a number of table tombs of historic interest. One marks the resting place of the beloved Bartholomew Yates, who served for many years as Rector, and taught at the College of William and Mary. A complete list of grave markings has been made.

In 1840 the church was revived in Middlesex. By that time the roof of Christ Church had fallen in, the woodwork had rotted and a large tree had grown in the center aisle. In 1840 the building was restored and has continued in use until the present time. In 1921 Christchurch School for boys was founded by the Rev. F.E. Warren.[2] The upper church is no longer standing.

Hannah Cheadle

(543-544;481) Hannah Cheadle married Richins Brame, the son of John and Mary Dabney Brame. John and Mary were married November 15, 1674 in Middlesex County. Her maiden name has been determined from a Masonic apron handed down for three hundred years in the Brame family. It is said to have been presented to John at his marriage.[3] After the death of Richins, Hannah married Thomas Burch of King William County. Hannah Burch died in Caroline County about 1740.[4]

(546-553;484-491)
Gen. 9 (8)   **JOHN CHEADLE II**

The earliest Quakers in Caroline County appear to have been members of the Cheadle, Chiles, Hackett, Hubbard and Terrell families.[5] It was they, with a few others, who made up the membership of the Caroline Friends Meeting at it formal beginning in 1739. To the Golansville Meeting House they and their children and their children's children came on First Day mornings for 114 years, gathering to "center down" in silence to "wait upon the Lord".[6]

The name of JOHN CHEADLE appears as early as that of any Quaker in St. Margaret's Parish, though he did not grow up in the Religious Society of Friends. He had been a communicant of Christ Church in Middlesex County where he married LETTICE SOUTHERN in 1713 and was mentioned in the parish register as late as 1724. He first appeared in 1728 in the Caroline County records, when he and Thomas Hackett jointly were granted 400 acres of land on the south branch of Polecat Creek.[7]

Where and how he became a Friend is not known, but it was in his home, as has been noted, that Friends commonly met in the 1730s before the Golansville Meeting House was built. Some of the "public Friends" of this period travelling in Virginia record staying with the Cheadles: John Fothergill and Thomas Chalkley from England in 1736 and 1738, respectively, and John Woolman from New Jersey in 1746.[8] Clearly a weighty Friend, John Cheadle served as Clerk of the Monthly Meeting from its beginning in 1739 to 1754. John's wife is not mentioned in the abstracted Cedar Creek Monthly Meeting minutes, but their six children who grew to adulthood all married within the Society.

Agatha and Ann Chiles, daughters of Henry and Mary Chiles of Hanover County, married brothers, David and Henry Terrell, and were the first of their family to become Friends. Agatha and David Terrell married about 1727, Ann and Henry Terrell in 1734. Both couples are said to have married by Quaker ceremony, but at least David and Agatha must have married under the care of the Cedar Creek Meeting since Caroline Friends were not organized in 1727. Later Manoah Chiles, the older brother of Agatha and Ann, joined the Caroline Meeting, probably shortly before his second marriage in 1742 to Anne Cheadle, a daughter of John.[9]

Thomas Hackett, identified in his land patent as "of Middlesex County", received 400 acres on the south fork of Polecat Creek in 1725, before Caroline County was created, and with John Cheadle acquired another 400, possibly contiguous to the first, in 1728.[10] Apparently he and his wife, Mary came to Caroline County from Middlesex County, shortly after selling their land there in 1724[11]. The names and birth dates of five of their children are given in the Christ Church Parish Register, Middlesex County, between 1715 and 1725[12].

John Hubbard, probably a member of the Virginia Quaker Hubbard family of York County, homesteaded 250 acres on the south side of the Mattapony River and north side of the South River in 1719.[13] He and his wife, whose name is unknown, had six sons (and possibly other children), two of whom, George and Peter, married Quaker women; a third Benjamin, became a major merchant in Caroline County and left the Society. Matthew, Richard and John, Jr. appear to have been other sons.[14] John Hubbard served as an overseer of the Caroline Meeting from 1741 until 1744.[15]

The two sons of WILLIAM and SUSANNAH TERRELL of Hanover County, David and Henry, who married Chiles sisters, were the first Terrells to become Quakers. They were the progenitors of a large clan of Quaker Terrells. David and Agatha had seven sons and five daughters, while Henry had five sons and five daughters: four children by Ann Chiles and six by his second wife, Sarah Woodson.[16] Most of these children and **their** children remained Friends, and Terrell men and women were faithful members of Caroline Meeting through all its 114-year history. Many more of this family moved to the Lynchburg area and joined the South River Meeting there.

A number of families joined Caroline Friends after their meeting house was built, including: the

Ballard brothers and their wives: Richard and Mary, and William and Sarah, and some of their children; Jason and Joel Meador, sons of Jonah; Thomas Stockton and his family, who came to Caroline in 1747, some of whom moved to Albemarle County; William and Mary MacGehee and one or two of their children; Nicholas Stone, born in England, and his wife Mary, a minister. Their son and three daughters married within the Society. Nicholas moved to New Garden Meeting in North Carolina after his wife's death in 1767.[17]

Others who joined were members of established Quaker families of other Virginia meetings who married into Caroline Meeting: the Clark, Crew, Hargrave, Harris, Johnson, Moorman, Ricks, Stanley and Winston families. Still others joined Caroline Meeting as newly-convinced Friends, such as members of the Cobb, Lewis, Maddox and Peatross families.

The Quaker world up to the mid-nineteenth century was in large measure knit together through the efforts of Friends travelling in the ministry; "public Friends", women as well as men, who left home for months or years to nurture the spiritual well-being of Friends meetings. Twenty-three of these public Friends mention in their journals visits to Caroline Meeting, from John Fothergill who visited in 1736 to Rebecca Hubbs in 1844. Of these, five made extended comments:

Edmond Peckover, 8th Month 1742, *...to a meeting in Caroline County...which hath been settled about eight or ten years, I think. There is a meeting house built, and a pretty company of Friends live in about four or five miles around it, perhaps about 40 or 50 in number*"[18]

William Reckitt, 1-1-1758, *A large and good meeting. The states of the people were spoken to...stayed with Menoah Chiles one night and John Chiles one night.*

Robert Walker, 1774, *...careless professors...Friends are the most out of order that I ever met with..."* (but he said the same thing of West River Meeting in Maryland when he visited soon after.)

William Matthews, 5-10-1776, *A close exercising time. Things appeared very much out of order.*

Thomas Scattergood, 11-31-1793, *To Caroline Meeting where was a gay mixed assembly...strength afforded to preach the everlasting gospel; it was an open good time; several members of Congress were present, one of whom came to me after I had got into the wagon and said 'Permit me to give you my hand'.*[19]

As the first organized body of dissenters in the county, Caroline Quakers had successfully asserted the right to worship according to the dictates of their conscience; this did not mean, however, that the exercise of their faith was without cost. The sheriff and his deputies visited their farms routinely to confiscate livestock or household goods when Friends refused to pay "priests' wages" or serve in the militia.

Property of the Cheadles was seized year after year through the 1740s and 1750s; Jason Meador's horse was seized in 1743; David Terrell's mare and Henry Terrell's table in 1746. *John Peatross suffered the seizure of one yoke of oxen on account of our testimony against war* about 1786; Thomas Terrell *one yoke of oxen and four cattle*; Pleasant Terrell *one mare & colt* for the same cause about the same time, and so on. These were heavy penalties with considerable financial loss to which the Friends were subjected[20].

Caroline Meeting when organized in 1739 was joined, as we have seen, with Cedar Creek Meeting in Hanover some twenty miles distant in a single Monthly Meeting. The Caroline Meeting was called interchangeably the Caroline Meeting or the Golansville Meeting, after the community in which many of these families lived and the meeting house was built. For many years they alternated the meeting place - and also the name - between the two locations. From this circumstance it also came to be called the "Circular" Monthly Meeting. For a time in the 1750s, Camp Creek Meeting at Poindexter in Louisa County was included as a third partner in the Circular Meeting. Remarkably, for the first thirty-six years of the Circular Meeting's existence, the Clerk (the responsible office for the meeting) always came from Caroline: John Cheadle served from 1739 to 1754; his son, Thomas from 1754 to 1758; and Samuel Hargrave (John's son-in-law) from 1758 to 1775.[21]

Along with a Clerk for the whole monthly meeting, there were also overseers, one or two of whom saw to the affairs of each constituent meeting, including Cedar Creek, Caroline and Camp Creek, and six preparative meetings: Fork Creek in Louisa County, Douglas in Orange County, Sugar Loaf Mountain in Albemarle, Johnson's in Amelia, Genito in Goochland, and briefly, South River Meeting near Lynchburg. Although in many instances women held these responsible positions, for the first thirty-six years no women appear to have been clerks or overseers in the Circular Meeting.[22]

Golansville Meeting lost a few members after 1784 when Virginia Yearly Meeting, following years of laboring with the issue to proceed in unity, reached the sense of the meeting that any Friends who continued to hold slaves would be disowned. At the same time, there were Friends who were actively concerned for the improvement of the conditions of the black people. Thomas Scattergood, while staying with Clark and Rachel Moorman when he visited in Caroline in 1793, wrote in his journal: *After dinner the black children [of freed black families] came in with their books to read their lessons. I was comforted in beholding such care and attention toward them. C[lark]s wife came in amongst the men, at the Yearly Meeting, to plead the cause of this people*[23].

Caroline Meeting lost many more members after 1800 when the Northwest Territory - Ohio and Indiana - opened up for settlement. Since this was declared slave-free by Congress, it drew Quakers from Virginia to move there by the hundreds. Between 1813 and 1833 six public Friends who visited Caroline all commented on the Meeting's diminished membership.

The undeniable effect of the slavery issue upon Caroline/Golansville Meeting along with others in Virginia should not obscure; however, the steady attrition caused by the Society of Friends' uncompromising stands on what was viewed as essential to a Friend's commitment. "Marriage out of unity" with Friends, i.e. marriage to someone not a Friend" probably led the list of those departures from standards enjoined by the Society that resulted in major losses of members. The Caroline Friends Meeting was "laid down"; its Meeting House at Golansville permanently closed in 1853.[24] George Fox Terrell was one of the last members of the Golansville Meeting.

The Society of Friends, or "Quakers" as they were frequently called, quietly and passively lived and practiced their beliefs. They come to Virginia by 1656 to escape religious persecution, and they were persecuted in Virginia. They were banished from the colony by 1658, and by 1661 the Virginia General Assembly passed a law that anyone who did not attend the Church of England for one month would be fined. It was not until 1688 that the Toleration Acts were passed which allowed for dissenting religious groups to hold services openly; however, they continued to be persecuted for not following the laws of the colony. The Quakers were the single largest religious group next to the Church of England. They quietly and passively lived and practiced their beliefs. It will surprise you to know that:
* they pioneered in economic development in the Industrial Revolution of the 18th century.
* they pioneered in many early social inventions such as banking and insurance.
* they also pioneered in establishing fixed prices for commodities instead of the custom at that time of "haggling".
* they pioneered quietly for the right of women to vote.
* it was in Caroline County that they began the movement to abolish slavery within the entire Quaker community.

Members of the Society of Friends moved with their families northward from the lower Tidewater counties into the wilderness and fearlessly established their homes beyond the fringes of civilization, before Caroline County had even become a county. Their presence was recorded immediately following the establishment of the county in 1727. These earliest Caroline Friends were probably associated with the young Cedar Creek Friends Meeting in western Hanover County, but in the 1730s began meeting for worship in their own homes, notably the home of John Cheadle. By the following year the Caroline Quakers were sufficiently strong to be approved as a meeting by the Virginia Yearly Meeting. They built their own meeting house in the hamlet of Golansville; the first monthly meeting for business of the joint Caroline and Cedar Creek Meetings was held here on March 12, 1739.[25]

The meeting house site has been identified and is located in a copse of trees about 100 yards south of the Golansville crossroads and less than 100 feet west of the highway. The old burying ground lies a short distance west of the meeting house site; marked only with periwinkle and two gravestones of a later time. There is a court record of the land that was purchased for the meeting house site and an additional acre of adjoining land given to the Society for the cemetery.

It was this site that was visited over two hundred and fifty years later (in the fall of 1995), by descendants of these early Quakers (Herbert Collins, Arnold Ricks, Virginia and Jim Davis). From the remaining foundation of the meeting house and the evidence of the cemetery, these descendants described them for posterity in the quarterly, *TIDEWATER VIRGINIA FAMILIES: A Magazine of History and Genealogy*. The hope was to preserve this heritage. The cemetery site was bulldozed in early 1997, just after these articles appeared in the magazine. The above provides the only assembled documentation of the Meeting House of these stalwart people. There is now an ongoing effort to restore the cemetery and preserve the meeting house site.[26] John Cheadle and his family would surely have been buried in the Friends Cemetery.

John Cheadle
(551;489) Records for Rowan County, North Carolina show that John Cheadle and Samuel Hargrave each bought land in that county. John Cheadle, of Caroline County, purchased from Obadiah Harris 440 acres on Wolf Branch of Deep River, October 1767, recorded in January 1768. Samuel Hargrave of Caroline County purchased 240 acres on Horsepen Creek from James Britain on December 21, 1766, also recorded in the January court 1768.[27]

correction: It is believed that Mr. Campbell in his book, *Colonial Caroline*[28] erred in stating that Samuel Hargrave, Sr. was the son of William Hargrave. It is believed that William, the overseer for Benjamin Hubbard was actually William Hargrove and that Samuel Hargrave descended from Lemuel Hargrave of Surry County.[29]

(554-561;492-498)
Gen. 8 (7)   **THOMAS CHEADLE**

CHEADLE FAMILY

ANNE CHEADLE is the eighth generation in line of ascent from BERNARD HUTCHESON. THOMAS CHEADLE is the seventh generation through the line of NELLIE BUTLER, through THOMAS CHEADLE.

Gen. 10 <u>JOHN CHEADLE</u>	m	<u>MILLICENT HUGHES</u>
Issue: Thomas	m	Frances Godby
JOHN	m	LETTICE SOUTHERN
Hannah	m	(1) Richins Brame
	m	(2) Thomas Burch
Gen. 9 <u>JOHN CHEADLE</u>	m	<u>LETTICE SOUTHERN</u>
Issue: Millicent	m	Arminger Trotter
John	m	Elizabeth Hargrave
Thomas		died in infancy
ANNE	m	MANOAH CHILES
THOMAS	m	JUDITH WOODSON
Mary	m	David Garland
Martha	m	Samuel Hargrave
Gen. 8 <u>THOMAS CHEADLE</u>	m	<u>JUDITH WOODSON</u>
Issue: MARY	m	JAMES HARRIS
John	m	
George		d.s.p.
Thomas	m	dis mcd
Sarah	m	Henry Chiles
Ursula	m	George Harwood
Judith	m	William Clark
Lucy	m	James Clark
Elizabeth	m	Bolling Clark
Jacob	m	(—?—) Chiles

Notes

1. C.G. Chamberlayne, *The Vestry Book of Christ Church Parish, Middlesex County, Virginia, 1663-1767* (Richmond: Old Dominion Press, 1927) 5-6; also see pp.x-xv, 8-9.
2. This history has been presented by Mr. Carroll Chowning to guests visiting the church, and also appears on the present church bulletin. Used with permission. Also in *TVF* 1: 127-130.

3. Arden H. Brame, Jr., II, *"Early History of the Brame-Brim Family, 1674-1725 in Middlesex County, Virginia and Devonshire, England, 1544-1666", English Genealogist* VI(n.d.): 96-102.

4. Correspondence with James E. Cockerham, 424 W Main St, Jonesville, NC 28642 (1993).

5. "*Early Caroline County Quakers*" ,*TVF* 5(1996): 221-226.

6. Jay Worrall, *Notes on Caroline County Friends.*

7. Hinshaw VI:232; V.L.H. Davis, *TVF* 2nd ed. 484-486; T.E. Campbell, *Colonial Caroline, a History of Caroline County, Virginia.*(Richmond: Dietz, 1954) 315. A plat of the land of Thomas Cheadle, his son, in the division of his estate, has survived. It totaled 928 acres.Caroline Co. Court Records, Acc. No. 26675, Library of VA. The land is identified as adjoining the land of John Hampton, whose land can be found today on the southeast corner of the intersections of US 1 and CR 601. The plat shows the bounds of his land as adjoining the land of Manoah Chiles, Robert Quarles, Anthony New, Christopher Terrell, Richard Tyler, Cobb, Allen, Hackett and Johnston.

8. Thomas Chalkley, *Journal of Thomas Chalkley.* 2nd. ed. (London, 1751) 305-307, also cited in Stephen B. Weeks, *Southern Quakers and Slavery.* (Baltimore: John Hopkins UP, 1896) 85; John Fothergill, *Life and Travels of John Fothergill*, Friends Library. Vol. 13: 419. John Woolman, *The Journal of John Woolman.* (J.G. Whittier Edition), rep. (Secaucus, NJ: Citadel Press, 1972) 60.

9. Hinshaw 273-275; *W&M Q* (1) 18:106-107; Dicken 165, 195; Davis 270-271, 246-249.

10. Land Patent Book 12:260; Book 13:276. Both patents adjoined the land of Hayle. This land does not appear to have been near Hackett Creek, which flows into Polecat Creek from the north about five miles east of Golansville.

11. *Middlesex County Court Order Book 6*, 100.

12. National Society of Colonial Dames of America, *Parish Register of Christ Church, Middlesex County, Virginia.* (Richmond, 1897). 91, 98, 103, 109, 117.

13. Land Patent Book 11:4.

14. Hinshaw VI:182, 249; Campbell 443, 490.

15. Hinshaw VI:249; Campbell 175, 380.

16. Hinshaw VI:273-275; Ibid.; *W&M Q*; Davis 270-271; Ibid., Dicken.

17. Hinshaw, passim.

18. *Edmond Peckover's Journal.* (London, 17[--]) 97.

19. Peckover 97; William Reckitt, *Life and Gospel Labors of William Reckitt.* (London, 1783) 81; John M. Moore "*English Quaker Ministers' Visit to Colonial American, 1773-1775*", *Quaker History.* (1989) 78:107-108; William Matthews, *William Matthew's Journal.* Matthews Papers, Maryland's Historical Society, Baltimore; Thomas Scattergood, *Journal of the Life and Religious Labors of Thomas Scattergood.* (Philadelphia, 1874) 125.

20. Hinshaw VI:232, 233, 259, 262, 276.

21. "*Early Caroline County Quakers and Their Meeting House*", *TVF* 5(1996) 159-163.

22. Hinshaw VI:224, passim.

23. Scattergood 138.

24. James P. Bell, *Quaker Friends of Ye Olden Times* 1905 (Baltimore: Clearfield, rep 1991 263.

25. *TVF* 5(1996): 159-163.

26. Excerpted from a talk presented (VLHD, 4/1997.) before the Caroline County Historical Society; and "*Early Caroline County Quakers*"; *TVF* 5(1996): 221-226.

27. *Rowan County, North Carolina Deed Book 6* 504, 505.

28. T. Elliott Campbell, *Colonial Caroline* (Richmond: Dietz, 1954) 381.

29. Correspondence (1998) Julia H. Painter, 6320 Howell Pl, Virginia Beach, VA 23464, a descendant of Samuel Hargrave, who referred to the book by Dorothy P. Beebe, *The Hargrove Family Study. Surry County Will Book 9* 415.

Conjectural Sketch of Golansville Meeting House c.1739

JOHN SOUTHERN I

Gen. 10 (9)

JOHN SOUTHERN is identified as having come to the colony on the *George* in 1620, is listed in the muster of the inhabitants of James Cittie taken the 24th of January 1624 and in the muster of Mr. Edward Blaney.[1] In 1623/4 at the regular session of the General Assembly the law was passed that each male over the age of sixteen was to receive four pounds of the best merchantable tobacco, in leaf, before October next. In 1626 he is listed at Blunt Pointe in the patents granted by Order of the Court with 40 acres of land.[2] He also acquired an additional fifty acres of land in James Citty for transporting William Soane. The land that John owned on Jamestown Island was described as being in two parcels, one twelve acres, a neck of land parted by a marsh from the land of Johnson and bounded northward by Back River, westward by the marsh Tucker's Hole and southward by the highway leading to Black Point. The other twelve acres was near the former, adjoining the land of Mary, wife of Gabriel Holland, west on the land of John Johnson and near the land of Thomas Passmore.[3]

Mr. John Southerne was present at the Grand Assembly held in James Citty the 21st of February 1631/32 as a Burgess from James Citty. John Southern was a person of some standing for he served in many capacities, among them as clerk, issuing warrants, executor and administrator of estates, released Governor Yeardley from his bond, was an appraiser and an arbitrator, juryman and served in many other areas of significance between the years 1623 and 1629. [4]

In 1652 the twenty-four acres described above was repatented by Edward Travis and described as being the land granted John Southern and identified further as formerly granted John Southern Senior.[5] Thus there were two generations of John Southerns in the colony of Virginia. While the direct relationship found between this John Southern and the John Southern listed on the Rent Roll of 1704 in Middlesex County and charged with 100 acres of land is not established,[6] it is believed that this is father and son. The name John Southern has not appeared in the records of the colony in so far as has been determined except in these two locations; the time frame would be appropriate to assume this relationship.

John Southern arrived in the colony of Virgin just after the colonists on Jamestown Island were beginning to settle beyond the James Fort and the immediate New Town area. While he must cope with the rigors of a new country and completely unfamiliar climate and surroundings the settlers were beginning to consider themselves a more cohesive and stable society. What follows sets the stage for the community in which John Southern lived and made his contribution to the stability of the colony.[7]

Presented here are excerpts from the "APVA Newsletter"[8] commemorating the momentous find of the 1607 James Fort. While the complete articles are printed in the newsletter it is in keeping with the philosophy of TVF that this major historic discovery be noted in the magazine.

In 1994...the APVA embarked upon a major archaeological investigation, *Jamestown Rediscovery*. With the same determination and teamwork of the founders, the APVA has "pulled off" the major find in the archaeological history of our nation. Once again attention has been paid to Jamestown. This time the APVA has the distinct honor of announcing that the original 1607 fort has been found.[9]

The discovery dispels the long held belief that James Fort, site of the first permanent English settlement in North America, was lost to the James River.[10] On 12 September 1996, The Honorable George Allen, Governor of the Commonwealth of Virginia proclaimed the finding of the site of the original 1607 James Fort.

'The Virginia Company, which was started at Jamestown, was the first Old World commercial venture started in the New World. Thus, from the Jamestown Fort foundations we all are reminded that on this unequaled hallowed ground the foundation of free people and free enterprise was begun.

From this birthplace rose the spirit that formed a great state - a great nation - and the ideals emulated by people all across the world. The ambitious, adventurous and enterprising spirit that gave rise to the original fort is the same spirit that has led us to its discovery today.

The resourceful efforts and skill of Dr. Kelso[11] and his team are to be commended. When the conventional wisdom indicated that the fort was lost to the mighty James River, these inquiring men and women had a much better idea. They literally dug in! The leaders and members of this private organization which helped make this discovery possible are to be praised.'

In the words of Dr. Kelso[12], 'James Towne is the symbolic 'Cornerstone of America'; the foundation of our form of government, law and predominant language began in this place. We have found the 'box' and briefly peeked inside. In three seasons of excavation, only about five percent of the fort and none of the town has been archaeologically investigated...How do we know that we have found the fort?

You may think when you view the site that all you see is dirt; --make that mud...But that is because ancient Virginia, the time we are talking about here...was a time of the Wooden Age, when almost everything was made of timber and earth. So what is left for archaeologists are not brick foundations, but rather stains in the soil where wooden walls decayed away...along with the clay pits and wells back filled with lost or discarded trash and garbage that has been excavated and can be dated.'

'Jamestown (1893-1907) did not suffer from a lack of attention. It has been admired, surveyed, dug, covered, re-dug, excavated, planned, charted, built, destroyed, eroded, saved, fenced, planted, beautified, blessed, walked on and defined for more than 350 years. The history of Jamestown has captured the imagination of historians and visitors for a very long time.'[13]

Despite all the attention mentioned above, during the years following the near abandonment of the Jamestown settlement, almost everything was done to Jamestown except to protect it - until the entrance in the late 1800s of two of the APVA's founders, Mrs. Cynthia B.T. Coleman and Miss Mary Jeffery Galt...In 1889 a legion of ladies accepted the responsibility of saving Jamestown from the 'ravages of time', allied themselves to incorporate what is today the nation's oldest statewide historic preservation organization, the **Association for the Preservation of Virginia Antiquities**....

Since 1901, and periodically through the years, Jamestown has been searched and researched in efforts to locate the remains of the settlement and the original 1607 James Fort. In the process, the APVA ladies and archaeologists subsequently uncovered such treasures as the foundations of the brick church, statehouse foundations, tombs and graves, structures, houses, boundaries, artifacts and ditches. The elusive dream of discovering the fort, however, remained on the APVA's wish list until the early 1990s, when the Association began turning the dream into a reality.

The original Jamestown Fort stands as an instructive reminder of America's humble, but courageous and noble beginnings. It is also a reminder of our unique and storied history - and of our bright, shining future.

If John Southern built on his land on Jamestown Island, his home place house would have been such as described by Dr. Kelso. The house would have been a post-in-ground house of wattle and daub, with a well nearby and an area of wooden fencing for his crops.

(addition)
Gen. 9 (8)   **JOHN SOUTHERN II**

JOHN SOUTHERN owned land on Perrots Creek,[14] the creek that flowed into the Rappahannock just northwest of Sunderland Creek. It was just beyond where the Upper Chapel was built on the ridge between the two creeks. His land lay adjacent to David George. He patented eighteen acres of new land there in 1714, adjacent to the land on which he lived.[15] Just how long John had been in the colony is not known.

John Southern, gentleman, patented twenty-four acres on the Island of James City on November 1, 1627.[16] It was located *north on the Back River, south on the highway to Black Point and west on the marsh called Tuckers Hole*. In 1652 when the land was purchased by Edward Travis, it was described as formerly granted to John Southern, Senior. John Southern was first listed in the muster at James City of 1624, having come to the colony in *George* in 1620.[17]

John Southern was a Burgess from James City during the session of 1629-1630.[18] It cannot be stated definitively that this was the ancestor of John Southern of Middlesex County, but it is believed that he was.

It is also believed that the wife of John Southern of Christ Church Parish was Catherine Southern who died on December 31, 1715.[19] Her death was recorded in the parish register, but no identifying information was included in the entry.

John Southern died in Christ Church Parish on October 1, 1728. He had made his will on October 3, 1726 and had signed it himself.[20] John left his land to his three sons. To John and Edward Southern he left each a moiety (half) of one tract of land, and to his son William Southern, he left the plantation on which he lived, containing 200 acres, as well as, the additional land he had patented. If William had no heirs, the land was to go to John's daughter, LETTICE CHEADLE, the wife of JOHN CHEADLE.

John especially wanted to be sure that his loom and his harness were not disposed of. He wanted his children to have the use of these possessions and he directed them to keep them in good repair. His will was recorded on February 4, 1728, and Edward Southern was named the executor. John's estate was valued at £38/19/3, and listed among his personal property were several books of several sorts. This further places him of the same social and educated status as John Southern of Jamestown. It is unusual for books to be included among the possessions of the early settlers. John did not name his wife, which is further evidence that she had died earlier.

John Southern the son, married Margaret Kidd February 17, 1720 and had sons: William, born August 16, 1722, Benjamin born October 29, 1730 and Joseph Southern born February 7, 1733 and daughters Susanna born July 22, 1725 and Averilla born December 25, 1738.[21] John Southern died October 21, 1759.[22] Edward Southern was baptized May 23, 1703, his marriage date is not recorded, but it is believed the entry for the birth of Jane, the daughter of Edward and Mary on August 23, 1745, was his daughter.[23] William Southern married Mary Saunders August 3, 1730, had a son, William born December 22, 1734 and a daughter, Sarah born October 31, 1740. William Southern died November 17, 1742.[24]

SOUTHERN FAMILY

Gen.11	JOHN SOUTHERN	m	UNKNOWN
Gen.10	JOHN SOUTHERN	m	CATHERINE
Issue:	John	m	Margaret Kidd
	Edward	m	Agatha (—?—)
	William	m	Mary Saunders
	LETTICE	m	JOHN CHEADLE

(561-564;499-501)

Gen. 8
JEREMIAH DUMAS

JEREMIAH DUMAS, or Jerome as he may have originally been called arrived in Virginia on the ship *Mary and Ann* near Hampton on July 20, 1700 with the first load of settlers for the Marquis de la Muce and Charles Sailly settlement later made at Manakin on the James River above Richmond.[25] They were received with kindness by Governor Francis Nicholson, and many of the wealthier Virginians contributed to the needs of the new arrivals. There were altogether 207 men, women and children, and they were weary of the trip. Their destination had been changed and they suspected it had been to the advantage of those in power. They were right; they would settle in the area of the now extinct Monocan Indians which would require little clearing of land, but they would also provide a buffer between the settled areas of the wealthy landowners and the Indians to the west.[26] Jeremiah was born about 1681 in St. Fort, Saintonge, France, the son of Jeremie Dumas and Susanne Faure.[27]

The land that was granted Jeremiah was reported to be on Fire Creek where it enters the James River. Since he had apparently spent some time in England before coming to Virginia he was acquainted with English customs and he did marry a Virginia woman of English descent. He married about 1702, UNITY SMITH, of New Kent County, said to be the granddaughter of Mary Croshaw White (the daughter of Major Joseph

Croshaw); however, the descent from Governor Yeardley is questioned. One daughter, Mathen, probably his first child, was baptized in the Anglican Church and the family was more closely associated with the English. Possibly for that reason and his young age, he was not in the forefront of the French activity and is not always included in the lists of the settlers of Manakintown. In 1701 Jeremiah Dumas is shown in the Quit Rent Rolls with 250 acres of land in New Kent County.

There are several references to Dr. Jeremiah (Jerome) Dumas. There is no evidence that he had medical training. He may have had an aptitude for medical matters and the inventory of his estate may have caused the conclusion that he had medical training. It may have been an honorary deference to his abilities. Jeremiah died in 1734. The children of Jeremiah and Unity Smith Dumas were:

Benjamin Dumas was born in 1705 in New Kent County and died in 1776 in Anson County, North Carolina. He married about 1725 Frances Clark, born about 1706 in New Kent County and died in 1752 in Anson County. He married second Martha McClendon, born before 1755 and died in 1766 without children. Benjamin and Frances had children: Benjamin, Jr., born c.1728, died 1796, married Jamima McLendon and second, Ruth Serdon; David Dumas, born c.1730, died c.1803, married Sarah Moorman, born 1738; Sarah Dumas, born c.1730, died before 1760 in Anson County, married Edmund Fleming Lilly; Jeremiah Dumas, born c.1735, died without issue c.1760; and Frances Dumas, born 1740, died c.1766, married in 1758 Francis Smith. Benjamin and his first wife lived in Louisa County from 1742 until 1750, then moved to Anson County, North Carolina; possibly operating the Dumas ferry across the PeeDee River.

Temperance Dumas was born about 1711 and married Robert Yancey, born 1714, the son of Charles Yancey and Miss Bartlett. Temperance married second, Prewid Hix of Louisa County. Her children were: Martha Yancey who married a Mr. Ellis; the Reverend Robert Yancey; Charles Yancey; Jeremiah Yancey and David Hicks (Hix) and Unity Hicks, who married William Thomasson, April 18, 1786.[28]

DUMAS FAMILY

Gen. 8 JEREMIAH DUMAS		m	UNITY SMITH
Issue:	Mathen		(p) died young
	Temperance	m	(1) Robert Yancey
		m	(2) Prewid Hicks (Hix)
	SARAH	m	BENJAMIN HARRIS
	Benjamin	m	(1) Frances Clark
		m	(2) Martha McClendon
	Jeremiah		d.s.p.

Notes

1. John Frederick Dorman and Virginia M. Meyer, *Adventurers of Purse and Person, Virginia 1607-1624/25* 1956 (Richmond: Dietz Press, rev. 1987) 31.
2. Hotten 273.
3. *Virginia Land Records* (Baltimore: Genealogical Publishing Co, 1982) 203, 490, 525.
4. H.R. McIlwaine, ed., *Minutes of the Council and General Court of Colonial Virginia*, 2nd ed., 1924 (Richmond: VA State Library, 1979) 8, 51, 55, 56, 65, 69, 101, 103, 117, 144, 150, 165, 178, 182, 184, 199.
5. Nugent 270-271.
6. Louis des Cognets, Jr., *English Duplicates of Lost Virginia Records* 1958 (Baltimore: Genealogical Publishing Co, rep 1990) 131.
7. "Jamestown Rediscovery, Jamestown is America's Hometown," *TVF* 5(1997):208-210.
8. *APVA Newsletter*, Vol. XV, No.3. 204 West Franklin St., Richmond, VA 23220. Used with permission Mr. Peter Dun Grover, Executive Director, APVA.
9. Governor George Allen, Press Conference, Jamestown. 12 Sept. 1996. Remarks announcing the discovery of the original 1607 James Fort to national and international media representatives and an assembled audience.
10. Samuel Yonge, *The Site of Old "James Towne"*. (Richmond: APVA, 1903).
11. See Dr. William Kelso, *Jamestown Rediscovery I: Search for 1607 James Fort* and *Jamestown Rediscovery II*. Published by the APVA, Richmond, 1995 and 1996. Available from the APVA at the above address for $5.95 ea., plus postage.
12. Dr. William M. Kelso, *Jamestown is America's Hometown*. Speech at the 12 September press conference held by the APVA. Dr. Kelso is the APVA Director of Archaeology.
13. Dr. Richard T. Couture, *To Preserve and Protect: A History of the Association of the Preservation of Virginia Antiquities*. (Richmond: APVA, 1984). Chapt. 3.

14. *Land Patent Book 9* 546.
15. LP Book 10 132.
16. Book 1, (1) 55.
17. Hotten 225.
18. John Bennett Boddie, *Colonial Surry* 1948 (Baltimore: Clearfield, rep. 1992) 165.
19. Colonial Dames 173.
20. *Middlesex County Will Book B* 353.
21. Colonial Dames 111, 118, 123, 130, 148.
22. *TVF* 2(1993):162.
23. Ibid., 158.
24. Ibid., 111, 140, 151.
25. John H. Wilson, *The Dumas Families, vol 1* Fort Worth, TX: privately printed, 1986) 4, 7,10. 1212 West El Paso St, Fort Worth, TX 76102. Much of what follows comes from this work.
26. Priscilla Harriss Cabell, *Turff & Twigg, The French Lands, vol one* (Richmond: privately printed, 1988) 9. P.O. Box 17091, Richmond, VA 23226.
27. Wilson 7-28.
28. W. Mac. Jones, ed. *The Douglas Register* 1928 (Baltimore: Genealogical Publishing, 1985) 46.

MIDDLESEX COUNTY

156

WILLIAM RUFFIN

Gen. 10

No further research has been done on the Ruffin family. Dr. Claiborne T. Smith, Jr., M.D., Lyndon H. Hart, III and David Gammon, all well-known and respected genealogists are compiling a history of the Ruffin family that should be published this year (1998). It would be superfluous to attempt to add to their expertly researched work.(568-579;505-515)

Gen. 9   **ROBERT RUFFIN I**
(580-585;516-521)

William Ruffin

(578;513) William Ruffin married Faith Gray, the daughter of William Gray, who was the son of Thomas Gray, the *Ancient Planter*.[1] William Gray was probably born about 1648 and lived on land near the Ruffin family. He served as a justice of Surry County, also as sheriff and was a member of the House of Burgesses from 1710 until 1712. He married Elizabeth Jarrett, the daughter of Richard Jarrett. His will was recorded on November 18, 1719, and in it he named his children: William, Gilbert, Mary Gray, Faith Ruffin and Priscilla Gray.[2]

PRIME FAMILY

Gen.10 EDMUND PRIME	m	(—?—) RIDLEY
Issue: ELIZABETH	m	(1) George Watkins
	m	(2) ROBERT RUFFIN I
Mary	m	John Price
John	m	Martha (—?—)
Phyllis	m	(1) Thomas White
	m	(2) William Edwards
a daughter	m	(—?—) Wright

Gen. 8   **ROBERT RUFFIN II**
(586-595;522-530)4e

Gen. 7   **JOHN RUFFIN**
(596-605;531-539)

Gen. 6   **FRANCIS RUFFIN**
(596-604;531-539)

RUFFIN FAMILY

Gen. 10 WILLIAM RUFFIN	m	UNKNOWN
Issue: ROBERT I	m	ELIZABETH PRIME WATKINS
Gen. 9 ROBERT RUFFIN I	m	ELIZABETH PRIME WATKINS
Issue: Olivia	m	William Chambers
Elizabeth	m	
ROBERT II	m	ELIZABETH WATKINS

William	m	(1) Faith Gray
	m	(2) Sarah Crafford Newsum
Jane	m	

Gen. 8	ROBERT RUFFIN II	m	ELIZABETH WATKINS
	JOHN	m	MARTHA HAMLIN
	Joseph	m	
	Benjamin	m	Lucy Simmons
	Edmund	m	Anne Simmons Edmunds
	Mary	m	
	Martha	m	
	Elizabeth	m	(1) William Kinchen
		m	(2) Richard Cocke

Gen. 7	JOHN RUFFIN	m	MARTHA HAMLIN
Issue:	Robert	m	Mary Clack Lightfoot
	William	m	(1) Mary Bland
		m	(2) Lucy Cocke
	Anne	m	Hartwell Cocke
	Elizabeth	m	George (J. M.) Nicholas
	John	m	d.s.p.
	Martha	m	Robert Newsome
	Thomas	m	d.s.p.
	FRANCIS	m	(1) Hannah Cocke
		m	(2) SUSANNA HARRISS

Gen. 6	FRANCIS RUFFIN	m	(1) Hannah Cocke
Issue:	John	m	
	Thomas		(p) died young
	Robert	m	
	Hannah	m	Caulfield Seward

	FRANCIS RUFFIN	m	(2) SUSANNA HARRISS
Issue:	Martha	m	(1) Thomas Edwards
		m	(2) Jack Faulcon
	William		d.s.p. unmarried
	ELIZABETH ANNE	m	REUBEN BUTLER
	George		died young
	Erasmus		died young
	Francis	m	(1) Mariah Wilson
		m	(2) Mary Augusta Robinson
	Susanna	m	Wm. H. T. Browne

(605-609-540-542)

Gen. 8,7

WILLIAM HARRISS II

correction: William Harris and his wife Lucy of Albemarle Parish and Sussex County were confused with WILLIAM HARRISS of Surry County. At the time the connection was made between the two families only the entries in the Albemarle Parish Register had been found, and since the name Hamlin Harris was unusual, it was assumed that the family was one and the same. The will of William Harris of Sussex County was recorded in the Sussex County Court on April 18, 1782[3], thus he died some fourteen years before William Harriss of Surry County. In his will he named his wife, Lucy and children who had been recorded in the parish register: Joseph, Reuben, Lewis, Nathan, Elizabeth (Rogers) and Lucy (Tudor). No connection has been found between this William Harris and the William Harriss who was the father of Susanna, Elizabeth and Hamlin Harris of Surry County, although the name Hamlin is of interest, and it is also of interest that William of Sussex did not name a son, Hamlin in his will.

HARRISS FAMILY

Gen. 8	WILLIAM HARRISS I	m	MARY SHORT
Issue:	WILLIAM	m	UNKNOWN
	Thomas	m	
Gen. 7	WILLIAM HARRISS II	m	UNKNOWN
Issue:	Hamlin	m	Margaret Belscher
	Elizabeth	m	Archibald Campbell
	SUSANNA	m	FRANCIS RUFFIN

(609-611;543-544)
Gen. 11

WILLIAM SHORT I

(611-613;544-545)
Gen. 10

WILLIAM SHORT II

(613-615;545-548)
Gen. 9

WILLIAM SHORT III

The location of the Short plantation *Spring Garden* was found to be near the intersections of CR 600 and CR 602, north of SR 40. The homeplace was visited about 1991 with the thought of visiting the family graveyard. While the owner knew of the site, the grave of the later William Short, thought to have been buried there had been moved, it is believed to Hollywood Cemetery in Richmond.

SHORT FAMILY

Gen.11	WILLIAM SHORT I	m	ELIZABETH (—?—)
Issue:	WILLIAM	m	MARY (—?—)
	Sarah	m	George Middleton
	Thomas	m	
Gen.10	WILLIAM SHORT II	m	MARY (—?—)
Issue:	WILLIAM	m	SUSANNA (—?—)
	Elizabeth	m	
Gen. 9	WILLIAM SHORT III	m	SUSANNA (—?—)
Issue:	William	m	Martha (—?—)
	Thomas	m	
	MARY	m	WILLIAM HARRISS

Notes

1. Meyer and Dorman 341.
2. Ibid.
3. *Sussex County Will Book D*, 1782-1789 22.

STEPHEN HAMLIN I

Gen. 10

Presented here is a tract map of the Weyanoke area that will be used as a framework for discussing the owners as families, neighbors and business associates.[1] This is of particular interest because it not only definitively places the land of Stephen Hamlin I, but also of his neighbors and associates. The map has been plotted from Land Patent Records, with selected deed record data superimposed. Each tract is captioned with the name of the owner, size, date of patent, and reference book and page number in Virginia Land Patents. References cited on the map are not repeated in the end notes.

Although some new neighbors were total strangers when they selected their land, most had some prior connection — family, religion, politics or business. It was even more common to find marriages between young men and women who had grown up as neighbors. From the existing data these associations and land ownerships have been found:

Ferdinando Austin Before Robert Brookes secured his patents, Ferdinando Austin/Aston/Ashton had acquired land in that area by virtue of two patents. The first, on 25 Feb 1653 mentions only vague bounds — *...on N. side of James Riv. & E. side of Queens Cr., Ely. On Moses Run, S. on Mr. Horsmandine & Mr. Hamblin.* By sketching bounds from Brookes to Horsmanden, thence to the Hockaday/Minge tract and so on around by way of Queens Creek and Robert Brookes line to Moses Run, we enclose about 1760 acres. This is only slightly more than one would expect, given the tendency to understate areas as discussed above. By a second patent, dated 5 Jan 1664, Austin extended his patent to include 1500 acres. The bounds are again vague —*...on No.& South side of the head of Moyses Run, bounding S. on Henry Cantrell's land, now in possession of Mr. Horsmanden, S. on Mr. Hamelins land Wly. on Queens Cr. Run & Nly. On the head of Pease Hill Sw. 1200 acres by patent 25 Feb 1653 and 300 acres...* By extending the hypothetical bounds of Austin's land around the eastern end of Brookes' lines to Pease Hill Sw. (now Barrows Creek) and thence down to the Cantrell/Horsmanden/Byrd line, we can enclose another 300 acres for a total of 2060 acres.

STEPHEN HAMELIN Like Austin, Hamelin (Sr) secured a patent at a time before precise bounds were recorded. In 1650 he claimed 1250 acres *...bounded S. upon the heads of Wionoke, E. upon Matshcoes Cr. & land of Mr. Cantrell, W. towards old mans Cr. and Queens Cr....* In 1666 Stephen Hamelyn (Jr.) was granted 1400 acres, *...provided that the Widdow & Relict of sd. Stephen Hamlyn, dec'd, bee noe way prejudiced...* This is presumed to be the original 1250 acres plus 150 additional, for which there was no charge, and so must have been due from a purchase. The 150 acres thus acquired may be the 150 patented to Richard and Henry Blankes five months before, since there is no further reference to the Blankes family after the date of patent.

Stephen Hamlin (Sr) owned land in York County before acquiring his 1250 acres in Charles City County. His land in York lay along the Queen Creek just north of the present community of Plantation Heights. His neighbors there included John Broche and Richard Major, about two miles to the east, and Henry Tyler, about a mile to the south.

William and Mary Byrd The tract which was patented to the Byrds in 1686 has been studied in detail by the William and Mary Center for Archaeological Research and the results published in 1992. Information in that report will appeal to those searching the Byrd family connections.[2]

Stephen Hamlin II

[619;550] It appears from the records of Charles City County that are extant that Stephen Hamlin II had daughters that had not been previously identified. It seems that there were two daughters, one of whom married a Mr. Cocke and one who married a Silvanus Stokes.[3] Abraham Hamlin gave land to a niece, Mary Cocke and land to probably a second nephew, Jones Stokes, as well, using the same pattern. There is also a Hamlin Stokes who is a brother to Jones Stokes.[4]

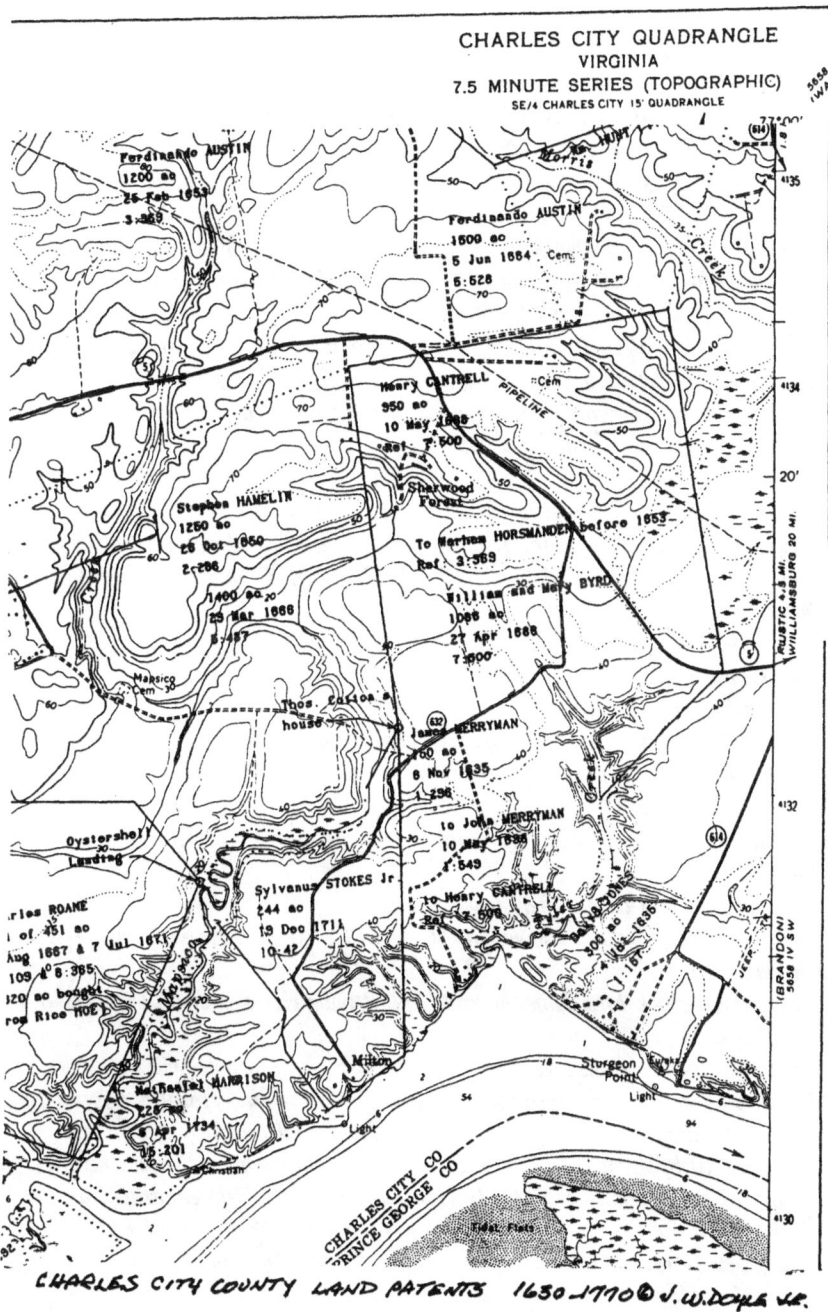

CHARLES CITY COUNTY LAND PATENTS 1630-1710 © J. W. DOYLE JR.

Abraham Hamlin

(619;550) The above information, identifying Abraham Hamlin as the uncle of daughters of Stephen Hamlin II verifies that Stephen and Agnes Hamlin were his parents. These legacies were a part of his will, that apparently has not survived, and it would appear that he was unmarried.

Charles Hamlin

The will of William Rookings (II), recorded March 16 1715[5], gave a bequest of land known as the *Greens* to his daughter, Susannah, the wife of Charles Hamlin.

JOHN HAMLIN

The account of the Charles City County land owners is very revealing in presenting who is whose neighbor. It is interesting that the Byrds were neighbors of the Hamlins, and the diary of William Byrd presents some interesting insights, not only about himself but about the Hamlin family. It should be realized, however, that by this date ELIZABETH HAMLIN, the widow of JOHN HAMLIN and her family were living across the James River in Prince George County at *Maycock*. The river was no barrier to friendships and business transactions, as seen by the frequency with which the Hamlins came to visit the Byrds. Following are some excerpts from his diary for the years 1709-1712 and for the year 1720.[6]

[1709, 3/26] I rose at 6 o'clock and read three chapters of Hebrew and 200 verses of Homer's Odyssey. *I said my prayers, and ate milk for breakfast. I danced my dance. I wrote a letter to England. My river sloop came about noon from Appomattox with 25 hogsheads of tobacco. I ate tripe for dinner. Before we had dined Mr. Hardiman came to see me but would not eat. In the afternoon Peter Hamlin came also. We played at billiards.*

[4/17] I went to church [Westover, no doubt], where were abundance of people, among whom was Mrs. H-m-l-n [Hamlin], a very handsome woman. [She was a generation older than the 35-year-old Byrd].

[6/11] When I came home I found Dick [RICHARD] HAMLIN and [Mistress] who had been taken by [a slow poison] about five years ago.

[7/3] Mr. Anderson and Captain Hamlin called there on the way [Byrd was at the Harrisons at the time].

[7/19] Peter Hamlin came to see me.

[8/2] Mrs. Hamlin was to see me.

[9/5] I sent for Mrs. Hamlin and my cousin Harrison about 9 o'clock and I said my prayers heartily for my wife's happy deliver, and had good health, good thoughts, and a good humor, thanks be to God Almighty. [Mrs. Byrd had borne a son, Parke.]

[9/6] Mrs. Hamlin and my cousin Harrison went away about 9 o'clock and I made my [satisfaction] to them for that kindness.

[9/29] Mr. Peter Hamlin came after it was dark.

[12/11] Colonel Eppes, Captain Llewellyn, Mr. Dick Cocke, Mr. Hamlin and Mrs. L[-?-] came and dined with us after church services.

[12/12] About 12 o'clock Mrs. Hamlin and Mrs. B-r-d-r came over and stayed to dinner...The company went away about 3 o'clock.

[1/15] I sent my English letters over the river to Peter Hamlin who will go on Tuesday next to England.

[2/15] My wife was indisposed again today so that I sent for Mrs. Hamlin...About 10 o'clock Mrs. Hamlin came and soon after her Mrs. Bolling, the widow...They both stayed and dined with me.

[2/25] We played at billiards till 12 o'clock; then Mr. Harrison, his wife, and Mrs. Stith came and soon after them Robin Mumford and Captain Hamlin [it is probable that the references to Captain Hamlin refer to John Hamlin II], who all dined with us...In the afternoon they played at cricket, at which the Captain sprained his thigh.

[3/12] In the afternoon we walked again about the pasture and then we heard guns as if a ship was coming to Swinyards. Mrs. Hamlin went away soon but Mr. C-s stayed until 8 o'clock.

[4/5] Mrs. Hamlin came and told us Mr. Harrison was still very bad. [5/18] Mrs. Hamlin came to see the child, whose fever continued. [5/27] Mrs. Hamlin came to see them [the children, Mr. Byrd's baby boy died June 3].

[9/27] About 9 o'clock Peter Hamlin came over who came lately from England in the ship "Betty". I lent him a horse to Colonel Hill's.

[11/5] Mrs. Hamlin stayed and dined with us and I ate boiled pork. In the afternoon Mrs. Hamlin went away and I took a long walk about the plantation and found all things in good order.

[1711, 1/16] In the afternoon Mrs. Hamlin came to see us and to have some salt.

[2/13] About 12 o'clock I got there and met several people there to do busines with and gave my letters to Peter Hamlin [at Prince George County Court].

[3/13] I rose at 8 o'clock and read nothing because Mr. Peter Hamlin came to see me and told me the

"Harrison" was come in and had abundance of goods for me. I lent him a horse to go to Colonel Hill's. [Byrd recorded on June 18 that Colonel Hardiman's son had the small pox on board Colonel Harrison's vessel and that nobody would go near him.]

[3/17] About 12 o'clock Dick Hamlin came for rights likewise.

[6/24] I went with him to church, where I saw Peter Hamlin, who had no letters from Barbados for me. People were afraid of him because one of his people had the smallpox.

[6/25] I sent for Mrs. Hamlin who came presently [Byrd's wife had a miscarriage].

[6/27] When my wife heard that Peter Hamlin had the smallpox she said that she should have them likewise because his mother had been there two nights ago and she had laid on her sheets [Mrs. Byrd died of smallpox in London in 1716].

[7/5] Poor Peter Hamlin died of smallpox, for want of attention.

[7/30] Dick Hamlin came to ask me whether Dr. Cocke would come to his brother [if] sent for to him, who had the smallpox. I told him he would.

[10/11] About 10 o'clock came Captain H-n-t to buy planks and soon after him came Captain Drury Stith and after him Captain John Eppes, Captain Sam Harwood and Captain Hamlin. I persuaded them to stay and dine before we went to the martial court and fined as many people as came to 4500 pounds of tobacco.

[10/13] Mrs. Hamlin came to account with me and would borrow money of me but I had the discretion not to do it. [Actually Elizabeth Hamlin was quite well off in her own right].

[1712, 2/28] Lucy Hamlin came just before dinner and it then began to thunder and rain very violently.

[8/5] I sent Mrs. Hamlin some bark [cinchona bark, the source of quinine].

[1720, 5/18] After dinner the Colonel and I settled accounts and then he went away and then came Mrs. Hamlin and Mrs. Duke and stayed about an hour and ate some cherries and then went over the river, and I took a walk about the plantation.

[5/21] In the evening I took a walk and met Mr. Harrison who had been at Mrs. Hamlin's who was very sick. We consulted what to do and resolved to let her blood. She went and in returning told me that our patient was better.

[5/23] Called at Mrs. Hamlin's to inquire how she did and found her a little better.

[5/25] After dinner we played at dice and I lost a pistole and in the evening took leave and went to visit Mrs. Hamlin and found her very bad and I gave her the best advice I could then came home, talked to my people and learned that Jenny was sick.

[5/26] Billy Hamlin came to get some barley cinnamon water for his mother and I sent half a pint. Mrs. Hamlin very ill.

[5/31] Ben Harrison and Mr. Cargill and I went to Mrs. Hamlin's who we found still sick, did not see her.

[6/8] Mrs. Hamlin died yesterday morning.

[6/10] After dinner we walked to the church to see poor Mrs. Hamlin buried and hear her funeral sermon. [The text suggests that Mrs. Hamlin was buried at the old Westover Church Cemetery, about 200 yards upstream from William Byrd's residence; a beautiful riverbank site, where few grave markers exist in modern times, and non for Mrs. Hamlin].

[6/14] I read some Latin until one o'clock when Mr. Randolph of Weyanoke, Major John Eppes, Mr. Harwood and Billy Hamlin came to dine with me and I ate roast mutton.

[11/1] About 9 o'clock Mr. Brook and [Mr.] Banister went to the Falls and about ten I committed my family to Providence and went with Major Bolling, Mr. Mumford and Ben Harrison and Billy Hamlin to "Green Springs" and there everybody left me and I went to visit my Aunt by myself and ate some boiled beef for dinner.

Peter Hamlin

(625;556) It would appear from the accounts of Peter Hamlin in the diary of William Byrd, and that he appeared to be a contemporary of the sons of Elizabeth Hamlin, that he was another son of John and Elizabeth. He would not have been named in her will since he died at an earlier date. The order for the appraisal of the estate of Peter Hamlin was dated November 1711 in the Prince George County court record. The inventory of his estate was presented by Elizabeth Hamlin and recorded on April 8, 1712.[7] It was signed by Thomas Harnison (his mark T), Gilbert Hay, and John Lett and sworn before Mr. Cha: Goodrich. Peter

Hamlin's estate was valued at £32/16/0. He apparently was unmarried. It is interesting to note how the personal property of a single man of status varied from that of the usual freeholder's possessions. Peter owned, among other things: 4 pair of shoes, 2 pair boots, 3 hats, 1 wig, 2 quadroons, 1 small chest, a parcel of books, 5 shirts, 1 neckcloth, 5 hankerchiefs, 1 white jacket, 1 suit bound in blue, 1 suit bound in black, 2 good suits of cloth, 1 cloth jacket, 3 weskets, 1 great coat, 8 pair stockings, 1 pair small curtains for walking, 10 knives and forks, 1 punch bowl, 1 silver ring and 1 gold mourning ring, 1 gun, 1 violin and 1 small trunk.

Sarah Hamlin

(625;555) correction: Sarah Hamlin married Micajah **Lowe**, not Rowe as originally written. Micajah Lowe identified his wife as Sarah and his mother-in-law as Mrs. Elizabeth Hamlin. He further identified Micajah Perry as his uncle and went on in the bequests in his will to name Susannah Lowe, Mary Lowe and Johanna Jarrett as his sisters. His will was dated **January 20, 1702** and proved **17 March 1703/4** (these dates differ from the information as recorded by Sherwood).[8]

(626-632;556-562)
Gen. 8

RICHARD HAMLIN

HAMLIN FAMILY

Gen.10 <u>STEPHEN HAMLIN I</u>		m	<u>AGNES (—?—)</u>
Issue:	Stephen II	m	
	Charles	m	Susanna Rookings
	Thomas	m	(—?—) Wynd widow
	JOHN	m	ELIZABETH TAYLOR
	Abraham	m	unmarried
Gen. 9 <u>JOHN HAMLIN</u>		m	<u>ELIZABETH TAYLOR</u>
Issue:	John	m	Ann Goodrich
	RICHARD	m	ANN HARNISON
	Sarah	m	(1) Micajah Lowe
		m	(2) Rev. John Cargill
	Elizabeth	m	Thomas Ravenscroft
	William	m	
	Lucy	m	William Epes
	Hannah	m	Thomas Cocke
	Peter		unmarried
Gen. 8 <u>RICHARD HAMLIN</u>		m	<u>ANN HARNISON</u>
Issue:	Sarah	m	William Hatt
	Thomas	m	
	Richard	m	
	MARTHA	m	COL. JOHN RUFFIN
	Elizabeth	m	

(632-635;563-565)
Gen. 9

THOMAS HARNISON

HARNISON FAMILY

Gen. 9 <u>THOMAS HARNISON</u>		m	<u>ELLINOR BLAYMORE</u>
Issue:	ANN	m	RICHARD HAMLIN
	Elizabeth	m	Robert Hall

164

(636-640;566-570)
Gen. 10

RICHARD TAYLOR

TAYLOR FAMILY

Gen.10 RICHARD TAYLOR	m	(1) Mary Perkins widow	
Issue: Richard	m	d.s.p.	
RICHARD TAYLOR	m	(2) SARAH BARKER	
Issue: ELIZABETH	m	CAPT. JOHN HAMLIN	
Frances	m	Richard Bradford	
Sarah		d. s. p.	
Katherine		d. s. p.	
John	m	Henrietta Maria	

BARKER FAMILY

Gen.11 WILLIAM BARKER	m	FRANCES (—?—)
Issue: SARAH	m	RICHARD TAYLOR
John	m	(—?—) Drew
Elizabeth	m	

(641-646;571-574)
Gen. 10,9

JOHN WATKINS II

JOHN WATKINS was granted the administration of the estate of his mother, Mrs. Elizabeth Brewster, deceased as recorded in the Surry County Court Order Book May 4, 1675. Henry Watkins provided the security for John.[9]

WATKINS FAMILY

Gen.10 JOHN WATKINS I	m	ELIZABETH (—?—)
Issue: JOHN	m	ELIZABETH SPENCER
Henry		d.s.p.
a child		

Gen. 9 JOHN WATKINS II	m	ELIZABETH SPENCER
Issue: Robert	m	
ELIZABETH	m	ROBERT RUFFIN II
John	m	Ann d.s.p.
Henry	m	
William	m	
Mary	m	

(646-652a;575-579)
Gen. 10

ROBERT SPENCER

SPENCER FAMILY

Gen.10 ROBERT SPENCER	m	(1) (p) ANNE TABERER
Issue: Anne	m	John Whitson
ELIZABETH	m	JOHN WATKINS II
Robert Spencer	m	(2) Elizabeth White
Issue: Ann		
Jane		

165

TABERER FAMILY

Gen.11	WILLIAM TABERER	m	
Issue:	William	m	
	Joshua		d.s.p.
	Thomas	m	Margaret Wood widow
	ANNE (p)	m	ROBERT SPENCER

Notes

1. This account of adjoining land owners and the plotting of their lands has been compiled by LtCol James W. Doyle, Jr., 2923 Tara Trail, Beavercreek, OH 45434-6252, and appears in *"Charles City County Land Grants, Neighbors and Families", Tidewater Virginia Families: A Magazine of History and Genealogy,* 6(1997): 5-16.

2. Charles M. Downing, *The Origins of Sherwood Forest, Charles City County, Virginia,* (A report by the College of William and Mary, Williamsburg, Virginia, 1992).

3. Contributed by Forrest King, 9815 Fosbak Drive, Vienna, VA 22182. Inferred from Charles City County Court Records.

4. Benjamin B. Weisiger, III, *Charles City County, Virginia, Wills & Deeds, 1725-1731.* (Richmond: privately printed, 1984) 9,31, 33.

5. *Surry County Book 6 224.*

6. *The Secret Diary of William Byrd II of Westover, 1709-1712; The London Diary 1717-1721 and Other Writings William Byrd of Virginia.* Contributed by Forrest King, 9815 Fosbak Drive, Vienna, VA 22182.

7. *Prince George County Deeds & Wills, Book B, 1710-1713.* 121-122.

8. Lothrop Withington, *Virginia Gleanings in England.* (Baltimore: Genealogical Publishing Co, 1980) 43.

9. *Surry County Court Orders, 1671-1682* 95.

SECTION VI

THE LEE ANCESTORS

JAMES PETTYJOHN I

Gen. 10

(695-700;587-592)
Gen. 9   JOHN PETTYJOHN

(701-704;593-596)
Gen. 8   JAMES PETTYJOHN II

(705-707;597-599)
Gen. 7   **ABRAHAM PETTYJOHN**

Correspondence with Robert Scott Davis, Jr[1] has supplied information about Jacob Pettyjohn that fits well with Jacob Pettyjohn of Amherst County. He believes that the Jacob who appeared in Jackson County, Georgia about the time that Jacob Pettyjohn disappeared from the records of Amherst County were one and the same. He further believes the suggested daughter of ABRAHAM PETTYJOHN was Mary, who married James Staton of Buckingham County. In the next generation Jacob Rogers married Mary Staton on June 18, 1818; Jackson County records indicate that Mary's mother was Mary Pettyjohn Staton, sister of Jacob Pettyjohn. Jacob Pettyjohn was the administrator of the estate of Mary Staton, January 2, 1809.[2]

It is further believed by Mr. Davis that Jacob may well have married a Elizabeth Staton. Buckingham County, the home of the Statons was just across the river from Amherst County. There is recorded a deed in Amherst County in 1790, where Jacob Pettyjohn and Lucy, Rebecca, Mary and Nancy Staton jointly sell property. This property may have belonged to William Staton mentioned earlier in the records.[3] Jacob may well have been acting for his wife's interest in this land. It is known that Jacob must have died in 1810, for his will was recorded on December 13, 1810.[4] He left his wife Betsy and named sons: James, Reuben, William and Abraham; and a daughter, Sally Kirkpatrick. He named a nephew, Fleming Staton. He named as his executors his sons, Reuben and Abraham.

The letter of the Louisianna Pettyjohn Donnan to her sister-in-law, Louisa Pannill Pettyjohn confirms that Jacob and WILLIAM PETTYJOHN were brothers.[5]

(705;597) It appears that Robert and Elizabeth Pettyjohn Warren had a son, Abraham Warren. While this is not confirmed, the names, dates and associations make this a logical conclusion. Abraham Warren posted his bond for his marriage to Rebecca Staton on January 20, 1794 in Amherst County. His security was Jacob Pettyjohn, who also stated that Rebecca was of age and the daughter of William Staton. Abraham and Rebecca were married February 4, 1794.[6] Abraham Warren would have been the half-brother of Jacob and William Pettyjohn.

(708-715;600-607)
Gen. 6   **WILLIAM PETTYJOHN**

(709;601)   It has always intrigued this author as to the whereabouts of William and Jacob Pettyjohn during the 1780s. It seems that Jacob had a number of ties with the Staton family, but no such ties have been found for William. An inspection of the records of Franklin County indicate that William Pettyjohn was in that county during the 1780s and served on a jury several times.[7] William Pettyjohn also appeared in Bedford County and served as a juryman in that county in the 1780s. This may have been the William Pettyjohn of Amherst County.

710;602) The letter of Louisianna Pettyjohn Donnan must be taken at face value. Whether she had real knowledge of the maiden name of her grandmother one cannot know. Repeated search of the records did not reveal a close relationship with the Crewes family. Naming patterns of the times indicate several families that may be possiblities as to the identity of Elizabeth Pettyjohn. Her identity remains a mystery. Further research needs to be conducted with this family.

(716-728;608-617)
Gen. 5   **JOSEPH PETTYJOHN**

Mrs. Betty Winkler Roberts has kindly supplied copies of Family Bible records and a letter from Louisianna Pettyjohn Donnan for further information about Joseph's family.[8] She admits that the letter from Louisa is conflicting with some of the information that is now known, but it also fills in some gaps that have been left in the family history. Where Louisianna relates that her grandfather and his brother came into Amherst County together after the Revolution, she leaves one to speculate as to which revolution she refers and from whence they came. The letter and the Bible record will be transcribed as Louisianna has written them to her sister-in-law, Louisa Pannill Pettyjohn, the wife of Joseph Pettyjohn (II).

My Dear Louisa   *Lexington, Va Mch 23d 1910*

Recd your letter on yesterday asking me to send the old Bible to you by express It is in a dilapidated condition both backs off & as it might get lost, in expressing it--conclusion to copy the record in the Bible <u>word for word</u> as that was the portion that you and Joe was interested in- As I wrote Joe in Jan that I did not think that the old Bible would throw any light on what he wanted to know- for the family Pettyjohn was French Huguenots & they must have left their home after the Revolution[9] and one of them went South and I never heard my Father speak of him-suppose he did not know himself, I hear my bro Jesse say that a nice looking fellow from the west called at the Lynch House & wanted to know if they were related, as they spelt their name in same way-& he may have been one of the offspring of Jacob the bro that came over with my Grandfather-for they both landed in Maryland If I heard right & then separated the one going South & one to Virginia....I hope that my copying the old family Bible will be as satisfactory as I have it word for word copying just as it is even some lines that my Father writes in it-that had no connection with the record of births deaths & marriages....

William Pettyjohn Senior died 15 May 1822 aged 68 years
Elizabeth Pettyjohn died 6th Feb 1831 aged 72 years
Charles Mundy died 9th of June 1842
James Alexander Pettyjohn died Saturday evening June 12th 1847 as the clock struck one, age 8 years 16 days old
William Pettyjohn died Tuesday morning October 23 1849 as few minutes before 5. clock aged 25 years 18 days
Hugh died Friday evening Nov 2 1849 at 15 minutes before one clock aged nine years 21 days
Canning Pettyjohn died Tuesday evening 13th 1852 at 25 minutes after 4 clock aged 23 years 7 months & 24 days
Catherine Rucker wife of Geo M Rucker died 1st of June 1863 about 10 clock A.M. aged 39 years 10 months
Joseph Pettyjohn died at sunset Wednesday 25 October 1865 aged 68 yrs 8 mos & 2 days
Nancy Pettyjohn died at sunset Thursday March 28th 1867 [69 years] one month & 6 days
James Bruce Pannill Pettyjohn Born 18th November 1877
Joseph Pettyjohn Jr 3 of this name Born 21st Nov 1879
James Bruce Pannill died 15th P.M. Feb 21st 1880
George Pettyjohn died at 11.20 night of Thursday 6th 1893 age 28 years 4 months and seven days
Joseph Pettyjohn died 2.45 morning of Tuesday May 28th 1893 aged 58 years 6 months 27 days This was written in Bible by my Father
When a few Years are Come, then I shall go the way whence I shall not return Job 16 ch. 22 verse

Joseph Pettyjohn, Jr

(723;614) Joseph Pettyjohn married **Louisa Pannill** on November 15, 1866.[10] Joseph and Louisa bought or managed The Lynch House, the leading hotel in Lynchburg during the 1870s, when he gave it up in the 1880s his brother Jesse and his wife were the proprietors, when Jesse died his wife continued to operate the hotel. The hotel was advertised as in an unequaled location on centre of Main Street, a five minute walk from the depot at $2.00 per day. They offered an omnibus, baggage wagon and porters to meet all trains and the best sample of rooms in the city. Their table was unexcelled with meals and lodgings 50c each. They also advertised hot and cold baths.[11]

correction: Jesse Pettyjohn and his wife ran The Lynch House, as related in his sister, Louisianna's letter. The name of his wife is not known, but apparently he was married.

PETTYJOHN FAMILY

Gen.10 JAMES PETTYJOHN	m	ISABEL (—?—)	
Issue: James	m		
William	m		
Isabel	m	(1) Richard Lester	
	m	(2) John Oakman	
JOHN	m	SARA (—?—)	
Gen. 9 JOHN PETTYJOHN	m	SARA (—?—)	
Issue: Thomas	m	Elizabeth White	
JAMES	m	HANNAH (—?—)	
John	m	(1) Sara Dodd	
	m	(2) Hannah Willson	
William	m	(P) Elizabeth Claypoole	
Richard	m	Hannah (—?—)	
daughter	m	(—?—) Reed	
daughter	m	George Dodd	
Gen. 8 JAMES PETTYJOHN	m	HANNAH (—?—)	
Issue: James, Jr.	m	Esther (—?—)	
Samuel	m	Anne (p)Wright	
Thomas	m		
Jacob	m		
ABRAHAM	m	ELIZABETH (p) MARSH	
Lydia	m		
Sarah	m	(—?—) Nixon	
Elizabeth	m	(—?—) Abel	
Abigail	m	(—?—) Bignal	
Naomi	m		
Major	m		
Gen. 7 ABRAHAM PETTYJOHN	m	ELIZABETH (p) MARSH	
Issue: Jacob	m	Elizabeth Staton	
WILLIAM	m	ELIZABETH (—?—)	
Mary	m	James Staton	
Gen. 6 WILLIAM PETTYJOHN	m	ELIZABETH (—?—)	
Issue: Rhoda	m	Jesse Woodruff	
William	m	(1)	
	m	(2)Paulina Crews	
Mary (Polly)	m	Robert Ridgeway	
Elizabeth	m	(1) Alexander Watson	
	m	(2) (—?—) Wills	

171

JOSEPH	m	ANN MUNDY
Wiatt	m	Jane Cox
George Washington	m	Ann T. Reynolds

Gen. 7	JOSEPH PETTYJOHN	m	ANN MUNDY
Issue:	William		d.s.p. unmarried
	MARY ELIZABETH	m	ALFRED STITH LEE
	Charles	m	Sarah A. Pettyjohn
	Catherine	m	George M. Rucker
	Missouri	m	John V. Wheeler
	Louisianna	m	George W. Donnan
	Caroline	m	William Mason Waller
	Joseph	m	Louise Pannill
	Jesse		unknown
	James Alexander		died young
	Hugh		died young
	Canning		died young

Notes

1. Robert Scott Davis, Jr., Director Family History Program, Wallance State College, P.O. Box 2000, Hanceville, AL 35077 has provided confirmation to some of the speculation, and answers to some of the questions about Jacob Pettyjohn.

2. Mary Avilla Abel Hall Farnsworth, *Kith and Kin of Georgia Ridge, Crawford County, Arkansas* (Newton, KS: United Printing, 1973) 171; Miscellaneous Records of Jackson County, Georgia 43.

3. Bailey Fulton Davis, *The Deeds of Amherst County, Virginia* (Easley, SC: Southern Historical Press, 1979) 246, 46, 122.

4. *Jackson County Will Book A* 41.

5. Mrs. Betty W. Roberts, P.O. Box 70189, Richmond, VA 23255-0189 (1993).

6. Amherst County Marriage Bonds 1794.

7. Franklin County Minute Book Index.

8. Betty W. Roberts, P.O. Box 70189, Richmond, VA 23255-0189.

9. It is assumed that she meant the Revolutionary War since that is the period in which William and Jacob disappear from the Amherst County records, and she did not seem to have knowledge of their being in the county earlier.

10. Roberts.

11. Lynchburg City Directory, 1883, 1884.

172

Gen. 7 **ROBERT MUNDY**

(728;618)   The following entries for Thomas Munday of Essex County (as relate to the account in *Tidewater Virginia Families* magazine) have been researched by Marion S. Wattenbarger[1] and contributed to *TVF* to provide evidence that Winifred Munday was the daughter of Elizabeth Harrison Munday, daughter of Andrew Harrison, and was the wife of John Munday, and not Thomas Munday. as conjectured in Mr. Harrison's article[2].

The will of Thomas Munday was entered into the records, drawn 1702, probated 1703. The will named the wife, Sarah, maiden name possibly Pealle, based on the will of John Pealle 1700 in which he left his estate to the wife and children of Thomas Munday.[3] Each child was named and identified as son/daughter of Thomas Munday.[4] The Thomas Munday will named these sons: Thomas, eldest; John; Charles; Joseph and daughters: Hannah, minor; Frances; Mary; Martha. 14 June 1711 John Munday was appointed guardian of Charles Munday.[5]

The will of Elizabeth Reeves 4 May 1700/14 Jan 1711. She named her six children: Elizabeth, Henry, Rebecca, Joseph, Martha and Mary; grandsons: Edward Moseley and Thomas Munday; daughter Ann Reeves to be Executrix. Thomas Munday was witness.[6] (This was Thomas, eldest son of Thomas died 1703). 11 Aug 1707 Henry Reeves, Joseph Reeves, Thomas and Mary Munday, John Hawkins, John Parker an Administrative Bond on the estate of James Reeves, dec'd. 19 Aug 1707 Inventory of the estate of James Reeves presented by Mary Munday, wife of Thomas Munday, the late Mary Reeves, Admin. of James Reeves.[7]

Will of John Munday (son of Thomas died 1703) 27 Oct 1739/18 Mar 1739/40 St. Ann's Parish , Essex Co. The will named these children: Sons: John, Thomas, Joseph, Charles, **Harrison**, minor and Ambrose, minor. Daughters: Sarah Ware, Mary Ware, Margaret, Winifred, Tabitha. Wife and Executrix, **Elizabeth**.[8]

12 September 1734, *It is ordered William Harrison be surveyor of the new road from the Court house to deep run and that he have Saml Coleman's Benja. Rennolds', James Trice's, James Burden's, John Munday's, John Long's, Baldwin Collins' and Capt. Wm. Taliaferro's people to assist him in clearing the road.* (William Harrison was the uncle of John Munday).[9]

2. 12 September 1735, *It is ordered Nicholas Ware, John Long, Wm. Harrison and John Munday appraise the estate of Boldwin Collown.* It should be noted that two daughters of John (I) and Elizabeth (Harrison) Munday married men with the surname Ware. A sister (Margaret) of Elizabeth Harrison married a man with the surname Long.[10]

3. 8 October 1742, *Ordered that John Munday be surveyor of the road in the room of Robert Stuart.*[11]

12 March 1752, *On the motion of Sarah Munday, it's ordered she have administration of the estate of John Munday, who with John Long and John Newton acknowledged a bond. It's ordered Robert Taliaferro, John Hutchens, Thomas Samuel and Peyton Smith appraise the estate of John Munday.* 14 May 1752, *The inventory and appraisement of the estate of John Munday returned.*[12] 13 August 1752, *It's ordered James Ware, Henry Ware and John Garrett divide the estate of John Munday among his widow and children.* 21 September 1752, *The division of the estate of John Munday returned.*[13]

Winifred Munday, named as an orphan of John Munday, appears to have been the youngest child. It also appears that these children of John Munday were under age in 1752 when he died, and based on the entries in the court order books the following birth dates may be approximated:

James, 1737/8; had guardian named in 1752; became a guardian in 1758.

John, (III) 1739/40, bound himself to Wm Helton in 1753 and to Gabriel Mitchell in 1756; chose brother James as guardian in 1758.

Reuben, 1742, chose brother James as guardian in 1758.

Sarah, 1744, chose brother James as guardian in 1758.

Benjamin, 1746, John Long became guardian in 1758.

Edmond, 1748, John Long became guardian in 1758.

Winnie, 1750, John Long became guardian in 1758.

Note: The last six children are listed in the order in which they appear in the court order entries.

It appears that Sarah, wife of John Munday and mother of the children, remarried once, and perhaps twice. Certainly she was the wife of Benjamin Robinson in 1758 when they were ordered to bring Sarah Munday, orphan of John, into court.

(729;618-619) Further information has been found concerning the life of ROBERT MUNDAY that gives some indication of his date of birth and how he spent the early years of his adulthood. This may negate the possibility of the relationship with the Mundays of Essex and Caroline counties that has been related in the book, *Tidewater Virginia Families*. Then again, since it is difficult to judge the exact dates of birth of the various Munday children and of John Munday the father, due to the paucity of records, it is possible that Robert Munday was an older son as has been conjectured. The answer is found in further research, with the hope of finding other records.

John Munday could have been old enough to have a son the age of Robert Munday of King George County, and he may have been the son of a first wife of John Munday. Robert Munday, of Hanover Parish, King George County purchased 100 acres of land from Cornelius McCartie and Frances his wife of Hamilton Parish, King William County on July 2, 1747. This means that Robert Munday was of age at that time, probably being born by 1726.[14] The one question that arises concerning Robert and his relationship with the Essex and Caroline County Mundays is an earlier entry in a King George County Deed Book for 1728 which refers to land sold to a Robert Mundane.[15] Was his name spelled correctly and he of a different family, or was this careless spelling?

The Robert Mundy of interest to descendants of CHARLES MUNDY of Amherst County is that Robert was evidently married to a Mrs. Ginnings, as his first wife. A deed from Joshua Ginnings confirms that Robert was his stepfather (referred to as father-in-law in the deed), as he stated that the personal property transferred from Robert was in full satisfaction for all the right that Joshua had in his father's estate.[16]

It is confirmed from a deed dated July 8, 1776 that William was the son of Robert Munday. The deed was executed by *ROBERT MUNDAY and his wife CATHERINE, for the natural love and affection they have unto their son....* The land was described as being in King George County, Parish of Hanover containing 100 acres. Robert signed the deed with his mark and Catherine signed with her name. It was a deed of gift, and William sold the land in October of the same year.[17] This is not to imply that Catherine was the mother of William as she and Robert were not married until shortly before the deed was executed. It is believed that William died in Knox County, Tennessee in 1817.[18]

(730-736b;620-626)
Gen. 6

CHARLES MUNDY

MUNDY FAMILY

Note: This line is presented with the knowledge that the family of Robert Mundy may not have been correctly identified.

Gen.10 THOMAS MUNDAY		m	SARAH (—?—)
Issue:	Thomas	m	
	JOHN	m	ELIZABETH (—?—)
	Charles	m	
	Joseph	m	
	Hannah	m	
	Frances	m	
	Mary	m	
	Martha	m	
Gen. 9 JOHN MUNDAY		m	ELIZABETH HARRISON
Issue:	JOHN	m	SARAH (—?—)
	Sarah	m	(—?—) Ware
	Thomas	m	

Mary	m	(—?—) Ware	
Joseph	m		
Margaret	m		
Charles	m		
Winifred	m		
Ambrose	m		
Harrison	m		
Tabitha	m		

Gen. 8 JOHN MUNDAY	m	SARAH (—?—)	
Issue: (p)ROBERT	m	(1) (—?—) Ginney widow	
	m	(2) CATHERINE HAYNIE	
James	m		
John	m		
Reuben	m		
Sarah	m		
Benjamin	m		
Edmond	m		
Winnie	m	James Spradling	

Gen. 7 (p) ROBERT MUNDY	m	(1) (—?—) Ginney widow	
Issue: John	m	d.s.p.	
William	m		
Joshua	m		
daughter	m	James Lampkin	

ROBERT MUNDY	m	(2) CATHERINE HAYNIE	
Issue: CHARLES	m	MARY FISHBACK	

Gen. 6 CHARLES MUNDY	m	MARY FISHBACK	
Issue: Catherine	m	Henry Watts	
Alexander	m	Mary Dillard Christian	
ANN (NANCY)	m	JOSEPH PETTYJOHN	
Jesse	m	Louisa Neville	
Sallie		died young	
Mary	m	Rev. James Dillard	

Notes

1. 8716 NW 4th Place, Gainesville, FL 32607-1411.
2. *TVF* 5(1996): 30-38; 5(1997): 239-241; 6(1997): 32-38.
3. *Essex County Deed & Will Book 11, 1702-1704* 55.
4. *D & W Book 10, 1699-1702* 53.
5. *D & W Book 13, 1707-1711* 419.
6. *D & W Book 14, 1711-1716* 17.
7. *D & W Book 13, 1707-1711* 11, 33-35.
8. *Essex Co. Wills, Book 6, 1735-1743* 242.
9. J. F. Dorman, *Caroline County Court Order Book, 1732-1740, Pt.1, 1732-1734/5* 78(157); See also, *TVF* 5 (1997): 239-241.
10. CCCOB, 1732-1740, Pt.2, 1734/5-1737 18(308 page in orginal book in parentheses); *TVF* 5: 241. See the account of Elizabeth Harrison Munday in *TVF* 5(1997): 240-242, and *Andrew Harrison of Golden Vale Creek, Caroline (Essex) County. TVF* 5(1996): 30-38.
11. CCCOB 1740-1746, Pt.1, 1740-742/3 76(129).
12. Ibid., 61(300), 69(312).
13. Ibid., 86(336), 91(342).
14. Ruth and Sam Sparacio, *Deed Abstracts of King George County, Virginia, 1735-1752* 90.
15. Sparacio *Deed Book 1* 528-531.
16. Sparacio *Deed Book 4* 505.
17. Sparacio *Deeds, 1773-1783* 1193-1194, 1190.
18. Correspondence (1995) with Robert Jenkins, 3316 Craigie Ct, Napa, CA 94558.

Gen. 9   **PHILIPP FISCHBACH**

In the line of ascent from NELLIE BUTLER, JOHANNES HEIMBACH I would be Generation 11, JOST; thought to be his brother provided the line of descent through JOHANNES FISCHBACH II and would be Generation 12 from NELLIE BUTLER.

HEIMBACH FAMILY

Gen.13 JOHANN HEIMBACH	m	UNKNOWN
Issue: JOHANNES I	m	ELISABETH (—?—)
(p) JOST	m	UNKNOWN
Gen.12 JOST HEIMBACH	m	UNKNOWN
Issue: GEORG	m	ELIZABETH NIESS
Ehla	m	Henrich Nohe
Johannes	m	
Gen.11 GEORG HEIMBACH	m	ELIZABETH NIESS
Issue: CATHARIN	m	JOHANNES FISCHBACH II
Herman	m	
Philipp	m	(1) Margarethe (—?—)
	m	(2) Maria Fischbach
	m	(3) Margareth Jung
Hermann	m	
Jacob	m	
Clara	m	
Johan	m	
Gen.12 JOHANNES HEIMBACH I	m	ELISABETH (—?—)
Issue: JOHANNES	m	CLARA (—?—)
Georg	m	
Gen.11 JOHANNES HEIMBACH II	m	CLARA (—?—)
Issue: Maria Elsbeth	m	
Henrich	m	
Johan Jacob	m	
Anna	m	
Johannes	m	
ELISABETH	m	PHILIPP FISCHBACH.

Gen. 8   **JOHN FISHBACK**

(747;637) correction: The name of the second wife of JOHN FISHBACK was incorrectly transcribed from his will and has been repeatedly handed down incorrectly. Her name was **MARIA DOROTHEA FITER** (not Mary Daughtery), and she is believed to have died before 1753, her dower was owned by her son by that date.[1]

The lots owned by John Fishback were designated as Lot Numbers 3 and 5. Lot 3 was John's first full lot and was left in his will with the upper half to his son, Henry Fishback, the lower half to his widow and second wife, Mary Dorothea Fishback, and after his death to his son, Frederick. Henry Fishback died young and his eldest brother Frederick inherited his land. In 1753 Frederick Fishback deeded Lot 3 to Thomas Marshall, and this lot then came into the possession of John Hatley Norton prior to 1781.

Lot 5 was John Fishback's second full lot. In his will he left it to his daughter, Elizabeth who married John Peter Kemper, the eldest son of John Kemper the immigrant. The Kempers sold it in 1749 to Jacob Rector, son of Jacob and Elizabeth (Fishback) Rector and son-in-law of Peter Hitt, the immigrant. Jacob Rector deeded it in 1772 to Henry Utterback, the grandson of Melchior Brumback, who still possessed it in 1790.

In addition John also owned one-half of lot 1, which he left to his daughter, Catherine, the wife of John Rector. The latter must have sold it to his brother-in-law, Frederick Fishback, who in turn sold it to John Ariss in 1765 and Ariss sold it to William Nelson in 1766. It is interesting that John Fishback owned a total of 250 acres, instead of 150 acres as would have been expected. Since Lot 5 does not fit into the original land patent acreage, the survey must have showed that the Germanna group in fact had acquired a larger tract of land than they had thought. John may well have purchased this extra land from the other eleven men some time prior to the various deeds made in 1729.

It seems likely that the original cemetery of Germantown was near the church on the lower part of Lot 15, the Germantown Glebe. Large flat stones have been turned up in recent years when the land has been cultivated, which makes one think that this is compatible with the remains of the old church. The cemetery would have adjoined the church grounds.[2]

Harman Fishback

(750;640) The mother of Harman was Maria Dorothea Fiter. Catherine Fishback the first wife of Harman Fishback died before 1745 at Germantown, she was probably Anna Catherine Otterbach, born January 2, 1705, sister of Mrs. Kemper and Mrs. Holtzclaw.[3]

Note: The Germanna Foundation, P.O. Box 693, Culpeper, VA 22701 continues to hold an annual reunion of the descendants of the Germanna Colony at Germanna Community College every summer.

(753-758;642-646)
Gen. 7

JOSIAH FISHBACK

FISHBACK FAMILY

Gen.11 JOHANNES FISCHBACH I	m	LIESS (ELIZABETH)
Issue: Daniel	m	
JOHANNES	m	CATHARINA HEIMBACH
Gen.10 JOHANNES FISCHBACH II	m	CATHARINA HEIMBACH
Issue: Clara	m	
Johannes	m	
Jacob	m	Klara Becker
Jost	m	
PHILIPP	m	ELSBETH HEIMBACH
Gerlach	m	
Gen. 9 PHILIPP FISCHBACH	m	ELSBETH HEIMBACH
Issue: Clara		died young
Anna Els	m	Hans Jacob Rector
Maria Els	m	John Spilman
Agnes		died young
JOHANNES (JOHN)	m	(1) Agnes Hager
	m	(2) MARIA DOROTHEA FITER
Hermann (Harman)	m	Catherine Utterback
Maria Els	m	Melchoir Brumback

Gen. 8 JOHN FISHBACK	m	(1) Agnes Hager
Issue: Anna Catherine	m	John Rector
John Frederick	m	(1) Ann Holtzclaw
	m	(2) Eva Martin
Henry		died young
Elizabeth	m	John Peter Kemper

JOHN FISHBACK	m	(2)MARIA DOROTHEA FITER
Issue: Harman		died young
John Jacob	m	Sarah (—?—)
John Philip	m	(1) (—?—) Neville
	m	(2) Jane Reed
	m	(3) Winifred Nutt
JOSIAH	m	ANN NELSON

Gen. 7 JOSIAH FISHBACK	m	ANN NELSON
Issue: Sallie	m	Timothy Cunningham
MARY (POLLY)	m	CHARLES MUNDY
Jesse		unmarried
Lydia	m	Thomas Rossey
Josiah		unmarried
John	m	Lydia O'Bannon
Nelson	m	Ann Welsh

(758-759;647)
Gen. 9

HENRY NELSON

(759-761;647-649)
Gen. 8

JOHN NELSON

NELSON FAMILY

Gen. 9 HENRY NELSON	m	(1) UNKNOWN
Issue: Henry	m	Jean Goodwin
JOHN	m	SARAH WHITSON
Mary	m	John Mason
Elizabeth	m	Daniel Mason
Margaret	m	John Pownall
Henry Nelson	m	(2) (p) Sarah (—?—)
Issue: Lettice	m	
Susanna	m	
Frances	m	

Gen. 8 JOHN NELSON	m	SARAH WHITSON
Issue: Jesse	m	
John	m	Mary Young
William	m	Elizabeth Morehead
Lydia	m	Alexander Morehead
ANN (NANNY)	m	JOSIAH FISHBACK
Mary	m	(—?—) Rector
Margaret	m	
Jemima	m	Charles Utterback
Lettice	m	George Shumate
Sarah	m	

178

Gen. 11

JOHN HAYNIE

MORRIS FAMILY

Gen.12 NICHOLAS MORRIS	m	MARTHA (—?—)
Issue: Anthony	m	(1) (—?—) Kinge
	m	(2) Dorothy Sanford
JANE	m	CAPT. JOHN HAYNIE

(766-770;654-657)

Gen. 10

RICHARD HAYNIE

(770-771;658)

Gen. 9

ANTHONY HAYNIE

It has been difficult to establish the activities of ANTHONY HAYNIE; however, it is now known that Anthony Haynie was a churchwarden in Brunswick Parish in 1734.[4] Lamb's Creek Church in Brunswick Parish, King George County was an Anglican Church,[5] built in the last half of the seventeenth century, and replacing an earlier church in parishes that dated back to the first part of the century.[6] Lamb's Creek Church is north of US Route 301 on SR 206 and then east on CR 694 in the Graves Corner area. It is a simple but refined brick structure built between 1769-77 that achieved sophistication without ornamentation (over the door is inscribed in a brick the year 1770). Its design is attributed to John Ariss who is the documented designer of Payne's Church (now destroyed). The church is set in a wooded area, with only that area adjacent to the church building cleared. A natural stone is placed directly in front of the church with the face of the stone polished, that bears the inscription:

LAMB'S CREEK CHURCH
RE-ERECTED 1760-70
REMOVED FROM MUDDY CREEK CHURCH SITE
IN USE IN 1710.

The church is stark in its simplicity, both without and within. Oil lamp chandeliers still hang from the ceiling and oil lamp sconces are placed along each wall. The simple white wooden pews came from St. Peter's Church in Westmoreland County to supplement the slatted back benches from an earlier date. Its predecessor, Muddy Creek Church was about nine miles from Fredericksburg, the creek itself forming the boundary between King George and Stafford counties. Lamb's Creek Church became the church of Brunswick Parish. Mr. Anthony Hainy was churchwarden in the parish in 1734, and Mr. Charles Carter and John Champe in 1739.[7] Brunswick Parish was established in 1732 and Anthony was likely a churchwarden at Muddy Creek Church.

Union troops used Lamb's Creek Church as a stable during the Civil War, then the church was restored to use by the Episcopal Church in 1908. The church is in need of preservation and restoration at present and is inactive; being used only annually for a memorial service.

(772-774;659-661)

Gen. 8

CHARLES HAYNIE

HAYNIE FAMILY

Gen.11 CAPT. JOHN HAYNIE	m	JANE MORRIS
Issue: RICHARD	m	(1) Elizabeth Bridger
	m	(2) ELINOR (—?—)

Martha	m	
Elizabeth	m	Peter Presley
John	m	(1) Mary Sadler
	m	(2) Hannah Spaleigh
Anthony	m	Sarah Harris
Anne	m	(1) Thomas Harding
	m	(2) Luke Rowlands

Gen.10 <u>RICHARD HAYNIE</u>   m   (1) Elizabeth Bridger

Issue:			
	John	m	
	Bridger	m	Mary (—?—)
	Richard	m	
	Maxmillian	m	Mary (—?—)
	Elizabeth	m	(1) (—?—) Smith
		m	(2) (—?—) Elleston
	Katherine	m	Thomas Bearcroft
	a child		
	a child		

Issue:	<u>RICHARD HAYNIE</u>	m	(2) ELINOR (—?—)
	ANTHONY	m	ELIZABETH (—?—)
	Elinor	m	
	Charles	m	
	Ormsby	m	Sarah (—?—
	Samuel	m	
	Winifred	m	
	Ann	m	

Gen. 9 <u>ANTHONY HAYNIE</u>   m   <u>ELIZABETH (—?—)</u>

Issue:			
	Spencer	m	
	Bridger	m	
	CHARLES	m	ELIZABETH (—?—)
	Ann	m	(—?—) Strother
	Elizabeth	m	
	Winifred	m	
	Jane	m	
	Richard	m	
	John	m	
	William	m	

Gen. 8 <u>CHARLES HAYNIE</u>   m   <u>ELIZABETH (—?—)</u>

Issue:			
	CATHERINE	m	ROBERT MUNDY
	Anthony	m	Sarah Williams
	Winifred	m	

Notes

1. Charles Herbert Huffman, ed, *The Germanna Record* 2(1962):50.
2. Huffman 39, 24, 38.
3. Huffman 50, 52.
4. Bishop Meade, *Old Churches, Ministers and Families of Virginia* 1857 (Bowie, MD: Heritage, rep 1992) 187-192; *TVF* 3(1992): 217-219.
5. See *TVF* 3(1992): 217-219.
6. Calder Loth, *The Virginia Historic Landmarks Register* 1986 (Charlottesville, VA: University Press of VA, 1987) 221.
7. Bishop Meade, *Old Churches, Ministers and Families of Virginia, vol II* 1857 (Bowie, MD: Heritage Books, rep 1992) 187-192.

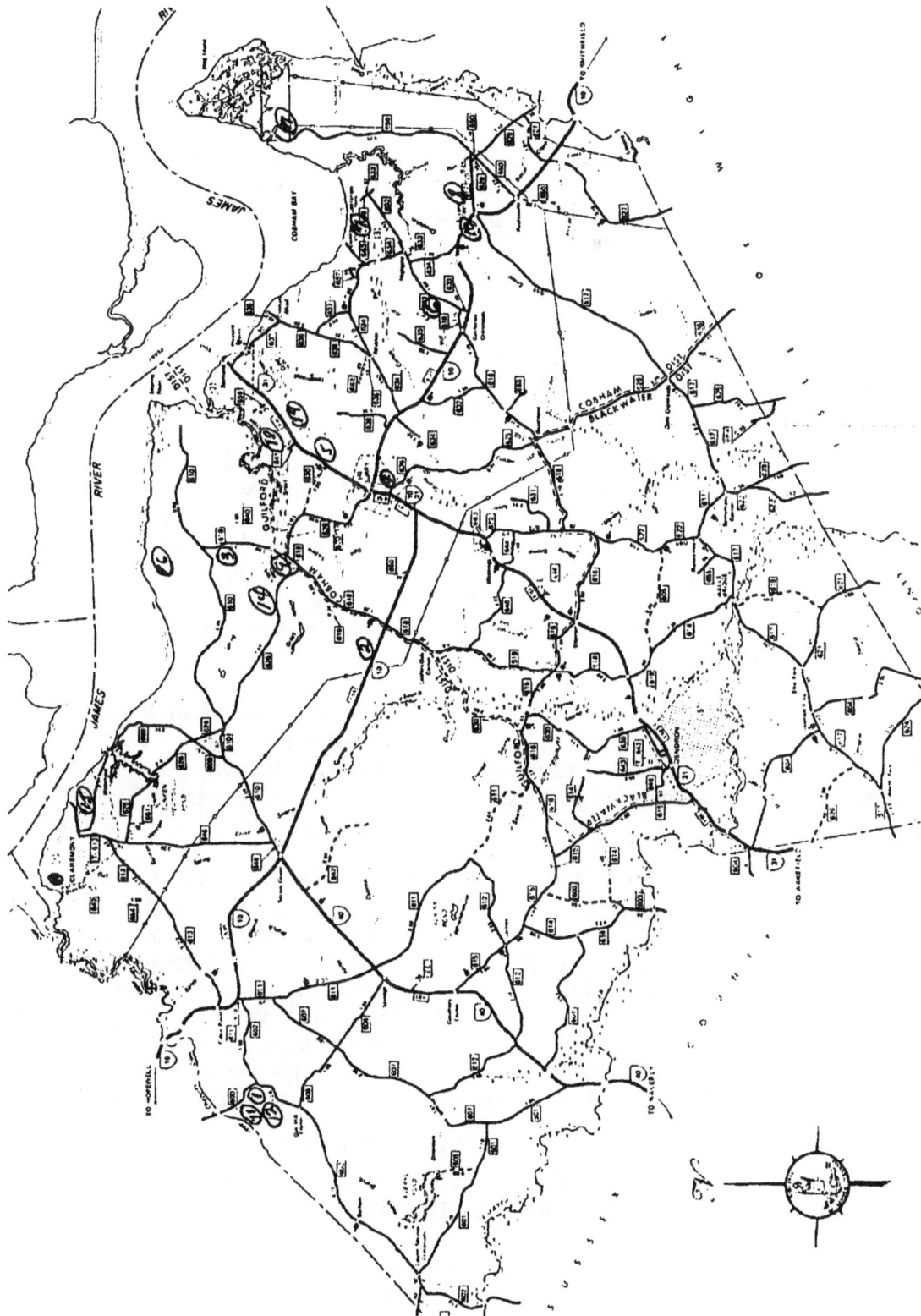

SURRY COUNTY

Gen. 9   **FRANCIS CLEMENTS**

It had seemed that FRANCIS CLEMENTS just "appeared" in Surry County; it is now known from the Fishmongers' Company records of apprentices bound for foreign plantations that Francis Clements was an apprentice bound to John Scampion for Virginia aged 23, 1683.[1] It is further known that his birth date was the year 1650. The records of apprentices bound in London to plantation service began in 1683 with entries in the Lord Mayor's Waiting Books. Francis rose from the status of an apprentice to a substantial citizen of Surry County, and furthermore married well.

(662;669) correction: Francis Clements married Elizabeth Meriwether, **the daughter of Nicholas Meriwether, and William and Francis were the brothers of Elizabeth, as was Captain Nicholas Meriwether.** Nicholas Meriwether, the father was clerk of the court and a justice in Surry County as early as 1655 and died before March 4, 1678/9.[2]

When research was begun it was not clear whether Francis Clements had been married twice prior to his marriage to LYDIA LAKER Bleighton, but with records that have since been researched it can be deduced that Francis married Elizabeth Meriwether Clough. An entry dated January 5, 1685, in the Surry County Court Orders states: *The difference between Mr. Fra. Clements as marryeing Mrs. Eliz. Clough, Exre. of Mr. John Clough and Mr. James Cane is refrd to xt. Cort.*[3] From the entry in the Surry County court records, April 21, 1695, concerning William Meriwether, deceased, it is shown that Captain Francis Clements and Elizabeth his wife and Nicholas Meriwether were appointed the administrators of his estate. Elizabeth and Nicholas were identified as sister and brother of William Meriwether.[4]

(664;671) The will of Francis Clements (II) is revealing in the naming and identification of the primary legatees of his estate.[5] Francis identified as his uncles Major Nicholas Meriwether and Captain William Browne (who had married Jane Meriwether, his mother's sister) and cousins William, David, Eliza, Jane, Sarah and Mary Meriwether, the children of Major Nicholas Meriwether and a legacy to Lydia Clements, mother-in-law (step mother).[6]

(663;670) Francis married a second time, Lydia Laker Bleighton, the widow of George Bleighton. Francis had risen to a position of status and respect in Surry County, his first marriage being fortuitous. His second was equally so. One only needs to read further in the account of Lydia's father, Benjamin to appreciate her heritage. It had not been known by this author that there was apparently a fairly significant group of dissenting Baptists in Surry and Prince George counties at this early date. A record was found of George Bleighton's association with the Baptists, but this seemed an anomaly for the times. The account of the life of BENJAMIN LAKER confirms that not only was he a force in the Baptist movement but he passed this on to his son-in-law. One wonders at the role of Lydia Laker Bleighton during her first marriage and the extent to which she adjusted her life to that of a respected Anglican communicant and wife of a justice in Surry County in her marriage to Francis Clements.

Gen. 8   **THOMAS CLEMENTS**

Gen. 7   **JAMES CLEMENTS**

Following is a re-evaluation of the relationship of JAMES CLEMENTS as the son of Thomas Clements, and therefore a descendant of LYDIA LAKER CLEMENTS, the daughter of Benjamin Laker, who was in the province of Carolina by 1680. The circumstantial evidence presented in the book, *Tidewater Virginia Families* was presented as the best proof available of the relationship of James and Thomas, and thus the descent from Lydia Laker Clements. Presented here is the response from a well-recognized genealogist, with the observation that the circumstantial evidence was stronger than had been implied, and is so strong that further evidence would indicate that a document had been found that actually stated the relationship.[7] Following is the analysis of the court order referring to James and Joshua (a known son of Thomas) Clements in connection with Ann Todd and John Todd. It is interpreted from this record in connection with the other evidence given, that it brings the status of circumstantial evidence as stated above.

A. Ann Todd's position was that she needed a *next friend* to pursue the suit against John Todd for her; this establishes her status as being one of the following: a minor female who had a right to the land; the wife of someone who was living whose surname was Todd, or an adult who was incapable of managing her estate.

B. Ann Todd would have had to acquire the land through a. inheritance as a devisee, as heir of one who died intestate or as one of the above through a chancery suit that did not survive; b. purchase of the land seems unlikely, and the circumstance relating to land purchased would not have led to a suit between her and her husband. c. a gift of the land seems more unlikely than as a devisee.

C. Considerations in the status of Ann Todd, was she: a. an adult, a minor, single or married, competent or incompetent. She must have been an adult, competent and capable of living alone but as an individual her status was that she could not hold the property in her own right without it being subject to conditions which were inconsistent with the circumstances connected with her acquiring an interest in it which conditions eventually led to the development of circumstances necessitating legal action.

D. It is known that Ann Todd was not *sui juris* (possessing full civil and social rights) because she had a *next friend* (one, an officer of the court, acting in her behalf, such as a married woman or minor). Ann was not a minor as she had no guardian, thus she was a married woman living with her husband, who would have been John Todd. Had he not been her husband, her husband would have been the one acting in her behalf.

E. It can be concluded that Ann Todd had an interest in the property which had been taken over by John Todd in the capacity of her husband, which capacity did not entitle him to having title to the property.

F. The only reasonable situation under the circumstances and laws of the times would have been that the house, yard and garden had been devised to her under the terms of a will with the provision that her husband not possess it or have right to it, but it was not devised to a trustee to hold for her.

G. It stands to reason that since she could not sue in her own right that her *next friend* would have been relative by blood, and most likely her brother, since the estate was too small to warrant payment of a legal fee.

H. The keystone of the evidence in the case is the disposition of the property by court order. It was to be deeded to James and Joshua Clements. Since James was not a party to the action but was appearing as an officer of the court to look after her interests other circumstances must have existed to warrant the judge ordering that it be deeded to both James and Joshua Clements, and thus as trustees.

I. It is concluded that Ann Todd was a sister of both James and Joshua Clements and that her father devised the house, yard and garden where she lived to be held by her and not by any husband that she had. The records further indicate indirectly that both James and Joshua were the executors of the will of their father, and as executors of his will under which Ann inherited the property, and brothers of Ann the Judge appointed both of them trustees.

J. With an understanding of the laws of inheritance of the times, it can only be concluded that Ann was a daughter of THOMAS and MARTHA CLEMENTS and James was a son, since it is established by the Bristol Parish Register that Joshua was a son of Thomas and Martha. This further explains the period of seven years absence from the parish records of children born to Thomas and Martha Clements.[8]

With the increased emphasis on the analysis of circumstantial evidence in establishing family relationships, the foregoing account provides a model for other researchers in understanding the legal system in effect, as well as the customs of the times.

(672;679) James Clements served under Colonel Theodorick Bland, November and December 1777 in the Third Troop of the Virginia Light dragoons in the First Regiment. For each month served he received Eight and one-half dollars, or £2/10 Virginia currency. James Clements signed his name for the receipt of his extraordinary pay.[9]

CLEMENTS FAMILY

Gen. 9	FRANCIS CLEMENTS	m	(1) Elizabeth Meriwether Clough widow
Issue:	Francis	m	d.s.p.
	FRANCIS CLEMENTS	m	(2) LYDIA LAKER BLEIGHTON widow
Issue:	Benjamin	m	Judith Parker
	THOMAS	m	MARTHA (—?—)
	Mary	m	William Browne, Jr.
	Elizabeth	m	
Gen. 8	THOMAS CLEMENTS	m	MARTHA (—?—)
Issue:	John (p)	m	Mary (—?—)
	Rebecca	m	
	Freeman	m	
	JAMES	m	LUCRETIA COTTON
	Ann	m	John Todd
	Thomas	m	
	Robert	m	
	Lockie	m	
	Joshua	m	
Gen. 7	JAMES CLEMENTS	m	LUCRETIA COTTON
Issue:	James		d.s.p.
	Jeremiah	m	Mary Lee
	Rebecca	m	Richard Moore
	Elizabeth	m	Benjamin Figg
	SARAH	m	(1) LODOWICK LEE
		m	(2) Thomas Lee
	a son		died in infancy

Notes

1. Peter Wilson Coldham, *The Complete Book of Emigrants, 1661-1699*. (Baltimore: Genealogical Publishing Co, 1990) 443.
2. Weynette Parks Haun, *Surry County, Virginia Court Records, 1652-1663*, Book 1 (Durham, NC: privately printed, 1986) 61 243 Argonne Dr, Durham, NC 27704; Haun, Book 3 245.
3. Haun, Book IV 504.
4. Eliza Timberlake Davis, *Wills and Administrations of Surry County, Virginia, 1671-1750* 1955 (Baltimore: Clearfield, 1980) 94.
5. Davis, 32.
6. Sarah Travers Lewis (Scott) Anderson, *Lewises, Meriwethers and Their Kin* 1938 Baltimore: Genealogical Publishing Co, 1995) 144, 148.
7. William M. Mann, Jr., M.D., Genealogist, OFFNC, Correspondence April 1995.
8. Churchill Gibson Chamberlayne, *The Vestry Book and Register of Bristol Parish, Virginia, 1720-1789*. (Richmond: Privately printed, 1898) passim.
9. William Fletcher Boogher, *Gleanings of Virginia History* (Bowie, MD: Heritage, 1993) 189, 198, 207.

Gen. 8   WILLIAM COTTON

Following is the a summary of the circumstantial evidence recounted in *Tidewater Virginia Families* to provide a more concise account of the relationships presented for consideration as a link to earlier generations.

The will of THOMAS COTTON of 1777 identified him as the father of William Cotton in his bequest to his son, WILLIAM COTTON and then to William's son, Wells Cotton. In the bequest of Thomas, to his son Thomas, of land he further identified the location of the land as being that on which he lived and as "the College Tenament".[1] No bequest of land was made to William; however, in so far as has been determined William was already living on this land. This conclusion is drawn from the fact that no reference has been found of William's ownership of land, and he was not listed in the Sussex Land Tax Records as being assessed for land taxes at any time.[2] His brother, Thomas (who is known to have lived on College Land)[3], likewise, was not assessed for land taxes and listed in the Sussex Land Tax Records. Those living on the College Land did not actually own the land, and thus did not pay county taxes on the land.[4]

It is further known that the Alsobrooks also owned land adjoining the "College Land".[5] This places the families in close proximity to each other. Many references showing an association between the two families appear in the *Albemarle Parish Register* as godparents are named in the baptismal records.[6] The study by Rutman and Rutman[7] of the network of families, their associations and marriages indicates that marriages during the colonial time period occurred between persons living in close proximity to each other. Thirty-six percent were between persons living within one-half mile of each other, and ninety-five percent between persons living no more than five miles apart.

While no primary documentation has been found to indicate that William Cotton married the daughter of SAMUEL ALSOBROOK (III) there is strong circumstantial evidence of this. The above information places the two families in close association. The naming of a son of William and Elizabeth Cotton, "Alsobrook Cotton",[8] is further evidence. Rutman and Rutman in their study of naming patterns of the colonial period show that typically, a son is named for the mother's father; either by given name or by surname of the mother.[9]

The extant Sussex County Guardian Bond shows conclusively that SAMUEL ALSOBROOK (III), whose estate was administered in December 1757, had a daughter ELIZABETH. Thomas Morris was appointed the guardian of John, Mary and Elizabeth Alsobrook in August 1758.[10]

It is believed that WILLIAM COTTON and ELIZABETH were married prior to December 1759, when the first entry for the birth of their child appears in the *Albemarle Parish Register*.[11] Extensive research has been conducted among the surviving county court records of Sussex County, both in the record books and among the loose papers. While no record has been found to show that Elizabeth or William Cotton, on her behalf, received the legacy belonging to Elizabeth Alsobrook, the Guardian Account Book (32-33) entry for 1761 lists only the other two orphans (John and Mary) of Samuel Alsobrook, in the account rendered by their guardian, Thomas Morris for the year 1761.[12]

While many of the county court records for Sussex County are extant, there are many gaps in the records, thus it is difficult to document the vital records of the residents of the county in the eighteenth century. No other family has been identified as closely with William Cotton as the Alsobrook family. No other person has been identified that may have been his wife. An extensive search of the available records for Sussex, Southampton and Greensville counties, where these families are known to have lived, and of the records of Halifax County, North Carolina, where a number of the Alsobrook and Cotton family members migrated, has failed to identify any other Alsobrook or Cotton of the same time frame that could have created this union.

It is therefore concluded that William Cotton, the son of Thomas Cotton of Sussex County married Elizabeth Alsobrook, daughter of Samuel Alsobrook of Sussex County.

The entry of the christening of LUCRETIA COTTON, daughter of William and Lucy Cotton in the *Albemarle Parish Register* in November 1762,[13] is confusing. When Boddie[14] made his abstraction of the births from the register, he made the correction that she was the daughter of WILLIAM and ELIZABETH COTTON.[15] There appears to be no doubt that Lucretia was, in fact, the daughter of William Cotton and Elizabeth, his wife. The William Cotton who was a contemporary of this William was married to Lucy, but they lived in Prince George County, as his will indicates. The William Cotton of Prince George County named his children in his will, and did not mention a daughter named Lucretia.

A compilation of the birth dates, in the parish register, of the children of William and Elizabeth Cotton gives a sequence of births that would place Lucretia in correct order among their children. That is: Selah, 1759; Jeremiah, 1761; Lucretia, 1762; Wells, 1763; Hardy, 1766; and Alsobrook, 1768.[16] Since there are entries for the births in the parish register of the children of John Cotton (of Sussex County) and his wife, Lucy (e.g. Jane, December 1744),[17] one would conclude that the Reverend Willie (the minister of Albemarle Parish at that time) simply confused the two when he made the entry. A commonplace mistake made by many in identifying those in a close community.

As a further confirmation that Lucretia was the daughter of William and Elizabeth Cotton is the naming of the children of James and Lucretia Cotton Clements, following the naming patterns of the time.[18] Their children whose names probably came from the Cotton family were: Jeremiah Clements, named for Lucretia's brother, and Elizabeth Clements, named for Lucretia's mother.

(678;684) correction: The reference for the birth of Jeremiah Cotton is found on **page 87** in the *Albemarle Parish Register* as transcribed by Richards, both the index and this author were wrong.

COTTON FAMILY

Gen. 9 THOMAS COTTON II	m	JEAN (JANE) (—?—)	
Issue:	Thomas	d.s.p.	
	Nathaniel	d.s.p.	
	WILLIAM	m	ELIZABETH ALSOBROOK
	Richard	m	Betty (—?—)
	Davis	m	
	Isham		
	Drewry	m	Phocbc (—?—)
	Henry	m	Sarah (—?—)
	Nary	m	

Gen. 8 WILLIAM COTTON	m	ELIZABETH ALSOBROOK	
Issue:	Sylvia	m	Richard Smith
	Jeremiah	m	
	LUCRETIA	m	JAMES CLEMENTS
	Wells	m	
	Hardy	m	Patty Saunders
	Alsobrook	m	

(680-683;686-689)

Gen. 7

THOMAS BONNER

BONNER FAMILY

Gen.10 THOMAS BONNER	m	(1) UNKNOWN	
Issue:	Frederick	m	Elizabeth Smith
	Chappell	m	Priscilla Smith
	SUSANNA	m	SAMUEL LEE
	Joan	m	Hicks Bonner

Thomas Bonner		m	(2) Jane (—?—)
Issue:	Elizabeth	m	Thomas Bonner
	Rebekah	m	Haitable Peebles
	Jane	m	Epps Reeves

Notes

1. Sussex County Will Book C. Copy of will from Sussex County Loose Papers.

2. Sussex County Land Tax Records, 1782-1804.

3. Sussex County Deed Book G.

4. Sussex County Land Tax Records, 1782-1804. Reel 321, Library of Virginia; Dennis Hudgins, *Cavaliers and Pioneers* vol 4 (Richmond: Virginia Genealogical Society, 1994); Land Patent Book 18, 315; Map of Sussex County, Virginia Department of Transportation; Gary M. Williams, Clerk of Sussex County Circuit Court, Letter, 13 Nov. 1991.

5. Land Patent Book 18 315.

6. Gertrude R. B. Richards, *Register of Albemarle Parish, Surry and Sussex Counties,1739-1778* 1958 (Easley, SC: Southern Historical Press, rep. 1984) passim.

7. Darrett B. and Anita H. Rutman, *A Place in Time, Middlesex County, 1650-1750* (New York: Norton, 1984) 104-105, Rutman and Rutman, *Explicatus* (Norton, 1984) 120-121.

8. Richards 184.

9. *Explicatus*, 88-93.

10. Sussex County Court Order Book, 1757-1761; Guardian Accounts; Sussex County Loose Papers, Sussex County Circuit Court Records, copy of Guardian Bond.

11. Richards 180.

12. Sussex Guardian Accounts 32-33.

13. Richards 147.

14. Boddie 31-32.

15. John Bennett Boddie, *Births, Deaths and Sponsors, 1717-1778, From the Albemarle Parish Register of Surry and Sussex Counties, Virginia.* 1958 (Baltimore: Clearfield, rep 1992) 31-32.

16. Richards 180, 87, 147, 182, 141, 184.

17. Richards 144.

18. *Explicatus*, 88-93.

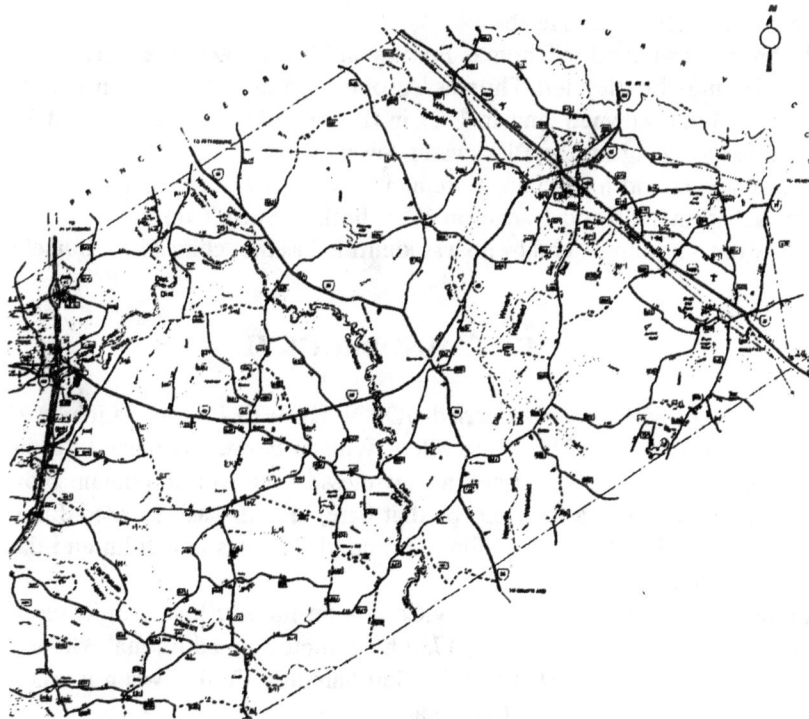

SUSSEX COUNTY

Gen. 11   **SAMUEL ALSOBROOK I**

      SAMUEL ALSOBROOK first appears in the records of Surry County in 1674 when he was listed as a headright for Benjamin Harrison. He was living on Benjamin Harrison's plantation in 1677 on the upper end of Southwark Parish, continuing to be listed as a tithable with Benjamin until 1679, alternately with others who listed him as a tithable, then again with Benjamin Harrison until 1688.[1] By 1689 Samuel was living between Thomas and John Ironmonger in the middle precinct of Southwark Parish.

      It is known that Samuel married MARY, the daughter of THOMAS and MARY HUX IRONMONGER, from the will of his brother, John Ironmonger. When the father of MARY ALSOBROOK died it was Samuel who was involved in the settlement of his estate. Both Samuel and Mary qualified as the administrators of the estate of Mary Ironmonger at her death in 1693.[2] This was granted *according to the said Alsobrooks wife being next of kin to the said deceased.*

      MARY IRONMONGER ALSOBROOK died sometime in 1695/6 with Samuel also dying between June 10, 1695 and September 1696. This is evidenced from the record with reference to the orphans of Samuel Alsobrook where an account of his estate mentioned *a child still at nurse at the home of David Andrews.* John Thompson was appointed the administration of Samuel's estate, he having died intestate.[3]

      Samuel and Mary left four known children all of whom were under age:[4]

      SAMUEL ALSOBROOK, in November 1708, chose Samuel Thompson as his guardian. Apparently he had taken over for his brother, John Thompson who had died. Samuel Thompson was empowered for and on the behalf of Samuel Alsobrook, son and heir of Samuel Alsobrook, deceased to gather and receive rent due on the estate.

      Mary Alsobrook married John High, the son of Thomas and Hannah Clements High. She was bound to William Foster until she reached the age of eighteen and on July 6, 1708 she took him to court as her indenture was over and she wanted the good new clothes he was suppose to give her. She had not married at that time as her name was still Mary Alsobrook.

      Thomas Alsobrook was bound to Thomas Bentley in March 1697. He married Sarah and they lived in Albemarle Parish. Thomas Bentley left Thomas Alsobrook a horse and furniture in his will. Thomas Alsobrook died in 1773. Thomas owned land in 1727 in the part of Surry County that later became Sussex County, his land described as being on the Blackwater Swamp.[5]

      John Alsobrook was bound to William Foreman in June 1697. He married Rachel Doles, a widow with a son Peter. John died in 1784 and Rachel in 1788, both in Surry County.

      There may have been a younger child who was identified as the "child still at nurse" when Samuel died.

addition
Gen. 10   **SAMUEL ALSOBROOK II**

      SAMUEL ALSOBROOK married JOAN HOWELL, the daughter of WILLIAM and REBECCA HOWELL.[6] On June 15, 1720, in the will of William Howell he named his daughter Joan as the wife of Samuel Alsobrook and Mary High signed as a witness.[7] The will of William Howell was written on May 9, 1718, thus his daughter Joan was married by that date, his will was recorded June 15, 1720. William Howell named his children in his will: sons, William, Edmond, Thomas and John and daughters, Joan, wife of Samuel Alsobrook and Elizabeth Fitchett.

      Samuel patented 200 acres of land in Surry County on the south side of Three Creeks, and up the creek to its beginning May 13, 1735. On May 12, 1750 he patented an additional 390 acres of land in Surry County.[8] Samuel and his family lived in what became Southampton County when it was formed in 1749 and from there moved to Halifax County, North Carolina.

      It is not known when Joan died, but later records identify his wife as Mary. Samuel had a number of children, some who stayed in Virginia and his will in made in Halifax listing those perhaps by his second wife. Samuel died in Halifax County, North Carolina with his will being recorded in 1766.[9] He made his will in Halifax County, listing perhaps only those children by his second wife. He named sons Howell, Hewitt and David. His son, Samuel Alsobrook III stayed in Virginia and married Agnes Morris, the daughter of Thomas Morris and they had three children: John, Mary and ELIZABETH.

addition
Gen. 9   SAMUEL ALSOBROOK III

SAMUEL ALSOBROOK lived in Sussex County, on land that adjoined the "College Lands"; this was land that had been deeded to him by his father.[10] The entry concerning this deed was recorded in the court order book, and stated that *a deed of Feoffment between Samuel Alsobrook senior in the parish of Albemarle and county of Sussex of the one part and Samuel Alsobrook junior of the same parish and County of the other part was acknowledged by the said Samuel Alsobrook senior and by the Court ordered to be recorded. 8th July 1754.*[11] Many references appear in the *Albemarle Parish Register* showing the Alsobrooks named as godparents in the baptismal records to other families known to live in that area.[12]

Samuel Alsobrook married AGNES MORRIS, as is known from the later will of her father, THOMAS MORRIS. At the time that he wrote his will Samuel had died and Thomas named his daughter Aggy Bass, for Agnes had married Arthur Bass by this date (1782)[13] Thomas Morris died in Greensville County, his will was written February 9, 1782 and recorded January 23, 1783. He named his wife, Boyce Morris and his children in his will: sons, Chislon, Henry and Jabez and daughters: Bethiah Brewer, Agga Bass and Sarah Davis.

Samuel Alsobrook died in Sussex County before December 16, 1757, when his estate was ordered to be administered by the court.[14] The following year Thomas Morris was appointed the guardian of John, Mary and ELIZABETH, the orphans of Samuel Alsobrook.[15] The extant Sussex County Guardian Bond shows conclusively that Samuel Alsobrook, whose estate was administered in December 1757, had a daughter Elizabeth. Thomas Morris was appointed the guardian of John, Mary and ELIZABETH ALSOBROOK in August 1758.[16]

It is believed that William Cotton and Elizabeth were married prior to December 1759, when the first entry for the birth of their child appears in the *Albemarle Parish Register.*[17] Extensive research has been conducted among the surviving county court records of Sussex County, both in the record books and among the loose papers. While no record has been found to show that Elizabeth or William Cotton, on her behalf, received the legacy belonging to Elizabeth Alsobrook, the Guardian Account Book entry for 1761 lists only the other two orphans (John and Mary) of Samuel Alsobrook, in the account rendered by their guardian, Thomas Morris for the year 1761.[18]

While no primary documentation has been found to indicate that William Cotton married the daughter of Samuel Alsobrook, there is strong circumstantial evidence of this. The above information places the two families in close association. The naming of a son of William and Elizabeth Cotton, "Alsobrook Cotton" is further evidence.[19] The customs of the naming patterns of the colonial period show that typically, a son is named for the mother's father; either by given name or by surname of the mother.[20]

ALSOBROOK FAMILY

Gen.11 SAMUEL ALSOBROOK I	m	MARY IRONMONGER
Issue: SAMUEL II	m	(1) JOAN HOWELL
		(2) unknown
Thomas	m	Sarah Bentley
John	m	Rachel Dole, widow
Mary	m	John High
Gen.10 SAMUEL ALSOBROOK II	m	(1) JOAN HOWELL
Issue: SAMUEL III	m	AGNES MORRIS

```
other children
not named
Samuel Alsobrook II              m      (2) unknown
   Howell
   Hewit
   David
```

```
Gen. 9 SAMUEL ALSOBROOK III      m      AGNES MORRIS
Issue:    John                   m
          Mary                   m
          ELIZABETH              m      WILLIAM COTTON
```

Notes

1. *"Tithables, Surry County"*, *Magazine of Virginia Genealogy* 22(1984); 23(1985); 24(1986).
2. *Weynette Parks Haun, Surry County, Virginia, Court Records, 1691-1700, Book V* (Durham, NC: privately printed, 1991) 243 Argonne Dr, Durham, NC 27704.
3. *Surry County Court Order Book 2* 173; Book 5 158a.
4. This account and the following account of this family has been contributed by Grace High Lawrence, 1508 Springhill Terrace, Dothan, AL 36303.
5. William L. Hopkins, *Surry County, Virginia Deeds 1684-1733* 1991 (Athens, GA: rep 1994) 130.
6. All of these records are taken from O.B. Film #0034129 and can be found in *Weynette Parks Haun, Surry County, Virginia, Court Records, 1700-1711, Book VI.* (Durham, NC: Privately printed, 1992).
7. *Surry County Will Book 7* 272.
8. *Land Patent Book 15* 485-486, Book 29 233.
9. *Halifax County, North Carolina, Will Book 1* 198.
10. Information about the Alsobrook family has been supplied by Doris Y. Stone, Williamsburg, VA.
11. *Sussex County Court Order Book 1754* 34.
12. Richards passim.
13. *Greensville County Will Book 1* 28-30.
14. *Sussex County Order Book, 1757-1761* 112; Will Book A 92-94.
15. *Sussex County Court Order Book, 1752-1761* 196.
16. *Sussex County Court Order Book, 1757-1761*; Guardian Accounts; Sussex County Loose Papers, Sussex County Circuit Court Records, copy of Guardian Bond.
17. Richards 180.
18. *Sussex County Guardian Accounts*, 1761 32-33.
19. Richards 184.
20. Rutman, *Explicatus*, 88-93.

BENJAMIN LAKER

BENJMAIN LAKER is considered to be one of the First Families of North Carolina, that is he settled in the Province of Carolina, which later became the State of North Carolina before the 12th day of July 1729. He arrived in the Proprietary of Carolina by 1680.[1]

While there may not be agreement as to how to spell the name of Benjamin Laker, there is agreement that he was deputy to one of the Lords Proprietors of Carolina. He is known to have bought land in Perquimans Precinct, (Albemarle County, North Carolina) shortly after 1680. His name is variously spelled Laker, Larker and as he signed his will (the original), Lakar.[2] Benjamin Laker was a resident of Betchworth Parish, Surrey County, England and a member of the family of that name living in southern Surrey County in the vicinity of the towns of Guildford, Dorking and Reigate. A number of the citizens of that area played an important role in the eighteenth-century and nineteenth-century Baptist history of North Carolina. Benjamin Laker is known to have been a staunch dissenter.[3]

The Lords Proprietors of Carolina were cognizant of this group and this situation and were seriously committed to religious liberty as a basic constitutional principle in the colony. The Proprietors went so far as to publish a number of promotional pamphlets in order to give widespread assurances of religious liberty in Carolina. Benjamin's decision to emigrate came about this time (1671). He seems to have left England with sufficient funds to begin his life in Carolina as a man of substance. He purchased 400 acres and settled with his wife and family of six children to the life of a planter.

The climate of Carolina was difficult for Benjamin's family, and two of his children, his son and oldest daughter died within a short time. His wife ELIZABETH and two other daughters dying later. In 1688 his daughter, Sarah married Thomas Harvey, then a member of the Council and subsequently deputy governor from 1694 to 1699. Benjamin married a second time, and a third time to Juliana Hudson Taylor. While it is not stated, it would seem that his daughter, LYDIA LAKER was a daughter of Elizabeth and came to Carolina with her father and mother. His daughter, Ruth to whom he left a legacy in his will must have been a daughter of a subsequent marriage. He did not name a son in his will.

During the 1680s Benjamin had been made a commissioner of the peace for Perquimans Precinct and early in 1690, Governor Philip Ludwell gave him a deputation to represent in Albemarle one of the Lords Proprietors, consequently raising him to the governor's Council and to the benches of the highest courts of the colony. He seems to have sat regularly as one of the judges in the high court of justice from the beginning of 1691 until the end of 1696, except for his attendance at the Council in 1695 and 1696. In 1697 he stepped down from the Council and lived as a private gentleman until his death.

Benjamin Laker made his will April 7, 1701 and died April 8, 1701. It is interesting that he made specific bequests of books expounding his Baptist faith to his daughter, Sarah Harvey and to George Bleighton, the husband of his daughter, Lydia. He left Sarah his Thomas Grantham's treatise on the General Baptist doctrine; somewhat unfortunate as the widow Sarah married Christopher Gale, an ardent Anglican churchman. George Bleighton seems to have followed the Baptist teachings of Benjamin, for it is known that he was a Baptist dissenter in Surry County, Virginia at a time when there were very few acknowledged dissenters. George received the copy of *Exposition of the First Five Books of Moses*. Benjamin left his land to his beloved wife, Juliana to be at her disposal and also a Negro girl and a mare. The rest of his property was to be divided equally between his wife and his daughter, Ruth. He named his wife the executrix of his estate.

Benjamin would be considered the "Father of North Carolina Baptists", although this title was bestowed on another at a later time. George Bleighton carried his Baptist faith to Surry County and was associated with the Baptist dissenters there. After his death in 1703 other dissenters were able to appeal to the General Assembly of General Baptists in London and in 1714 Robert Norden went to Virginia as a minister. He appeared in the court in Prince George County in 1715 and subscribed the oaths required of dissenting ministers. The records show that Lydia Laker Bleighton Clements was a supporter of Robert

Norden. Lydia Clements husband, Francis Clements was a justice in the court of Surry County, clerk of the Surry County Court and a Burgess to the Virginia General Assembly. For him to have held these positions he would have been of strong Anglican Church affiliation.

BENJAMIN LAKER

Gen.10 BENJAMIN LAKER		m	(1) ELIZABETH (—?—)
Issue:	oldest daughter		died young
	son		died young
	Sarah	m	(1) Thomas Harvey
		m	(2) Christopher Gale
	LYDIA	m	(1) George Bleighton
		m	(2) FRANCIS CLEMENTS
	2 daughters		died young
Benjamin Laker		m	(2) unknown
Issue:		m	(3) Juliana (—?—)
	Ruth		

Notes

1. William M. Mann, Jr., M.D., P.O. Box 8605, Rocky Mount, NC 27804 and Greer Suttlemyre, Jr., PhD, *Order of First Families of North Carolina, Proprietary Policy and Development of North Carolina, 1663-1729.*
2. Secretary of State Wills, SS875 1/8, SS/AR original, North Carolina State Archives, Raleigh, North Carolina.
3. William S. Powell, ed., *Dictionary of North Carolina Biography, vol 4* (Chapel Hill, NC: The University of North Carolina Press) 3-5. The account of Benjamin Laker following comes from this source.

Gen. 9   **THOMAS EDWARDS**

THOMAS EDWARDS was claimed as a headright by Edward Oliver when he patented 500 acres of land called *Pynie Point*, on the east side of the Chickahominy River on May 1, 1638.[1] A Thomas Edwards was to be transported from London to Virginia on the *Philip*, after examination by the Minister of Gravesend, June 20, 1635. He was listed as being twenty years old.[2] Thomas Edwards was also listed as a headright for Colonel Abraham Wood who patented 2073 acres of land at Fort Henry on the south side of the Appomattox River in Charles City County on September 16, 1663.[3] This is the area in which Thomas Edwards later owned land himself.

Thomas Edwards was identified in the court records as owning land adjacent to the land of Samuel Tatum on Second Swamp in 1711.[4] In the will of John Butler of Prince George County, Thomas Edwards is given the option to purchase 150 acres of land belonging to John on the upper side of the great branch of Warwick Swamp adjoining land at Indian Fields.[5] Samuel and Thomas Lee were appointed processioners of the land between Second Swamp and Warwick Swamp, as recorded in the *Vestry Book of Bristol Parish*[6]. It was not until the *Prince George County, Wills and Deeds, Book B* was returned to the clerk of the circuit court in Prince George County from an estate settlement (in a plain brown wrapper, no less) that much new information came to light about the early residents of the county. This book is the second book of records and oldest extant records of the newly created Prince George County. It is the first record of the identity of FRANCES EDWARDS, the daughter of Thomas and MARY EDWARDS and the wife of SAMUEL LEE.[7] Samuel Lee and his wife Frances acknowledged the receipt from Mary Edwards, the administrator of the estate of Thomas Edwards, deceased *all that part of the Estate of the said Dece^d as was or is due too me to me [sic] the said Samuell Lee as marrying the said Ffrancis [sic] Daughter of the said Thomas Edwards Dece^d and due hereby Acquitt, Release and Discharge the Said Mary Edwards and her heirs for Ever from the same. Witness my hand this 12th Day of January 1713.* It was signed with the mark S of Samuel Lee and witnessed by Samson Meredith and Thom Simmons (his mark S).

Little is known of Thomas Edwards beyond his association with the Tatums and the Lees. He had died before July 5, 1712 when the inventory of his estate was recorded in the county court. His estate was valued at £89/5/4 and appraised by James Thweatt, Matthew Anderson and John Thweatt. Mary Edwards, his relict and administrator presented the inventory and it was recorded. His personal property consisted of the following:

> 20 hed of cattle young & old, 69 hogs young & old
> 1 mare & coalt 1 horse 4 sheep 1 horse 1 colt
> 1 trooping sadle 1 pr pistoles and 1 sword
> 4 pads 1 old Stadle [sic] 5 wonty [sic]
> 1 Chest 1 Table 1 old feather bed 1 rugg & blanket 1 bed Stead hide & cord
> 1 old Clock bed & blanketts old 1 brass Kettle Qt 1 Small Kettle
> 20 wt of puter 6 puter plaits 1 Tankard 1 brass Skimr
> 2 Iron wedges 1 Iron possell 2 old Casge & old tubbs
> 1 pr of old unfixed pistols & some old Iron 1 old grind Stone
> 1 old spinning wheal old Ciar fraims 1 pr Shott mould
> 1 pr Spatter lashes 2 old Sifters 1 pott rack 1 Kersey Coat
> 1 old Coatt 1 Wescoatt 1 pr briches 1 old bagg
> 1 frying pann 5 glass bottles Duffill Coat
> 3 old Cairs & old horse collar 1 Iron pott of 24wt Ditto of 40wt
> 1 Indian man 20lb 1 Indian girl 10lb

A list of the persons to whom Thomas Edwards was indebted, to a total sum of £4/7/0 included the following: Robert Hunicutt for 4 pr shoes; Peter Michele; Tho. Clay; John Winingham; Edward Winingham; John Scott 150lb pork; John Weaver; Mr. Hatch; Nath Urvin; and Capt Robert Bolling.[8] In the final settlement of the estate the names of John Ledbetter, Peter Fairfax, William Marrow and Thomas Simmons and Capt Robert Bolling were added. The names of those to whom payments were made were added: Widow Mavery, Samuel Lee and (—?—)y Lee Junr.

It is known that Thomas and Mary Edwards had a son John, for he was identified as his son in a land survey of May 14, 1711. John Edwards owned 50 acres of land on the south side of Second Swamp.[9] John Edwards and his wife Elizabeth recorded the birth of a Negro named Cooke in the Bristol Parish Register on January 22, 1721/2. John Edwards was appointed along with John May, Jr. to procession the land from Indian Town Run to the Bristol Parish line in 1746 and again in 1749.[10]

(684-686;690-691)

Gen. 11 **NATHANIEL TATUM**

Some researchers have written of an earlier date of birth (1599) for NATHANIEL TATUM, which would have meant that he was twenty years old when he came to Virginia.[11] This is not consistent with the identification that he was one of the Bridewell Orphans, nor with the research of Edward O'Donoghue who extracted the list of names and stated that they were children between the ages of eight and sixteen. Not only was Nathaniel identified in the muster of 1624/5 as being twenty years old,[12] making him fourteen years old when he was appointed to go to Virginia February 27, 1618/19.[13] He would not have been detained at age twenty, and would have been too old to have been among the group of boys shipped to Virginia.

The land of Nathaniel Tatum has now been identified as adjoining the land of Colonel Francis Epes at City Point in what is now the town of Hopewell. City Point is the point of land at the confluence of the Appomattox and James rivers. Nathaniel was in heady company, for a Bridewell orphan. Your author has flown over the land owned by Nathaniel and after visualizing it without the industrial complexes that line the rivers, it would have been a magnificent setting for his plantation of at least 600 acres in Virginia, in great contrast to his life in London.

Nathaniel and his wife ANN TATUM had children not listed in *Tidewater Virginia Families*. Their order of birth seems to be different from that listed also.[14]

Mary Tatum

Mary has been listed first in some accounts of the life of Nathaniel primarily because she is listed as his daughter among the headrights Nathaniel Tatum claimed in his land patent. It is not known who she married.

SAMUEL TATUM See biographical sketch

John Tatum

John Tatum seems to have been born about 1635 and his will was probated September 15, 1673. His wife was Elizabeth Wheeler, a widow, who married when John died, John Good.[15] John Tatum made a will proved September 15, 1673, however the will is now lost. John Tatum left a daughter, Elizabeth.[16]

Nathaniel Tatum

(686;691) Nathaniel appears to have been born about 1637 as he was referred to as Junior by 1656, which would seem to imply that he was an adult. He married Mary Robinson; this is inferred from the many associations of Nathaniel with Christopher Robinson and the fact that he named a son Christopher.[17]

Isaac Tatum

No further information has been found about Isaac; however, several accounts of the life of Nathaniel include him as a son.[18]

SAMUEL TATUM

SAMUEL TATUM is believed to be the oldest son of Nathaniel Tatum and was born about 1630. There are descendants of Rebecca Temple who identify Samuel's wife as Mary Moore.[19]

Nathaniel Tatum

(688;693) Peter, the son of Nathaniel and Elizabeth Tatum married Mary Epes, the daughter of Littleberry Epes.[20]

Rebecca Tatum

(688;693) Rebecca Tatum married William Temple of Warrockhock Swamp in what became Prince George County. William, along with Samuel Tatum and Richard Ligon were issued a patent for 1022 acres of land on the south side of the Appomattox River in October 1690.[21] Their known children were: Samuel Temple, Thomas Temple, William Temple and John Temple.[22]

Samuel Tatum

(688;693) The records of the *Bristol Parish Register* are interesting in that John is entered as the son of Samuel and Phoebe Tatum with a birth date of June 7, 1710; William, son of Samuel and Elizabeth Tatum, born June 26, 1717; Elizabeth the daughter of the same, born November 29, 1718; and Francis, son of Samuel and Mary Tatum born April 17, 1721. There does not seem to be another Samuel Tatum of the same generation and the same time. At the vestry session of November 14, 1734, Samuel Tatum was ordered to be levy free.[23]

TATUM FAMILY

Gen.11 <u>NATHANIEL TATUM</u>		m	<u>ANN (—?—)</u>
Issue:	Mary	m	
	SAMUEL	m	MARY (—?—)
	John	m	Elizabeth Wheeler widow
	Nathaniel	m	Mary Robinson
	Isaac	m	
Gen.10 <u>SAMUEL TATUM</u>		m	<u>MARY (—?—)</u>
	Nathaniel	m	Elizabeth (—?—)
	ANN	m	HUGH LEE II
	Rebecca	m	William Temple, Sr.
	Samuel	m	(1) Phoebe (—?—)
		m	(2) Elizabeth (—?—)
		m	(3) Mary (—?—)
	Mary	m	Richard Carlisle
	Barbara	m	Thomas Mitchell

Notes

1. Louise Pledge Heath Foley, *Early Virginia Families Along the James River, Their Deep Roots and Tangled Branches: Charles City County — Prince George County, Virginia vol II.* 1978 (Baltimore: Genealogical Publishing Co, rep 1990) 10.
2. Peter Wilson Coldham, *The Complete Book of Emigrants, 1607-1660.* 1987 (Baltimore: Genealogical Publishing Co, rep 1992) 150-151.
3. Foley 28-29.
4. *Prince George County, Wills & Deeds, Book B, 1710-1713* 81.
5. Benjamin B. Weisiger, III, *Prince George County Wills & Deeds, 1713-1728.* (Richmond: privately printed, 1973) 41.
6. C. G. Chamberlayne, *The Vestry Book and Register of Bristol Parish, Virginia, 1720-1789.* (Richmond: privately printed, 1898) 55.
7. *Book B* 269
8. Book B 136-137, 186.
9. Weisiger 91.
10. *Vestry Book* 296, 125, 140.

11. Meyer and Dorman 595; David A. Avant, Jr *Some Southern Families vol 3* (Tallahassee, FL: 1989) chart; among others.
12. Coldham 1: 12, 36, 53.
13. Bridewell Royal Hospital Papers, Personal Papers, Accession No.26237, Library of Virginia, Richmond, VA.
14. Correspondence Doris Y. Stone, Williamsburg, VA.
15. Stone; Meyer and Dorman 596; Avant 584. See also *Charles City County Order Book*, 1667-1679 286.
16. *Charles City Order Book, 1687-1695* 142.
17. Stone. Avant 585.
18. Stone; Meyer and Dorman 595.
19. Stone; Avant 585; Temple, *William Temple of Prince George County, Virginia* 353.
20. Avant 586.
21. Land Patent Book 8:86.
22. Avant 587-588.
23. Register 372, 71.

PRINCE GEORGE COUNTY

Gen. 12   **THOMAS IRONMONGER**

      William Ironmonger, Elizabeth Ironmonger and Francis Ironmonger were claimed as headrights of Mrs. Anne Bernard in land that she patented in 1651 in Northumberland County. They were claimed again in a patent by Anne Bernard. In 1663 William Ironmonger patented land on the Corrotoman River in Lancaster County and in 1664 he patented land in Gloucester County on the Ware River. He sold the Lancaster County land in 1666.[1] No evidence has been found to connect this William Ironmonger with THOMAS IRONMONGER of Surry County, other than the name relationship of the surname Ironmonger, an unusual name.

      MARY HUX was the daughter of JOHN HUX and JANE (Joan) GRAY and was surely born in Surry County. She married THOMAS IRONMONGER. The will of her brother William Hux gives evidence to the fact that she was the daughter of John Hux in his bequest to her two daughters *the two daughters of my brother Ironmonger, Susannah to have the land that Thomas Ironmonger lives on, and Mary the land that I live on*....He appointed his brother, Thomas Ironmonger and his brother John Ironmonger as the executors of his estate.[2]

      Mary may have been older than her brother, William for Thomas Ironmonger was born between 1630 and 1635. He gave his age in a deposition in 1684 as being age forty-nine or thereabouts. In 1690 he gave his age in another deposition as being age sixty.[3] Thomas Ironmonger died in 1691 for his inventory was entered in the Surry County Court Records on July 7, 1691. His wife, Mary was the administratrix of his estate. The brother John Ironmonger had died by January 19, 1691/2 for Mary Ironmonger testified as to John's nuncupative will, in which he left property to his brother's son and daughter and to his cousin (i.e. nephew), Samuel Alsobrook's two children.[4]

      Mary Hux Ironmonger died in 1693, with administration of her estate being granted Samuel Alsobrook and Mary, his wife on May 2, 1693. This shows that Mary Ironmonger, the daughter of Thomas Ironmonger mentioned in the will of William Hux, had married Samuel Alsobrook. It is probable that the daughter Susannah had died young, for the son and daughter mentioned in John Ironmonger's will as his brother's children were apparently younger children of Thomas, that is the children, Ann and Thomas.[5]

IRONMONGER FAMILY

Gen.12 THOMAS IRONMONGER		MARY HUX
Issue: MARY IRONMONGER	m	SAMUEL ALSOBROOK I
Susanna		died young
Ann	m	
Thomas	m	

addition

Gen. 13   **JOHN HUX**

      Joan or JANE GRAY as she is interchangeably called in the court records was born in 1618; she was reported as being six years old in the muster at James Citty in 1624. She would have grown to womanhood in what became Surry County. She married JOHN HUX of Surry County, who was born in 1612 or 1613, from a deposition that he gave in 1652, stating that he was forty years old or thereabouts. In 1659 in another deposition he gave his age as forty-six. The second deposition concerned land that was related to the estate of THOMAS GRAY, his father-in-law.[6]

      JOHN HUX, among others who testified, stated that Thomas had given land to his daughter, Joan, and John Hux further deposed that he had married the daughter, Joan (Jane) and that he received twenty-five acres of the land from her father as her share. John and Jane Hux had two known children, William and MARY. After the death of his first wife, John Hux married a second time, Mary and died before May 4, 1668 when his widow appointed John Harlow, whom she subsequently married as her attorney.[7]

The son, William did not marry, and made his will October 31, 1676 giving his land to his nieces, Susannah and Mary Ironmonger. His will was recorded May 1, 1677.[8]

HUX FAMILY

Gen.13 <u>JOHN HUX</u>	m	<u>JOAN (JANE) GRAY</u>	
Issue: MARY HUX	m	THOMAS IRONMONGER	
William Hux		d.s.p.	

addition

Gen. 14   **THOMAS GRAY**

While later biographers have stated that Thomas Gray came in the *Starr* in 1608, an inspection of the lists compiled by Captain John Smith of the first three supply ships, and other records of that time do not list Thomas Gray among the earliest settlers. This account of Thomas Gray is extracted from the extant records and compiled accounts of his life.[9] THOMAS GRAY, from the designation, *Ancient Planter* was in the Colony of Virginia before 1616; he was so identified when he patented land on August 27, 1635. The 550 acres of land was described as on the south side of the main (James) river, over next to James Citty, on Cross and Rolfe's creeks, in what was to become Surry County. His patent of 550 acres was due him, with 100 acres due him as *an ancient planter at or before the time of Sir Thomas Dale according to a charter of orders from the late Treasurer and Company, dated November 18, 1618.* An additional 50 acres was due for his first wife, ANIS (Annis) Gray, and 50 acres for his "now" wife, Rebecca, and 350 acres due for the transportation of his two sons, William Gray and Thomas Gray and five servants. This additional land adjoined land that was already in his possession.

A colonist in Virginia by the year 1616 was entitled to 100 acres of land provided he paid his own passage and had dwelt in the Colony for three years when application for land was made. In accordance with a predetermined policy of the Virginia Company, no individual assignments of land were made during the first seven years of the Colony's existence. The policy of granting patents for acreage to settlers was inaugurated during the latter part of the time of Sir Thomas Dale, Governor form 1611 until 1616. Those entitled to this land were designated as Ancient Planters.[10] Thomas Gray was identified as an *Ancient Planter*.

Thomas was listed in the muster of James Citty taken January 14, 1624, with Margaret his wife and William his son, age three and Jone (JANE) his daughter age six. The space for the names of the ships, given in many of the muster listings, was left blank in this instance. Thomas Gray had at this listing eleven barrels of corn, 2 pounds of powder, ten pounds of shot, a fixed piece (musket), suit of armor and five swine.[11] It appears that Thomas was about thirty-one years old, as he deposed in March 1653/4 that he was sixty or thereabouts. Thomas continued to patent land, forfeited some for failure to plant, but ultimately took out a new patent for 800 acres of land in March 1852/3.[12] This land was described as adjoining the land of John Kemp at the head of Smiths Fort Creek.

A record has survived in the records of St. Peter, Paul's Wharf, London of the marriage of Thomas Gray to ANIS (Annis) VALENTINE. She had died before the muster of 1624 and Margaret was listed as his wife, or so the record has been transcribed. He had married Rebecca by September 11, 1626 when she deposed before the General Court that *good weif Wright did tell her this deponent That by one token wch this deponent had in her forehead she should burye her Husbande.* Thomas survived Rebecca and married again about 1645, by whom he had young children, named as orphans in a controversy over land with John Corker in 1662.

There seems to be some discrepancy in the extant records as to the chronology and identity of the wives and children of Thomas Gray. Mr. John Boddie has listed them as he inferred their relationships from the record as follows:[13]

The children of Thomas Gray, Sr. by his first wife, Anis: Joan (Jane) Gray, born 1618 and William Gray, born 1621 and who appears last in the patent of Thomas of 1635; he apparently died young.

The children of Thomas Gray, Sr. by Rebecca: Thomas Gray, born c.1625-28; Rebecca Gray, born 1628-1630; and Francis Gray, born c.1630-1635.

The children of Thomas Gray from his last marriage: William Gray, born c.1648-1649; John Gray, born 1651-1652 and Thomas Gray, born c.1652-1653.

Mr. Boddie has apparently studied the Surry County records closely and for descendants of the above named children it would be worthwhile to read his account and to confirm the identifications in the original records. As an accepted descendant of Jane Gray, this author will not relate the conclusions drawn about the identities and ages of the other Gray children.

Thomas Gray must have died before November 2, 1658, for his son, Francis Gray transferred a patent to his brother, Thomas. The following spring Luke Mizell testified in court that he had been a servant to Thomas Gray, Senior who was deceased and he said he had heard that Thomas Gates had given fifty acres of land to their son, Thomas and daughter Jane.

GRAY FAMILY

Gen.14 THOMAS GRAY *Ancient Planter*[14]	m	(1) ANIS (ANNIS) VALENTINE
Issue: JOAN (JANE)	m	JOHN HUX
William (I)		died young
Thomas Gray	m	(2) Margaret
children listed believed to be 3		
Thomas Gray	m	(3) Rebecca
Rebecca	m	Daniel Hutton
Francis	m	Mary (—?—)
William (II)	m	Elizabeth Jarrett
John	m	Mary (—?—)
Thomas	m	

Notes

1. Nugent 1:211, 278; 437; 514; 561.
2. John Bennett Boddie, *Historical Southern Families, vol XVII* (Baltimore: Genealogical Publishing Co, 1972) 89-90.
3. Elizabeth Hogg Ironmonger, *Ironmonger and Connections Updated, Iremonger-Ironmonger* (Berryville, VA: Virginia Book Co, 1972); Weynette Parks Haun, *Surry County, Virginia Court Records, 1691-1700, Book V*   (Durham, NC: Privately printed, 1991).
4. Ibid.; Boddie 90-91.
5. Ibid.
6. Virginia M. Meyer and John Frederick Dorman, *Adventurers of Purse and Person, Virginia, 1607-1624/25* 1956 (Richmond, VA: Dietz, rev 1987) 340; Boddie 88-89.
7. Ibid.
8. Ibid.
9. Meyer and Dorman 339-345; Boddie 81-91; Nugent 31.
10. Meyer and Dorman xxiii.
11. Meyer and Dorman 35.
12. Nugent 271.
13. Boddie 84-85.
14. As listed in Meyer and Dorman 340.

ABBREVIATIONS

Acc. No.	Accession Number
APVA	Association for the Preservation of Virginia Antiquities
b	born
c.	circa, approximately
CCCCOB	Charles City County Court Order Book
CCCOB	Caroline County Court Order Book
CR	County Road
d	died
dis mcd	dismissed, married contrary to discipline
dis mou	dismissed, married out of unity
d.s.p.	died without issue
Ibid.	reference cited just before
LVA	Library of Virginia
MVA	*Magazine of Virginia Genealogy*
Mss.	Manuscript
m	married
NGS	National Genealogical Society
NPS	National Park Service
n.d.	no date given
p	place
(p)	probably
SR	State Route
TVF	*Tidewater Virginia Families: A Magazine of History and Genealogy*
US	United States
VBVR	Virginia Bureau Vital Records, Virginia Health Department
VCU	Virginia Commonwealth University
VDOT	Virginia Department of Transportation
VHS	Virginia Historical Society
VMHB	*Virginia Magazine of History and Biography*
VSL	Virginia State Library
W&M Q	*William and Mary Quarterly*
WPA	Works Progress Administration

MAPS AND DIAGRAMS

INDEX

NFN No first name given; NLN No last name given

Abbott
  Fanny 102
Alexander
  Mary 137
Allen
  Elizabeth 71, 73
  Emma 112
  George 5, 152
  Littleberry 27
  NFN 147
  William 4
  Wilson 118
Allison
  Elizabeth 120
  Hannah 120
  John 120
  Robert 120
Alsobrook
  Agnes 189
  David 189, 190
  Elizabeth 185, 186, 189, 190
  family 185
  Hewit 190
  Hewitt 189
  Howell 189, 190
  Joan 188
  John 185, 188-190
  Mary 185, 188-190, 197
  Rachel 188
  Samuel 185, 188-190, 197
  Sarah 188
  Thomas 188, 189
Alsop
  Samuel 113
Alvise
  William 75
Amis
  Martha 86
Anderson
  Barttelott 76, 77
  Eliza 76
  Elspet 129
  Jane 92
  Matthew 193
  Mr. 162
  Robert 141
Andrews
  Lewis 43
Andros
  Edmond 58
  Sir Edmond 58
Ariss
  John 177, 179
Armistead
  Anthony 121
Arnett
  Mary 75, 78
Arnott
  Thomas 141
Arthur
  Ann 11, 12
  James 11
  Margaret 11
Ashton
  Ferdinando 160
Aston
  Ferdinando 160
Augustine
  St. 125

Austin
  Ferdinando 160
Babcock
  William 48
Bacon
  Elizabeth 4
  Nathaniel 4, 83, 85
Baetz
  Brian 18
  Jenifer 18
  Zachary 18
Baker
  George 23
  Samuel 65
  Thomas 23
Baldwin
  Elizabeth 25
  Joanne 81, 86
Ball
  William 106
Ballard
  Mary 148
  Richard 148
  Sarah 148
  William 148
Banister
  Mr. 163
Barker
  Elizabeth 165
  Frances 165
  John 165
  Robert 120
  Sarah 165
  William 165
Barnes
  Jane 68
Barnett
  Ann 47
Barney
  Edward 126
Barnhouse
  Nicholas 85
Bartlett
  Miss 155
Baskervyle
  John 60
Bass
  Agnes 189
  Arthur 189
Bassett
  Anna Marie 140
  Burwell 140
  William 83
Bates
  Alice 130
  Ann 130
  Anne 130
  Elizabeth 130, 138
  George 58, 129, 130
  Hannah 129, 130
  Isaac 130
  James 130
  John 129, 130
  Marcia 13, 43
  Mary 130
  Sarah 130
  Susanna 127, 130
  William 13

Baugh
  Agnes 24
  James 24
Baughs
  Ann 46
  James 46
  William 46
Baxter
  John 100
Baylor
  John 142
Bazille
  Leon 91
Bearcroft
  Thomas 180
Becker
  Klara 177
Bell
  Bersheba 118
  Bethia 118
  David 118
  Elizabeth 117
  George 117, 118
  Jemima 118, 133, 134, 138
  John 117, 118, 135
  Martha 71, 73, 118
  Mary 118
  Moore 118, 122
  Nathan 117, 118, 134-136
  Rebecca 118
  Sarah 117, 118, 136
Belscher
  Margaret 159
Bennett
  Isabel 141
  John 141
Bent
  Miss 67
  Sarah 72
Bentley
  Sarah 189
  Thomas 188
Berkeley
  William 58, 83, 85
Bernard
  Anne 197
Betts
  Nannie 43
Beverley
  William 100
Bibb
  Agnes 75
  Ann 75-79
  Anne 67
  Benjamin 75-78
  Charles 66, 67, 75-79
  Christian 76
  Christiana 75, 78, 79
  David 67, 75-79
  Eleanor 67, 75-79
  Eliza 78
  Elizabeth 66, 75-77, 79
  Fleming 77
  George 77
  Henry 75-78
  James 75, 78
  John 67, 75-79
  Justina 75
  Knelly 77
  Lavinia 78

Burgess
    Pattie 6
Burgin
    Nancy 141
Burk
    Thomas 26
Burke
    Rebecca 15
    Thomas 102
Burnet
    Elizabeth 65
Burnett
    Elizabeth 144
    Overton 65
    Thomas 95
Burruss
    Agnes 77
    Charles 65, 66, 77
    Eleanor 77
    Elizabeth 65, 66, 70, 112
    Elliott 65, 66
    Frances 77
    George 70
    Henry 65, 66, 70
    Jacob 65, 75
    James 66
    John 65, 66, 70, 77
    Justina 75, 78
    Lucy 77
    Margaret 65
    Mary 66, 77
    Mary Jane 65
    Nancy 65, 66
    Rachel 65, 66, 70, 77
    Richard 9
    Rozelle 33, 34
    Sally 65, 70
    Sarah 77, 91
    Susanna 113
    Thomas 72, 77, 79
    William 112
Burton
    Robert 97
Burwell
    Abigail 4
    Lewis 4
Butler
    Ada 43
    Alfred 16, 17, 43
    Alice 36, 42, 43, 91
    Amanda 43
    Anderson 92
    Andrew 13
    Ann 43, 92
    Anne 36, 43, 91
    Arthur 43
    Bess 17
    Carolyn 17
    Celia 91
    Charleton 18
    Cora 43
    Crawley 19, 43
    Deborah 19
    Edward 91, 92
    Elizabeth 36, 43, 91, 92
    Franklin 91
    Frederick 91
    Gertrude 13, 43
    Grace 6, 43
    Harrison 43
    Isaac 42, 43, 91, 92, 112
    James 36, 43, 92
    John 38, 39, 43, 91, 92, 193
    Joseph 92

Butler
    Judah 42, 43
    Julia 43
    Kate 43
    Katherine 17
    Leland 91
    Louise 17
    Lucy 36, 43, 92
    Marcia 13
    Margaret 36
    Margery 36
    Mark 17
    Martha 91
    Mary 17, 36, 42, 43, 91, 92
    Mary Louise 17
    Melvin 17
    Molly 16
    Mrs. 6
    Nancy 91, 92
    Nellie 6, 28, 29, 43, 118, 127,
        138, 150, 176
    Nicholas 17
    Otho 91
    Patricia 18
    Patrick 91
    Polly 92
    Reuben 42, 43, 158
    Robert 6, 13, 18, 43, 48, 142
    Robert Emmet 43
    Robert Hardy 18
    Samuel 36, 37, 42, 43, 92
    Sara 43
    Sarah 26, 28, 36, 42, 43, 92
    Stefanie 19
    Susanna 42, 92
    Thomas 3, 26, 36-39, 42, 43, 91,
        92
    Valentine 91
    Virginia 17, 43, 91
    Virginia Grace 17
    Wealthean 36, 43
    William 13, 43, 76, 91, 92, 139
    William Fleming 43, 139
Byrd
    Mrs. 162
    Parke 162
    William 135, 160, 162, 163
Callis
    Thomas 101
Campbell
    Amey 34, 113
    Ann 116
    Archibald 159
    Atwell 112
    Dorothea 113
    Dorothy 112
    Elizabeth 111-113
    Elliott 111-113, 150
    Emma 112
    Felix 114
    Frances 32, 34, 114
    George 111, 113
    Henrietta 114
    Henry 114
    James 111-114
    Jane 111, 113
    John 112-114
    Joseph 31, 34, 78, 111-113
    Julia 111, 112
    Mannaseh 112
    Margaret 111
    Martha 114
    Mary 112
    Mary L. 111, 112

Campbell
    Matthew 111, 113
    Minnie 33, 34
    Nancy 113
    Noel 112
    Richard 112
    Sally 112
    Sarah 112-114
    Seth 69, 73, 113, 114
    Susanna 69
    Thomas 112
    William 111-113
    Winnie 112
    Zaccheus 111-113
Canals
    James River 142, 143
    Kanawha 142
Cane
    James 182
Cannon
    William 127
Cantrell
    Henry 160
Cardwell
    Ann 23
Cargill
    John 164
    Mr. 163
Carleton
    Eliza 25
Carlisle
    Richard 195
Carnal
    Patrick 112
Carneal
    Carolyn 11
    Patrick 112
Carr
    Agnes 59
    Ann 59
    Charles 59
    Elizabeth 59
    John 60, 76
    Mary 59
    Phoebe 59
    Sarah 59
    Susanna 59
    Susannah 59
    Thomas 59, 60, 66
    Walter 59
    William 59, 60
Carroll
    Kenneth 136
Carter
    Annie 32
    Besha 134
    Charles 179
    John 134
    Lucy 25
    Mamie 32
    Myrtle 34
    R.W. 32
    Susanna 43
Catlett
    Martha 106
Chalkley
    Thomas 147
Chamberlayne
    Churchill G 146
Chambers
    William 157
Champe
    John 179

205

Cleer
  Lucy 68
Clements
  Ann 183, 184
  Benjamin 184
  Elizabeth 184, 186
  Francis 182, 184, 192
  Freeman 184
  Hannah 188
  James 182-184, 186
  Jeremiah 184, 186
  John 184
  Joshua 183, 184
  Lockie 184
  Lucretia 186
  Lydia 182, 183, 191, 192
  Martha 183, 184
  Mary 184
  Nicholas 182
  Rebecca 184
  Robert 184
  Sarah 48, 184
  Thomas 182-184
Clough
  Elizabeth 182, 184
  John 182
Cobb
  family 148
  Nancy 91
  NFN 147
Cobbs
  Mary 77
  Nancy 92
Cocke
  Dick 162
  Dr. 163
  Hannah 158
  Hartwell 158
  Lucy 158
  Martha 43
  Martha Newsome 43
  Mary 76, 77, 160
  Mr. 160
  Pleasant 76, 77
  Richard 158
  Thomas 164
  William 76
Colburn
  Lucy 33
Cole
  Sarah 53
Coleman
  Cynthia 153
  Elizabeth 98
  George 69
  Hulda 98
  Jane 37, 98
  John 9, 73
  Julius 78
  Lindsey 70
  Lucy 70, 72, 73
  Molly 70
  Nancy 69
  Nanny 70
  Richard 70
  Robert 70
  Saml 173
  Samuel 98
Collier
  Charles 120
  Frances 25, 28
Collins
  Baldwin 173
  Edmund 134, 138

Collins
  Herbert 27, 111, 112, 149
  James 32
  John 114
  Ogenia 114
  Patsy 134
Collown
  Boldwin 173
Commandres
  John 4
Conner
  William 66
Copeland
  Philip 100
Corker
  John 198
Correll
  Thomas 85
Corry
  Edward 75
Corsby
  James 68
  Lucy 68
Corum
  Frank 105
Cotter
  John 57
Cotton 186
  Alsobrook 185, 186, 189
  Betty 186
  Elizabeth 185, 186, 189
  Hardy 186
  Jane 186
  Jeremiah 186
  John 186
  Lucretia 184, 186
  Lucy 186
  Phoebe 186
  Sarah 186
  Selah 186
  Thomas 185, 186
  Wells 185, 186
  William 185, 186, 189, 190
Couture
  Richard 153
Covington
  Ann 70
  Nanny 32
  Parthenia 32
  Richard 70
  Sarah 70
  William 32
Cox
  Elizabeth 122
  Jane 172
  Mr. 51
  Stephen 127
  Susanna 122
Craighill
  Thomas 77
Crawley
  Elizabeth 19
Creeks 179
  Acquia 32
  Acquinton 36
  Barrows 160
  Beaverdam 117, 126
  Bell 117
  Camp 148
  Cedar 147-149
  Cross 198
  Diascund 140
  Ducking Hole 66, 67
  Falling 141

Creeks
  Fire 154
  Fork 148
  Hickory 105
  Hill's 137
  Horn Quarter 64
  Horsepen 150
  Howards 70
  Jenito 126
  Lagrange 30
  Lamb's 179
  Mangohick 64
  Marrocosick 31
  Matadequain 129
  Mechamps 88, 129
  Mehixon 37
  Muddy 85, 179
  Nimcock 30
  Nominy 60
  Occupacia 100, 101
  Perrots 153
  Polecat 27, 147
  Queen 160
  Queens 160
  Rolfe's 198
  Sandy 86
  Sedgy 76
  Short 137
  Smiths Fort 198
  Sunderland 30, 153
  Three 188
  Totopotomoy 129
  Urbanna 30
  Wahrani 140
  Ward's 13
  Warrany 140
Crenshaw
  Eliza 143
Crew
  Andrew 121, 142
  Elizabeth 122
  family 148
  James 142, 144
  Jane 143
  John 121
  Judith 142
  Mary 121
  Micajah 133
  Sarah 121, 122
  Talitha 143
Crewes
  family 170
Crews
  Paulina 171
Crispe
  Elizabeth 130
Croshaw
  Joseph 155
  Mary 154
Cross
  Nathaniel 9
  Susan 9, 28
Crowshaw
  Joseph 129
Crue
  Margery 36
Crump
  Elizabeth 56
  John 56
Crutchfield
  Benjamin 11
  Margaret 11
Cunningham
  Timothy 178

Giles
  Susanna 58
Ginnings
  Joshua 174
  Mrs. 174
Glass
  Thomas 129
Glenn
  Mourning 141, 144
Glover
  Richard 23
Godby
  Frances 150
Gooch
  Albert 48
Goodloe
  Mary 134
Goodrich
  Ann 164
  Cha: 163
Goodwin
  Edward 104
  Jean 178
  Littleton 73
  William 141
Gordon
  John 59
Gore
  Charles 88
Gouldman
  Martha 138
Govan
  James 37
Grantham
  Thomas 23, 191
Grantland
  Elizabeth 36
  Walter 36, 43
Gray
  Anis 198
  Annis 198, 199
  Elizabeth 71, 157
  Faith 157, 158
  Fanny 71
  Frances 71
  Francis 199
  Gilbert 157
  Harriette 7, 29
  Isabel 73
  Isabella 71
  Jane 197-199
  Joan 197-199
  John 71, 199
  Margaret 198, 199
  Mary 71, 157, 199
  Peggy 71
  Phoebe 71
  Priscilla 157
  Rebecca 198, 199
  Sarah 71
  Thomas 157, 197-199
  William 157, 198, 199
Greenwood
  Grace 48
Gregory
  Mary 32
Grinstead
  Nancy 43
Groom
  Elizabeth 75
  Robert 75
Gross
  Deborah 11

Groth
  Lucy 43
  William 43
Grover
  Peter 152
Grubbs
  Elizabeth 141
  Nancy 141
Hackett
  family 147
  Mary 78, 147
  NFN 147
  Pleasant 70
  Thomas 9, 147
Haden
  Amy 31
  Ethel 31
  Jane 31
  Jeanie 31
  Joannah 31
  John 31
  Joseph 31, 34
  Mary 31
  Nelson 31
  Polly 31
  Rebecca 31
  Rhode 31
  Richard 31
  Susannah 31
Hager
  Agnes 177, 178
Hainy
  Anthor 179
Haley
  John 1 (
  Margaret 113
  Mary 134
  Meriday 113
  Nancy 134
  Sarah 134
  Stephen 134
Hall
  Alice 13
  Allison 7
  Cynthia 14
  Helen 65
  Robert 164
  Vernon 13
Hamlin
  Abraham 160, 161, 164
  Agnes 161, 164
  Billy 163
  Captain 162, 163
  Charles 161, 164
  Dick 162, 163
  Elizabeth 162-164
  Hannah 164
  John 162, 164
  Lucy 163, 164
  Martha 158, 164
  Mr. 160
  Peter 162, 163
  Richard 164
  Sarah 164
  Stephen 160, 161, 164
  Susannah 161
  Thomas 164
  William 164
Hampton
  Andrew 104
  Ann 106
  Anna 106
  Anthony 105
  Cary 106

Hampton
  David 104
  Elizabeth 104-106
  Frances 106
  Francis 104
  General 105
  George 104-106
  Grace 106
  Jacob 105, 106
  Jane 106
  Joane 104-106
  John 104-106, 147
  Laurence 105, 106
  Lydia 104
  Margaret 105
  Martha 106
  Mary 97, 98, 104, 106
  Philadelphia 106
  Reuben 105
  Richard 105, 106
  Sarah 104, 106
  Thomas 104-106
  Wade 105
  William 104-106
Hancock
  Jane 45
Hankins
  Dorothy 93
Hanson
  Susan 124
Hardiman
  Colonel 163
  Mr. 162
Harding
  Thomas 180
Hardy
  Annabel 43
  Jane 23
Hargrave
  Elizabeth 150
  family 148
  Joseph 77
  Lemuel 150
  Rachel 77, 79
  Samuel 150
  William 150
Hargraves
  Elizabeth 72
  Lucy 68, 72
Hargrove
  William 150
Harker
  Frank 43
Harlow
  John 198
  Mary 198
Harnison
  Ann 164
  Elizabeth 164
  Thomas 163, 164
Harrelson
  Anne 72
Harris
  Ann 141
  Anne 78, 144
  Barnabas 141
  Benjamin 135, 136, 141, 142,
    144, 155
  Christopher 141
  Dabney 141
  Elizabeth 9, 141, 143, 144, 158
  family 148
  Frances 141
  Hamlin 159

Harris
  Isabel 141
  James 9, 136, 141-142, 144, 150
  Jane 141
  Jemima 144
  Jeremiah 73, 144
  Jessie 141
  John 144
  Joseph 158
  Judith 136-139, 142, 144
  Lewis 158
  Lucy 144, 158
  Malcolm 76
  Malcolm H 39
  Margaret 141
  Martha 65
  Mary 141, 142, 144
  Mourning 141
  Nancy 141
  Nathan 158
  Obadiah 150
  Obediah 144
  Overton 65, 141
  Rachel 144
  Reuben 158
  Robert 140, 141, 144
  Samuel 141
  Sarah 141, 142, 180
  Temperance 141
  Thomas 144
  Tyree 141
  Unity 144
  William 65, 141, 142, 144, 158
Harris
  John 141
Harrison
  Andrew 173
  Ben 163
  Benjamin 188
  Edward 42, 91
  Elizabeth 86, 87, 173, 174
  Margaret 173
  Mr. 162, 163
  William 173
Harriss
  Elizabeth 158, 159
  Hamlin 159
  Susanna 158, 159
  Thomas 159
  William 158, 159
Hart
  Frederick 134
  Polly 134
Hartwell
  Alice 48
Harvey
  Jacquelin 142
  John 123
  Sarah 191
  Thomas 191, 192
Harvie
  Jacqueline 135
Harwood
  Besha 134
  George 134, 138, 150
  Mr. 163
  Rebecca 134
  Sam 163
  Winston 134
Hatch
  Mr. 193
Hatcher
  Harriet 71
  William 23

Hatt
  William 164
Hawkins
  John 173
Hay
  Gilbert 163
Hayes
  Elizabeth 25
  Hiram 25
Haynie
  Ann 180
  Anne 180
  Anthony 179, 180
  Bridger 180
  Catherine 175, 180
  Charles 180
  Elinor 179, 180
  Elizabeth 180
  Jane 180
  John 179, 180
  Katherine 180
  Martha 180
  Mary 180
  Maxmillian 180
  Ormsby 180
  Richard 180
  Samuel 180
  Sarah 180
  Spencer 180
  William 180
  Winifred 180
Heimbach
  Anna 176
  Catharin 176
  Catharina 177
  Clara 176
  Ehla 176
  Elisabeth 176
  Elsbeth 177
  Georg 176
  Henrich 176
  Herman 176
  Hermann 176
  Jacob 176
  Johan 176
  Johann 176
  Johannes 176
  Jost 176
  Margarethe 176
  Maria 176
  Philipp 176
Helton
  William 173
Henderson
  Elizabeth 112
  John 112
  Lucy 112
  Mary 112
  Mary L. 112
  Sarah 112
  Thaddeus 112
  Virginia 33, 112
Henly
  Frances 77
  Mr. 77
Herndon
  Edward 59
  Mary 85
Hewlett
  Fanny 72
  Frances 68
  Mary 68, 72
  Sarah 68
  William 68

Hicks
  David 155
  Prewid 155
  Temperance 155
  Unity 155
High
  Hannah 188
  Jonn 188, 189
  Mary 188
  Thomas 188
Hightower
  Deveriux 24
  Susannah 24
Hill
  Edward 57
Hilliard
  Benjamin 134
  Polly 134
Hines
  Grace 34
Hitt
  Peter 177
Hix
  David 155
  Prewid 155
  Temperance 155
  Unity 155
Hockaday
  Warwick 160
  William 81
Hodges
  Jenny 26
  Mr. 26
  Nancy 26
  Thompson 26, 28
Hodgson
  John 34
Hogan
  Clementina 71
  Mr. 71
Holland
  Gabriel 152
  Mary 152
Holliman
  Matilda 68
Holmes
  John 95
Holtzclaw
  Ann 178
Homes
  Aberconnaway 45
  Bellville 135
  Belvidere 135
  Cherry Grove 37
  Clifton 135, 142
  Cosbie's 4
  Green Springs 39
  Hampton Key 4
  Hickory Grove 32
  Hill's Creek 137
  Humanity Hall 91
  Jacob House 33, 136
  Kemp House 55, 57
  Kingsmill 4
  Level Green 6
  Littletown 4
  Maycock 162
  Meadowville 126
  Moldavia 135
  Mount's Bay 4
  Neck-of-Land 126
  Palestine 27
  Pettus 4
  Poplar Grove 97, 112

Jarrett
 Elizabeth 157, 199
 Johanna 164
 Richard 157
Jefferson
 John 3
 Thomas 59
Jeffries
 George 94
 Mary 95
 Sarah 94
 Swepson 95
 Thomas 95
Jennings
 Sarah 138
Jesse
 Joseph 71
 Mary 71
John 30
 Elizabeth 194
 Paul 4
Johnes
 Katherine 52
Johnson
 Agnes 121
 Ashley 117
 Cecilia 117, 118
 Elizabeth 65, 66, 70
 family 148
 John 117, 120, 121, 152
 Lucretia 117
 Martha 117
 Massey 121
 Rebecca 144
 Robert 23
 Sarah 73
Johnston
 NFN 147
Jones
 Ann 19
 Daniel 25
 Edmund 106
 Elizabeth 25
 Foster 141
 Frances 141
 Frederick 63
 James 19
 John 19
 Joseph 78
 Mary 24
 Mourning 141
 Roger 63
 Stephen 24
 Susan 19
 Thomas 63
 William 102
Jordan
 Marion 47
 Robert 122
 Samuel 129
 Thomas 122
Jung
 Margareth 176
Jurgens
 Carol 9
 Ellen 10
 John 9
 Susan 9
Keelling
 Elizabeth 101
 Mary 101
Kelly
 William 114

Kelso
 William 153
Kemp
 Richard 55, 57, 58
Kemper
 Elizabeth 177
 John 177
 Peter 178
Kenny
 Mary 89
Kidd
 Margaret 154
Killman
 Mary 113
 Sarah 113
Kimball
 Emily 124
 Gregg 136
Kimbrow
 Susanna 73
Kinchen
 William 158
King
 Elias 69
 Pamelia 69
Kingsmill
 Elizabeth 3
 Jane 3
 Richard 3
Kirk
 S. 146
Kirkland
 Catherine 68
Kirkpatrick
 Sally 169
Kyle
 Hazlett 139
 Lucy 138
 Virginia 138
Ladd
 Chlotilda 144
 Elizabeth 122
 James 118, 122
 John 121, 144
 Thomas 118, 136
 Unity 144
 William 121, 122
Lafarge
 Caroline 73
 Martha 71
Laker
 Benjamin 182, 191, 192
 Elizabeth 191, 192
 Juliana 191, 192
 Lydia 182-184, 191, 192
 Ruth 191, 192
 Sarah 191, 192
Lampkin
 James 175
Lanciano
 Claude 58
Lane
 Frances 32, 33
 Frank 32, 33
 Stuart 32
Lark
 Annamarie 18
 Carol 18
 Jenifer 18
 John 18
 Jonathan 18
 Scott 18
Larker
 Benjamin 191

Laub
 Virginia 43
Laughlin
 John 69
 Lucy 69
Ledbetter
 John 194
Lee
 Alfred 46-48, 172
 Alice 13, 43, 142
 Ann 46, 47
 Arthur 47, 48
 Catherine 48
 Chappell 47
 Charles 48
 Cuthbert 47
 Dallas 47
 Edward 45
 Elizabeth 47
 Evelyn 48
 Frances 46, 193
 Gertrude 48
 Hancock 102
 Hannah 45
 Henry 47
 Hugh 45, 47, 195
 Jane 45
 John 45
 L. Robins 47
 Littleberry 47
 Lodowick 48, 184
 Logan 47
 Marion 47
 Mary 46, 48, 184
 Matthew 47
 Nathaniel 47
 Percy 48
 Rebecca 47
 Richard 45, 47
 Robert E 13
 Samuel 46, 47, 186, 193, 194
 Sarah 47
 Susanna 48
 Thomas 45, 47, 184, 193
 W. Davis 47
 William 47, 48
Leiby
 Benjamin 14
 Cynthia 14
LeNeve
 William 140
Lester
 Richard 171
Lewis
 David 86
 Elizabeth 125
 family 148
 Fielding 67
 John 125
 Sarah 125, 127
 William 127
Lide
 Mary 120
Lieby
 Pamela 14
Lightfoot
 Mary 158
Ligon
 Richard 195
 servant 123
Lilly
 Edmund 155
 Sarah 155

213

Mitchell
  Elizabeth 111
  Gabriel 173
  Grace 71
  John 101
  Michelle B. 6
  Morris 71
  Reuben 111, 113
  Thomas 195
  Virginia 33
Mizell
  Luke 199
Moon 31
  Joannah 31
  Turner 31
Moore
  Archibald 94
  David 24
  Frederick 94
  Hannah 24
  John 24
  Martha 94
  Mary 94, 195
  Rebecca 118
  Richard 184
  Sally 94
  Sarah 93, 94
  William 94
Moorman
  Clark 144, 149
  family 148
  Micajah 72
  Nancy 137
  Rachel 149
  Sarah 155
Mordecai
  Rachel 140
  Samuel 140
Morehead
  Alexander 178
  Elizabeth 178
Morey
  Dennis 124
Morgan
  Miss 73
Morris
  Agnes 189, 190
  Anthony 179
  Bethiah 189
  Boyce 189
  Chislon 189
  George 82
  Henry 189
  Jabez 189
  Jane 179, 180
  Martha 179
  Nicholas 179
  Sarah 189
  Thomas 189
Morton
  John 94
  Rebecca 31
  William 31
Mosby
  Agnes 121, 122
  Benjamin 122
  Edward 122, 127
  Hannah 122
  Hezekiah 122
  Jacob 122
  John 122
  Joseph 122
  Mary 122
  Poindexter 122

Mosby
  Richard 122
  Robert 122
  Sabrina 122
  Sarah 122, 127
Moseley
  Edward 173
Moss
  Frances 24
  Nathaniel 95
  Ray 24
Mossom
  David 140
Motley
  Edwin 101
  Henry 101
  John 100, 101
  Tabitha 101
Mountains
  Blue Ridge 143
Mumford
  Daniel 93
  Edward 93
  Joseph 93
  Mary 93, 97
  Mr. 163
  Robin 162
Mundane
  Robert 174
Munday
  Ambrose 173, 175
  Benjamin 173, 175
  Catherine 174
  Charles 173-175
  Edmond 173, 175
  Elizabeth 173, 174
  Frances 173, 174
  Hannah 173, 174
  Harrison 173, 175
  James 173, 175
  John 173-175
  Joseph 173-175
  Margaret 173, 175
  Martha 173, 174
  Mary 173-175
  Reuben 173, 175
  Robert 173-175
  Sarah 173-175
  Tabitha 173, 175
  Thomas 173, 174
  William 174
  Winifred 173, 175
  Winnie 173, 175
Mundy
  Alexander 175
  Ann 172, 175
  Catherine 175
  Charles 170, 174, 175, 178
  Jesse 175
  John 175
  Joshua 175
  Mary 175
  Robert 174, 175, 180
  Sallie 175
  William 175
Myhill
  Ann 120
  Anne 120, 121
  John 120
  Joshua 120
  Judith 120
  Robert 120

Neblet
  Mary 24
  Sterling 24
Needles
  Mary 24
Negroes
  Adam 67
  Alice 66
  Ben 67
  Buck 64
  Cooke 194
  Coss 64
  Davey 64
  Dennis 64
  Dianh 77
  Hannah 77
  Harry 64
  Isabella 66
  Kitty 66
  Lucy 60, 66
  Maria 66
  Matt 64
  Minny 64
  Moses 95
  Rachael 64
  Spencer 66
  Tom 60
Neill
  Edward 57
Nelson
  Ann 178
  Edward 65
  Elizabeth 178
  Frances 178
  Henry 124, 178
  James 65
  Jemima 178
  Jesse 178
  John 178
  Lettice 178
  Lydia 178
  Margaret 178
  Mary 178
  Sarah 178
  Susanna 178
  William 177, 178
Netherland
  Robert 76
Nethery
  Mary 25
Neve
  Derek 14
  Kimberly 14
Neville
  Elizabeth 104
  Louisa 175
New
  Anthony 147
Newsome
  Robert 158
Newsum
  Sarah 158
Newton
  Betty 85
  John 173
Nicholas
  George 158
Nicholson
  Francis 154
Niess
  Elizabeth 176
Nohe
  Henrich 176

214

Perkins
  Mary 165
Petro
  John 30
Pettus
  Thomas 4
Pettyjohn
  Abigail 171
  Abraham 169, 171
  Betsy 169
  Canning 170, 172
  Caroline 172
  Catherine 170, 172
  Charles 172
  Elizabeth 169-171
  Esther 171
  George 170, 172
  Hannah 171
  Hugh 170, 172
  Isabel 171
  Jacob 169-171
  James 169-172
  Jesse 170-172
  John 171
  Joseph 170-172, 175
  Louisa 169-171
  Louisianna 169, 170, 172
  Lydia 171
  Major 171
  Mary 48, 169, 171, 172
  Missouri 172
  Nancy 170
  Naomi 171
  Reuben 169
  Rhoda 171
  Richard 171
  Sally 169
  Samuel 171
  Sara 171
  Sarah 172
  Thomas 171
  Wiatt 172
  William 169-172
Philipps
  Elizabeth 75
Phillips
  Dabney 24
  Elizabeth 78
  Martha 24
Pillman
  John 64
Pillow
  Elizabeth 97
Pleasants
  John 127
  Joseph 127
  Mary 127
  Robert 136
Pocahontas
  (Indian princess) 125
Poindexter
  John 76
  Mary 122
Pollard
  Ambrose 37
  George 37
  Martha 76
  Mary 37, 76
  Nancy 37
  Richard 76
  Robert 37
  William 76
Pool
  Charles 135

Porter
  Nancy 31
  Sarah 127
Pott
  Dr. 123
Pouncey
  John 83
Pouncie
  Roger 85
Povall
  Elizabeth 19
Pownall
  John 178
Presley
  Peter 180
Preston
  Edward 105
  Elizabeth 105
Price
  Amelia 97
  Ann 93, 96
  Anna 96, 97
  Elizabeth 97
  James 38
  John 93, 96-98
  Lennis 94
  Martha 94
  Mary 93, 94, 96, 97
  Polley 93
  Polly 94
  Richard 93, 96, 97
  Sarah 94
  Sophia 97
  Susan 97
  Susanna 96, 97
  Thomas 96
  Warner 97
  William 93, 94, 96, 97
Prime
  Elizabeth 157
  Martha 157
Purnell
  Elizabeth 93
Quarles 37
  Aaron 36, 37
  Frances 36, 43
  Jane 134
  John 36
  Margaret 36
  Mary 134
  Robert 147
  Roger 3 134
  Sarah 78
  Susannah 37
  Tunstall 37
Quinn
  Reuben 48
Raffensperger
  Jacqueline 14
Raine
  Mary 94
Raines
  Mary 46
  Shands 46, 47
Rand
  Henry 106
Randolph
  Molly 135
  Mr. 163
  Thomas 129
Ransone
  Ellen 10
  John 10

Ravenscroft
  Thomas 164
Reckitt
  William 148
Rector
  Catherine 177
  Elizabeth 177
  Jacob 177
  John 177, 178
Reed
  Jane 178
Reeves
  Ann 173
  Elizabeth 173
  Epps 187
  Henry 173
  James 173
  Joseph 173
  Martha 173
  Mary 146, 173
  Rebecca 173
Remington
  Lydia 33
Rennolds
  Benja. 173
  Phillip 112
  Sarah 112
Reynolds
  Ann 172
Rice
  Anna 28
  John 28
  Mary 140, 144
  Morton 28
Richards
  Buchan 39
  Eliza 39
  Gertrude 186
  John 39
  Mourning 66
  Penelope 39
  Richard 4
Richardson
  Agnes 127
  Ann 68
  Elizabeth 94, 95
  Frances 95
  George 94, 95, 98
  Giles 95
  James 68
  John 32, 94
  Joseph 95, 97
  Mary 94, 95
  Polly 94
  Rebecca 94, 95
  Rebeckah 94
  Sarah 95
  Susan 68
  Thomas 98
Richeson
  Elizabeth 94
  Frances 115
  George 94
  Giles 94
  Jesse 68
  Joseph 94, 142
  Mary 94, 95
  Polly 94
  Rebecca 94
  Selina 68
  Thomas 94
Ricks
  Alfred 137, 143
  Ann 139

Ricks
  Arnold 9, 135-137, 139, 143, 149
  Deborah 137
  Eliza 143
  family 148
  J. Hoge 143
  Julia 137, 143
  Martha 143
  Mary 137, 143
  Mary Ann 143
  Richard 9, 137, 143
Ridgeway
  Robert 171
Riggs
  David 57
Riley
  Price 15
  Veronica 15
Ring
  William 39
Risher
  Molly 16
Rivers
  Appomattox 53-54, 57, 162,
    193-195
  Back 152, 153
  Chickahominy 140, 193
  Corrotoman 197
  Deep 150
  James 3-5, 13, 41, 53, 124-126,
    136,142-143,152-154,162,194
  Kanawha 143
  Kentucky 71
  Mattaponi 3, 140-142, 147
  Mississippi 138
  North Anna 9, 78, 141, 143
  Ohio 143
  Pamunkey 3, 37-39, 63, 64, 83,
    88, 89, 126, 140, 141
  PeeDee 66, 67, 155
  Potomac 60
  Rappahannock 23, 30, 60
  South 24, 147, 148
  Susquehanna 118
  Ware 197
  West 148
  York 56, 83, 140, 141
Roberts
  Betty 170
Robins
  Logan 47
  Rachel 25
Robinson
  Benjamin 174
  Christopher 194
  George 77
  Joseph 9
  Lucy 77
  Mary 158, 194, 195
  Sarah 174
  Suzannah 77
Rodham
  Matthew 45
Rogannia
  Gregory 68
  Sarah 68
Rogers
  Catharine 69
  Elizabeth 158
  Jacob 169
  John 69
  Lucy 69
  Mary 169
  Sarah 69, 73

Rogers
  William 69
Rolfe
  Elizabeth 24
  John 125
Rookings
  Susannah 161
  William 161
Rossey
  Thomas 178
Rothman
  Marlene 14
Rouzee
  John 102
Rowe
  Micajah 164
  Sarah 164
Rowlands
  Luke 180
Rowzee
  Edward 101
Royall
  Mary 127
Rucker
  Catherine 170
  George 170, 172
  Lelia 137
Ruffin
  Alice 39
  Anne 158
  Benjamin 158
  Edmund 158
  Elizabeth 43, 157, 158
  Erasmus 158
  Faith 157
  Francis 158, 159
  George 158
  Hannah 158
  Jane 158
  John 158
  Joseph 158
  Martha 158
  Mary 158
  Olivia 157
  Robert 38, 157, 158
  Sterling 39
  Susanna 158
  Thomas 158
  William 157, 158
Rutherfoord
  Thomas 135
Rutherford
  John 111
  Julia 111
Sadler
  Mary 180
Sailly
  Charles 154
Sale
  Janey 102
  Joseph 71, 102
  Peggy 71
  Phoebe 98
  Rosy 113
Samuel
  Mary 69
  Thomas 173
  William 69
Sandy
  George 4
Sandys
  George 4
Sanford
  Dorothy 179

Saunders
  Fanny 71
  Lelia 137
  Mary 32, 97, 154
  Patty 186
  Reuben 71
  Sarah 32
  Suberta 34
  William 102
  Wren 32
Scampion
  John 182
Scattergood
  Thomas 148, 149
Sclater
  Crawley 19, 43
  Werter 43
Scott
  Charles 123
  John 27, 193
Serdon
  Ruth 155
Seward
  Caulfield 158
Shadrock
  Jeffrey 14
  Sherri 14
  Veronica 15
Shall
  Margaret 138
Shaver
  Kimberly 10
Shaw
  Jon. 53
Shelby
  John 70
Shelton
  Carolyn 11
  Deborah 11
  Frances 11
  Frank 11
  Hilda 11
  James 105
  John 11, 88
  Lorraine 11
  Paul 124
  Richard 11
Sheltons
  Ralph 59
Sheperdson
  Joseph 75
  Oney 75
Sheppard
  John 146
Short
  Elizabeth 159
  Jordan 71
  Martha 159
  Mary 71, 159
  Sarah 159
  Susanna 159
  Thomas 159
  William 159
Shumate
  George 178
Simmons
  Anne 158
  Lucy 158
  Thom 193
  Thomas 194
Simpson
  Amelia 138
  Annie 138
  George 138, 139

219

Tyler
  John 56, 60
  Lyon G 57
  Richard 147
Tyrrell
  Charles 81
  Joanne 81
  John 81
  Margaret 81
  Mary 81
  Robert 81
  Timothy 81
Urbach
  Cynthia 14
  George 14
  Marlene 14
  Veronica 14, 15
Urvin
  Nath 193
Utterback
  Catherine 177
  Charles 178
  Henry 177
Valentine
  Anis 198
  Annis 198
  Mary 24
Vandiver
  Bess 17
  Carol 18
  June 18
  Robert 17
Vaughan
  Anne 11
  Frances 11
  Gregory 11
  Joseph 94
  Lennis 94
Venable
  William 116
Vicars
  Thomas 58
Vitter
  Brittany 19
  Patricia 18
  Robert 19
  William 18
Vliet
  Elizabeth 5, 7, 29
  Gordon 5, 7, 29
Voinard
  Otelia 43
Wadding
  James 58
Wade
  Fay 54, 57, 75
  Margaret 105, 106
Wadkins
  Elizabeth 7
  Elizabeth Lee 5
  Harriette 7
  Helen 6, 7
  J. Thomas 6, 7
  James T. 7
  James Thomas 29
  Kyle 6
  Kyle Lee 7
  Richard 6
  Richard C. 6
  Richard Cleveland 7
  Robin 6, 7
  Sarah 6
  Sarah Tyce 7
  Thomas 6

Wadkins
  Tom 3
  Virginia Hutcheson 7
Wagstaff
  John 25
  Rebecca 25
Walke
  Susan 97
Walker
  David 13
  Nancy 75
  Robert 148
Wallace
  James 68
  Mary 68
Waller
  John 37
  Mary 37
  William 172
Ware
  Henry 173
  James 173
  Mary 173
  Nicholas 173
  Sarah 173
Wareham
  John 4
Waring
  Francis 82
  Thomas 100
Warner
  Thomas 86
Warren
  Abraham 169
  Elizabeth 169
  F. E. 146
  Rebecca 169
  Robert 169
Washington
  George 136, 140
  Martha 140
Waters
  Ann 141
  Elizabeth 141
  John 141
  Margaret 141
  Samuel 141
  Susannah 86
  Thomas 141
Watkins
  Ann 165
  Benjamim 120
  Elizabeth 93, 157, 165
  Henry 120, 122, 125, 165
  Jane 120
  John 165
  Joseph 93
  Mary 93, 122, 165
  Rachel 125, 127
  Richard 93
  Robert 165
  Susanna 122
  Thomas 120
  William 165
Watson
  Abner 93, 94
  Agnes 122
  Alexander 171
  Benjamin 94
  Frederick 94
  James 43
  John 94
  Joseph 94
  Mary 93, 94

Watson
  Polley 93, 94
  Richard 94
  Sarah 94
  Susan 94
  William 94
Watt
  Virginia 71
  William 71
Wattenbarger
  Marion 173
Watts
  Elizabeth 88
  Emily 105
  Hannah 136
  Henry 175
  James 88, 89
  John 88
Weathers
  Edward 98
Weaver
  John 193
Webb
  Doct: 94
Webber
  Henry 59
  Jane 59
Weisiger
  Benjamin 66
Wellstedd
  Alice 52, 71
Welsh
  Ann 178
West
  Joseph 64
  Thomas 124
Wheeler
  Elizabeth 194, 195
  John 172
Whitaker
  Alexander 125
White
  Aaron 66
  Elizabeth 171
  Ethel 31
  Mary 154
Whiting
  Henry 58
Whitlock
  Martha 143
Whitson
  Sarah 178
Wigdon
  Earl of 129
Wigglesworth
  Elizabeth 78
Wilkerson
  Nancy 141
Wilkinson
  Julia 143
Willes
  Th: 86
William
  the Conqueror 81
Williams
  Elizabeth 97
  Frances 24
  Jane 23
  John 60
  Sarah 24, 180
  Thomas 24
  Warner 97
Willie
  Reverend 186

Willis
  George 33
  Joanna 33
  Mary 33
Willson
  Elizabeth 113
  Hannah 171
Wilson
  Elizabeth 112
  Hannah 25
  Mariah 158
Wily
  John 76, 77
Winchester
  Arthur 36
Winingham
  Edward 193
  John 193
Winkler
  Betty 170
Winn
  John 43
  Miss 69
Winston
  Ambrose 137
  Amelia 138, 139
  Ann 19, 134, 139
  Anthony 117, 134, 138
  Benjamin 139
  Betsy 134
  Bowling 137
  Charles 137
  Chloe 137
  Edmund 134, 139
  Eliza 134
  Elizabeth 19, 137-139
  family 148
  George 33, 117, 118, 134-139,
    142, 144
  Harris 136
  Isaac 138
  James 117, 137, 139
  Jane 134
  Jefferson 134
  Jemima 133, 134
  John 134
  Joseph 137
  Judith 136, 137
  Julia 137
  Lelia 137
  Lindley 137
  Lucy 13, 137-139
  Margaret 138
  Martha 138
  Mary 69, 72, 137-139
  Nancy 134, 137
  Nathan 134, 139
  Nathaniel 118, 133, 134, 137,
    138, 139
  Patsy 134
  Patty 134
  Peter 19
  Philip 137
  Pleasant 134, 137-139
  Polly 134
  Rebecca 134, 138
  Sally 134
  Samuel 134, 138
  Sarah 134, 137, 138
  Susan 19
  Thomas 137-139
  Virginia 43, 137, 139
  William 134, 137, 138, 142
  Zalinda 137

Womack
  Martha 122
  Sarah 127
Wood
  Abraham 193
  Samantha 33
  William 117
Wooday
  Martha 117
Woodfolk
  Richard 78
Woodruff
  Jesse 171
Woodson
  Agnes 122
  Benjamin 127
  Charles 126, 127
  Deborah 123, 127
  Elizabeth 117, 118, 125, 127
  Jacob 127
  Jane 127
  John 123-127, 129, 130
  Joseph 122, 127
  Josiah 127
  Judith 127, 150
  Mary 127
  Rachel 125
  Richard 127
  Robert 123, 125-127
  Sarah 122, 123, 125, 127, 147
  Stephen 125, 127
  Susanna 127
  Tarleton 126, 127, 129
Woodward
  Elizabeth 48
Woolfolk
  Anne 78
  Augustine 78
  Betty 78
  Christiana 76, 78
  Elizabeth 66, 67, 72, 75, 77-79
  George 142
  John 78
  Joseph 75-79
  Mary 78
  Pitchegrue 26
  Richard 78
  Robert 78
  Sally 65
  Thomas 78
Woolman
  John 147
Wormley
  Aylmer 146
  Catherine 146
  Ralph 146
Worrall
  Jay 136
Worshing
  Sarah 28
Worsnam
  George 57
  William 57
Worsnan
  John 58
Wortham
  Charles 65
  Richard 118
  Sally 65, 70
Wright
  Ambrose 96
  Anne 171
  Archer 94
  Archibald 94, 97

Wright
  Elizabeth 96
  Emuella 114
  George 94
  Isbell 94
  John 33
  Lillie 33, 34
  Mary 94, 97
  Parthenia 28
  Polly 72
  Sally 94
  Sarah 93, 94
  Virginia 33
  William 94, 118
Wyatt
  Elizabeth 194
  Flora 144
  Henry 82
Wyld
  Daniel 60
Yancey
  Charles 155
  Jeremiah 155
  Martha 155
  Robert 155
Yarbrough
  Ann 134, 139
  Jeremiah 113
Yates
  Bartholomew 146
Yeardley
  Governor 152
Yonge
  Samuel 5, 152
Young
  Amelia 97
  Henry 39
  James 134
  Mary 95, 98, 178
  William 95, 96
  Williamson 95, 96
Younger
  Ann 93, 96

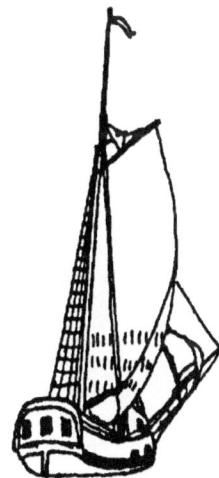